AF479304

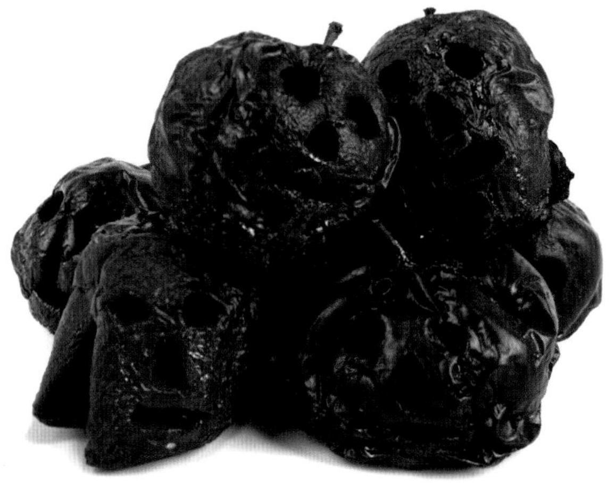

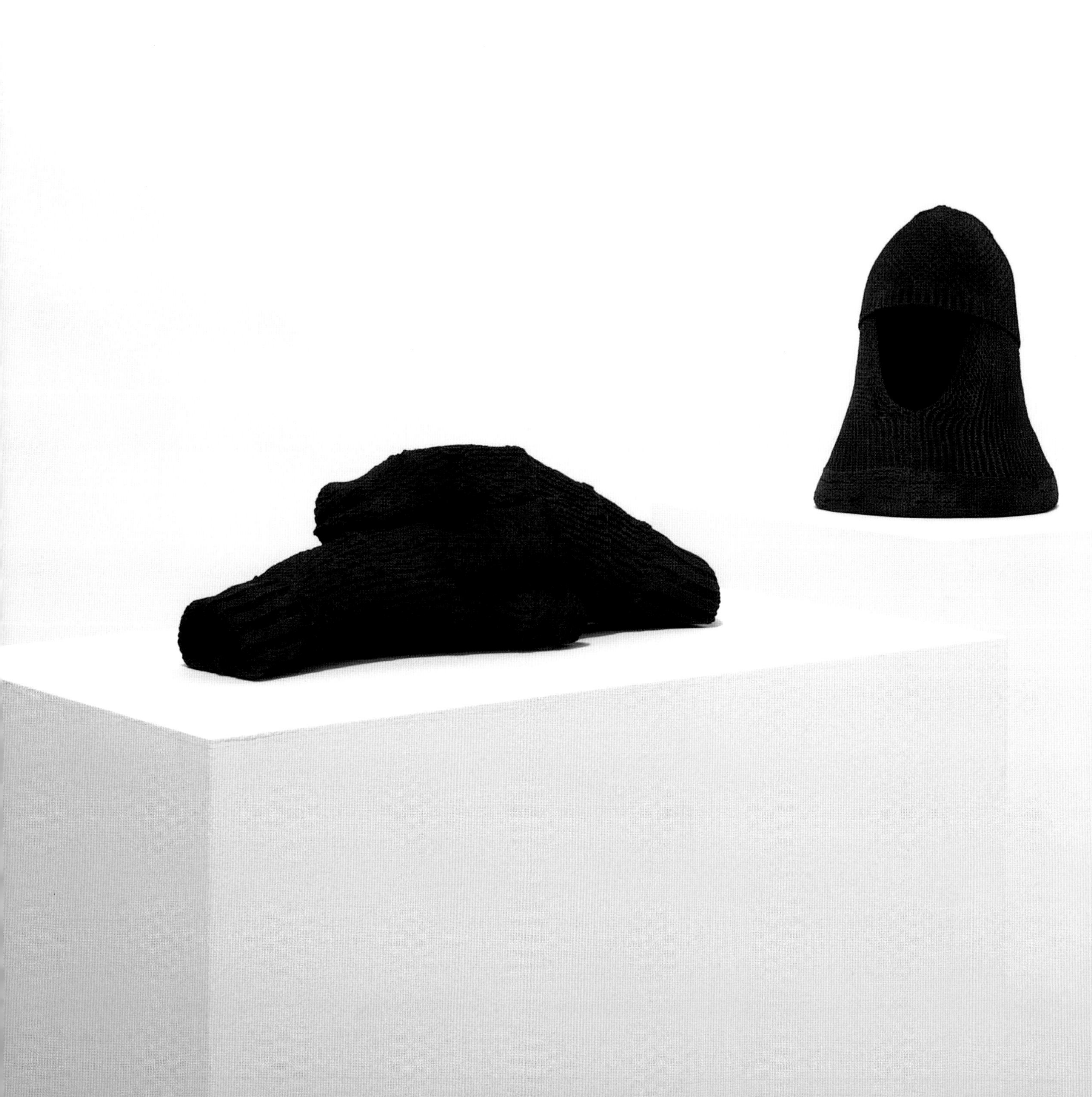

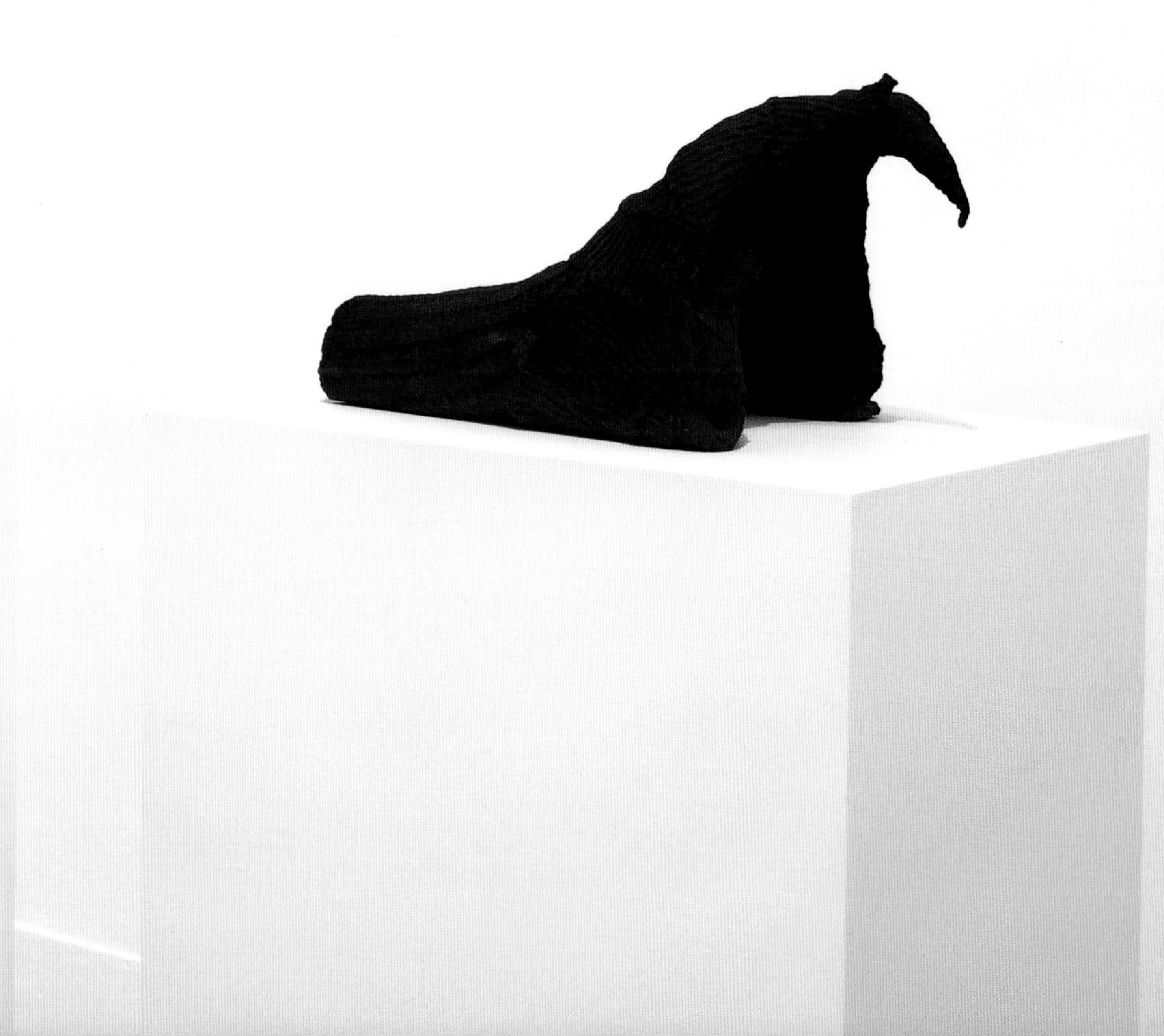

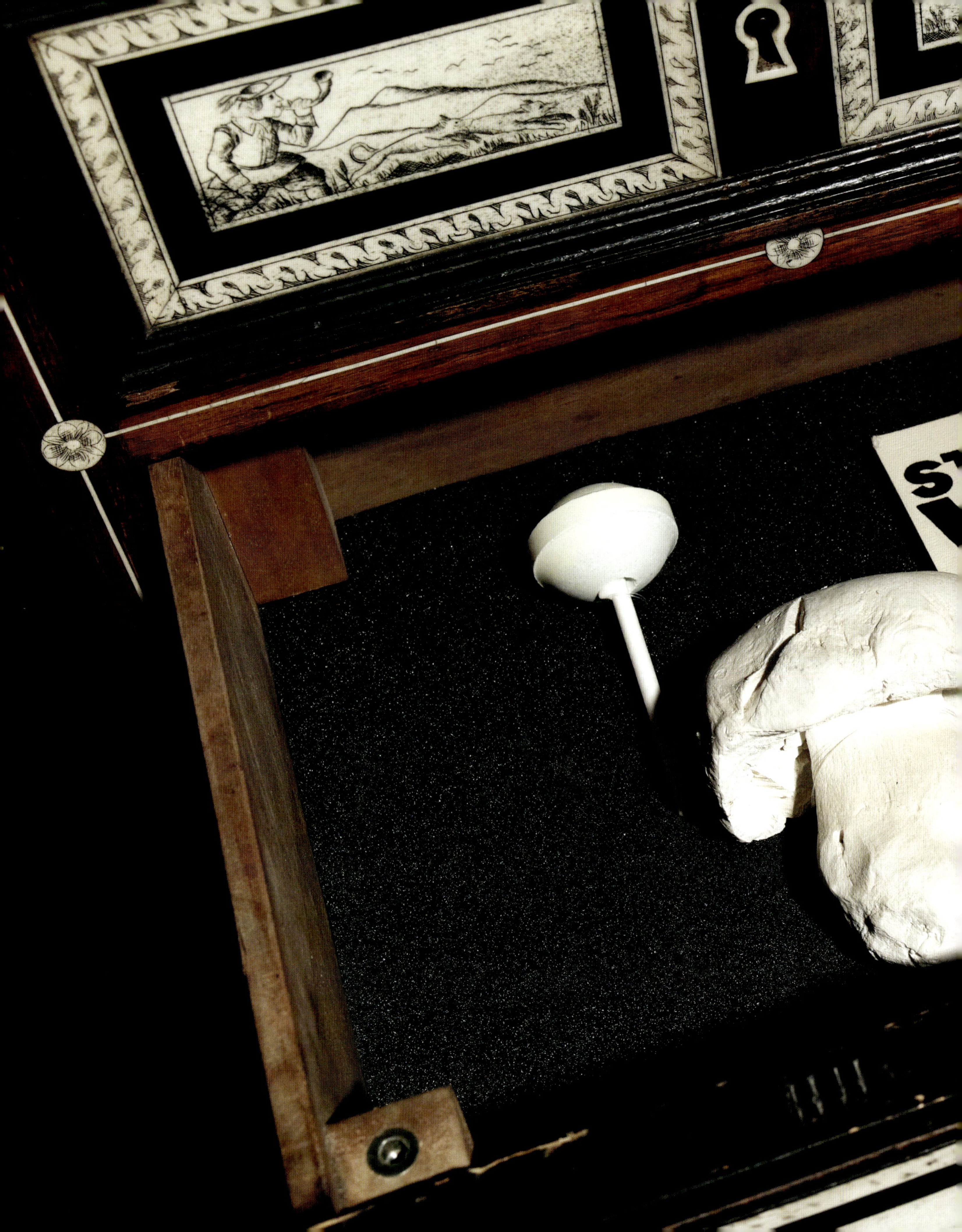

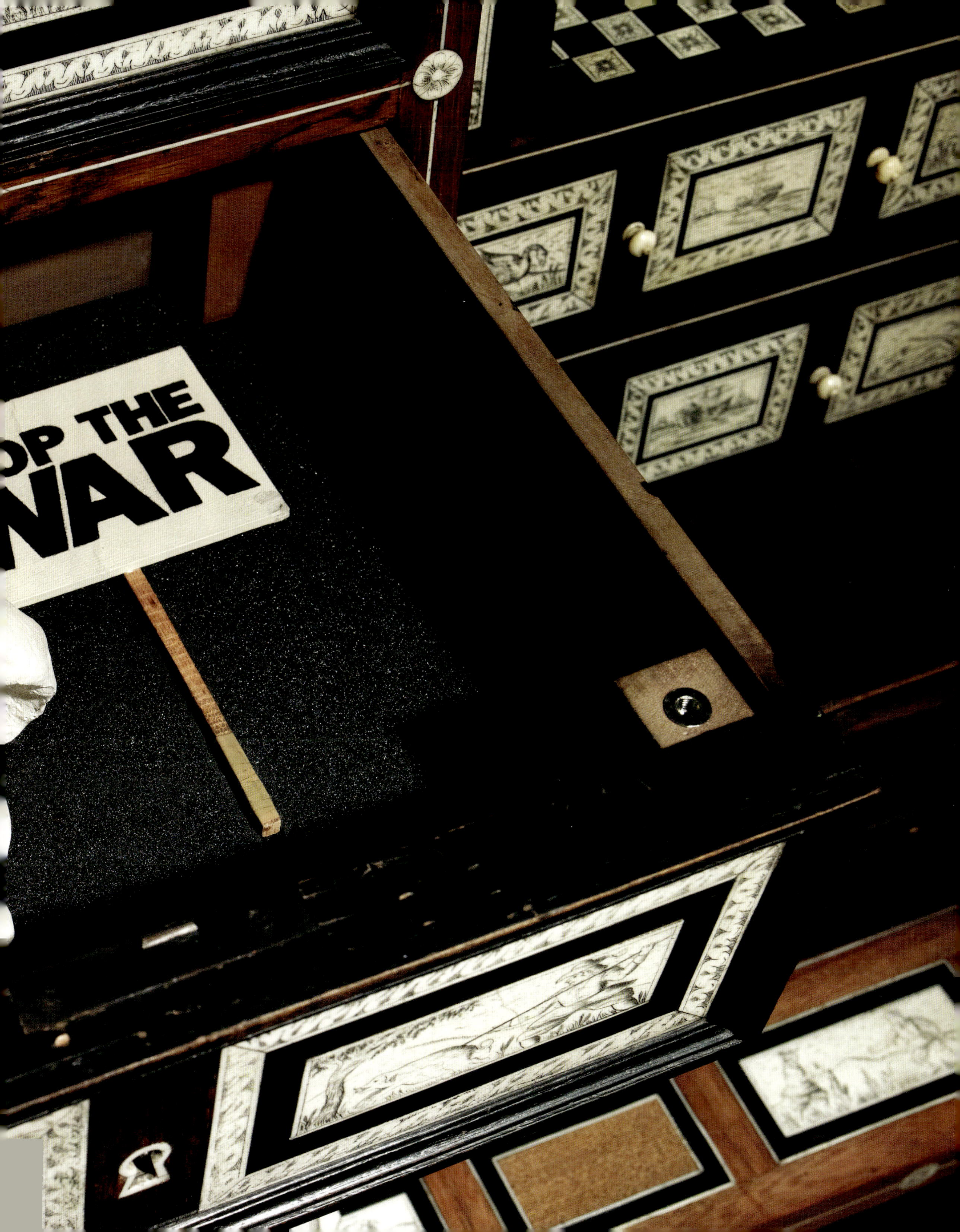
OP THE
WAR

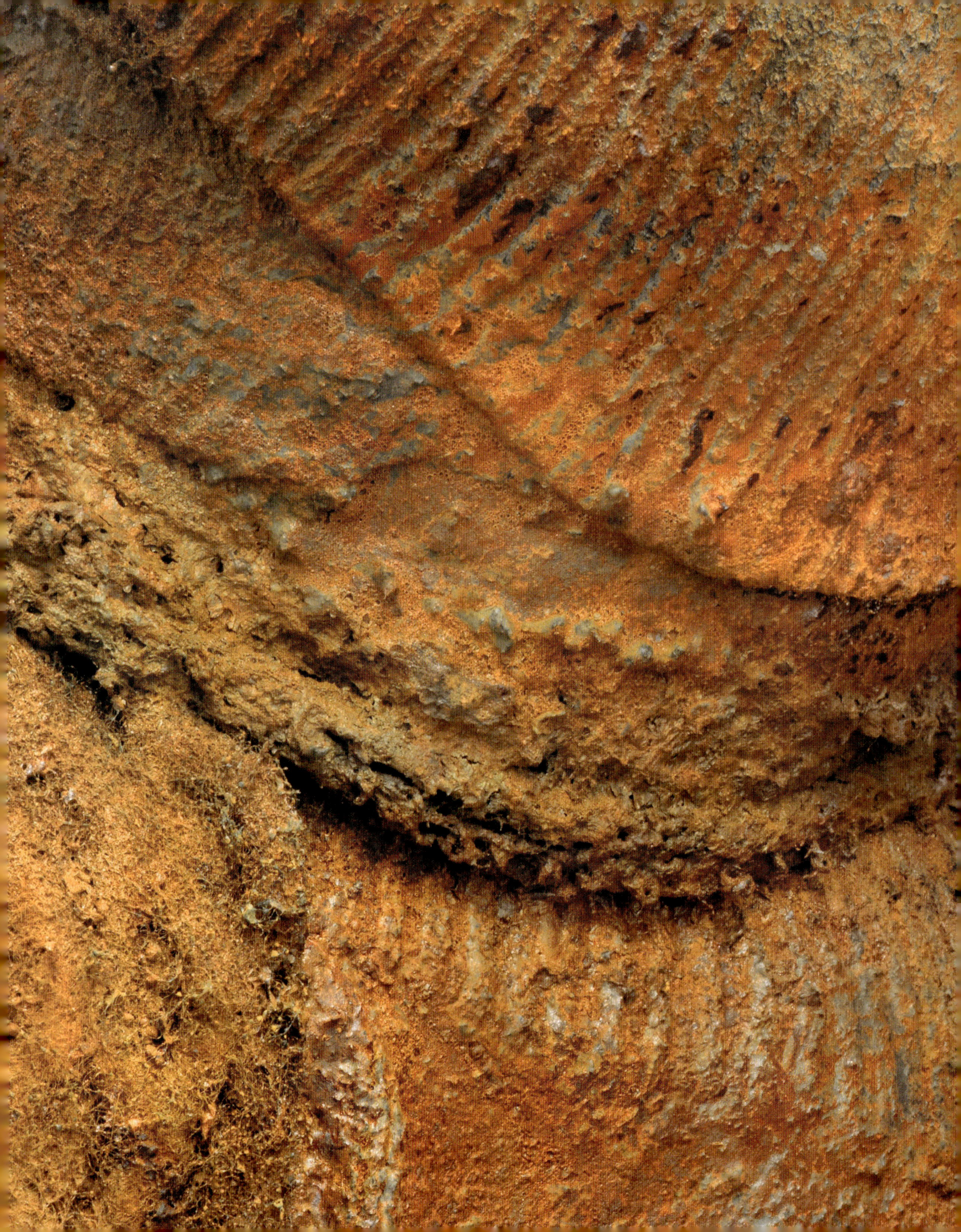

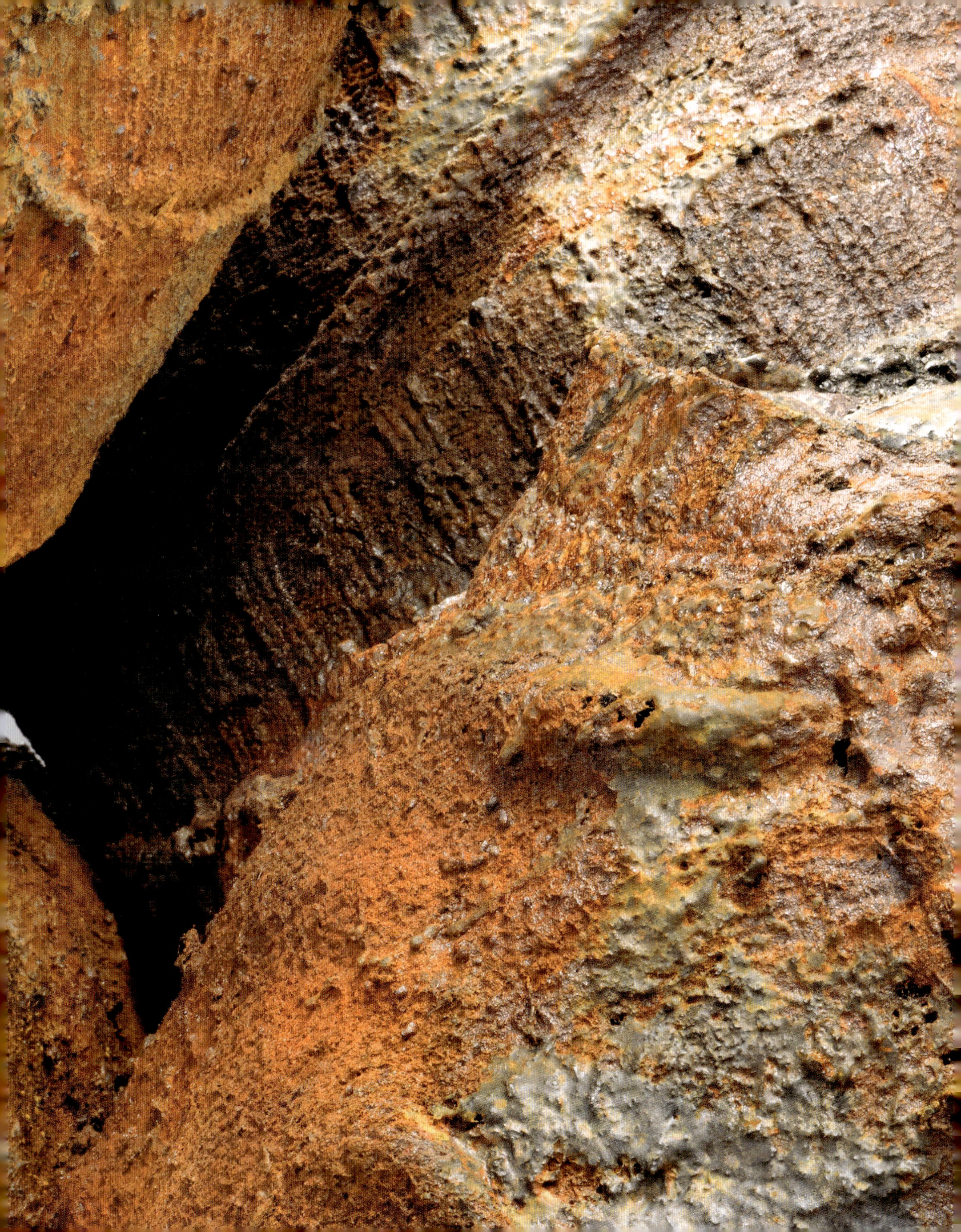

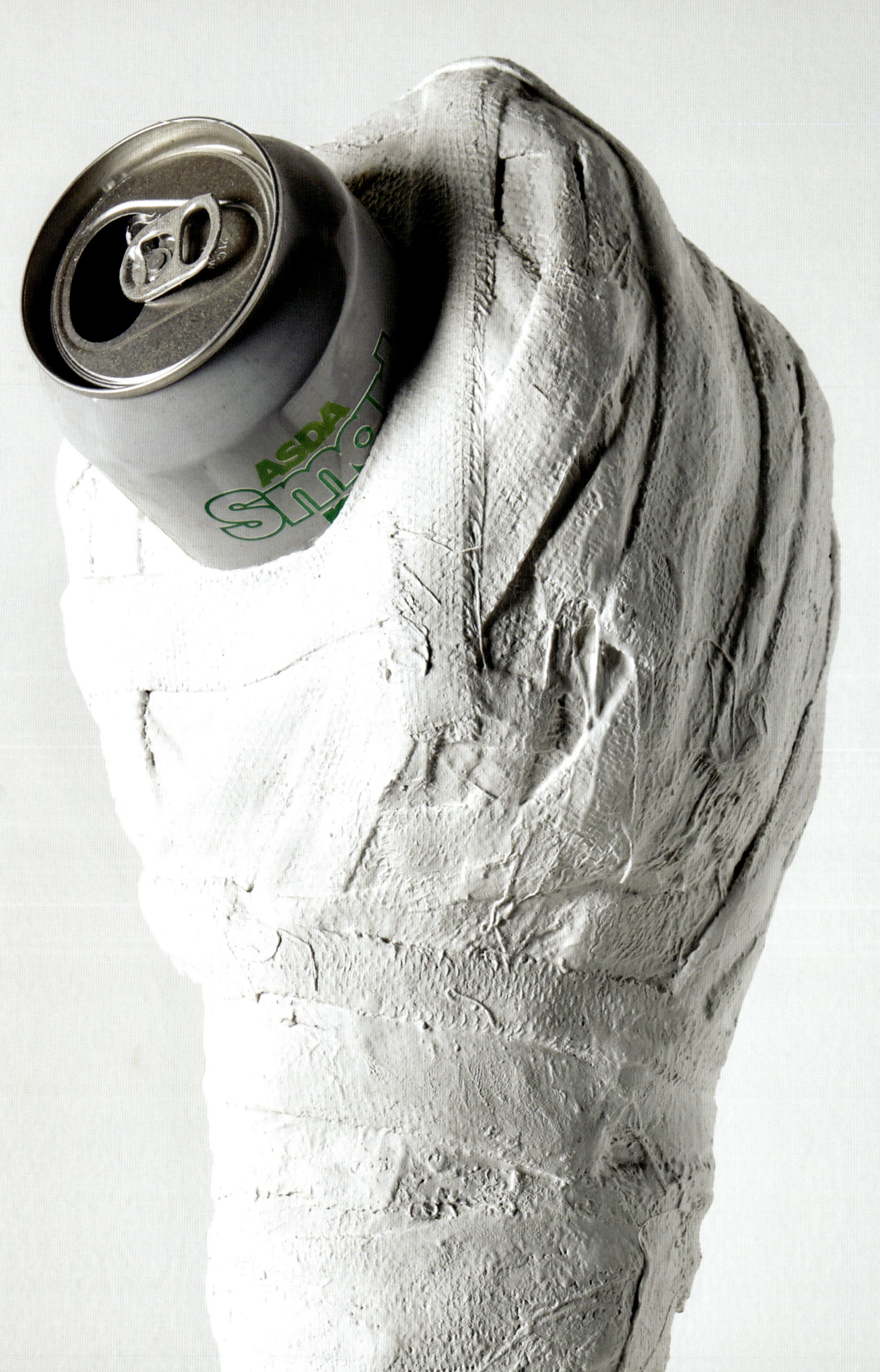
ASDA

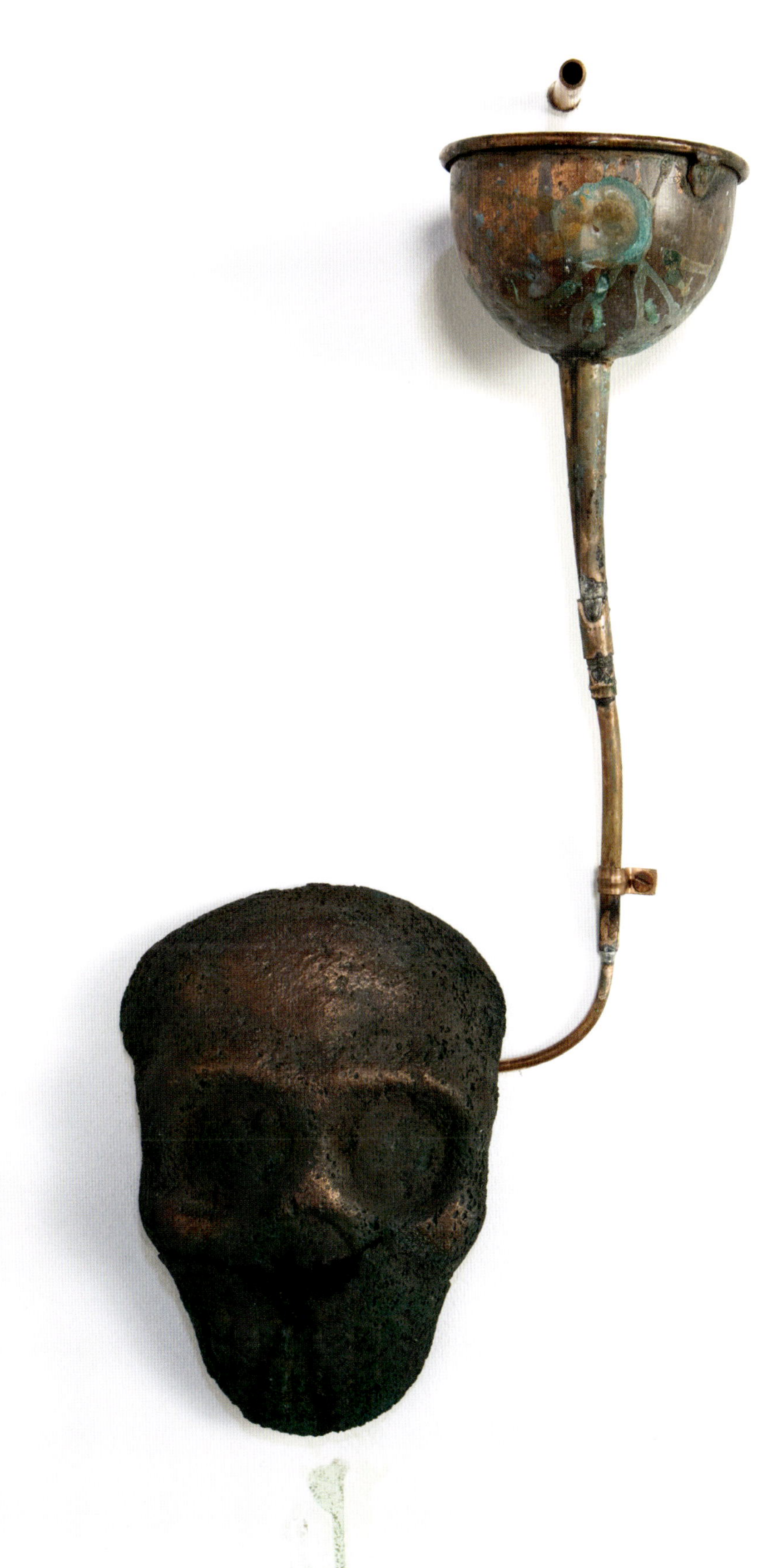

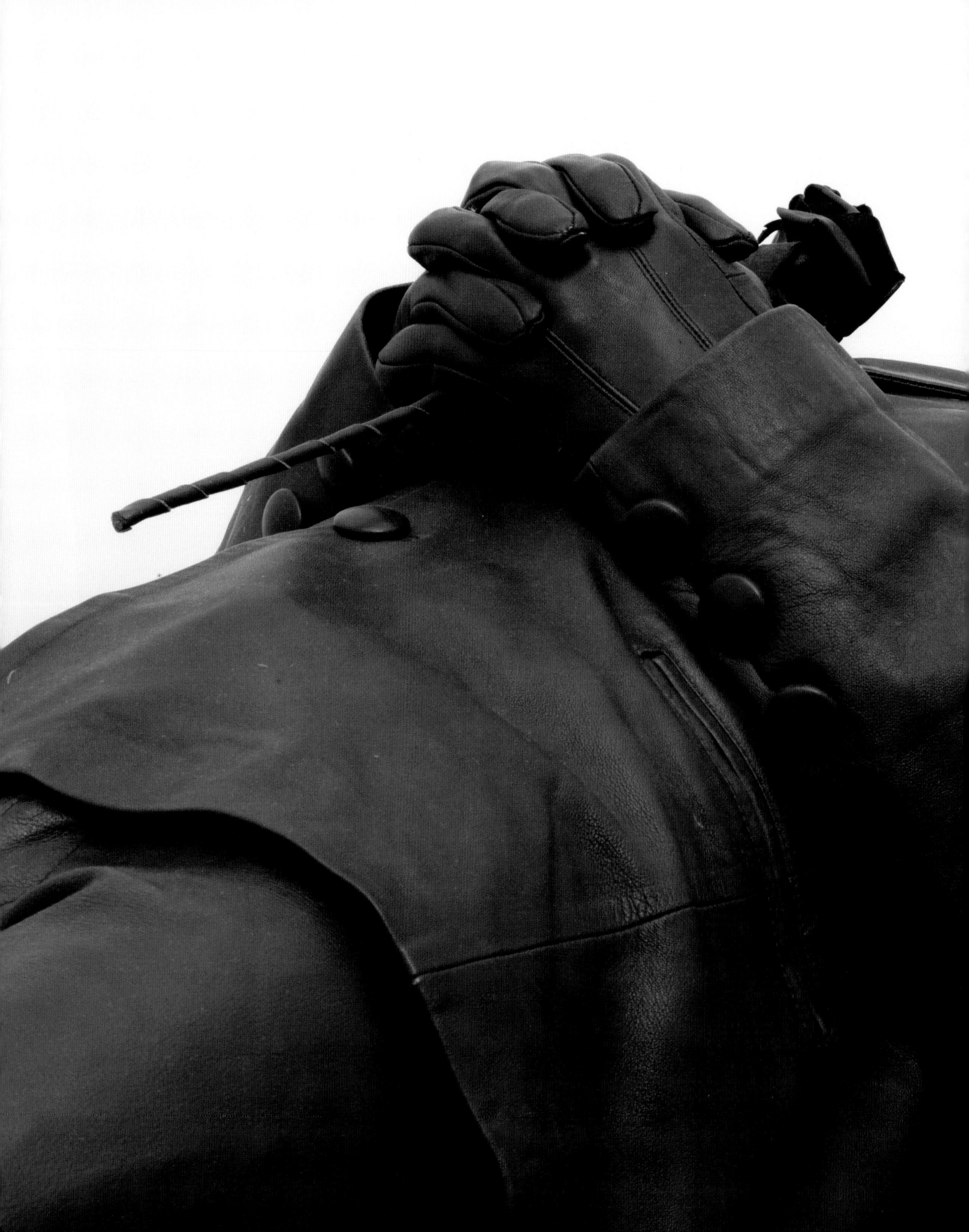

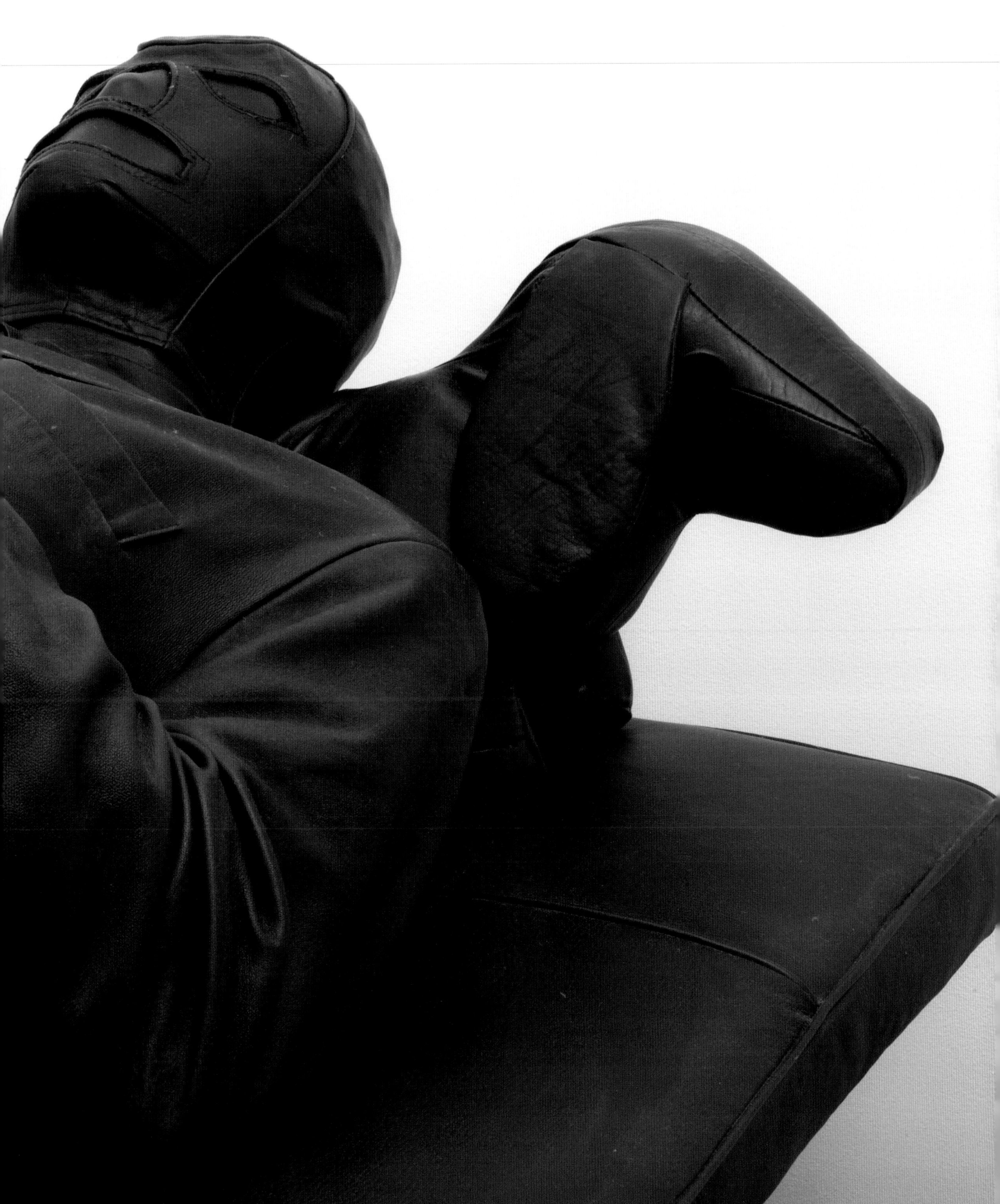

Des Hughes

I Want To Be Adored

ART/BOOKS

with texts by

Stephen Feeke

Bruce Haines

Harry Thorne

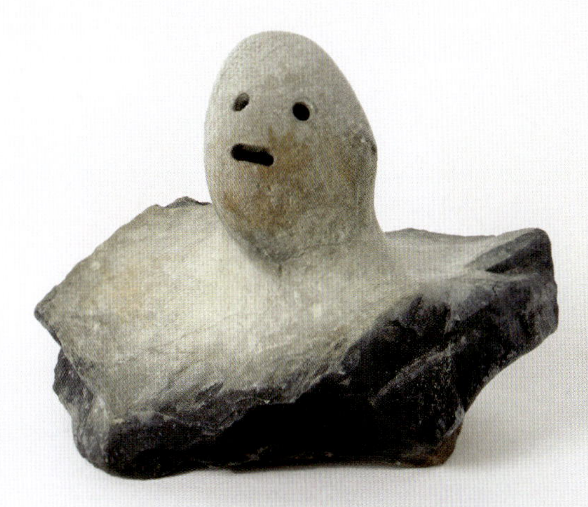

For Phil Hughes

page 1 *Burnt or Charred*, 2014, burnt apples, dimensions variable
pages 2–3 'Art Now: Beating the Bounds', 2009, Tate Britain, London
pages 4–5 Nottingham Contemporary, Small Collections Room, 2010, various works, mixed media
pages 6–7 *Rust Never Sleeps*, 2013, fibreglass, wool, resin and iron powder, 199 × 216 × 83 cm (detail)
page 8 *Drop Dead Gorgeous*, 2013, plaster and beer can, 52 × 15 × 10 cm (detail)
page 9 *The Lovely Faces*, 2008, resin, copper powder, copper pipe, funnels, copper horn, water and pump, dimensions variable (detail)
pages 10–11 *... the Terrible*, 2008, leather, mannequin and Poul Kjaerholm PK80 daybed, 200 × 100 × 60 cm (detail)
Title page *Infirm*, 2012, bronze, 9 × 12 × 9 cm

First published in the United Kingdom in 2018
by Art Books Publishing Ltd

Art Books Publishing Ltd
18 Shacklewell Lane
London E8 2EZ
Tel: +44 (0)20 8533 5835
info@artbookspublishing.co.uk
www.artbookspublishing.co.uk

British Library Cataloguing-in-Publication Data
A catalogue record for this book is available from the British Library

ISBN 978-1-908970-43-5

Designed by Art / Books and Des Hughes
Printed and bound in Latvia by Livonia

Distributed outside North America by
Thames & Hudson
181a High Holborn
London WC1V 7QX
United Kingdom
Tel: +44 (0)20 7845 5000
Fax: +44 (0)20 7845 5055
sales@thameshudson.co.uk

Available in North America through
ARTBOOK | D.A.P.
75 Broad Street, Suite 630
New York, N.Y. 10004
www.artbook.com

Contents

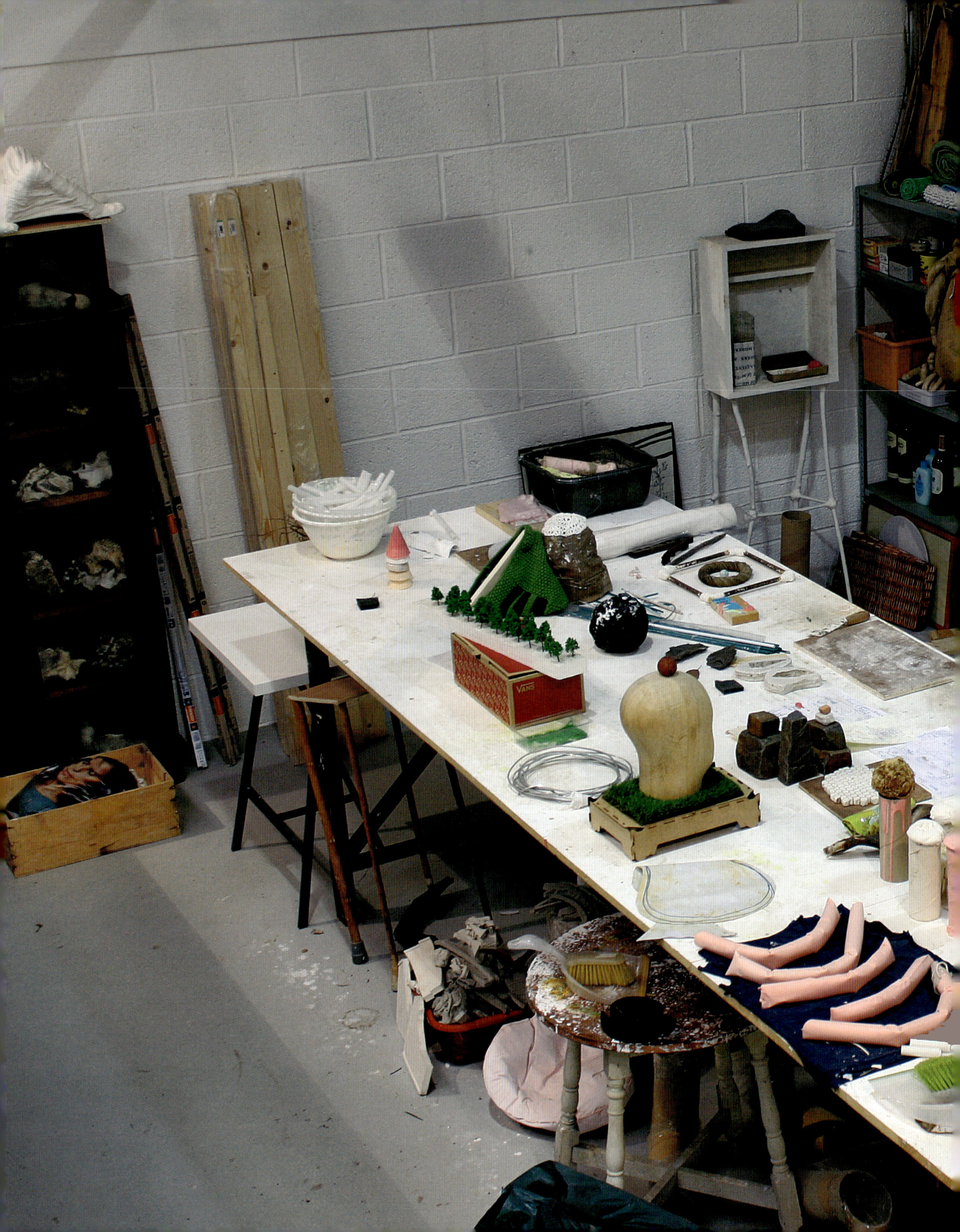
VANS

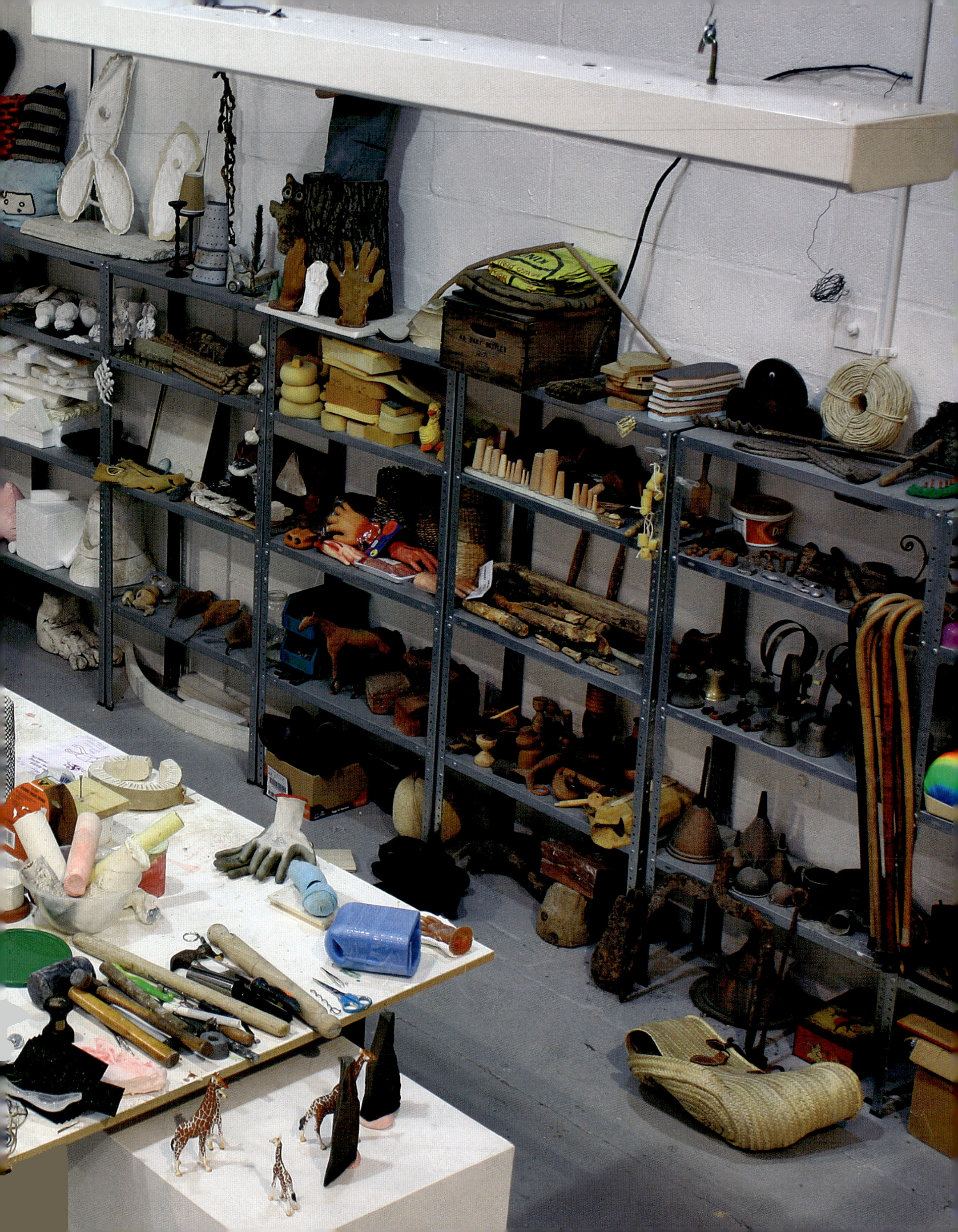

Sore Thumb 2004
Plaster bandage,
10 × 4 × 4 cm

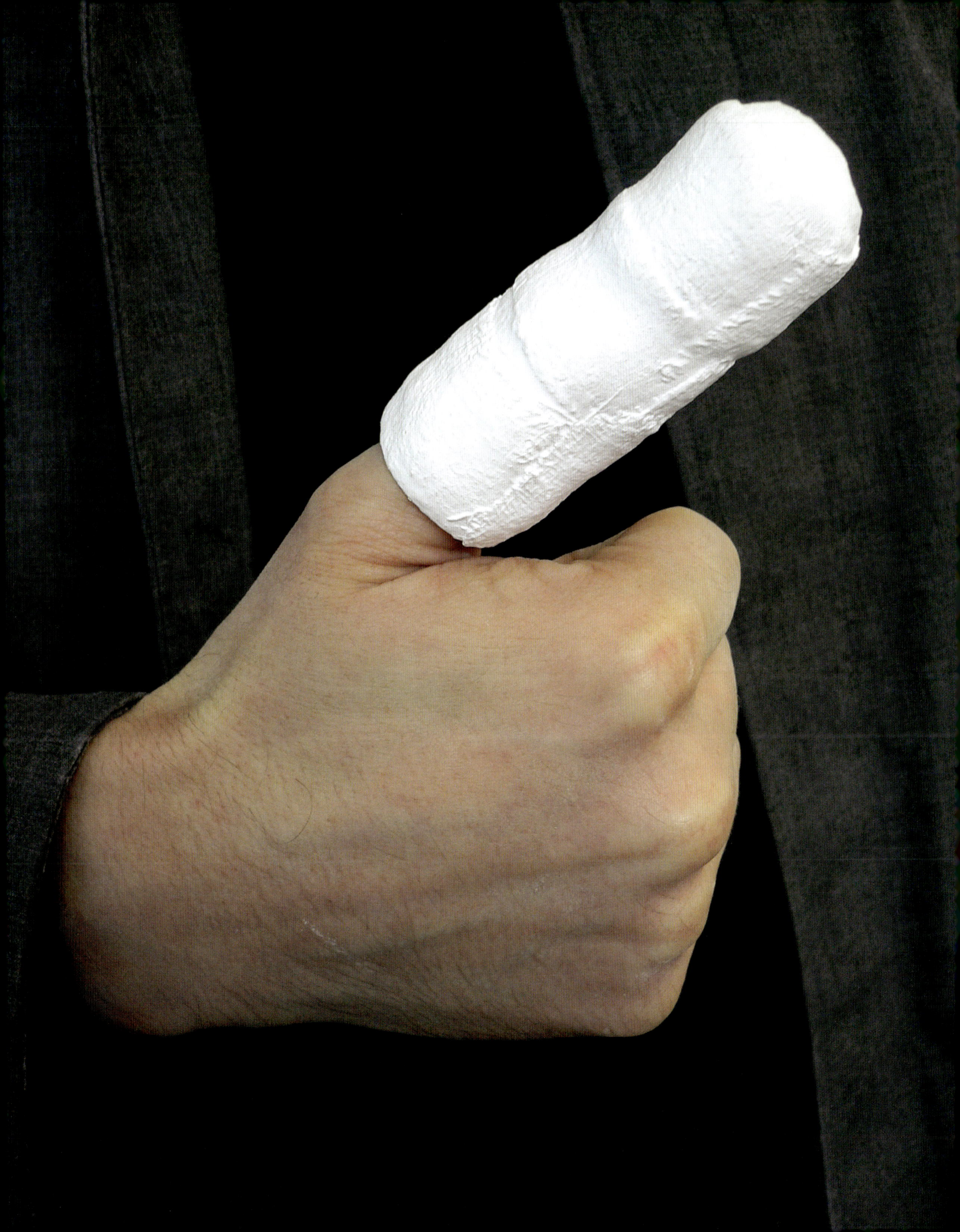

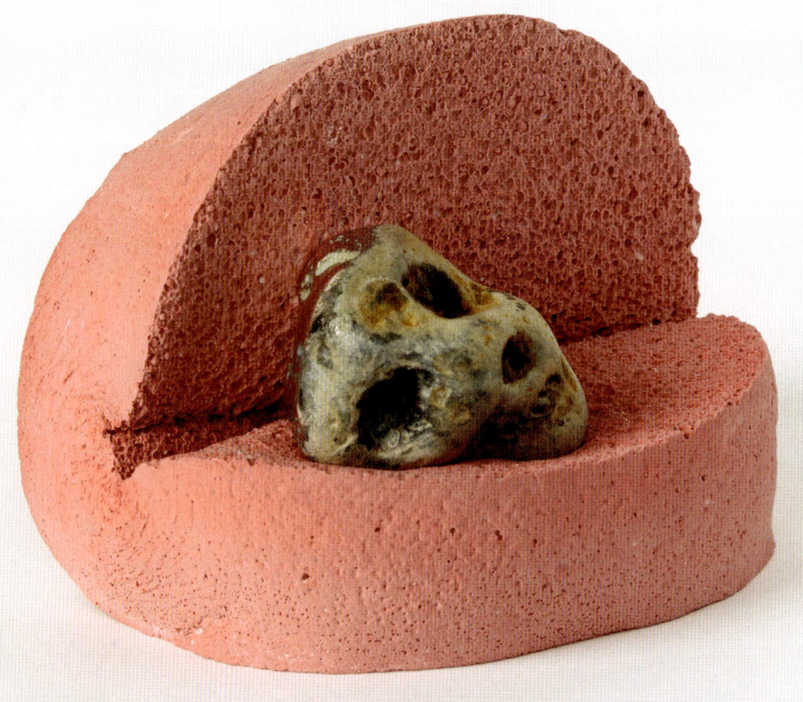

Split Lip 2012
Bronze and plaster,
7 × 9 × 7 cm

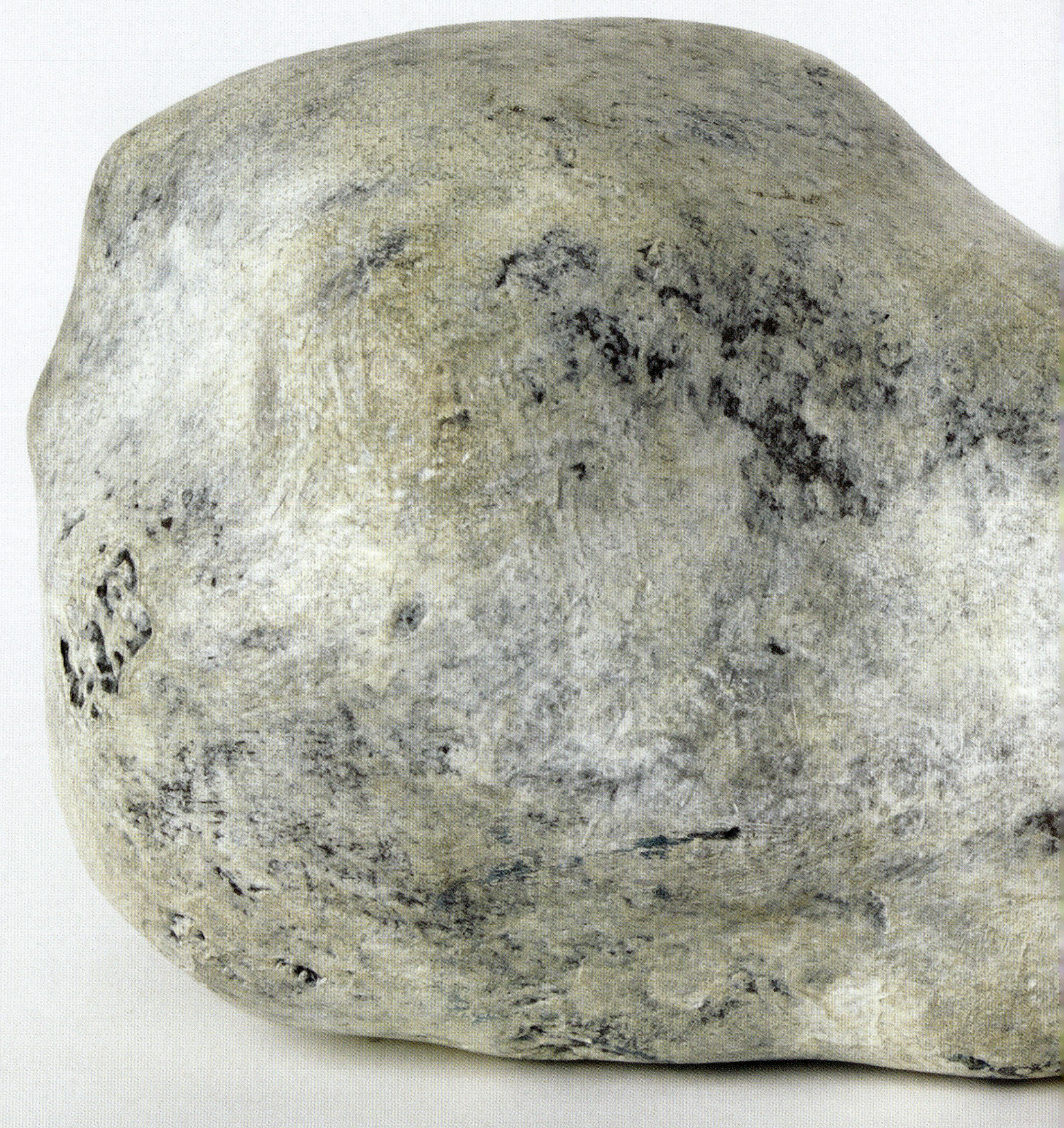

One Thing Leads To Another 2012
Bronze, plaster base, two pieces,
9 × 14 × 9 cm (large) and 5 × 5 × 4 cm (small)

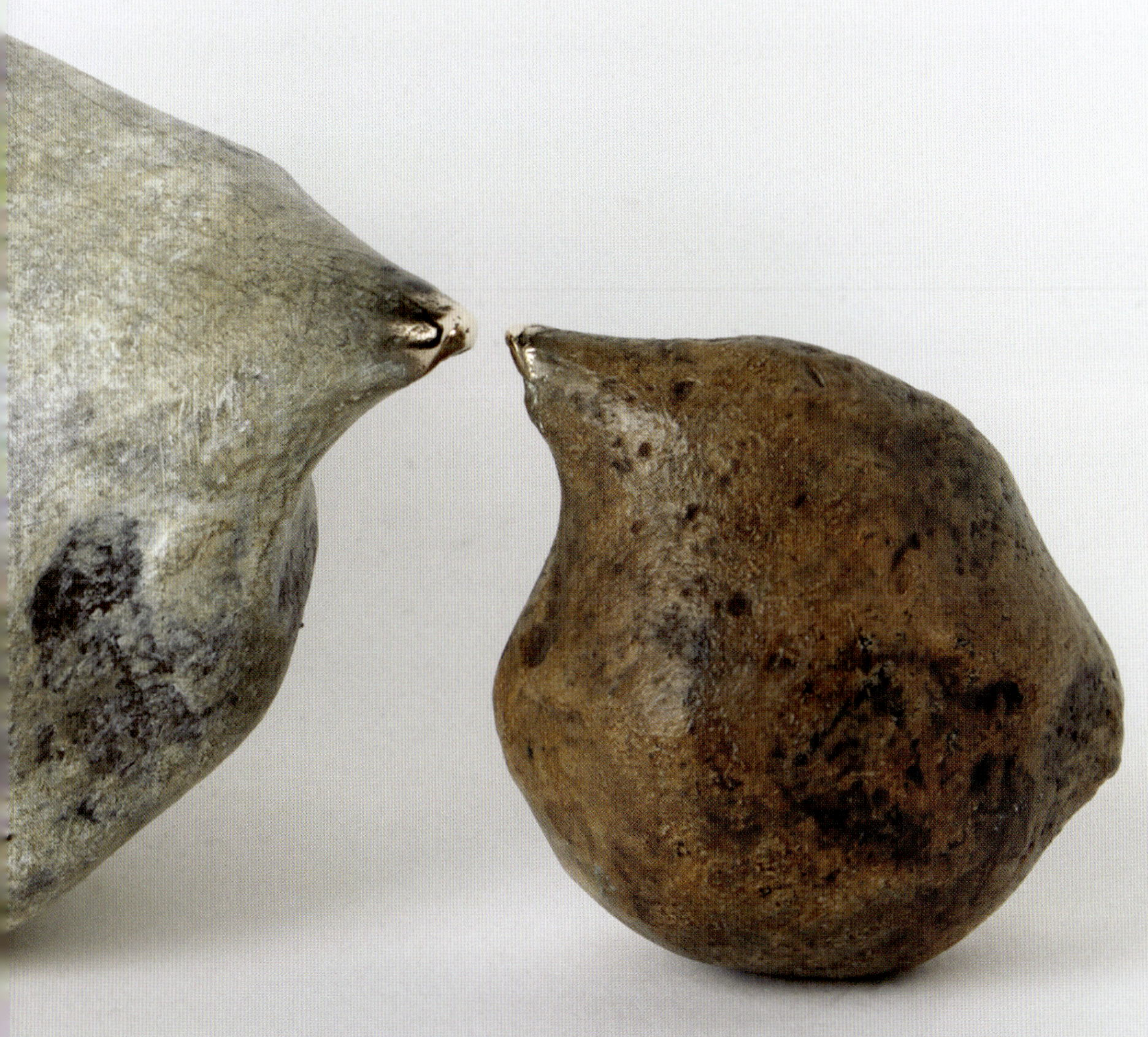

'I found this turnip for sale by the side of the road. The farmer had done all the work for me, it was oversized and misshapen and already looked like a grotesque face. The whole time I was casting it, I would put it on pieces of yellow sponge to stop it rolling onto the floor or scratching, but when I had the finished cast, it looked like something was missing. So I cast the foam as a base and it looked complete. I made it around the time that my dad died. Someone told me afterwards that organs and other body parts sit on pieces of sponge during an autopsy to soak up excess fluids and to stop them sliding about.'

Stump Still 2014
Resin, iron and plaster,
26 × 22 × 26 cm

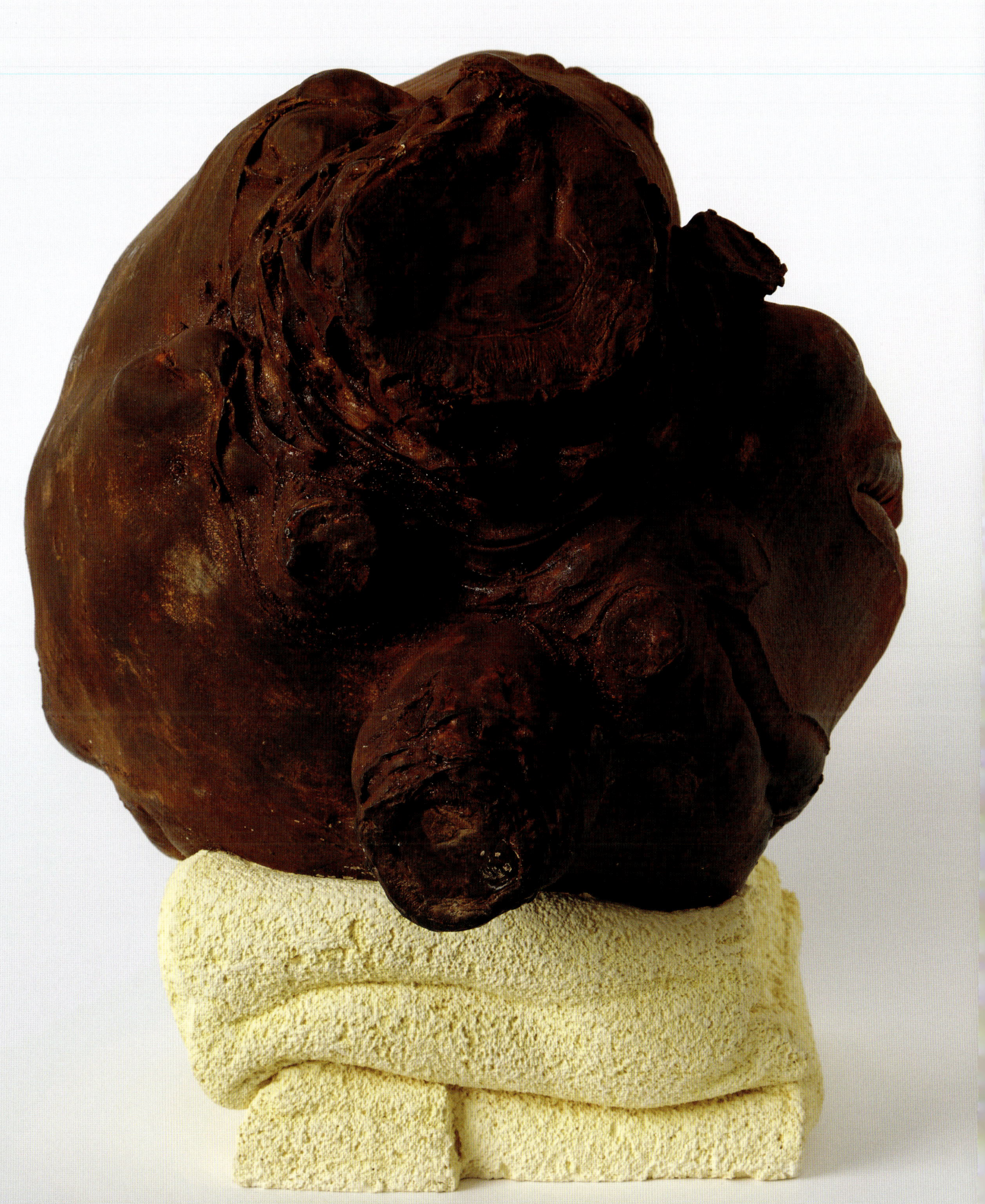

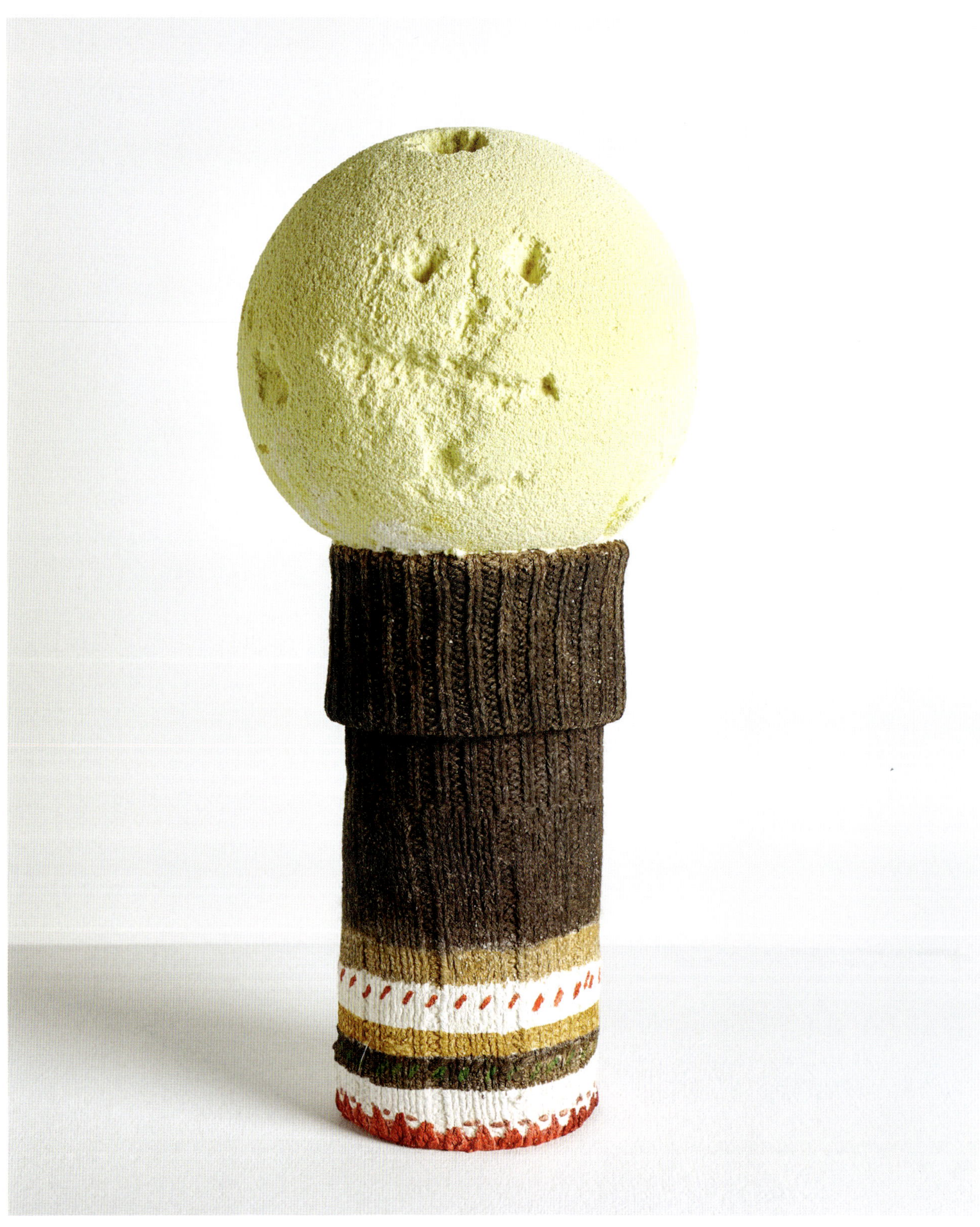

Planted 2017
Plaster and watercolour,
40 × 25 × 25 cm

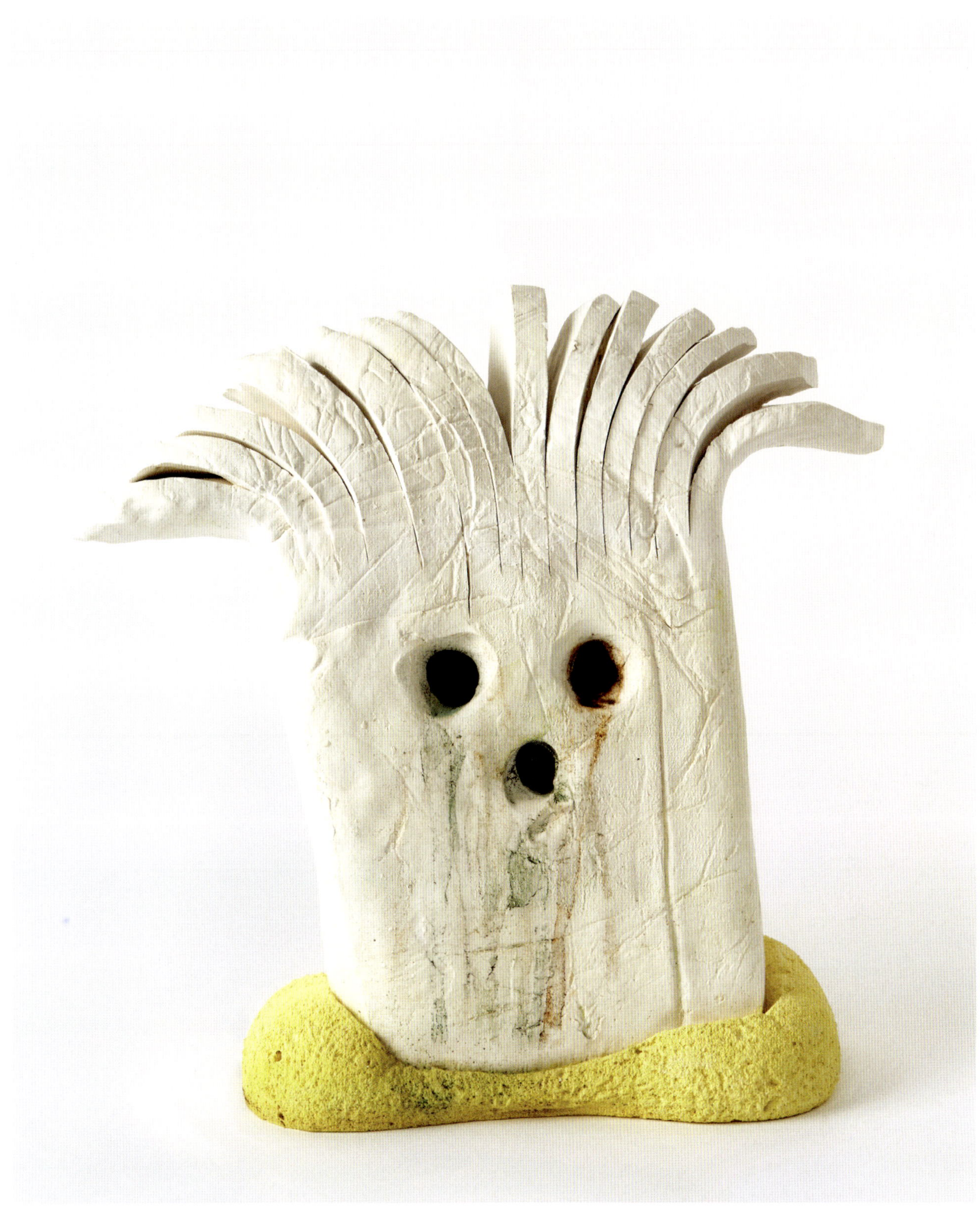

Suck It Up 2015
Plaster, bronze and copper,
30 × 33 × 13 cm

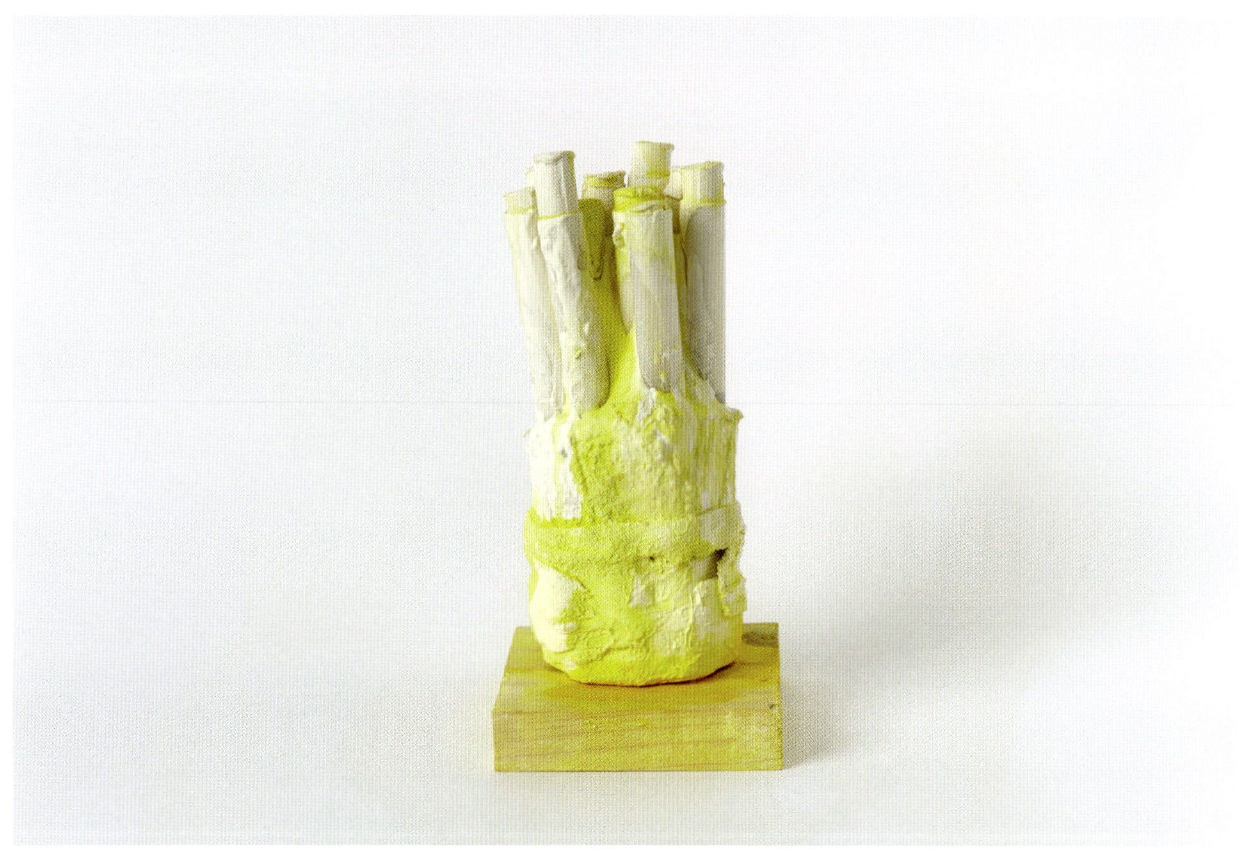

Razor Clams 2015
Plaster, plastic, scrim,
wood and watercolour,
19 × 9 × 9 cm

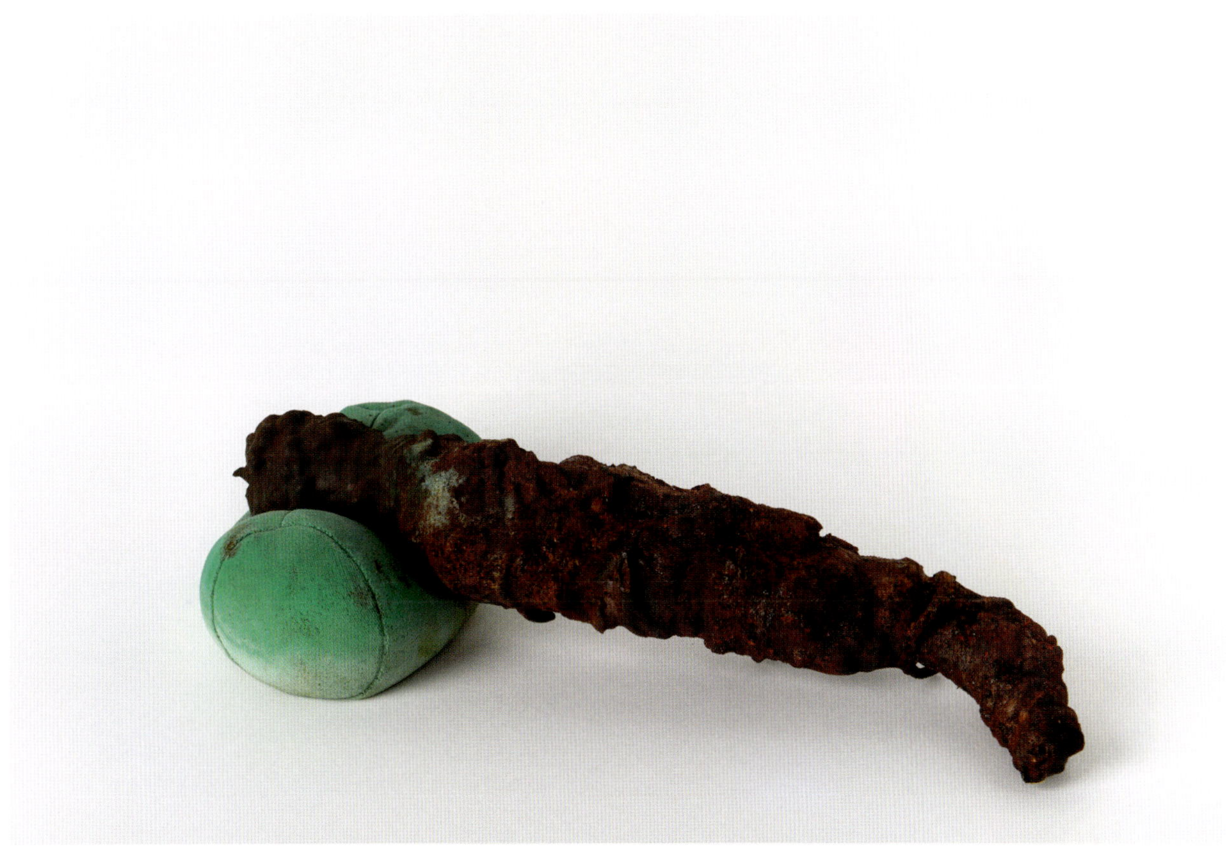

A Slender 2015
Resin, copper, iron and plaster,
7 × 31 × 14 cm

Alcoholic, Academic? 2015
Antique embroidery with cotton
silk cross-stitch on linen,
60 × 30 cm

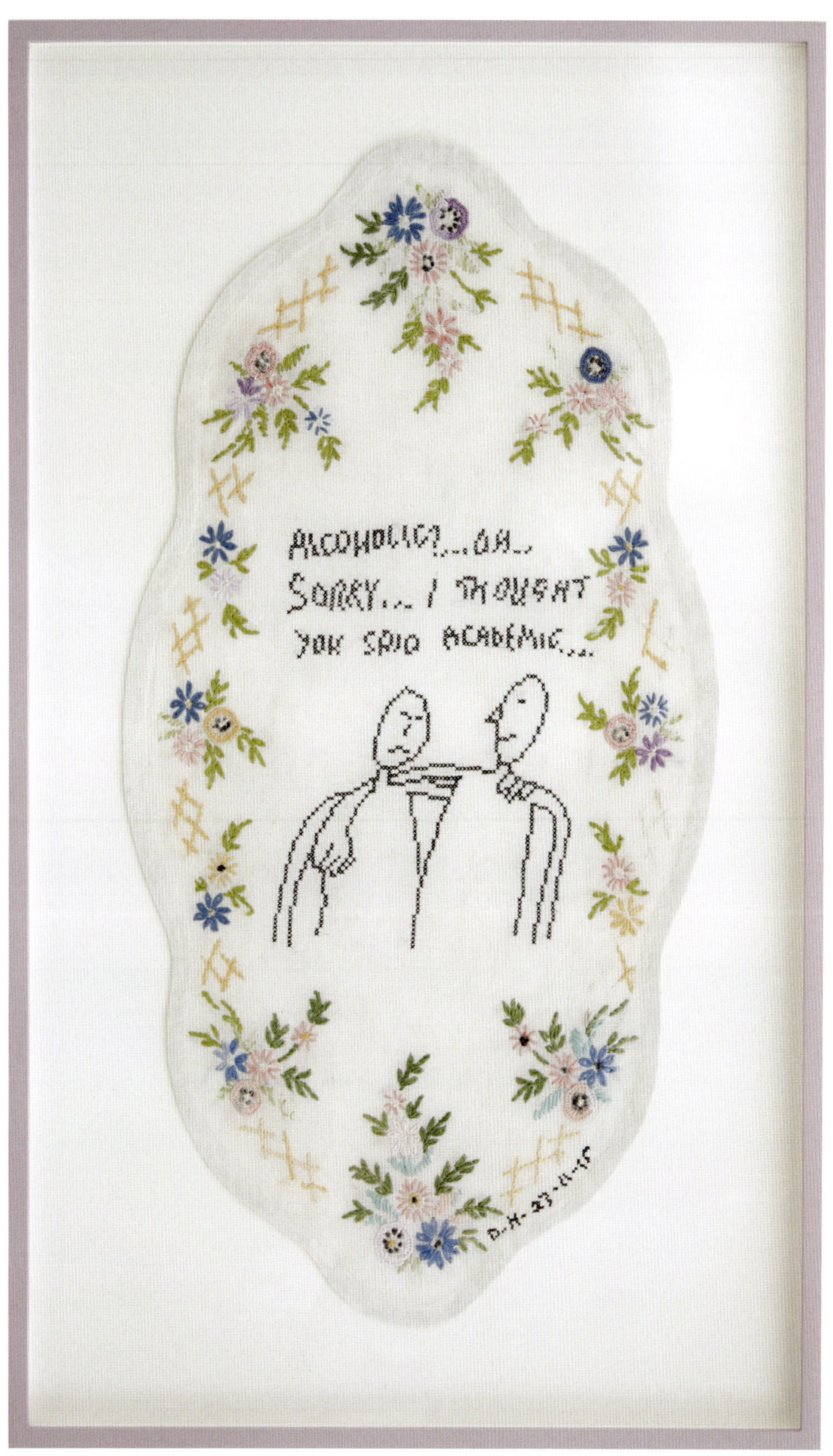
ALCOHOLIC?...OH...
SORRY... I THOUGHT
YOU SAID ACADEMIC...
D.H. 23-11-15

'When I was doing my MA at Goldsmith's, the tutors and I discussed at length the importance of collecting in my work. Door wedges, toy eyeballs, dog biscuits, red bits of litter picked up from the floor, etc., all which have been useful. For some reason, we decided that it might prove insightful to start a collection that was neither useful nor interesting. I began to collect the *What's On TV* guide, and I have done so every week for sixteen years. So far, it has taught me nothing.'

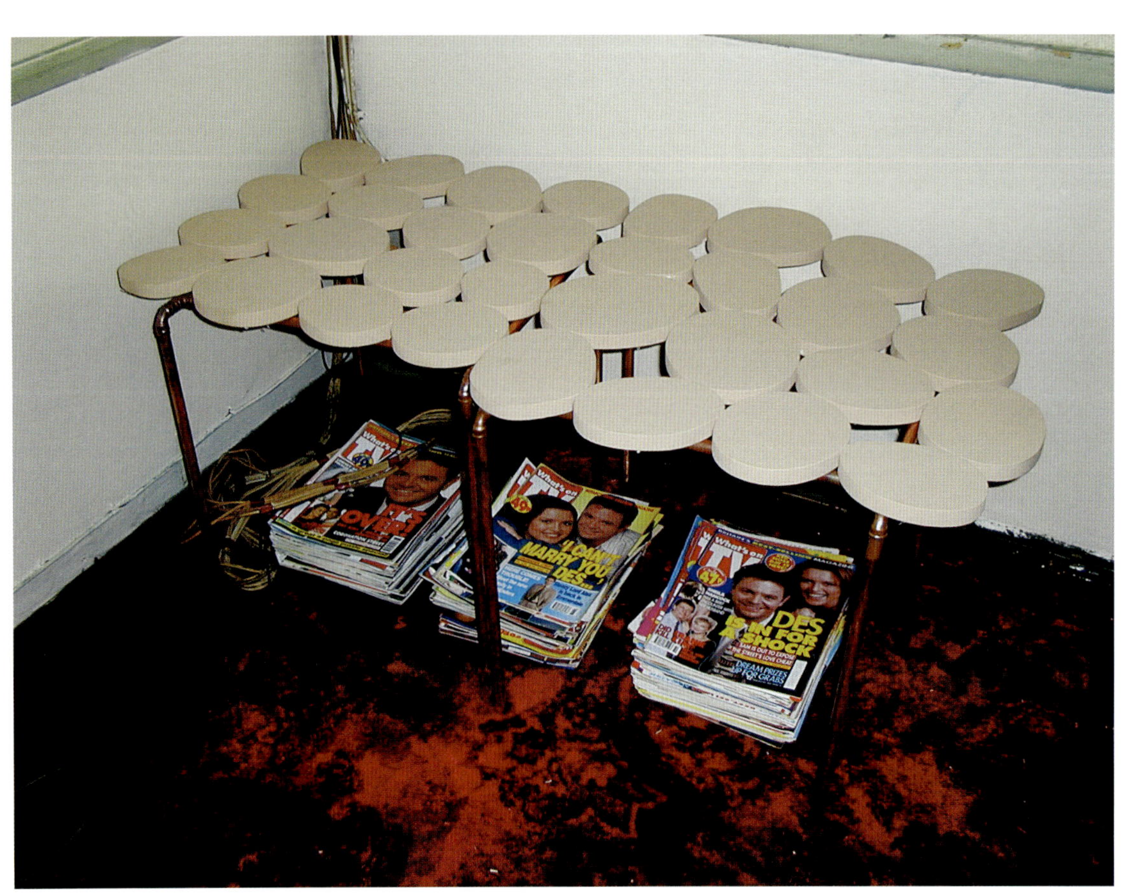

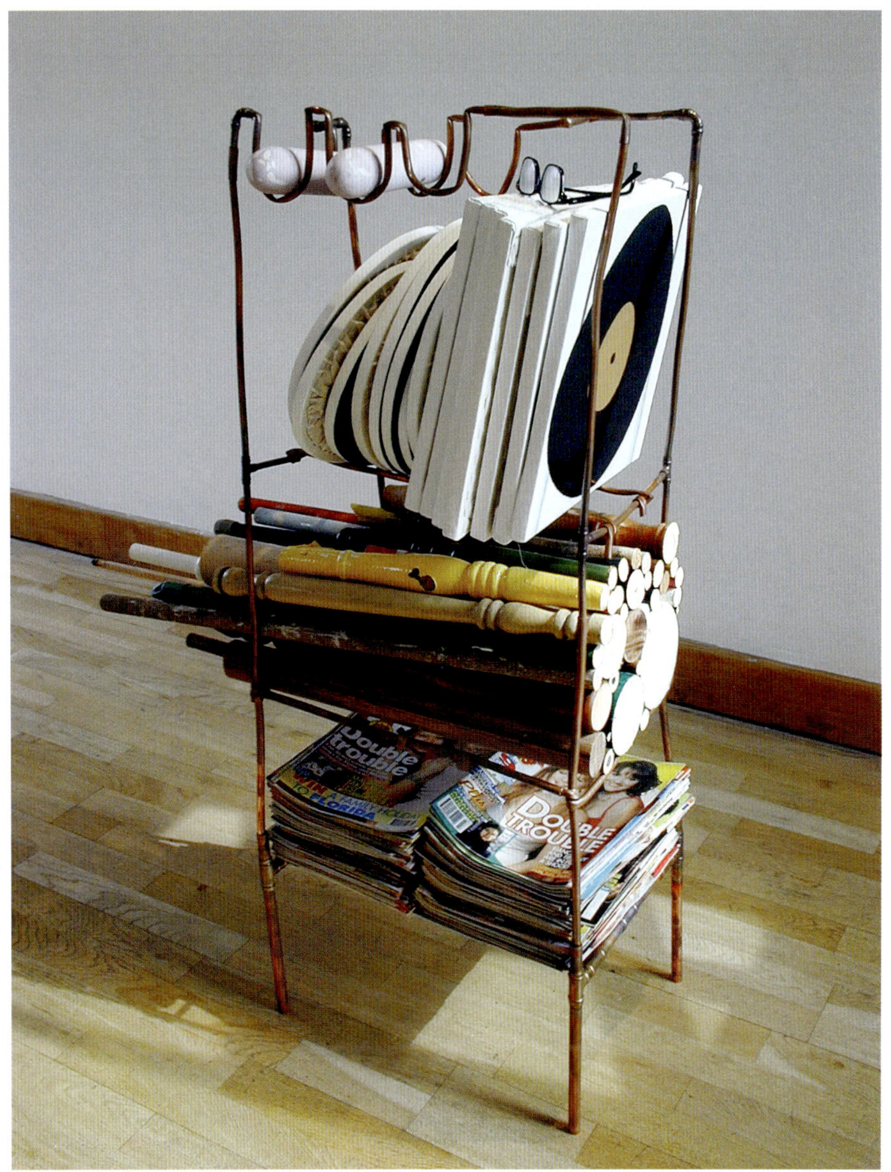

above

Who Hates Who and How Much 2002
Copper and mixed media, dimensions variable

opposite

What Was On TV 2001
Magazines, copper, MDF, canvas and acrylic, dimensions variable. Installed in an abandoned pub, Deptford, London.

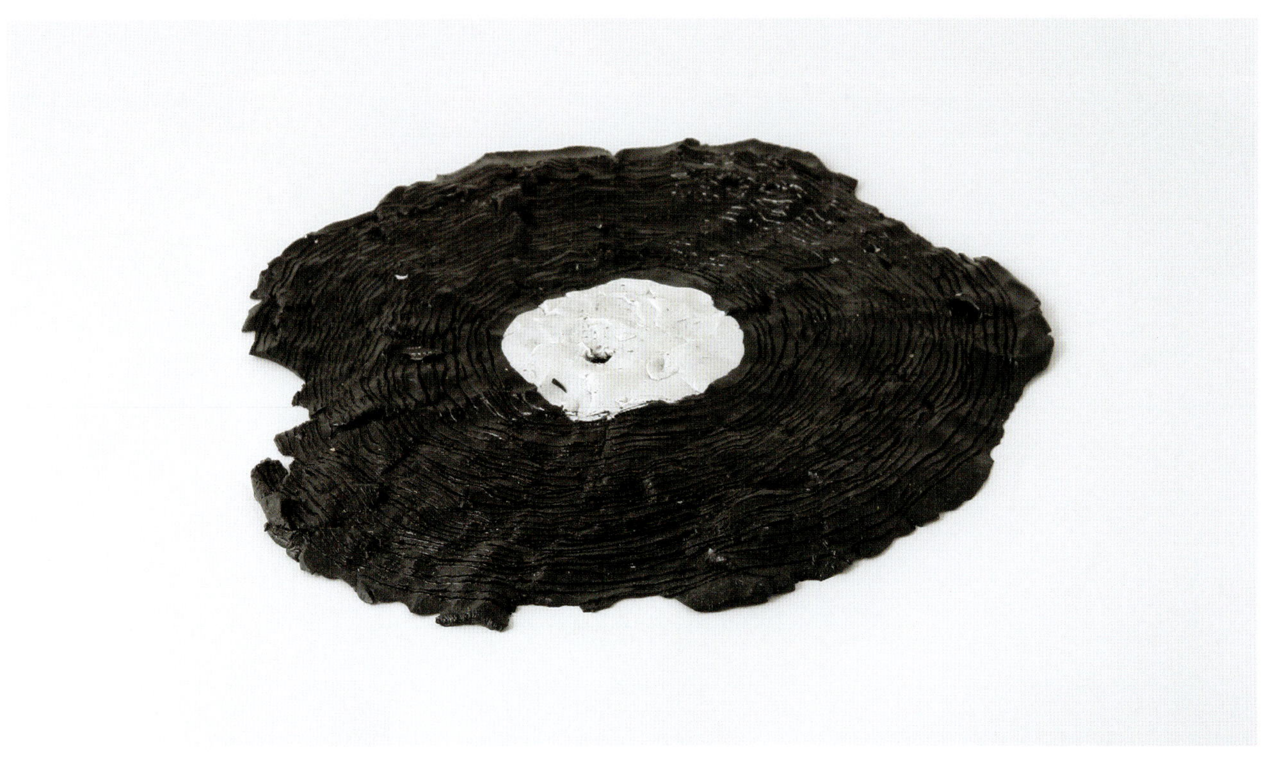

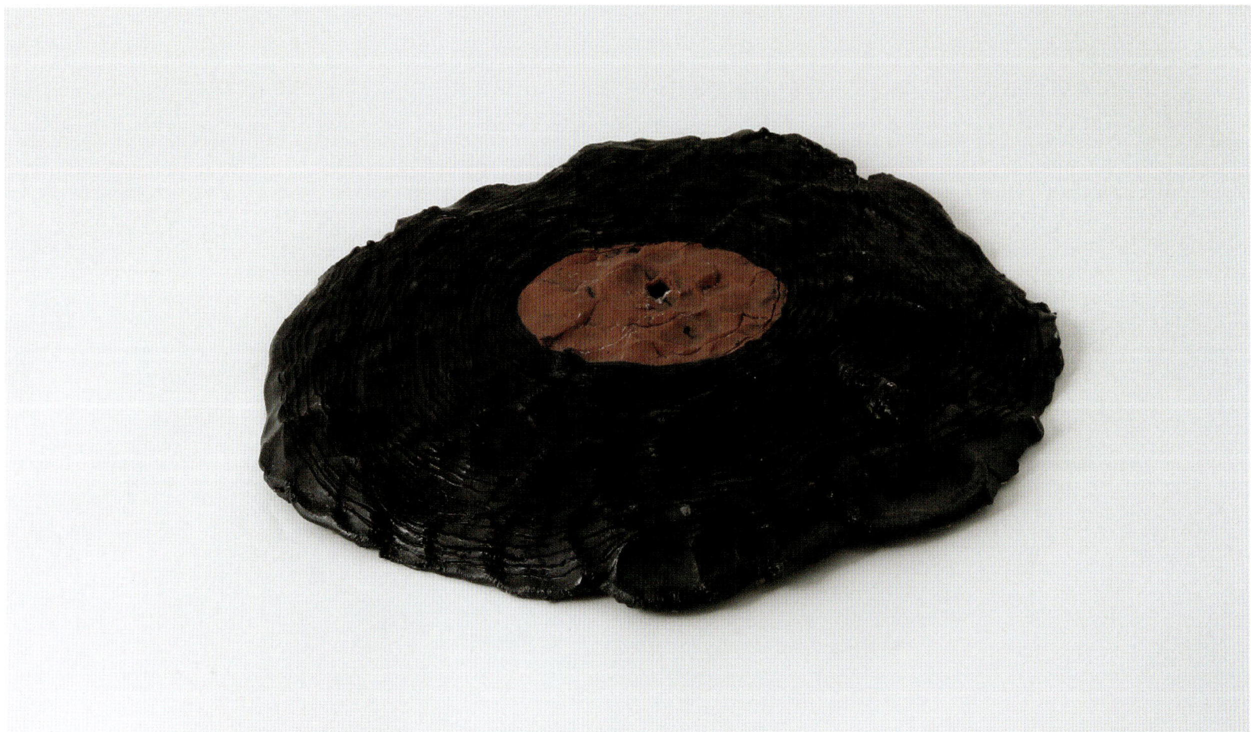

top

Record White Label 2002

Resin and pigment,

1 × 30 × 30 cm

bottom

Record Brown Label 2002

Resin and pigment,

1 × 30 × 30 cm

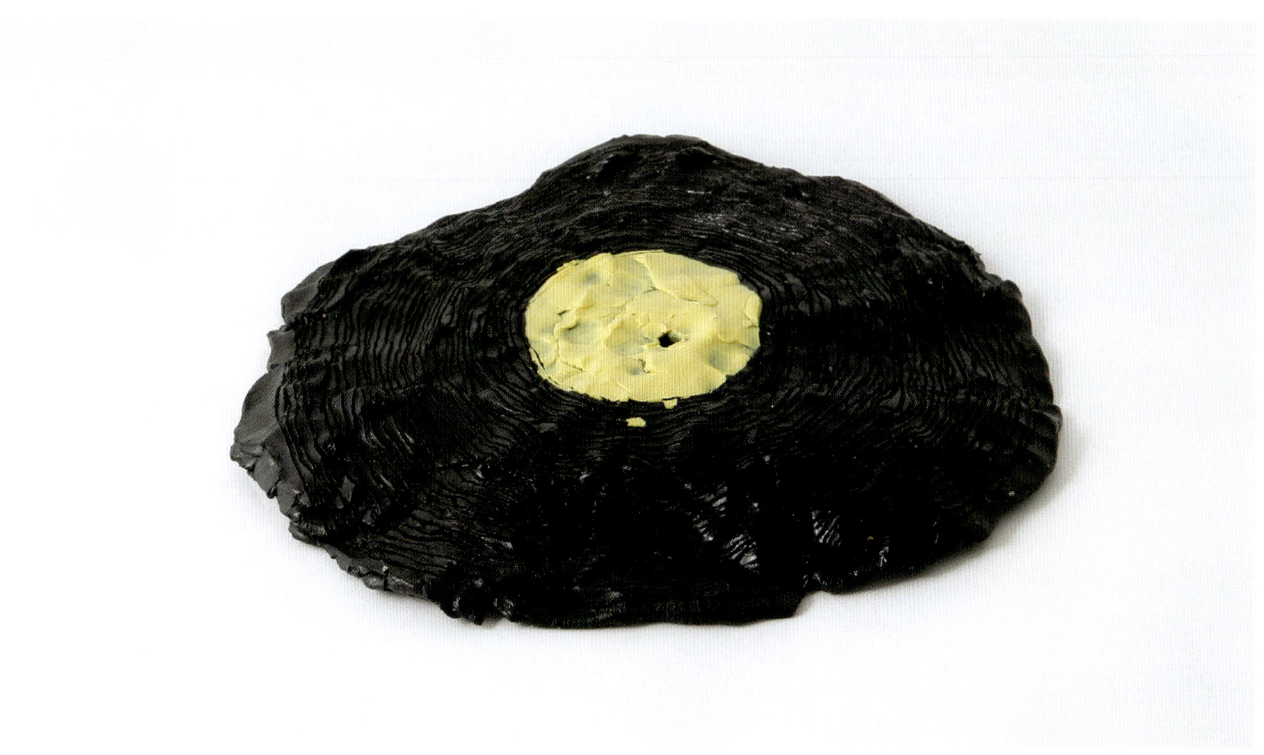

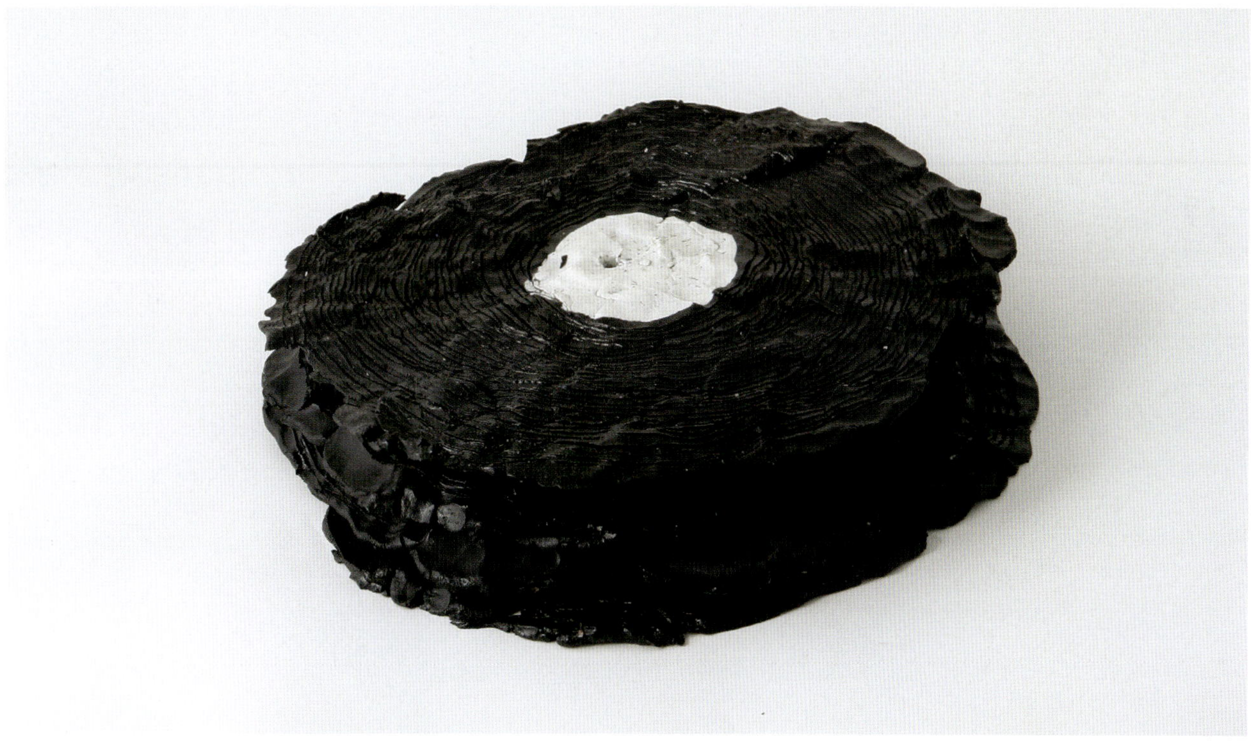

top
Record Yellow Label 2002
Resin and pigment,
1 × 30 × 30 cm

bottom
Stack of Records White Label 2002
Resin and pigment,
5 × 30 × 30 cm

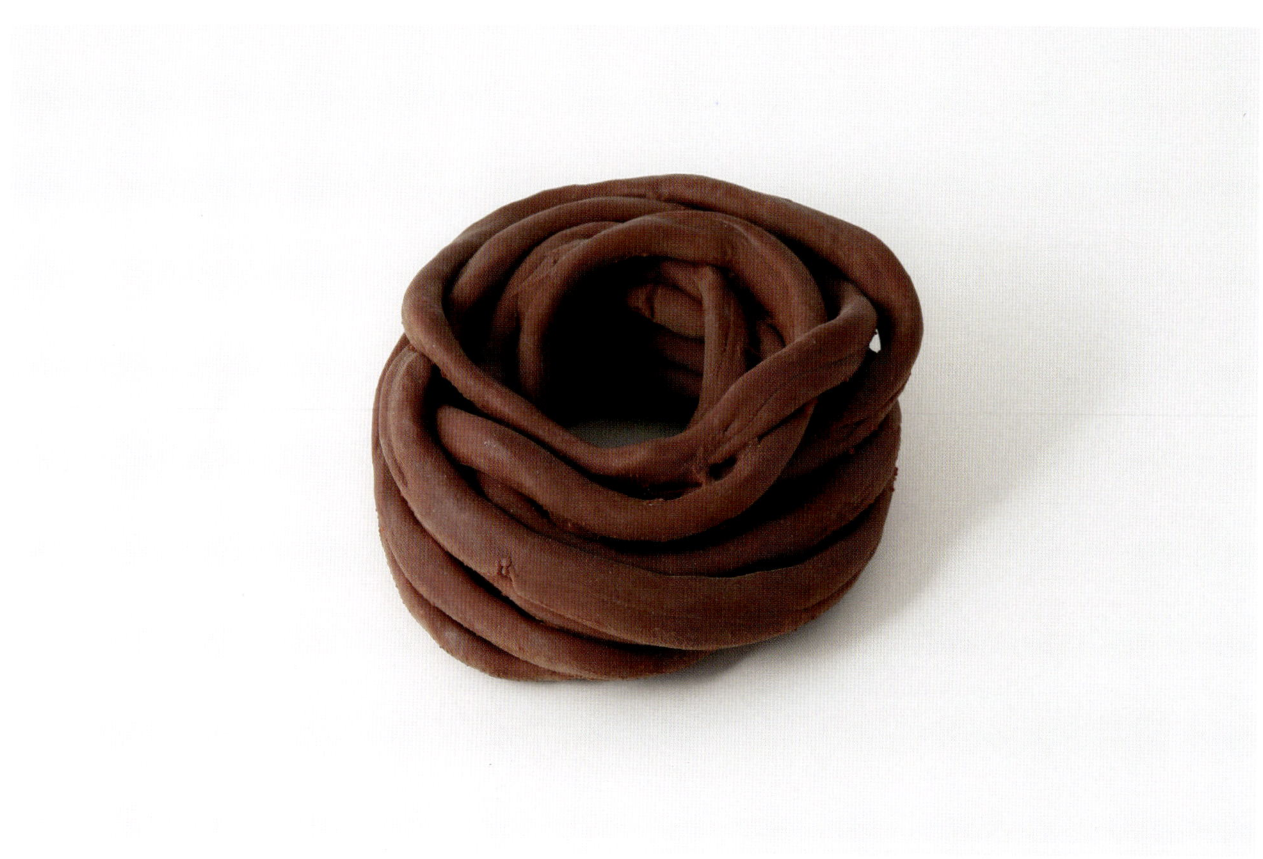

Ordure 2000
Latex and pigment,
80 × 150 cm

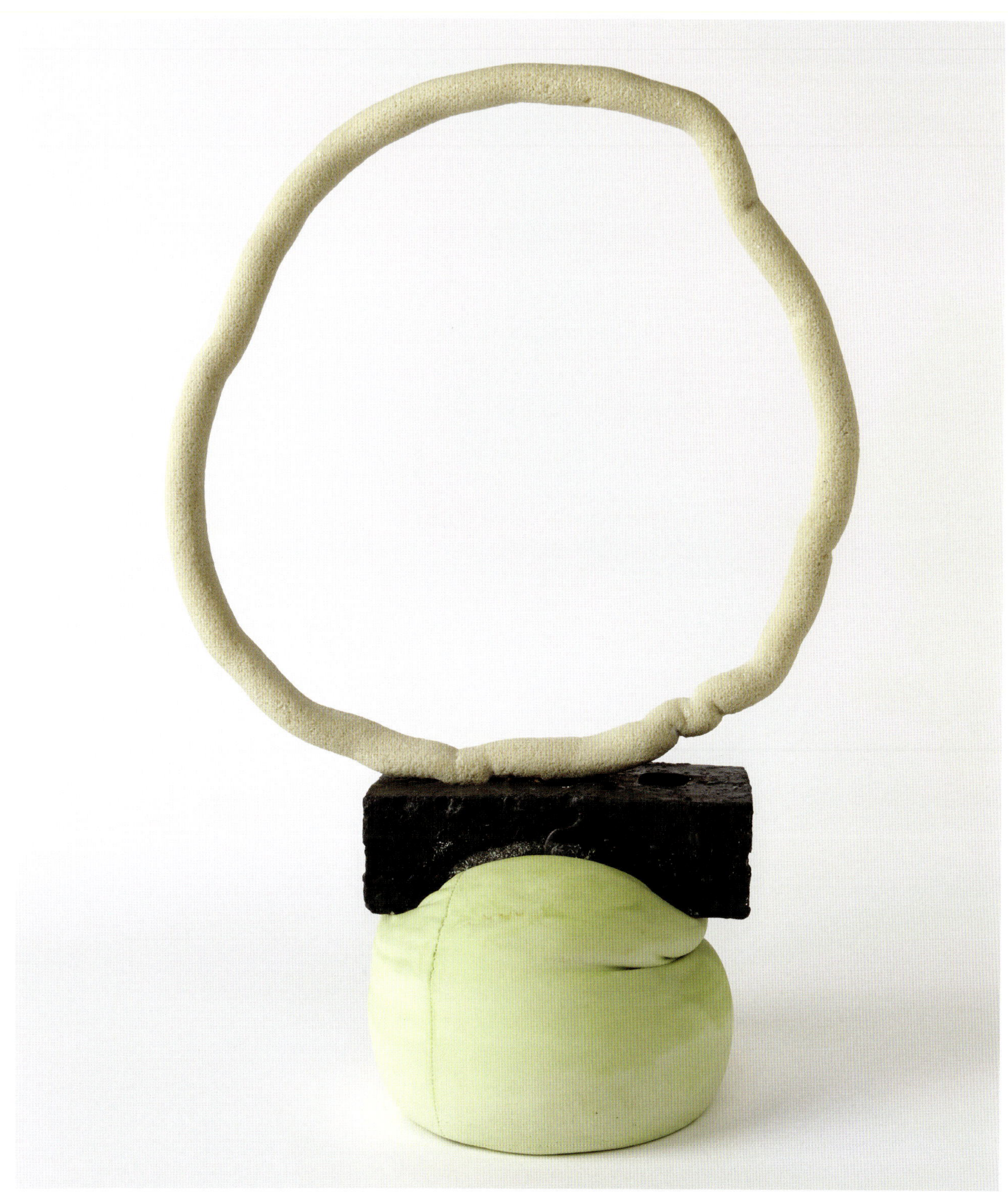

Threw It Through It 2015
Resin, plaster and iron,
57 × 40 × 20 cm

In a Brown Study 2011
Mixed media,
180 × 170 × 25 cm.
Installed in the studio.

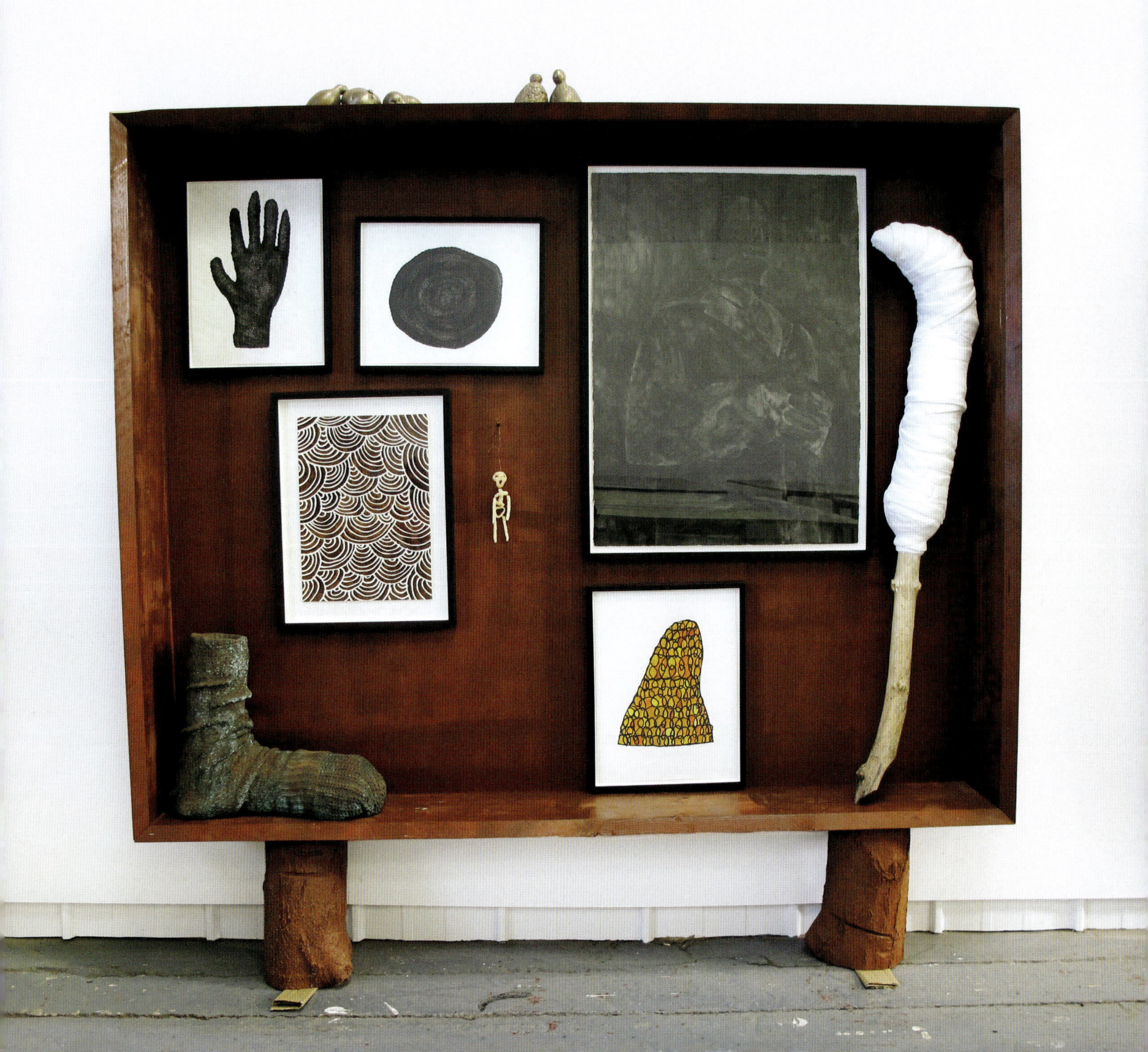

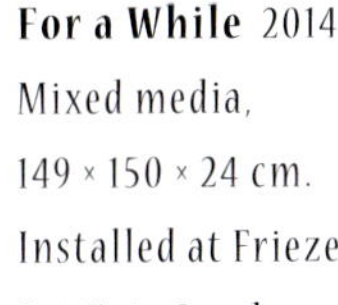

For a While 2014
Mixed media,
149 × 150 × 24 cm.
Installed at Frieze
Art Fair, London.

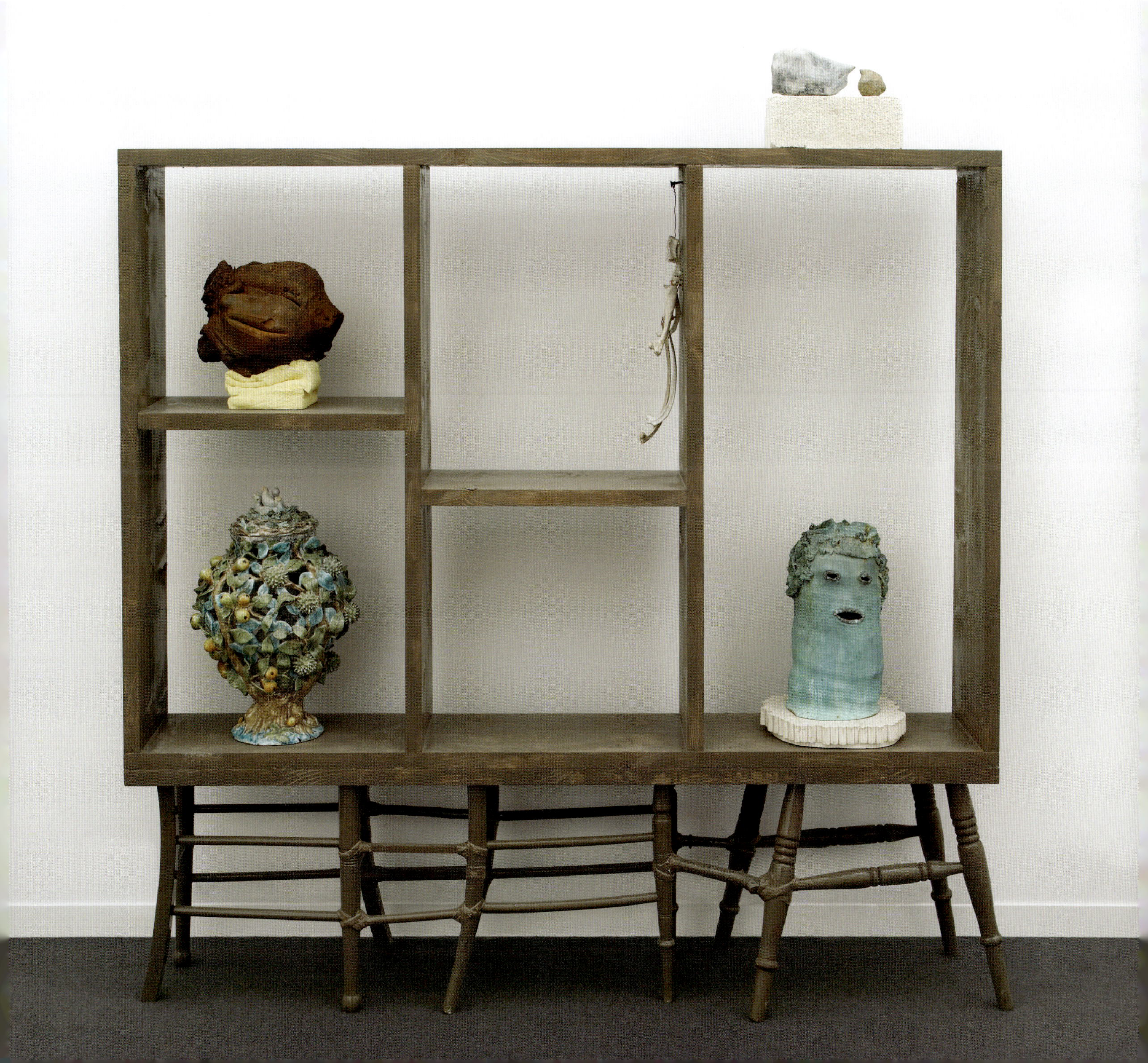

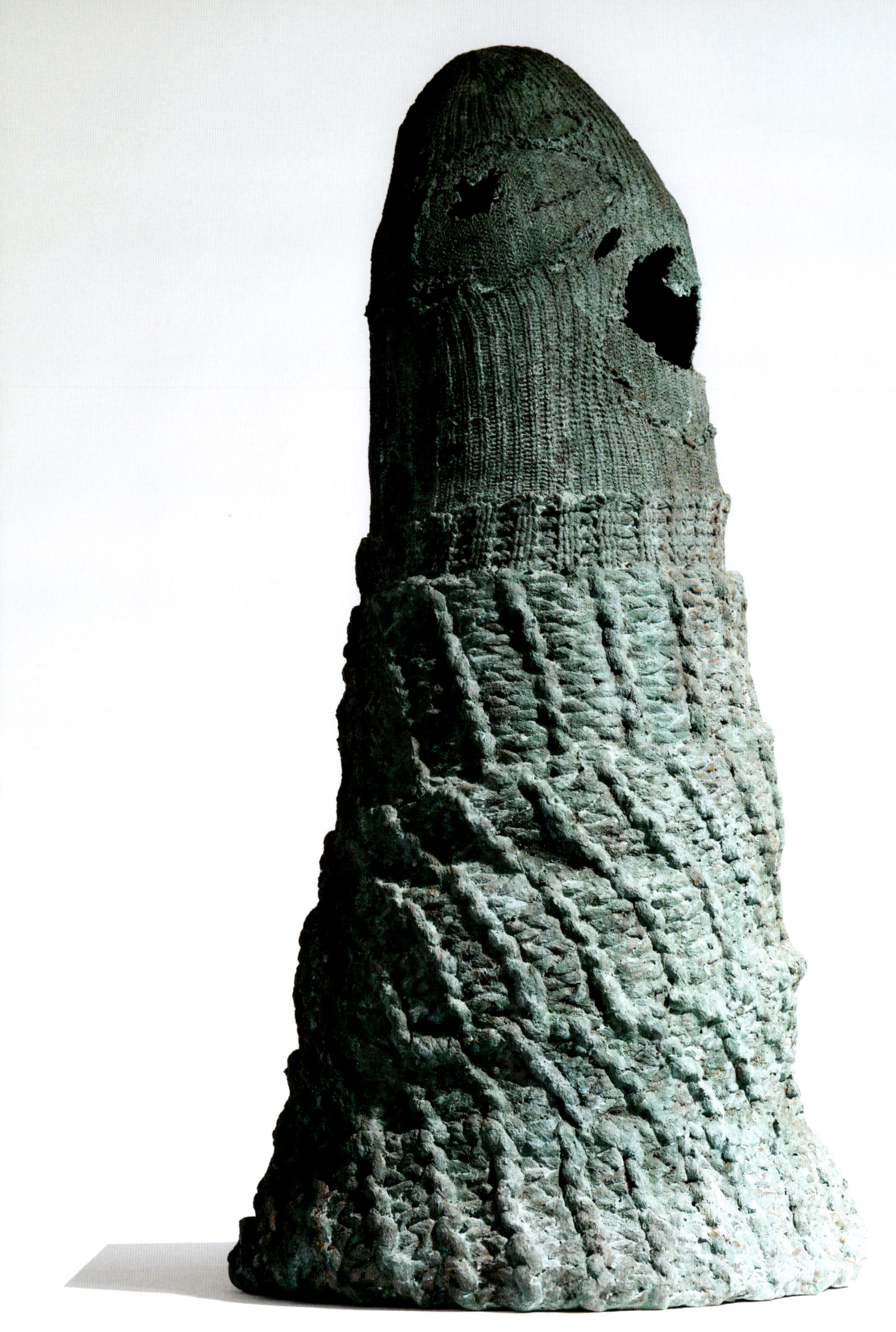

A Keeper of Heads

Bruce Haines

'A finger had poked its way out of the drain hole in the basin. A human finger. For a moment it froze, as if aware it had been discovered. Then it began to move again, feeling its wormlike way around the pink porcelain.'[1] So began the notice for Des Hughes's second exhibition at Ancient & Modern in London in 2013, which combined a typically diverse group of the most handmade of objects, including grinning charcoaled apples, hand-stitched embroidery and rusted cast resin-and-iron-powder sculptures of knitted, wrapped and teetering bodily forms. I wrote then as now that Hughes's practice has at its heart a wry humour, often manifest in his use of words in watercolours and thread, combined with a thorough immersion into the traditional materials of sculpture. A robust sense of imagery – he describes his art works as 'fending for themselves' – recalls classic British horror with a tender acknowledgment of the twentieth-century modernist canon, one that reimagines a pre-Romantic and more medieval moment, whose sombre world view was of the transience of life, the futility of pleasure and the certainty of death.

At Erno Goldfinger's former home at 2 Willow Road in Hampstead is an open 'cabinet' that forms a frame for the surrealist art collection contained inside. This device for containing things forms the basis for a series of sculptural installations by Hughes that bring together a delicate range of his watercolour drawings and resin casts. I encountered an early incarnation of these at the artist's old studio on a former Second World War airstrip in Herefordshire, a simple, picturesque environment where a lack of electricity meant he could work only until dusk. With their bases made variously from casts of tree trunks, or intertwined branches of young trees,

1 From Stephen King's 1990 short story 'The Moving Finger'.

The Grind Is So Ungrateful 2010
Copper, iron and resin, 68 × 40 × 40 cm

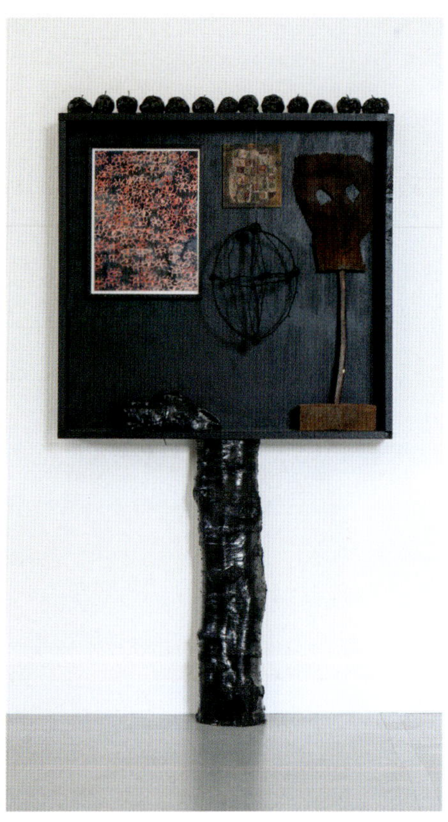

Mr Incomplete 2013
Mixed media, 157 × 90 × 15 cm

they were anticipating some kind of animation. I once took a small black version to an art fair in Basel, along the top of which were the aforementioned apples that had been baked to a crisp in the family's AGA oven. Each face carved Halloween-style into it had contorted into grimaces of the kind where pain and pleasure are indistinguishable. Beneath them within the frame was suspended a globe of black thorns and a delicate watercolour resembling an early twentieth-century abstract painting by Paul Klee, although Hughes's still life is of freshly baked hot-cross buns, all squished up against one another. A couple of Mexico-based artists mistook it for a piece of religious iconography from their own continent. It was, as with much of Hughes's sculptures, quite unlike anything else in contemporary art, more like reliquaries imagined in extraordinary places where they really have had to fend for themselves.

'The Moving Finger' quoted at the start of this account, and which does not end well for the watching protagonist, is the basis of a number of sculptures Hughes has constructed, cast using an enviable skill that by now we take for granted in his practice, but which enables an uncanny corporeality of his subjects. The degree to which one material can be made to mimic another in the traditional casting process is a kind of alchemical wonder to the uninitiated, just as technologies around 3D digital printing might also provide a quick shorthand to something similar on the factory floor. In this respect, Hughes looks back to traditions that were developed in medieval times. His various 'Hoods', among them *The Grind Is So Ungrateful*, evoke a kind of comedy knight's armour, though modelled from clay leaves or cast from forms modelled from chunky knitwear. That his work is sometimes also cast in bronze is interesting too when some is rendered equally powerfully, if not for longevity, in sticky tape. Medieval tombs are sometimes accompanied by an emblematic sculpture of man's best friend, a dog, a familiar motif to connect the living with the dead. Hughes has his own version, faceless but relatively

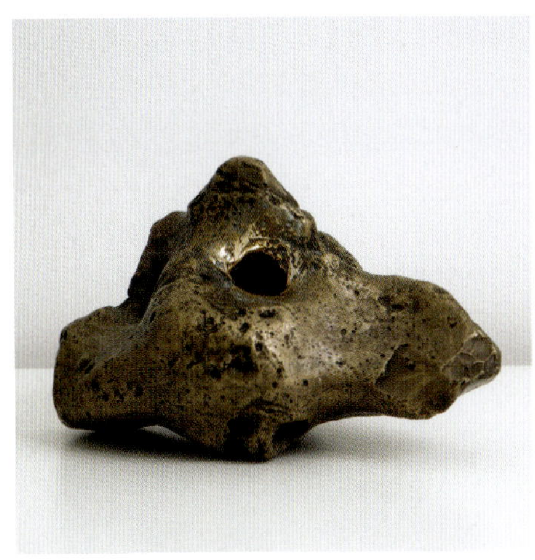

Norfolk Flint (with boring) 2007
Bronze, 18 × 28 × 16 cm

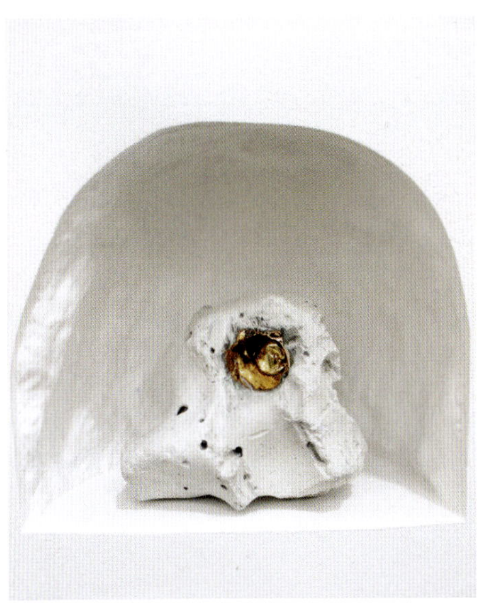

Stonut 2008
Bronze and crisp bag, 21 × 20 × 14 cm

Labrador in scale whose paw rests upon another of Hughes's own recurrent forms, the severed hand. One version of *Do You Think Of Me Often* (*pp. 122–3*), cast in bronze, rests in the sculpture garden of Whitworth Art Gallery in Manchester, a particularly poignant publically sited vessel for our times.

The reclining knight was the centre of *Endless Endless*, a theatrical installation at Frieze Art Fair in London in 2010 (*pp. 108–9*). An effigy on a large pedestal – the pedestal is an ongoing subject of fascination in Hughes's work, and at the centre of his most recent exhibition in Copenhagen – with a shallow pool of water in its belly, resembled the statuary found on the tombs of medieval dignitaries, but in this case could also be someone either drunk or asleep. Public sculpture of this type nearly always displays the ravages of time, a result of casual vandalism, religious aggression or the weather – changes generally not encouraged in art works. The torso is cast in resin mixed with iron powder so that as the water pools onto its surface, it continues to rust. Black mirrors, fittingly titled *Each Way* and based on witches' scrying glasses, surrounded the figure, into which visitors gazed at their soul, or adjusted their hair. Within alcoves set into the walls – themselves cast from carrier bags – were three small bronzes cast from flints dug from a field in Norfolk where Henry and Irina Moore and artist-friends including Ivon Hitchens, Barbara Hepworth and Ben Nicholson stayed on various occasions during the 1930s. Moore and Hepworth collected such flints and made studies of them. Hughes's versions, such as *Norfolk Flint (with boring)*, which resembles a skull, have polished parts at the inverse of where one would expect it; more normally it would be a prominence that would be rubbed smooth by people touching the work – as happens to the feet, hands, genitals, breasts and buttocks of historical monumental bronze figures; or in another, *Stonut*, a crisp packet is pushed into a hole, the bronze of the inside of a bag of McCoy's matching precisely the sheen of the polished bronze hole in which it is stuffed. There is a

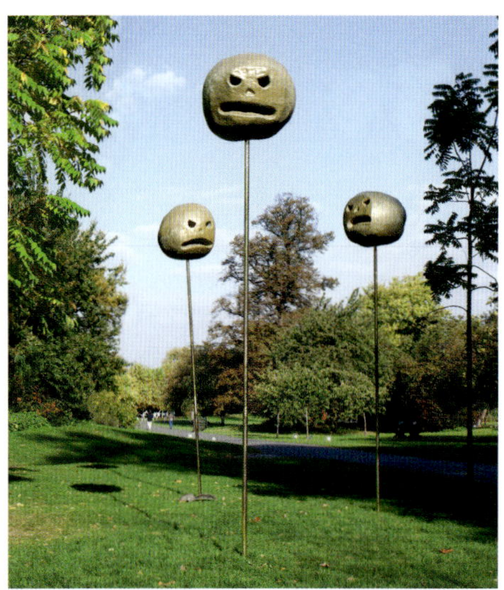

Angry Pins Frieze Sculpture Garden, Regent's Park, London, October 2011. Fibreglass, resin, brass powder and brass, 400 × 50 × 50 cm

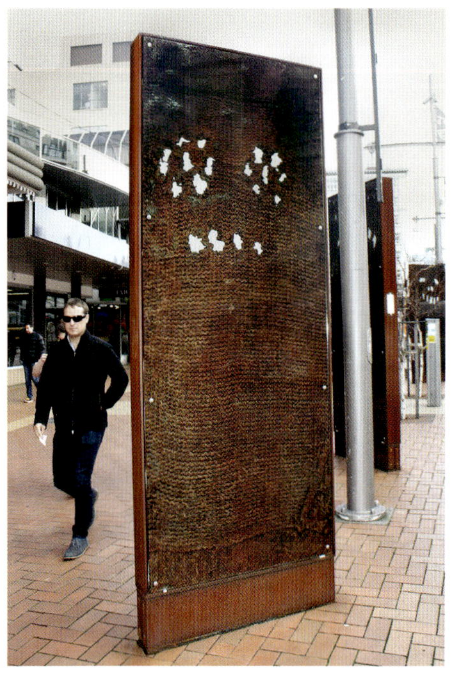

The Visitors Wellington city centre, New Zealand, 2015
Light boxes, 300 × 100 × 20 cm

subtly erotic dimension to these pieces, along with a mysterious essence that Moore and Hepworth would also have identified in such stones. In this sense, Hughes's work can also be seen as something of a fond tribute to British modernist sculpture, although clearly retaining its own identity.

Public art works *Angry Pins* and *The Visitors* demonstrate a marvellous possibility of greater public visibility of Hughes's work, where dry humour alleviates the anxiety of daily life. *Angry Pins* is hugely scaled-up version of a miniature sculpture by the same name (*p. 73*) that was made as part of a series called 'Thems' – small-scale works based on assemblages of overly familiar and non-traditional sculptural objects such as peas or nails. Each head of the pin features a grimacing face, as if it has been recently squeezed, atop tall metal pins set into the ground. *The Visitors* took their form from sheets of wool imbedded with rusted iron powder and punctured with holes in the rough outline of faces. Photographs of the sculptures (cannily avoiding shipping bills!) were set into light boxes and placed on the pavement in Wellington, New Zealand. Both works were subtly confrontational and funny, qualities rarely expounded in public art since Claes Oldenburg's own signature giant or floppy sculptures based on everyday objects.

It is appropriate that when he brought his most recent work to exhibition, in Copenhagen in 2017, Hughes did so under the title 'Keeper of Heads' (*pp. 46–56*). From the fourteenth to the seventeenth centuries, beheading was a common form of execution, usually reserved for the most important prisoners, and there was a more or less constantly changing display of decapitated heads on spikes at Tower Bridge in London, then the only crossing point into the City, grinning down on people passing beneath. Since the repatriation of a severed head with the rest of the body was seen as important in medieval times, the 'Keeper of Heads' had a vital role in protecting them. The head in *Good Boy* has its features turned inside out; or, in *Planted* (*p. 26*), they are almost obliterated,

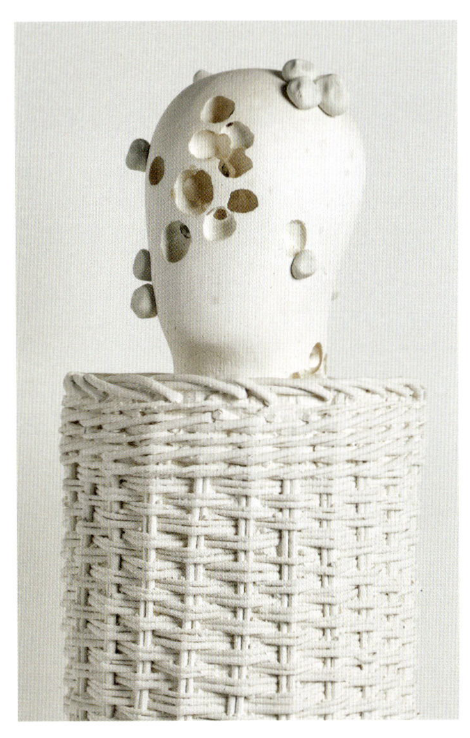

Good Boy 2017
Plaster, 76 × 35 × 35 cm

their gestures like emoji, pared down, clear. I think what we are witness to with these works is a process of getting there, about going gently on to find a point of balance between materials, pedestal, materiality and objective form, a teetering and tantalizing coming together of skills and mysterious visions that is about a theatre of display, one that begins in a studio that is the artist-as-collector's library of physical references. Among his most recent sculpture is *Stunt* (*pp. 47 and 48*), which seems to cock not one but three hats at the long, complex but joyous journey from which this body of work has come, and the as-yet-unknown path it will continue on next.

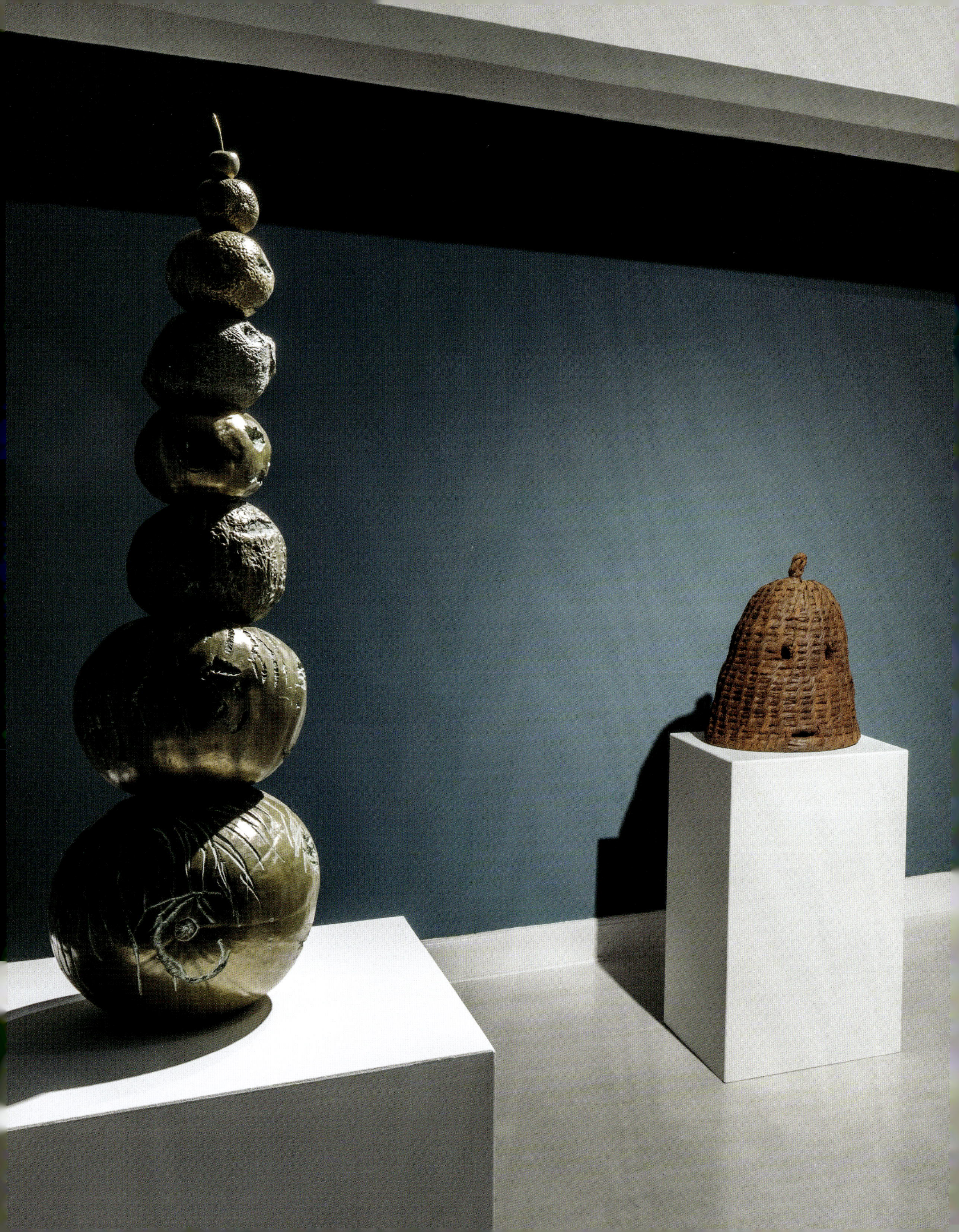

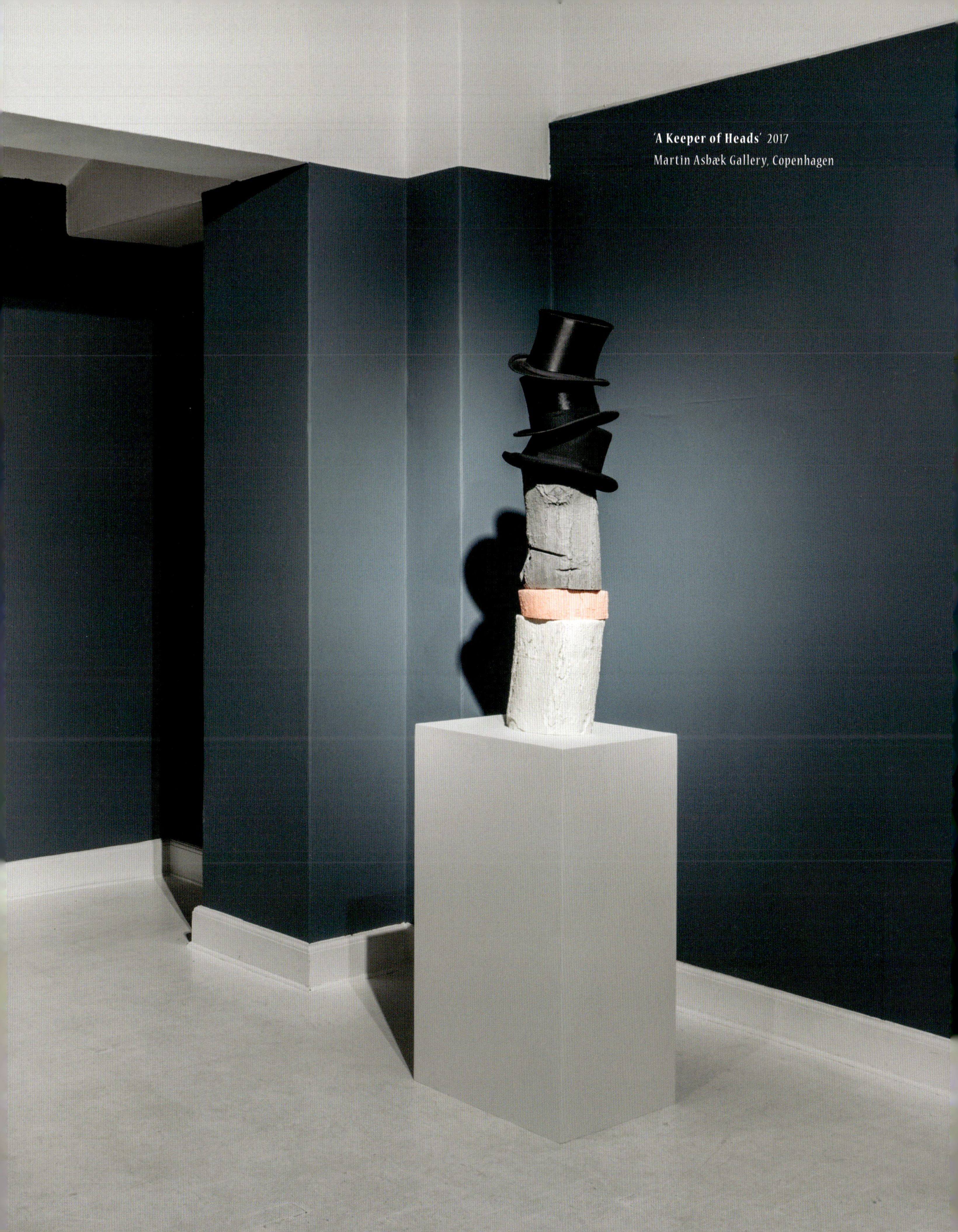

'A Keeper of Heads' 2017
Martin Asbæk Gallery, Copenhagen

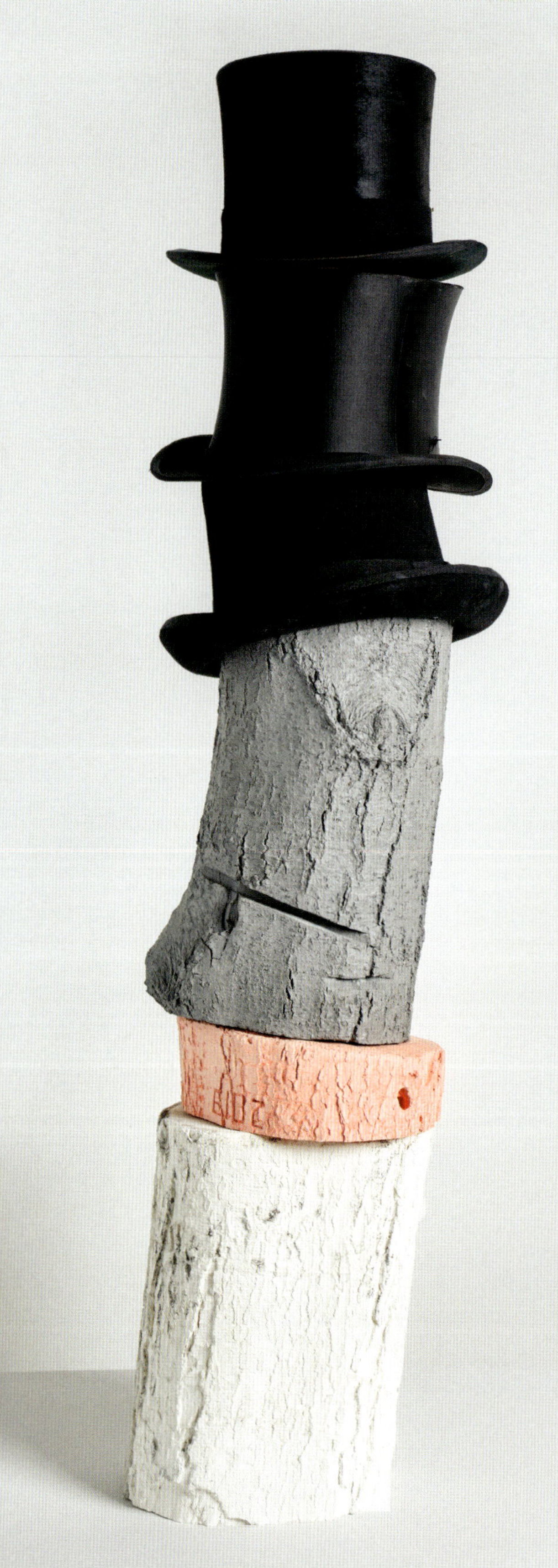

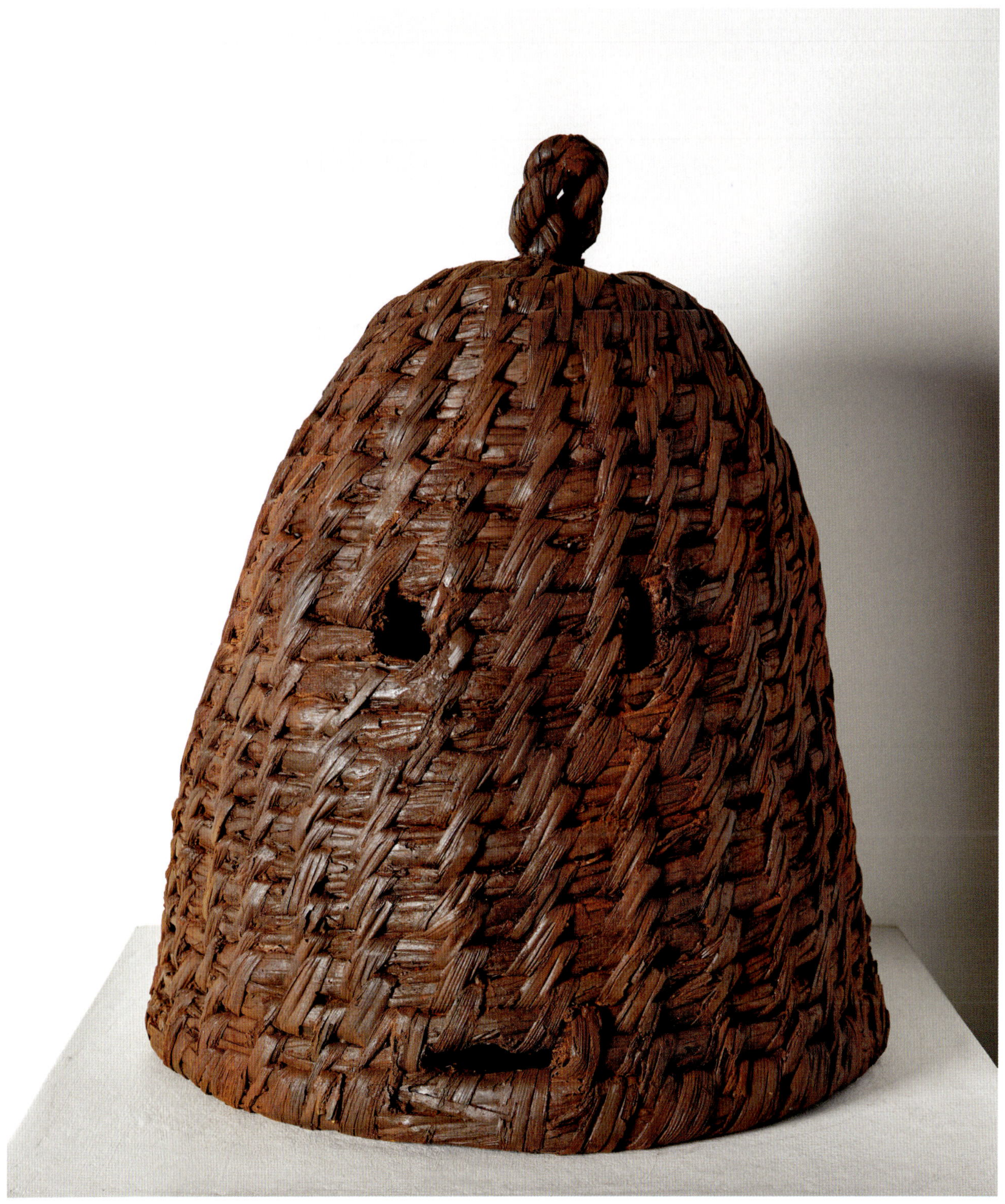

opposite
Stunt 2017
Plaster, aluminium, resin and top hats,
98 × 23 × 20 cm

above
The Bell 2016
Resin and iron powder,
50 × 43 × 43 cm

'Sometimes, the image is the most important thing. I'll have a clear picture of how I want the finished sculpture to look. In the case of *The Losing End*, I made the work very quickly and achieved the intended result. Yet with *Good Boy*, the process was all I had. All I knew was that I wanted the idea of "the mould" as a negative space and the positive "object" that comes out of it, to exist simultaneously in one place. Usually the mould belongs in the past, it stays behind in the studio while the sculpture goes out into the world. The small clay balls that I used were just the stooge that sets up the gag. I needed to keep revisiting the mould and reworking the materials until I felt that I'd got this point across. That process is equally as important to me as the final sculpture.'

The Losing End 2017
Resin and brass powder,
67 × 22 × 21 cm

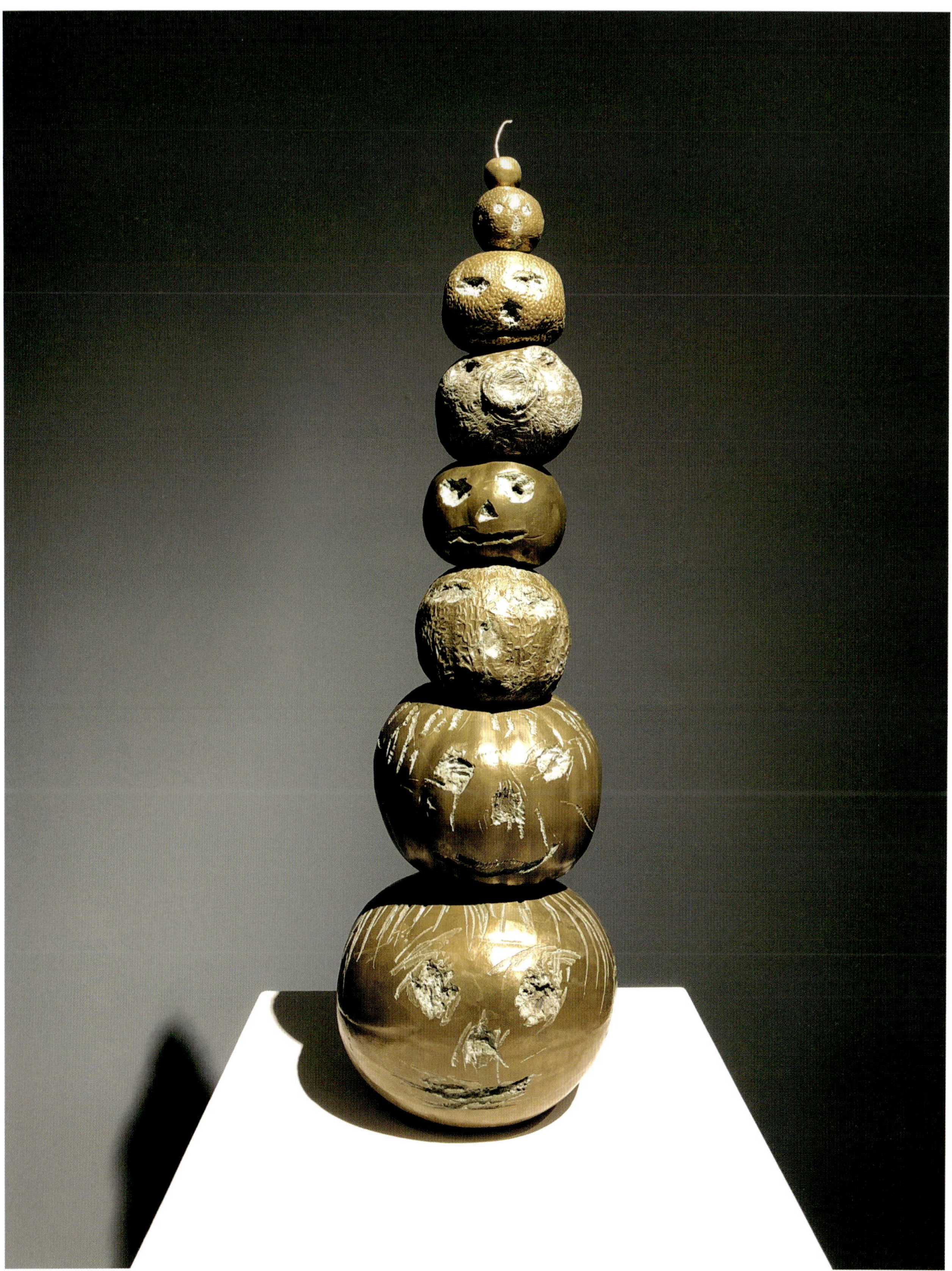

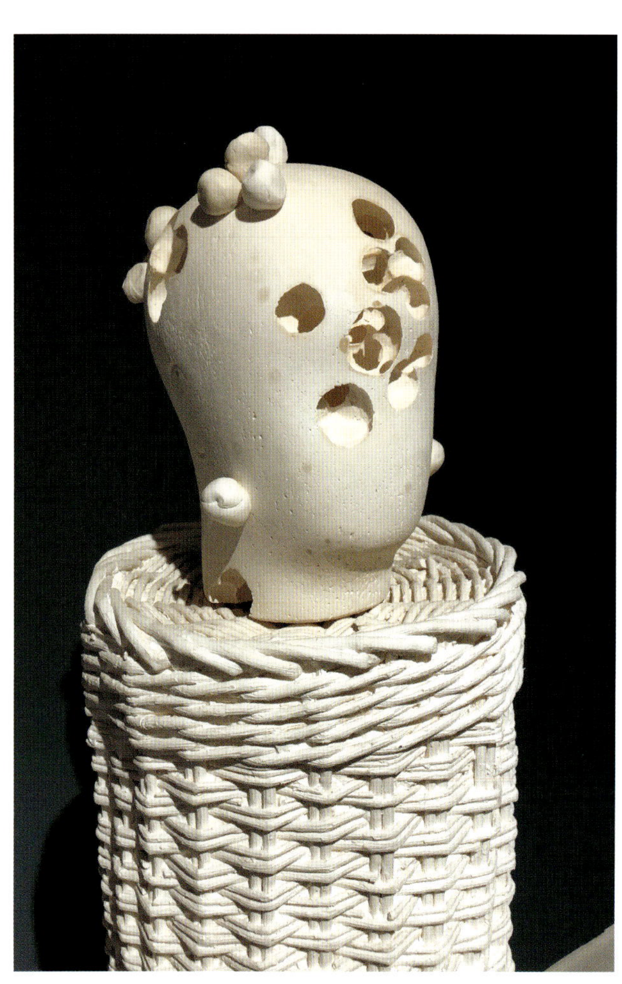
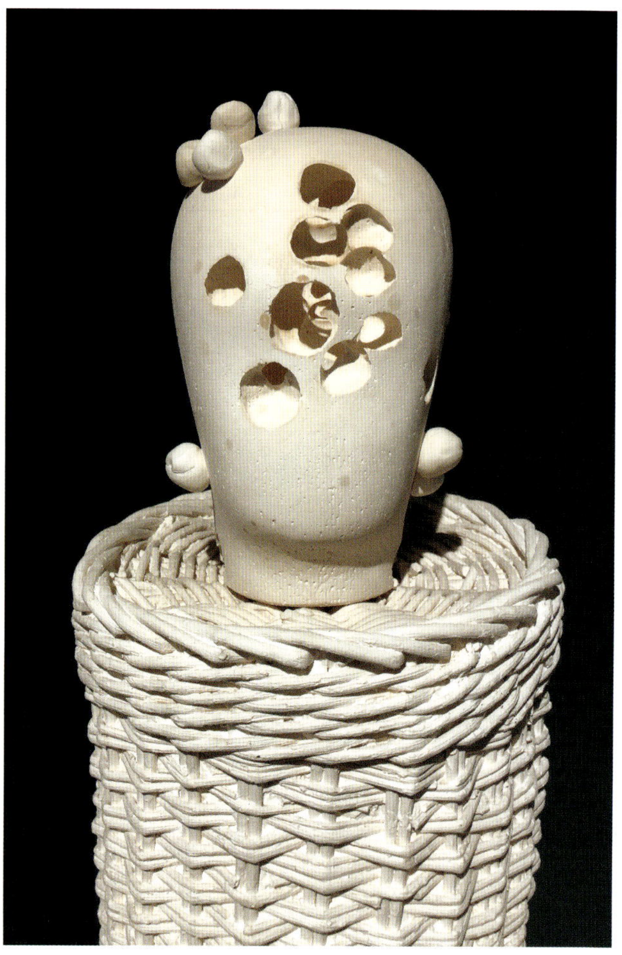

Good Boy 2017
Plaster,
76 × 35 × 35 cm

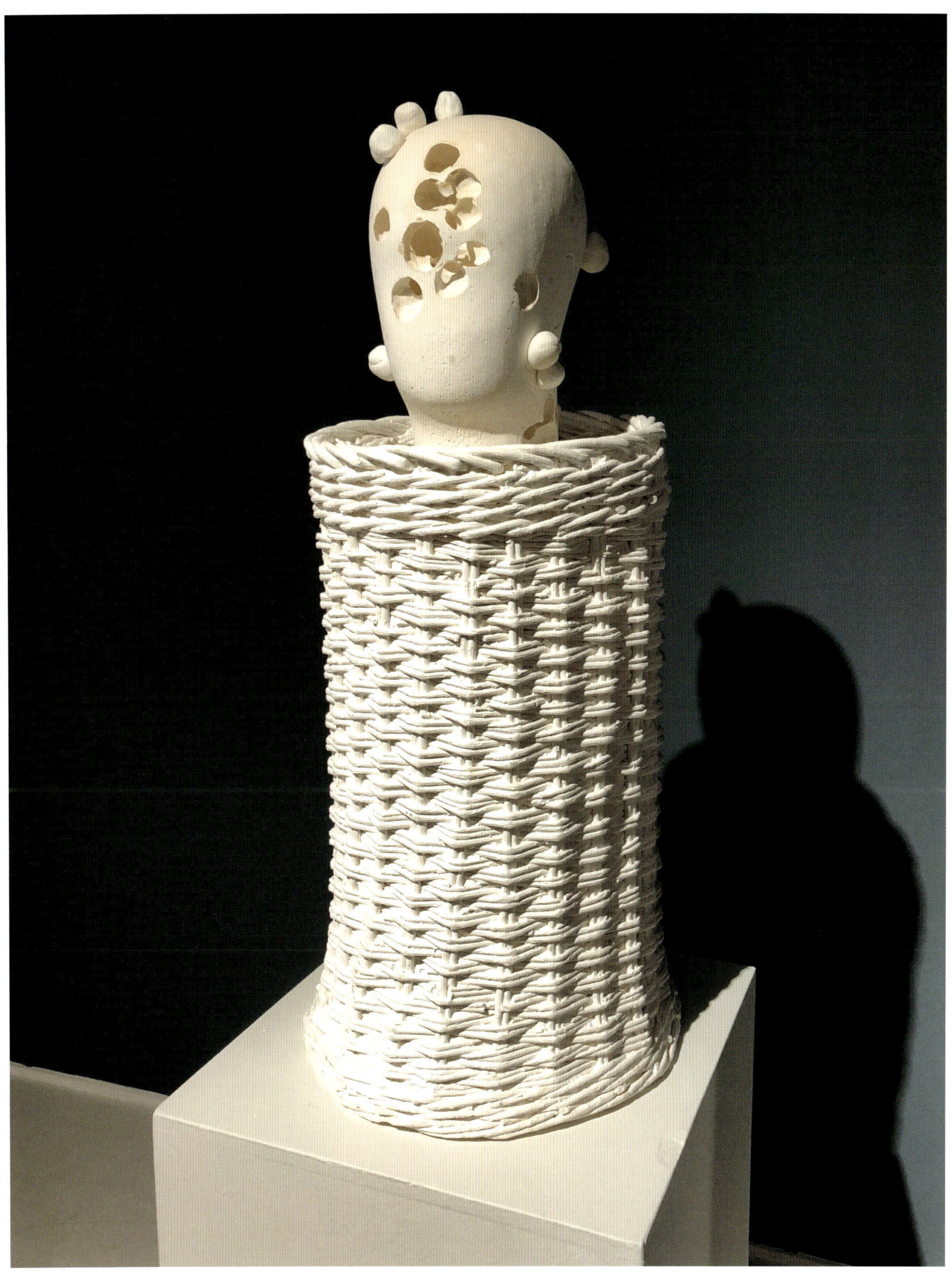

After the Best Before 2017
Brass and plaster,
155 × 100 × 91 cm
Installed at Martin Asbæk Gallery,
Copenhagen.

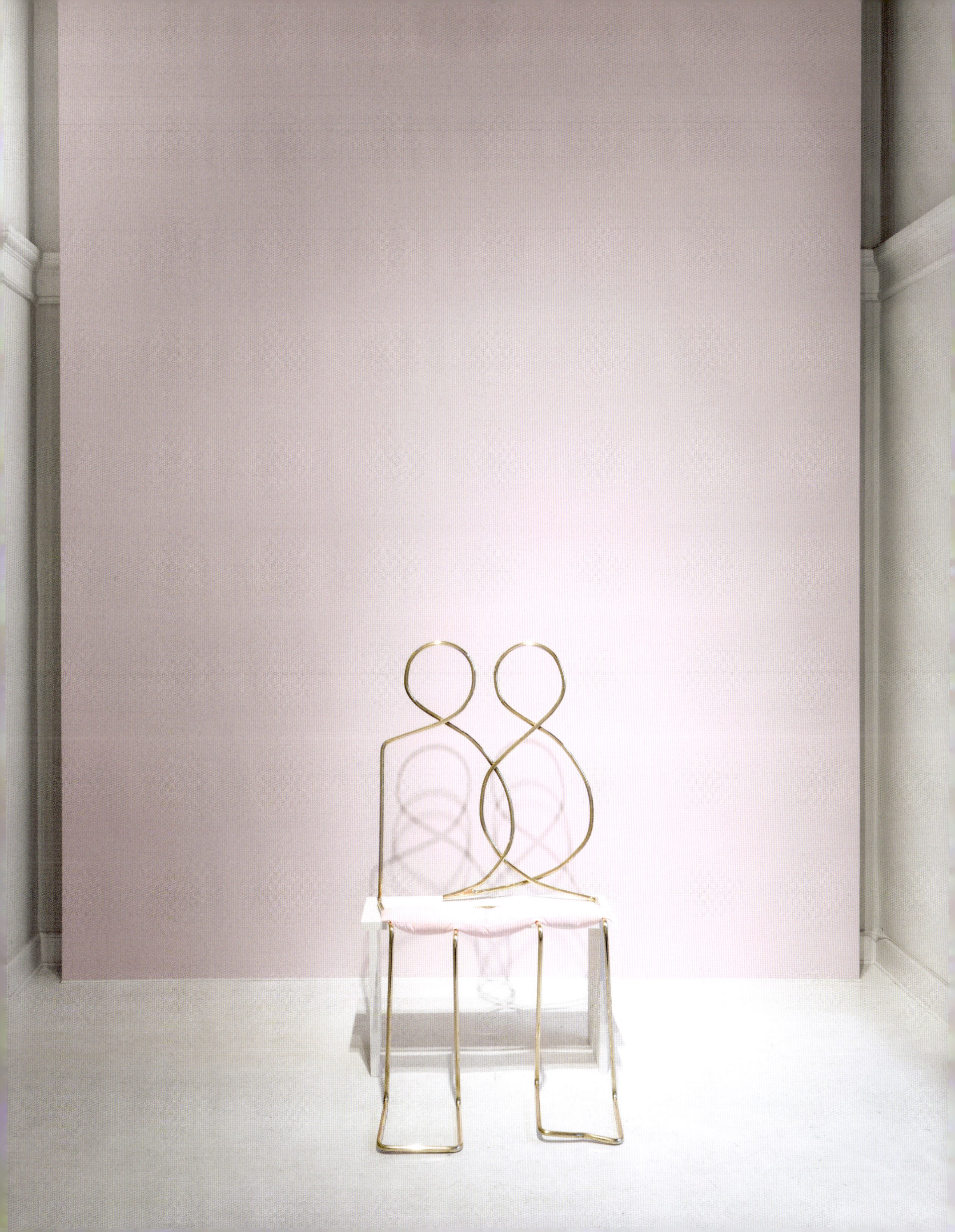

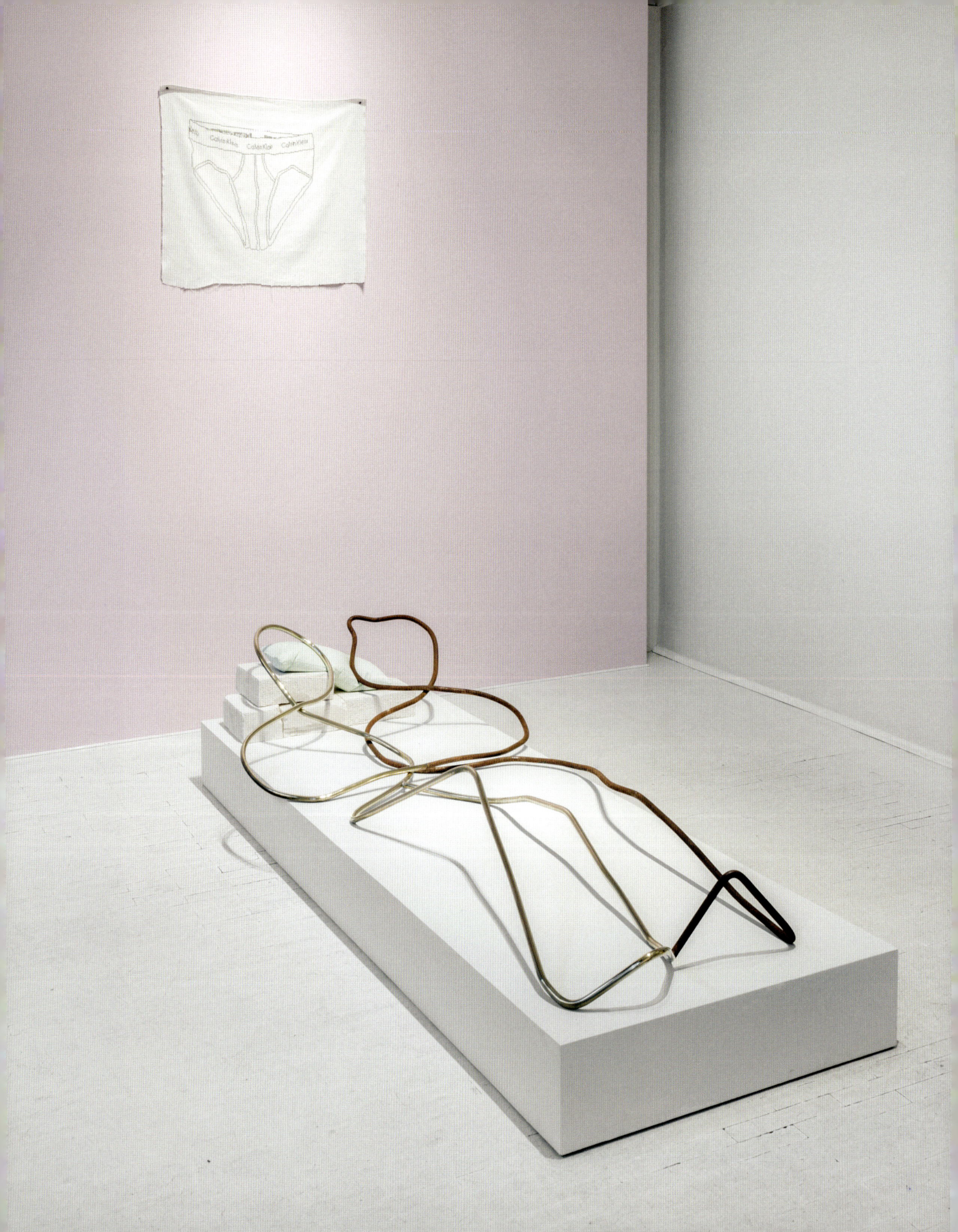

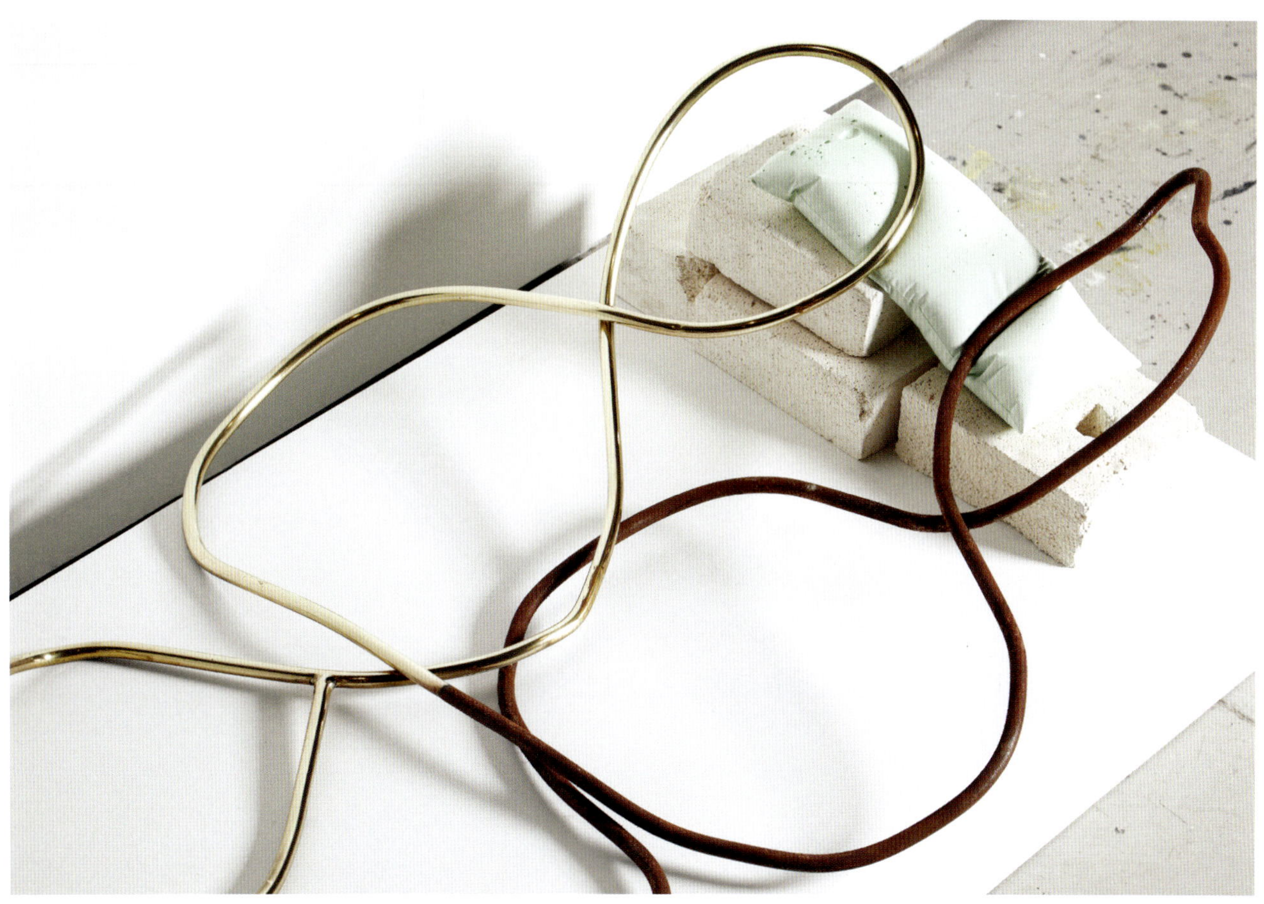

Torn Between Two Lovers 2016
Brass and steel,
22 × 240 × 93 cm.
Installed at Martin Asbæk
Gallery, Copenhagen (*opposite*)
and the studio (*above*).

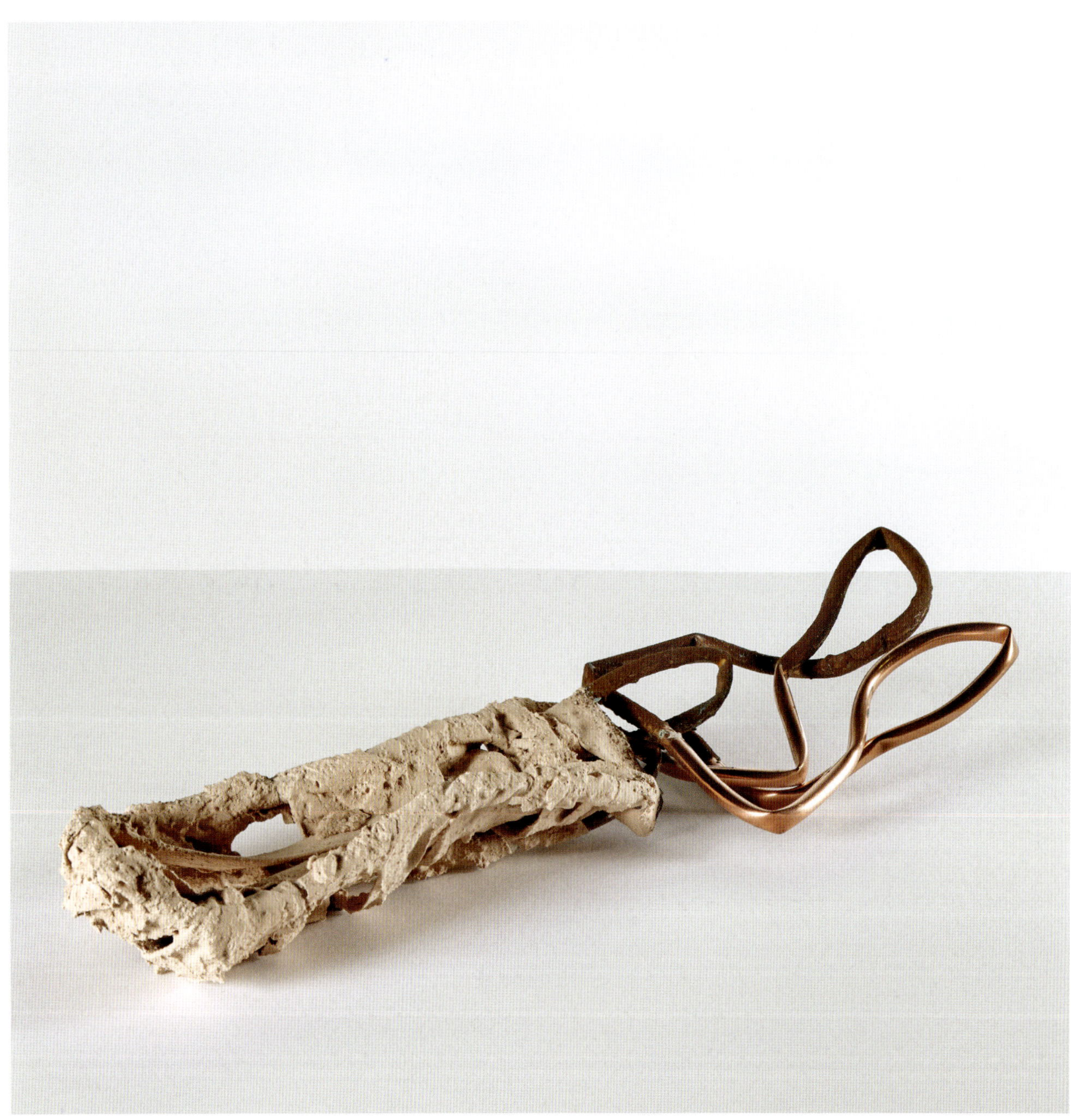

above

Maquette for Torn Between Two Lovers 2016
Building plaster, copper pipe and cloth,
10 × 51 × 18 cm

opposite

A Keeper 2016
Plaster, brass and twig,
14 × 23 × 12 cm

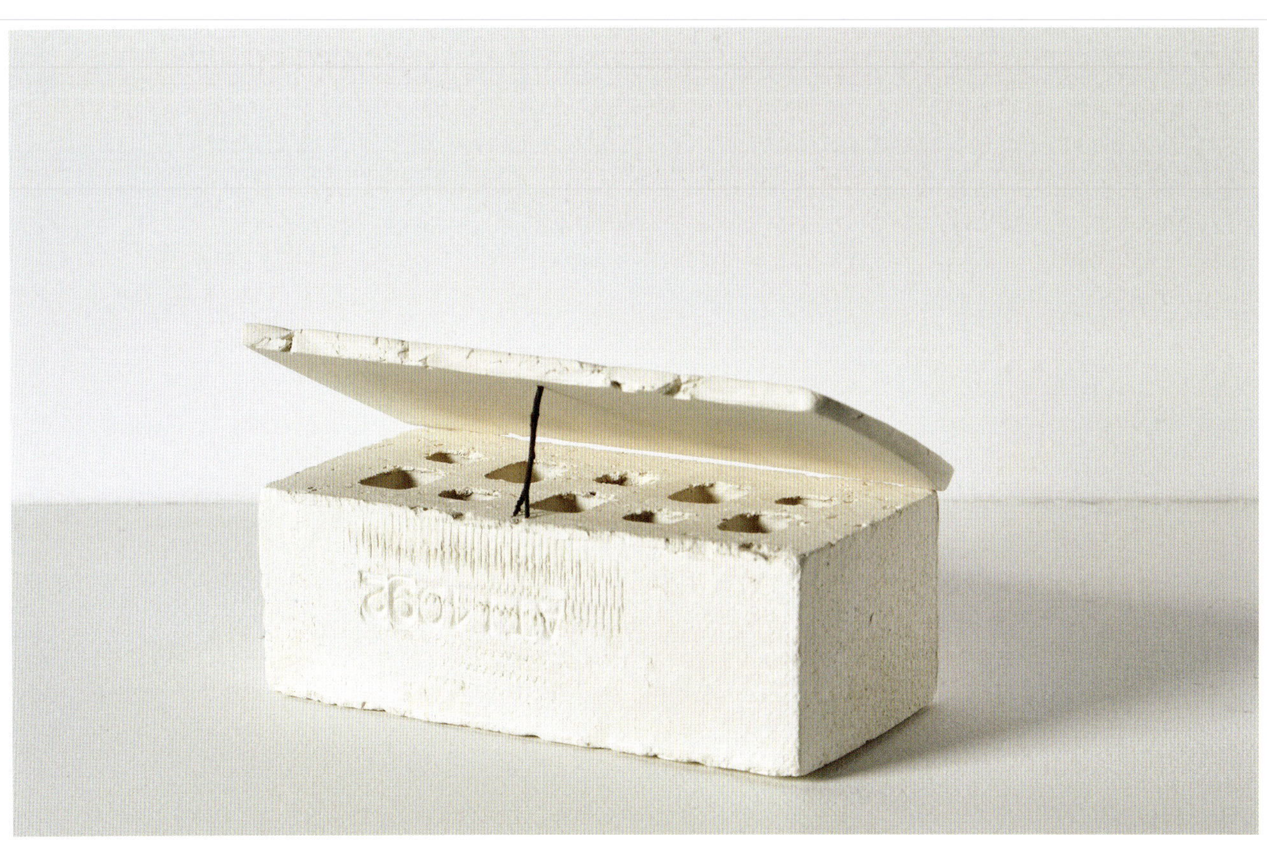

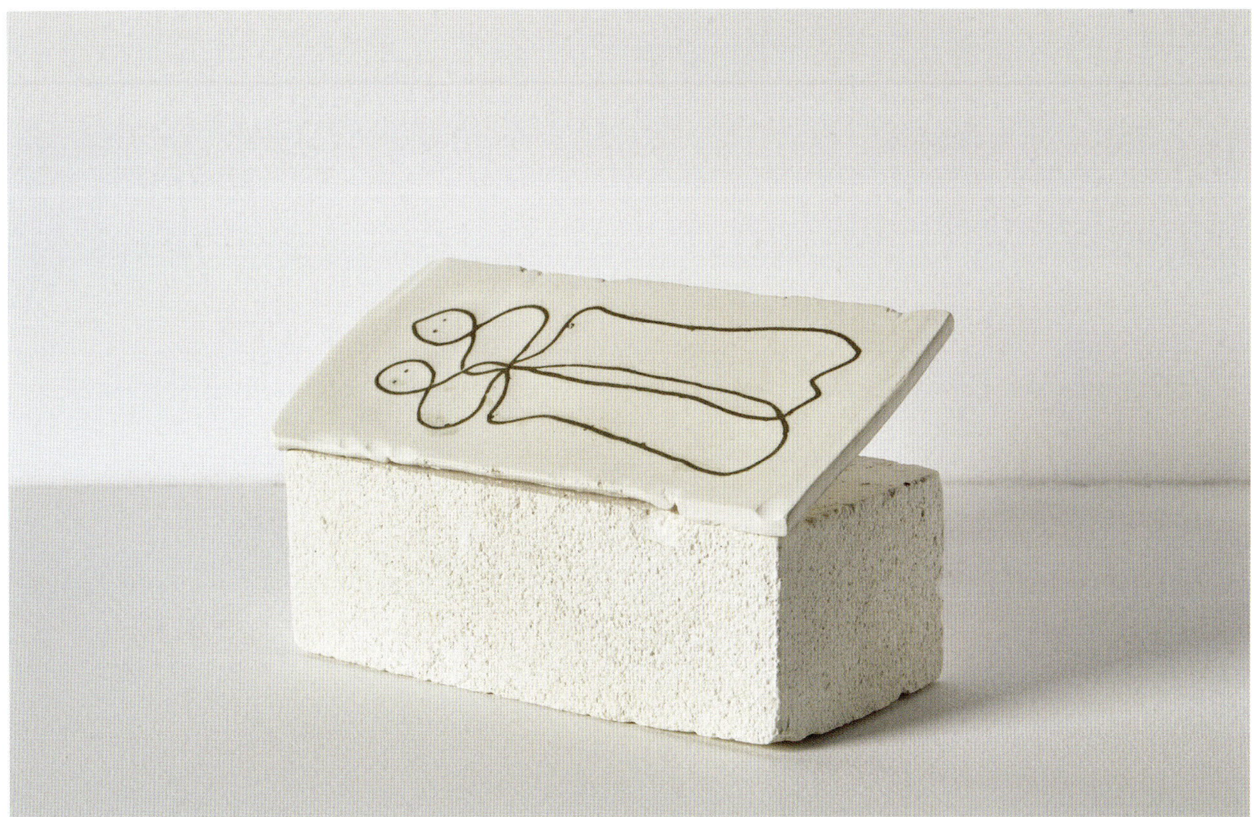

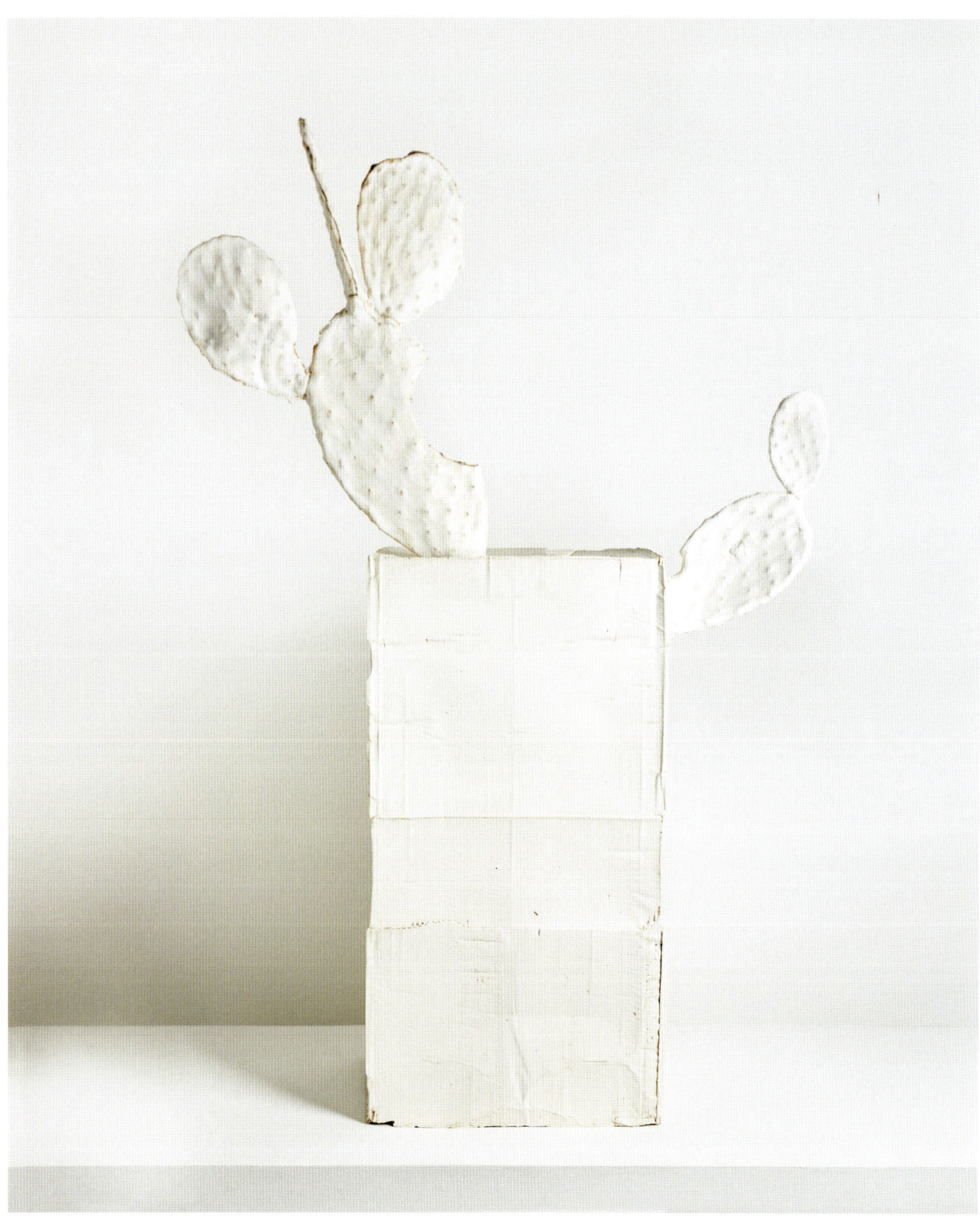

Badly Made But Well Travelled 2017

Plaster,

123 × 41 × 28 cm

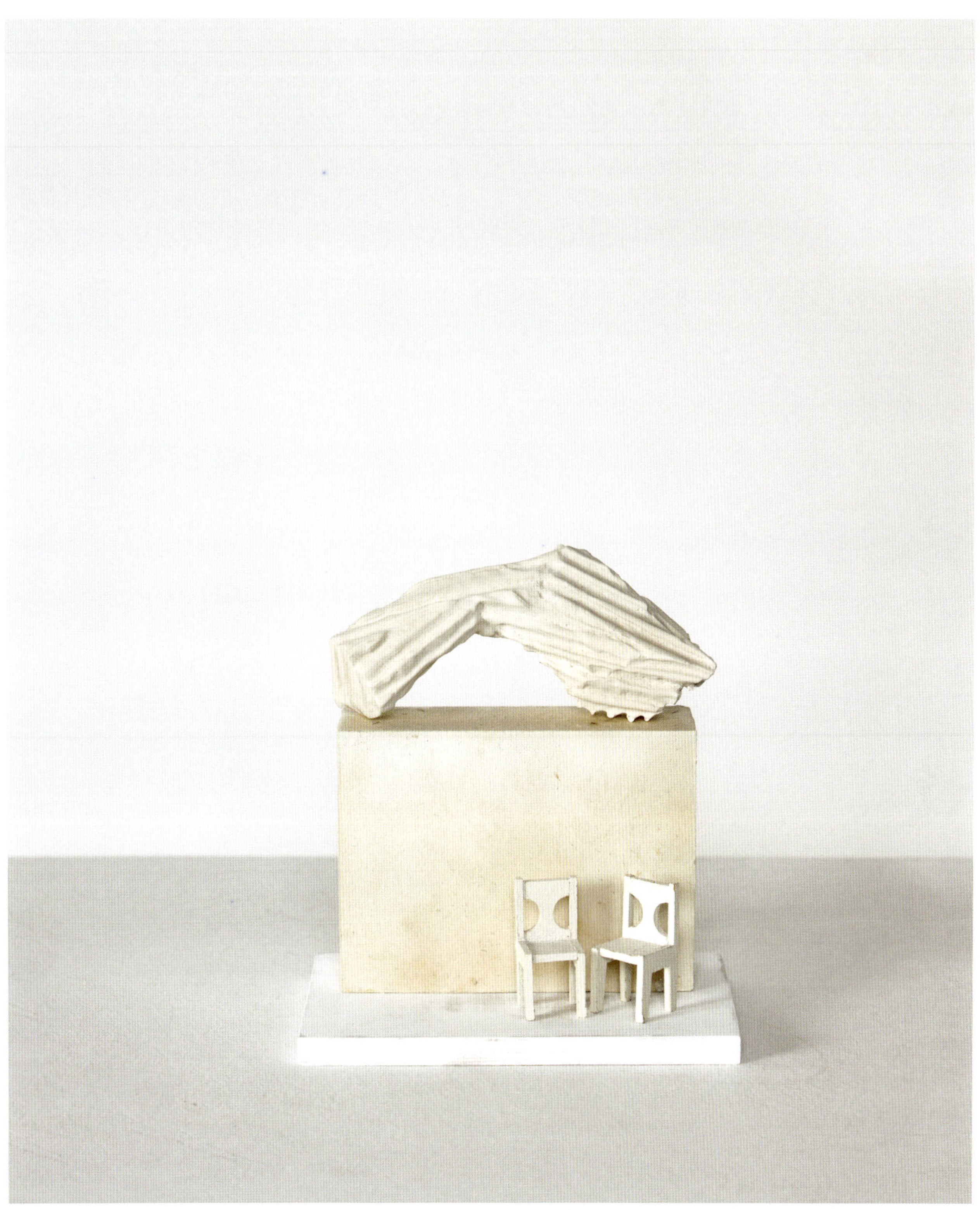

Public Sculpture with Two Chairs 2013
Plaster and wood,
20 × 20 × 14 cm

'When I discovered that you could cast an "almost" convincing metal cheaply and quickly in the studio by adding metals powders to resin, for want of a better subject, I started making clay copies of all the metal bits and pieces I had to hand: nails, screws, etc. I was hoping that my little twisted attempts would be more convincing when cast in metal. I made some of the nails to stick out of a wall to hang things on. Funnily enough, they had to be attached to real nails. After casting the first few, I felt that "some" wasn't enough and that it had to be "a lot of nails". I remembered it was the same logic that decided how tall Brancusi's *Endless Column* was. I kept the nails in a jar while I was making them, because that seemed to be the right way to store them. In the shed at least. I could never find the right way to show them in a gallery, so I just hand someone the jar when I want to show them. The sound of them rattling around has become a part of the work. It also meant that I knew when to stop making them.'

Jar of Home-Made Nails 1999–2002
Resin, aluminium powder and glass jar,
16 × 9 × 9 cm

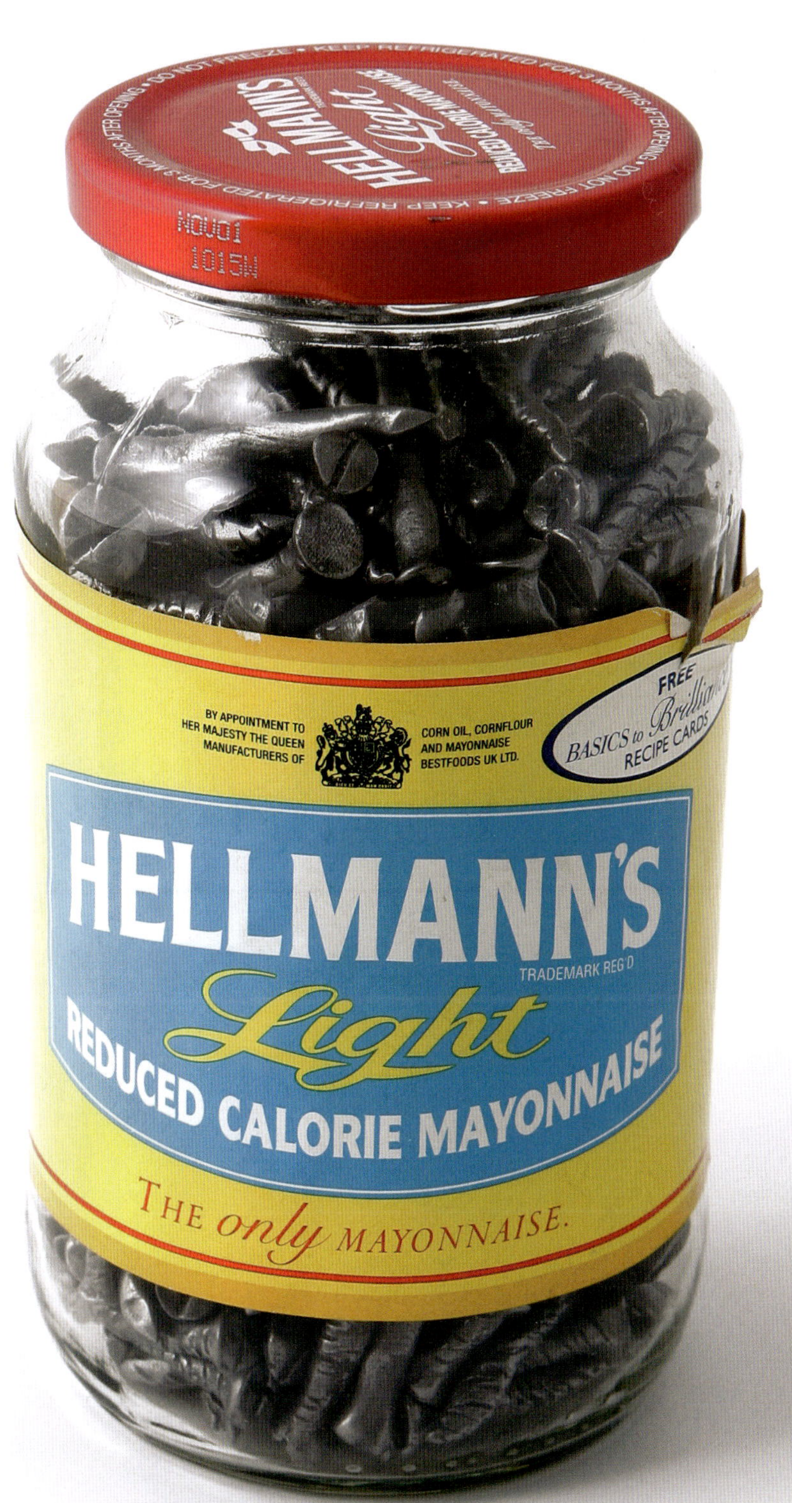
DO NOT FREEZE • KEEP REFRIGERATED FOR 3 MONTHS AFTER OPENING
HELLMANN'S
NOV01
1015W
BY APPOINTMENT TO HER MAJESTY THE QUEEN MANUFACTURERS OF
CORN OIL, CORNFLOUR AND MAYONNAISE BESTFOODS UK LTD.
FREE
RECIPE CARDS
HELLMANN'S
TRADEMARK REG'D
Light
REDUCED CALORIE MAYONNAISE
THE only MAYONNAISE.

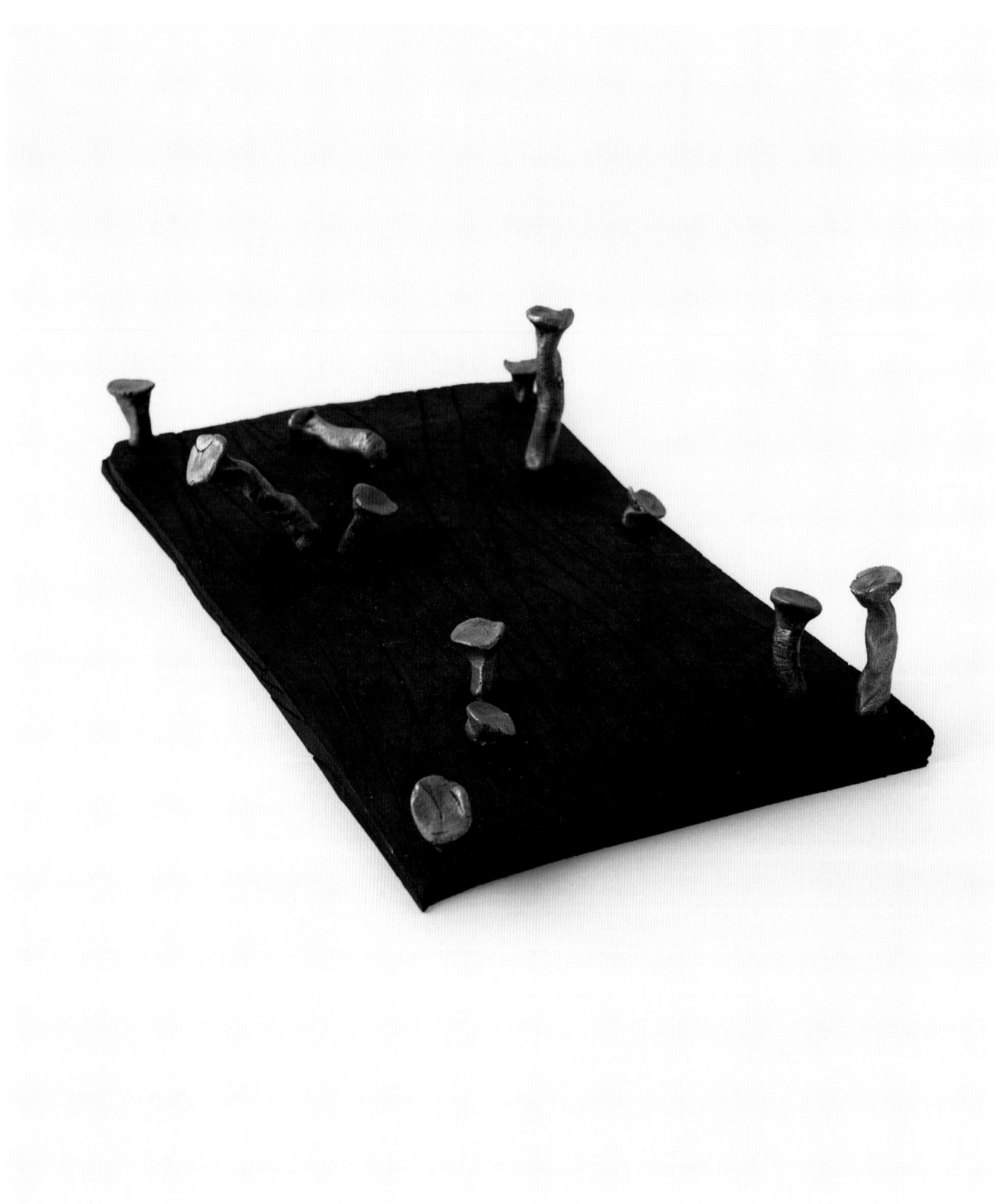

Warped Wood Nailed Badly 2000
Resin, pigment and metal powder,
6 × 13 × 23 cm

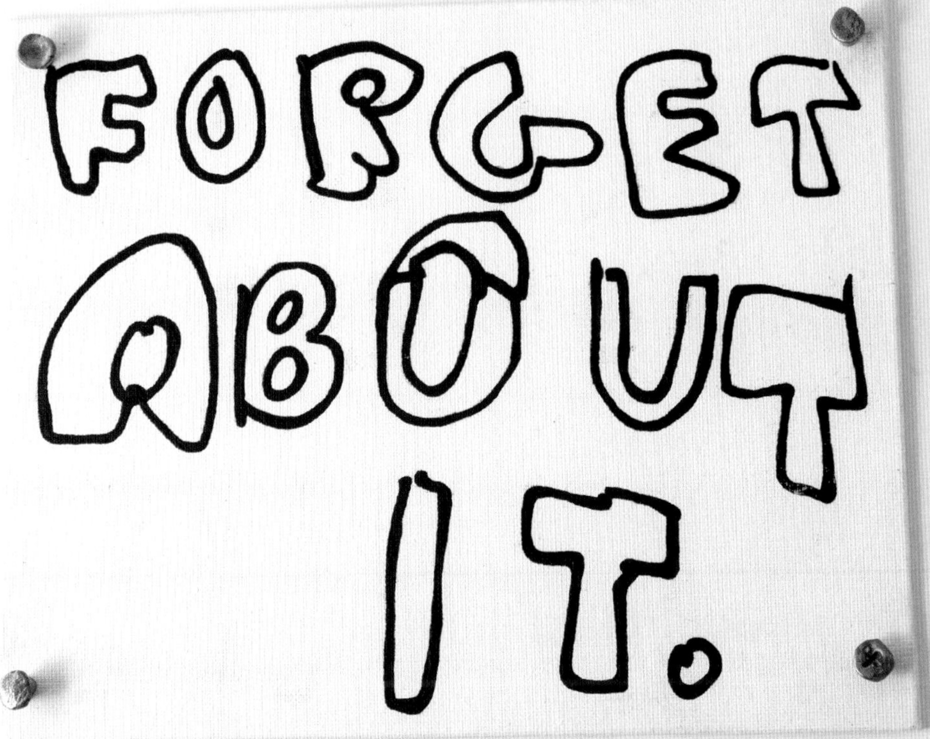

Forget About It 2002
Acrylic on board, resin
and aluminium powder,
20 × 27 × 2.5 cm

Rusty Nails and Screws (Pile) 1999–2000
Resin and iron powder,
dimensions variable

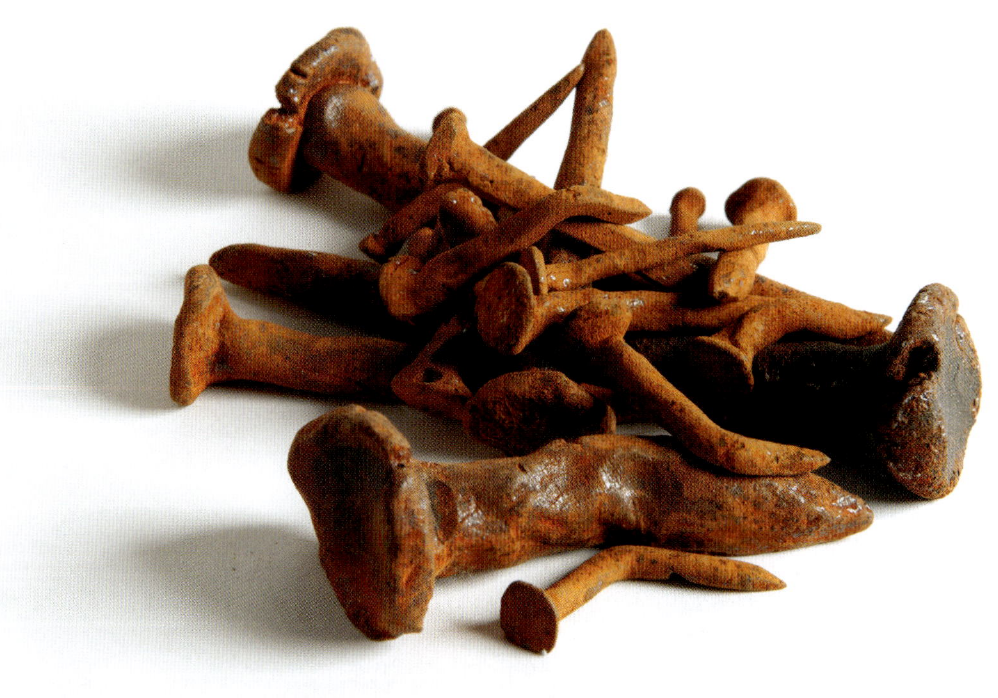

Rusty Nails and Screws (Fixed) 1999–2000
Resin and iron powder,
each 3 × 1 × 1 cm

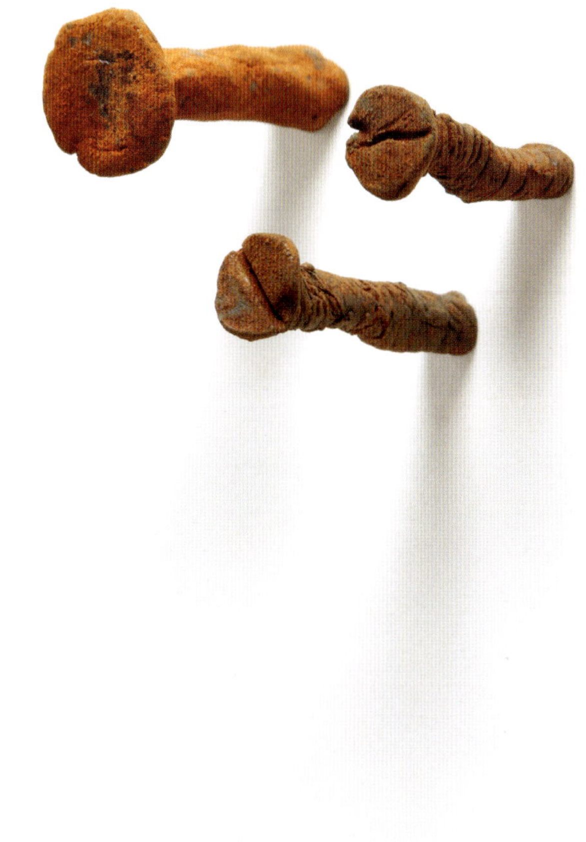

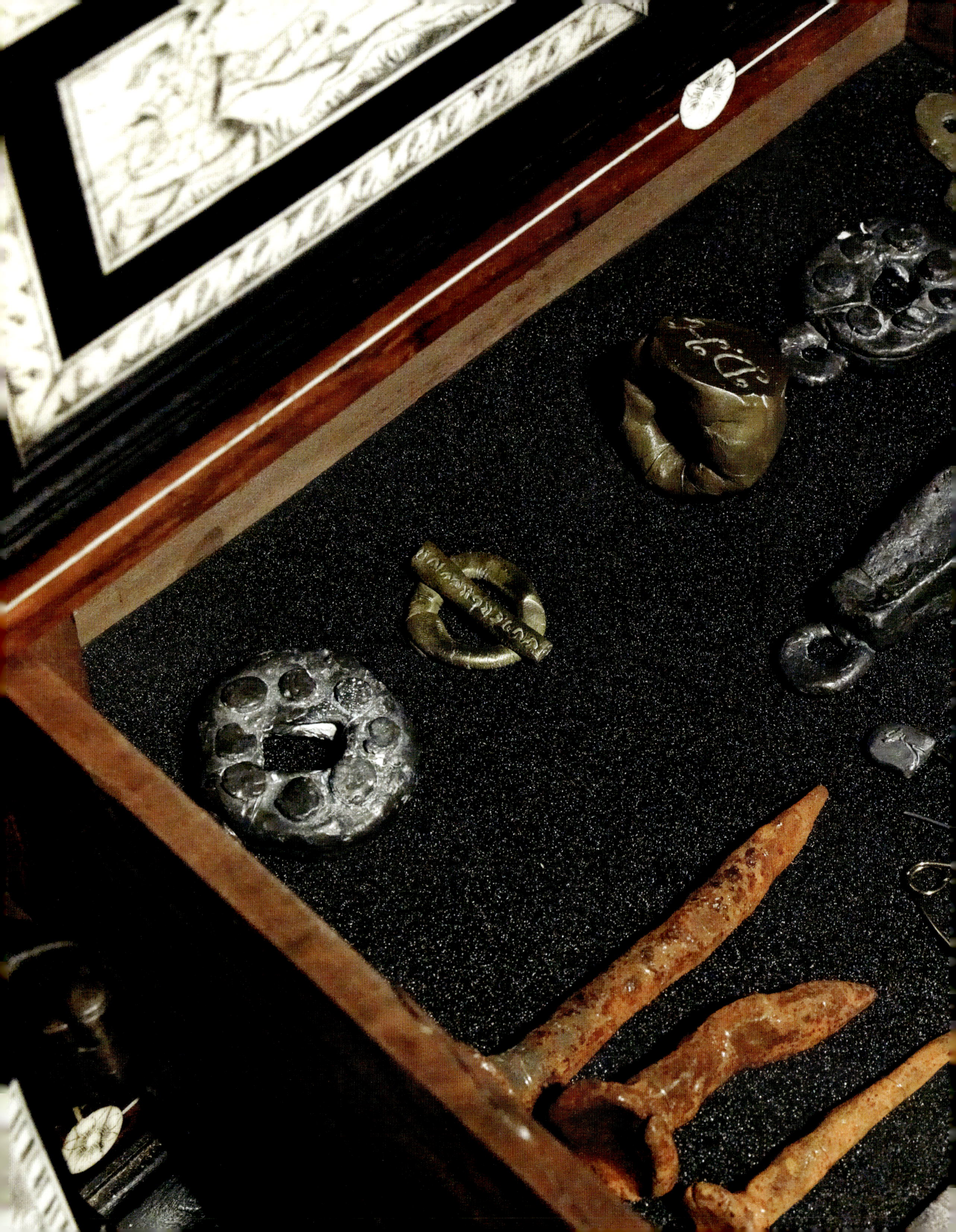

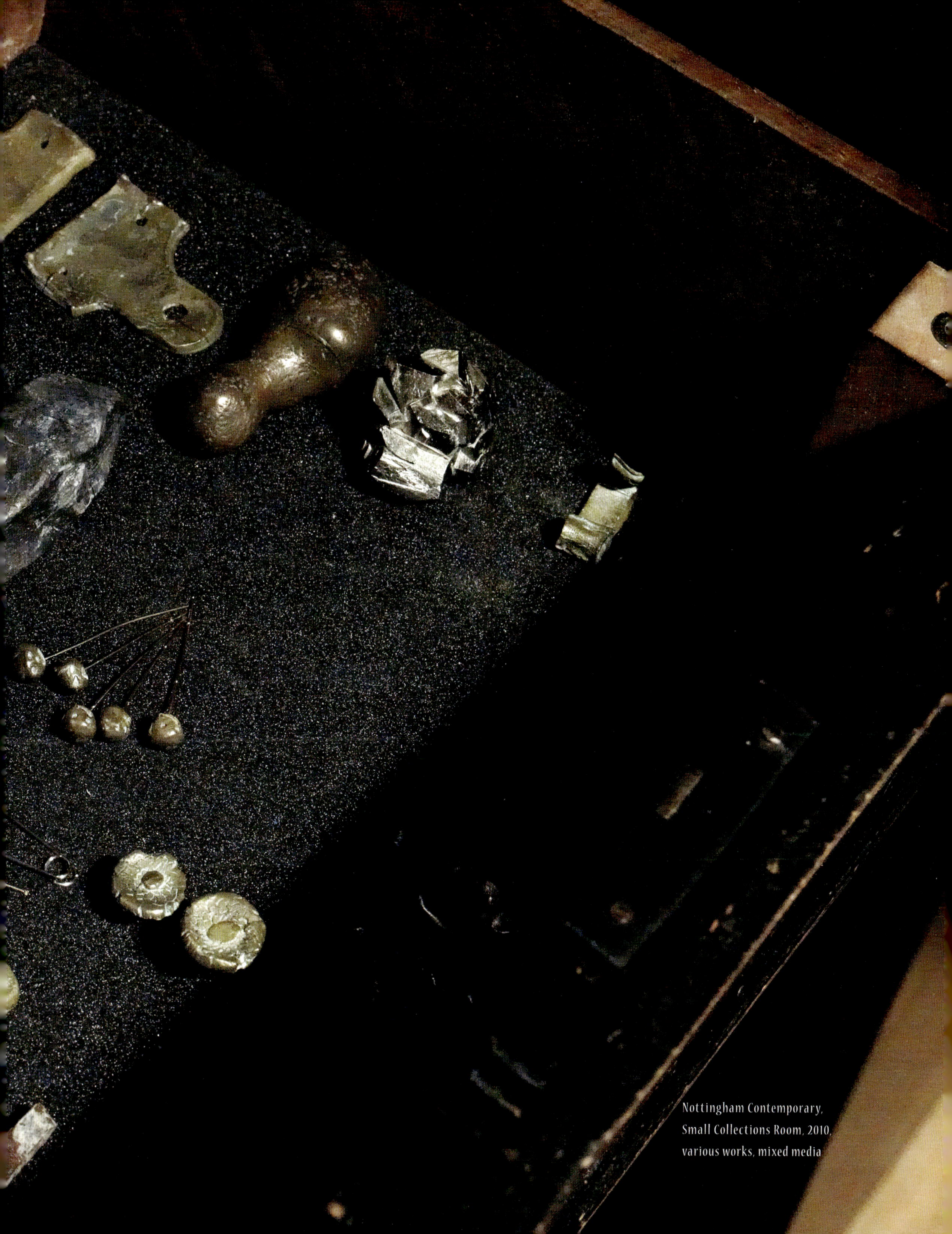

Nottingham Contemporary,
Small Collections Room, 2010,
various works, mixed media

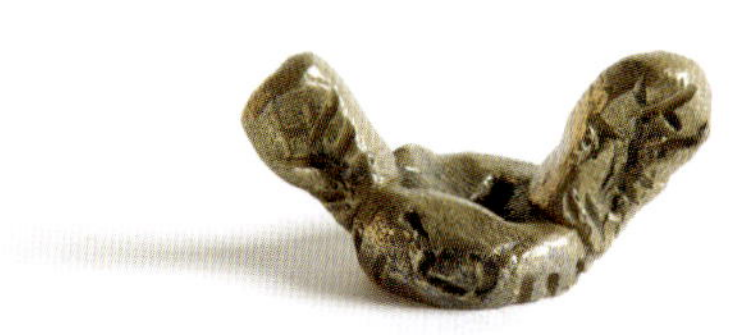

Wing Nut Fly 2003
Resin and brass powder,
1.5 × 2 × 1.5 cm

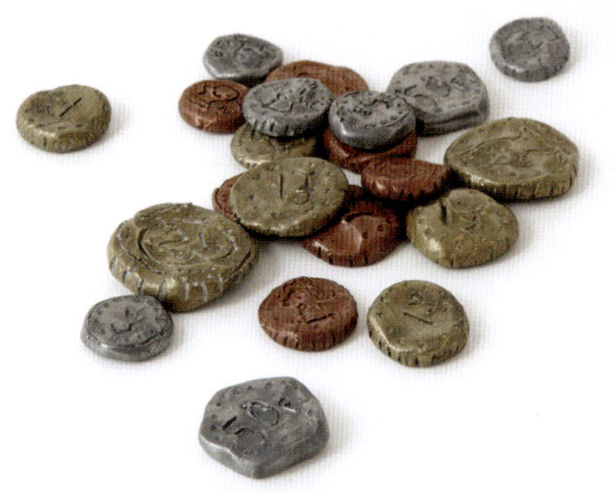

Some Money 1999
Resin and metal powder,
dimensions variable

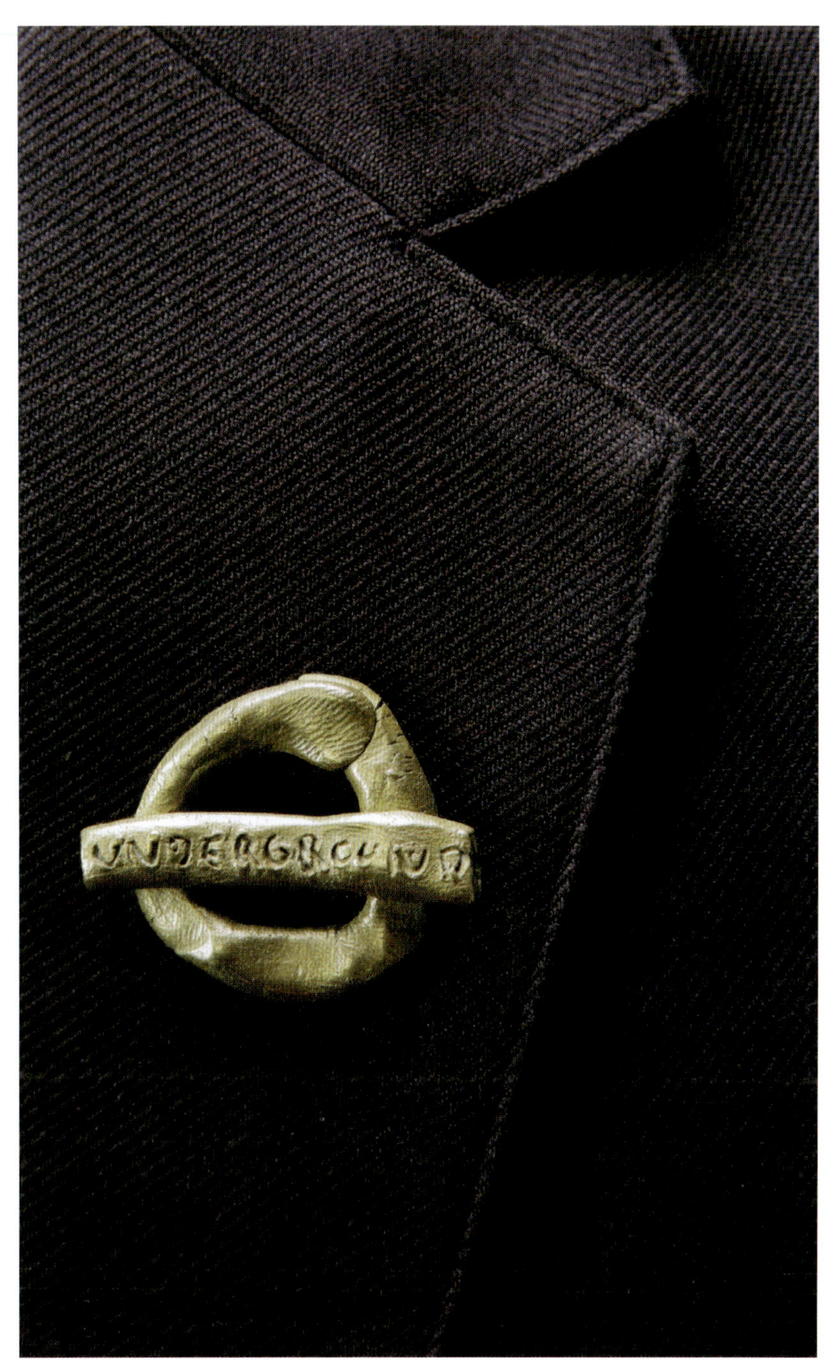

The Collector 2007
Badge on lapel made for poster commissioned by Art on the Underground to celebrate the centenary of the London Underground Roundel in 2008.

Drawing Pins 1999
Resin, brass powder and brass wire, dimensions variable

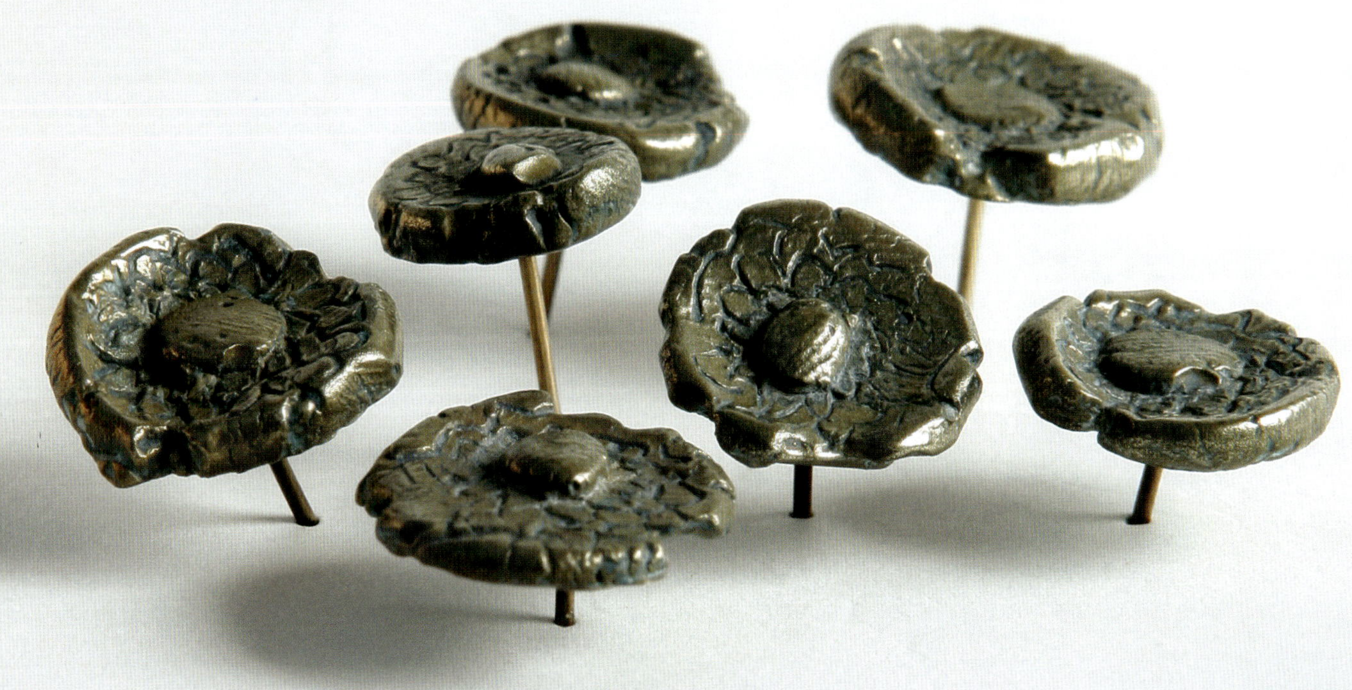

Angry Pins 1999

Resin, brass powder and brass wire,

5 × 0.5 × 0.5 cm

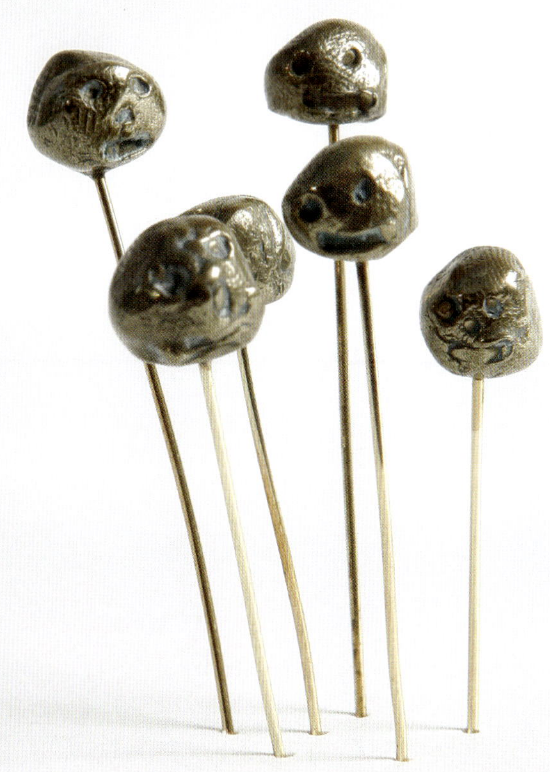

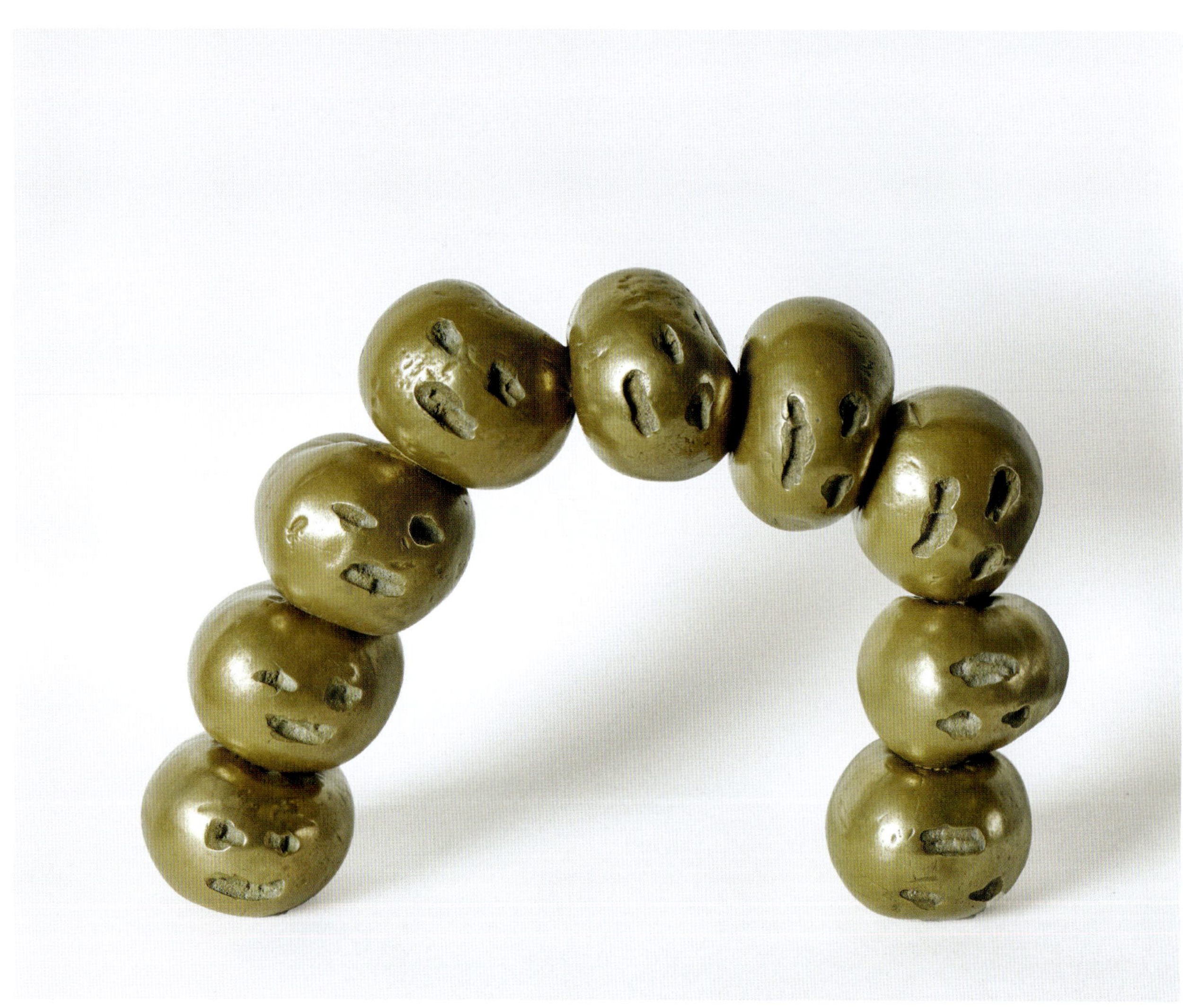

You Move Me 2018
Resin and brass powder,
22 × 35 × 7 cm

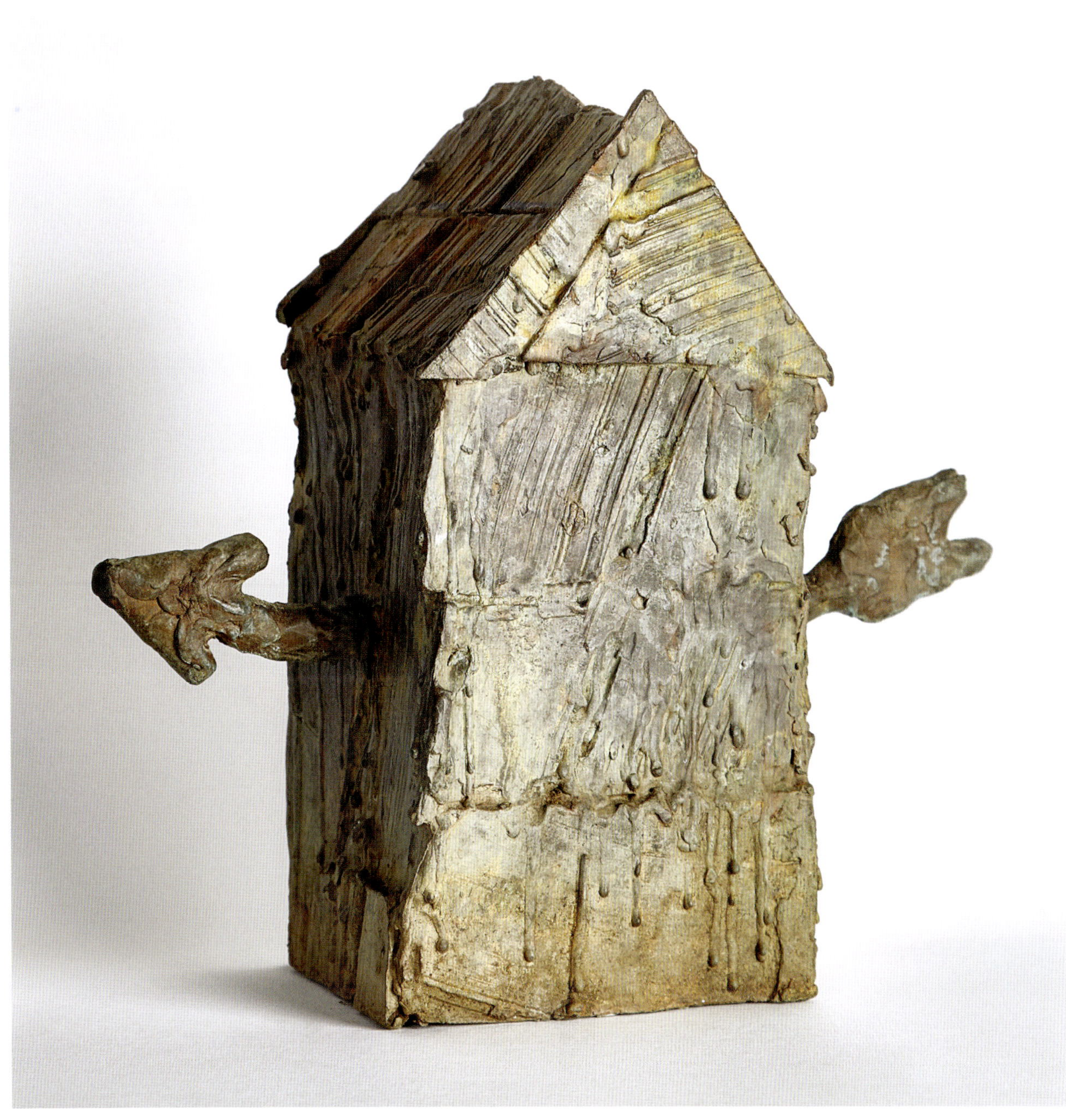

Wounded Bronze House 1989

Bronze,

25 × 25 × 20 cm

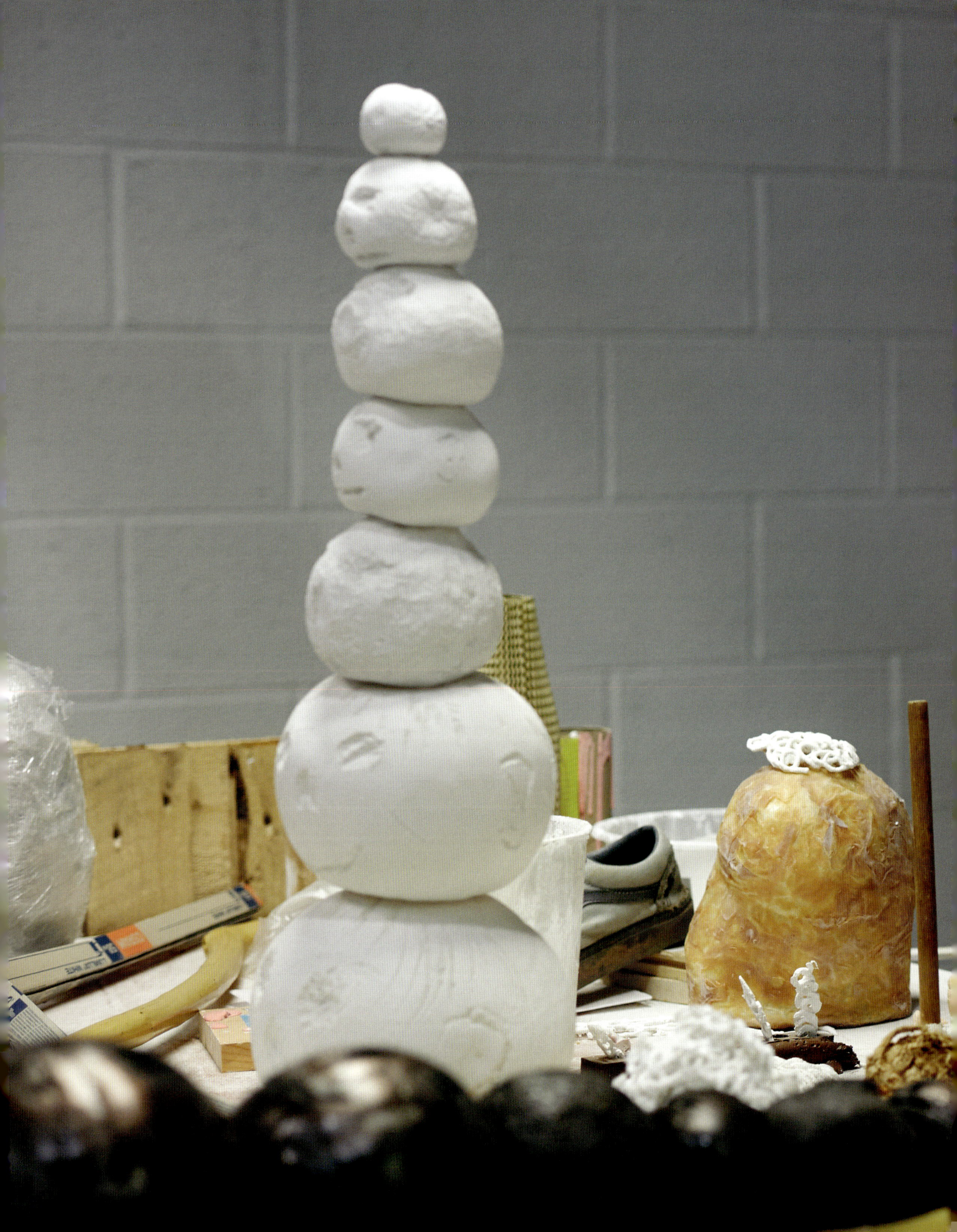

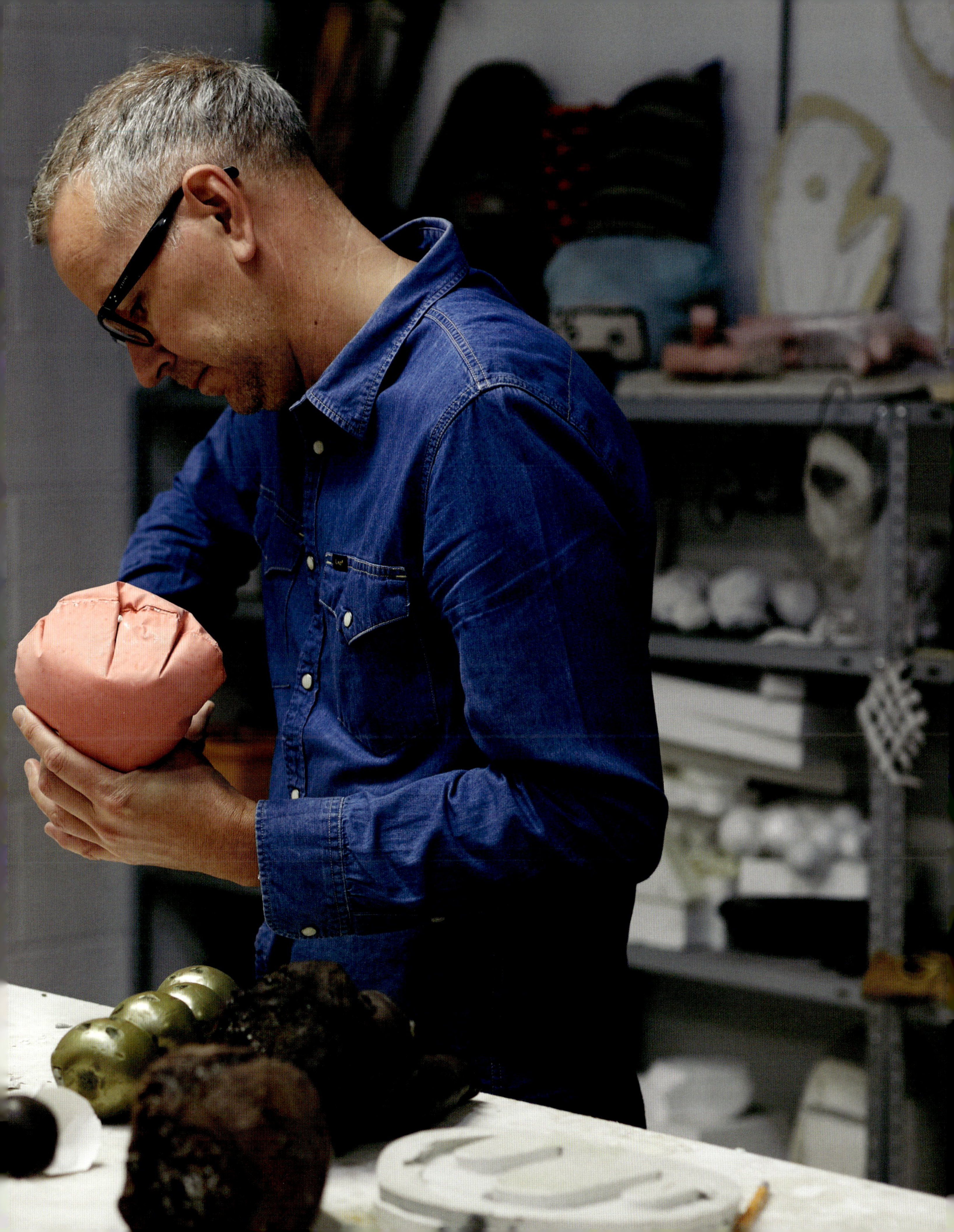

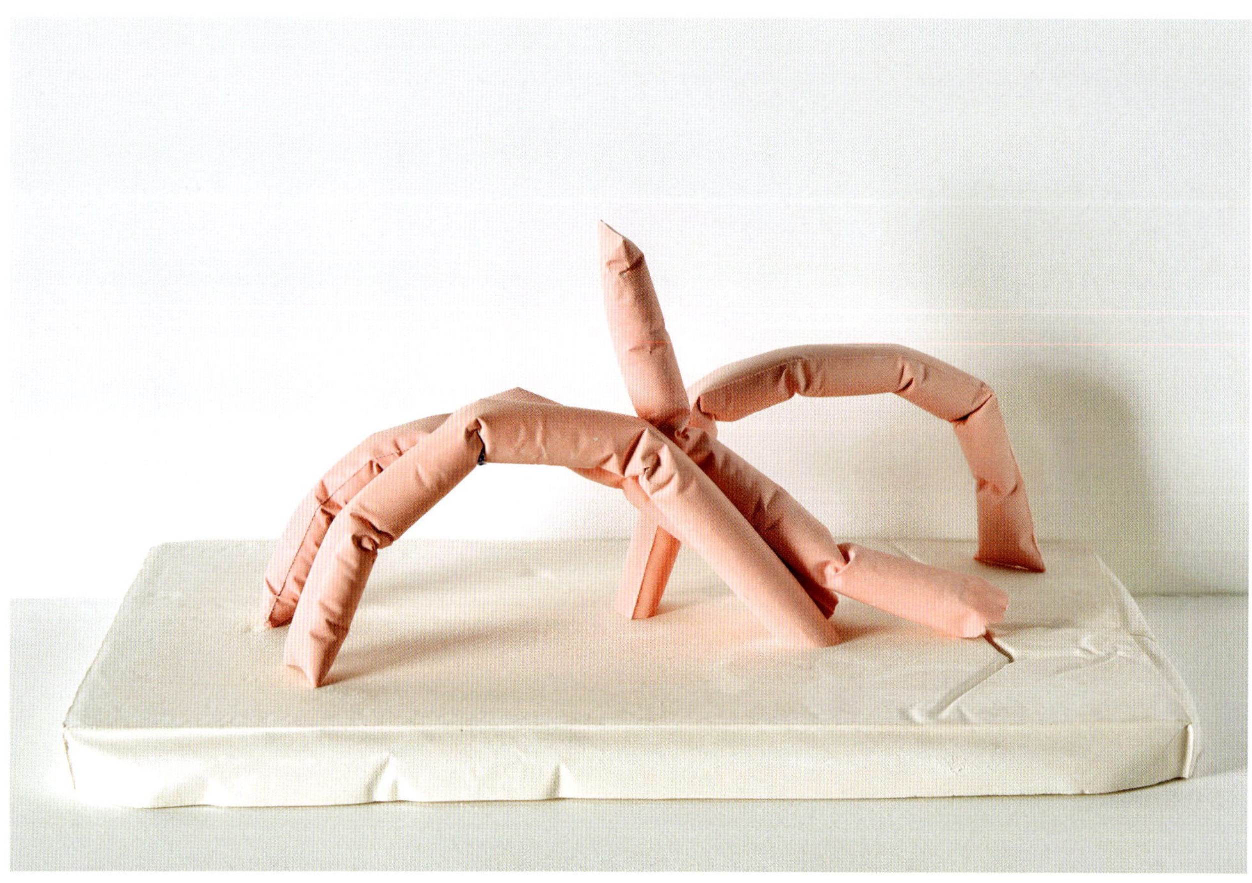

above
Greasy Pole 2008
Plaster and pigment,
27 × 60 × 38 cm

opposite
A plaster-and-pigment
work in progress in
the studio, 2018

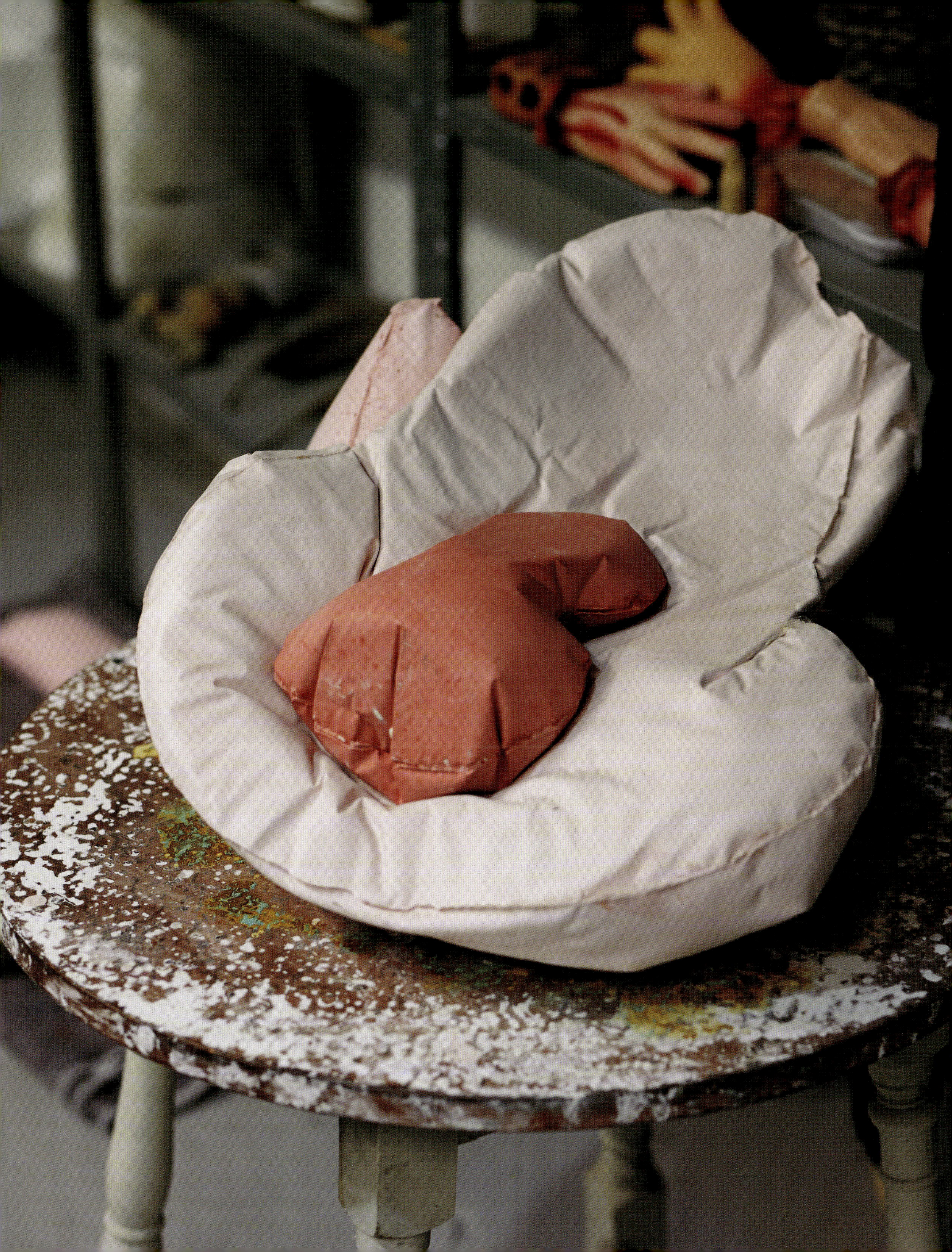

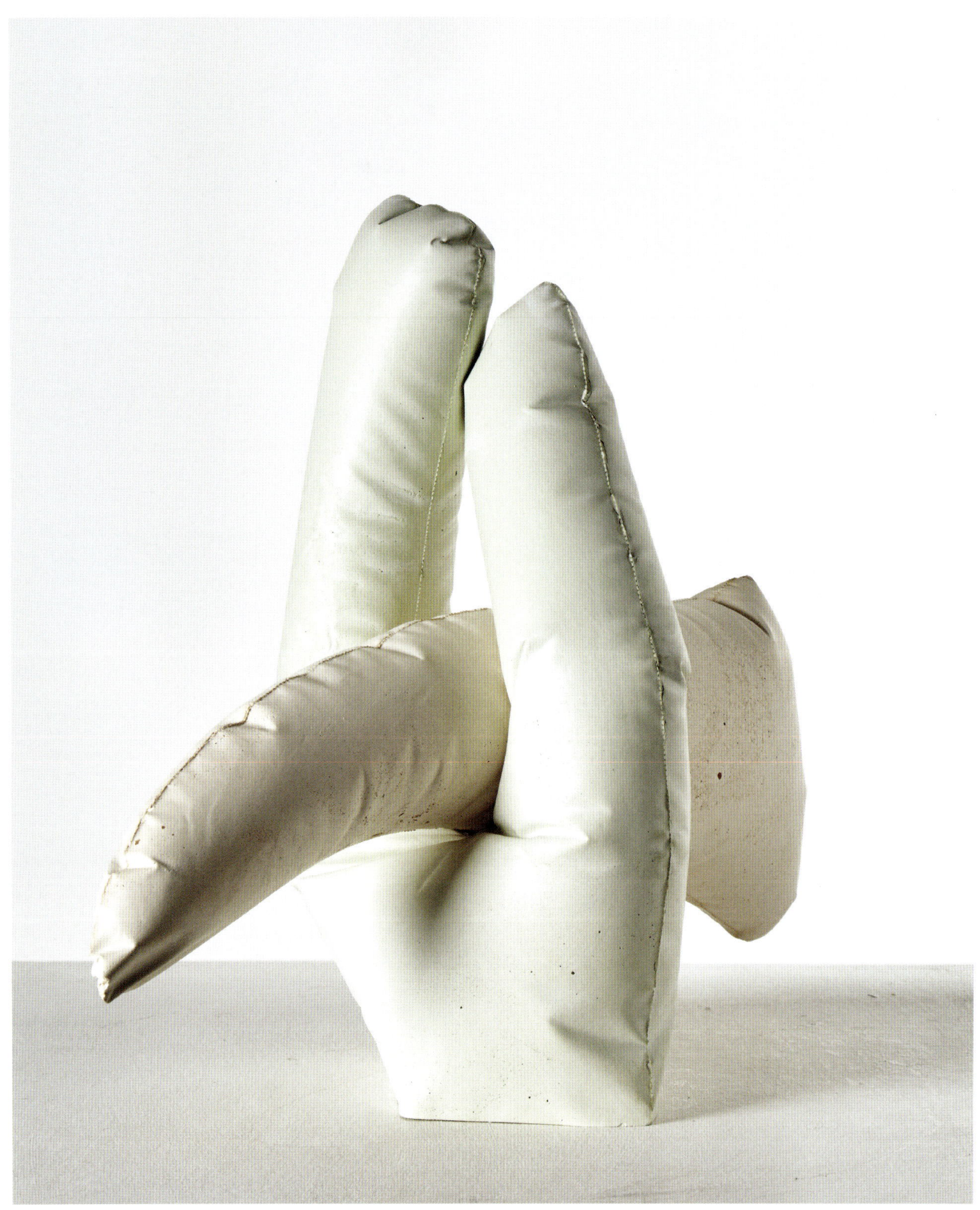

A Rush and a Push 2016
Plaster and pigment,
40 × 43 × 45 cm

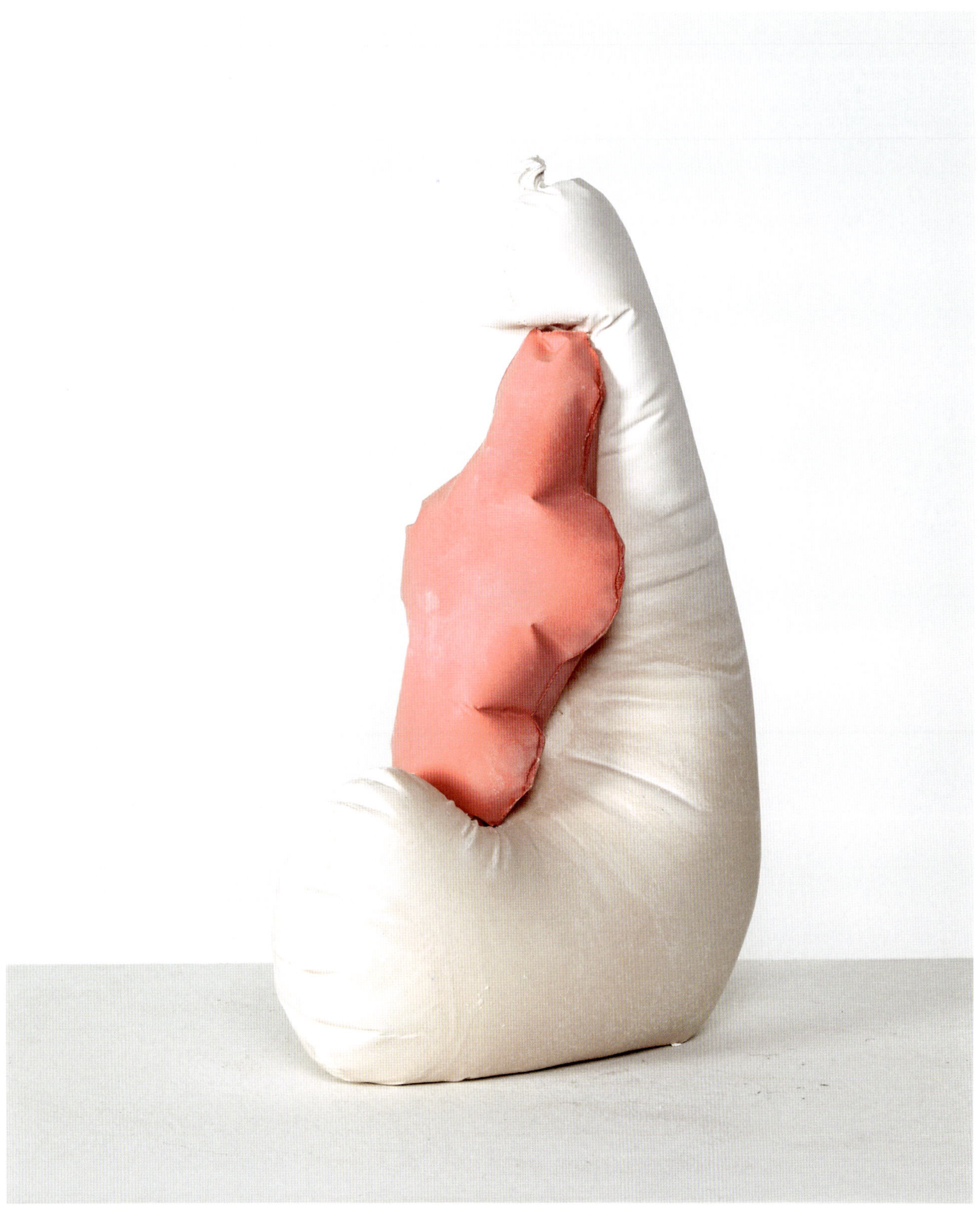

Mother and Child 2016
Plaster and pigment,
40 × 30 × 16 cm

'This is what happens when you put something in an AGA oven and forget about it. I obviously discovered it by accident, but the charred remains had a certain quality that was impossible to match in any other material. Light as a feather with a gloss so shiny that it looks wet. It is also unpredictable in the way it explodes and then stops dead. I started to carve apples like Halloween pumpkins, so I'd end up with these distorted, angry faces.'

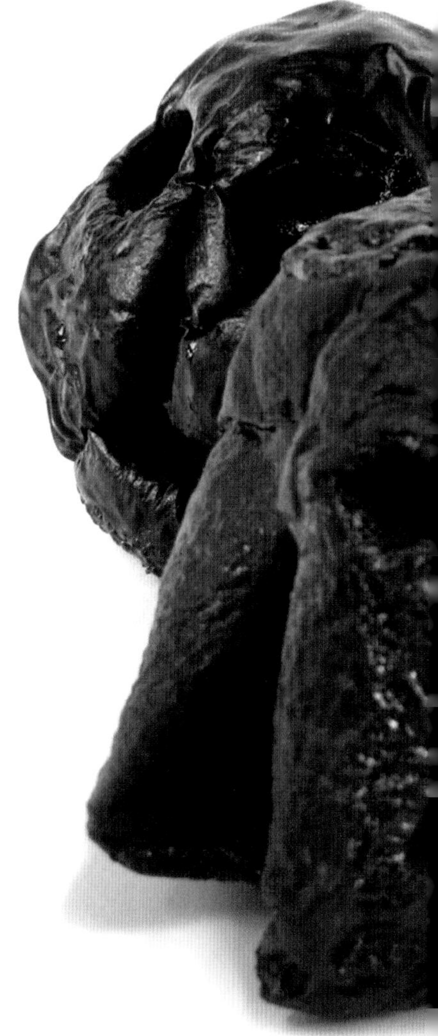

Burnt or Charred 2014
Burnt apples,
dimensions variable

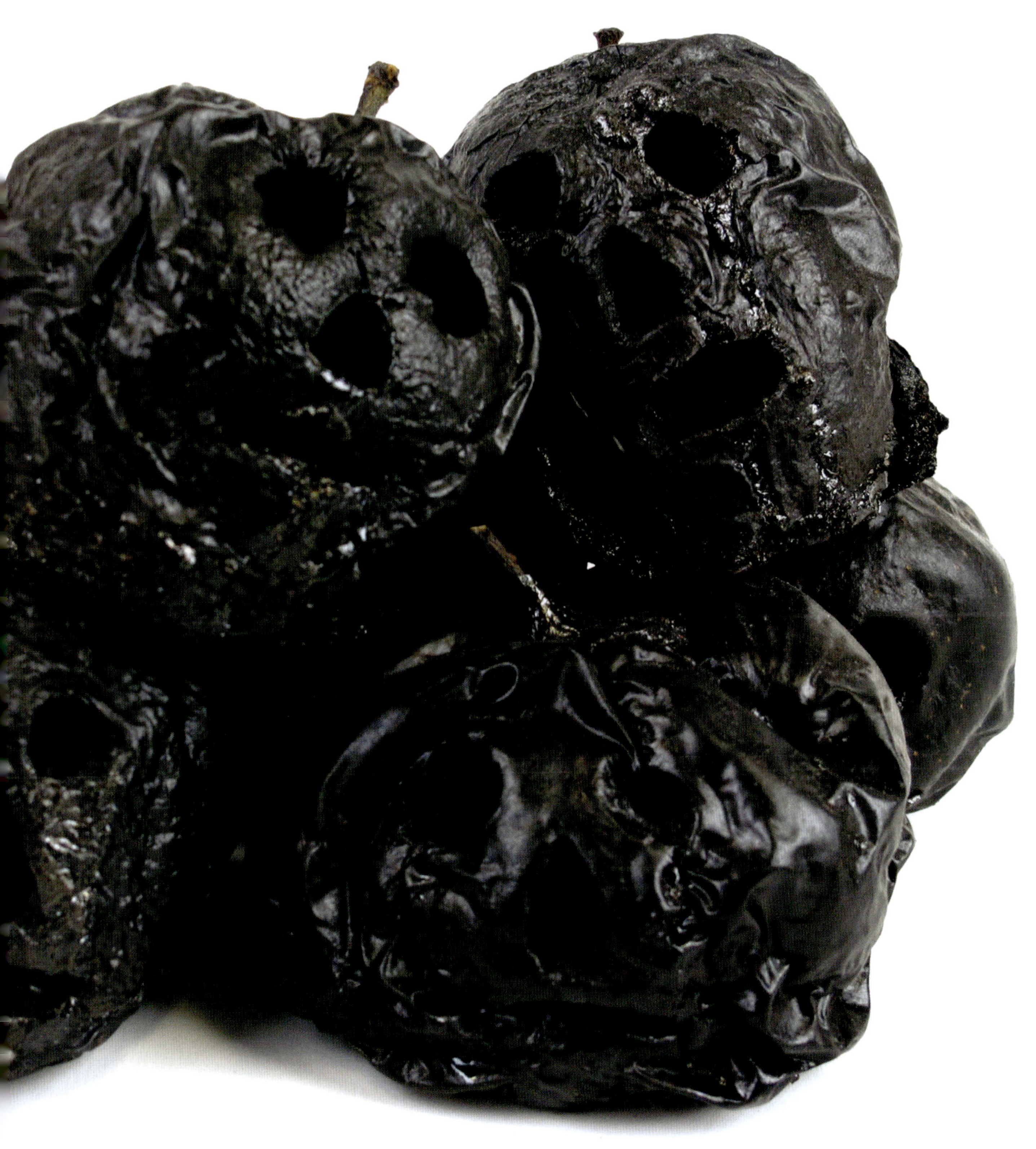

They Thinks We's Bumpkins 2015
Resin, copper powder and iron powder,
12 × 30 × 17 cm

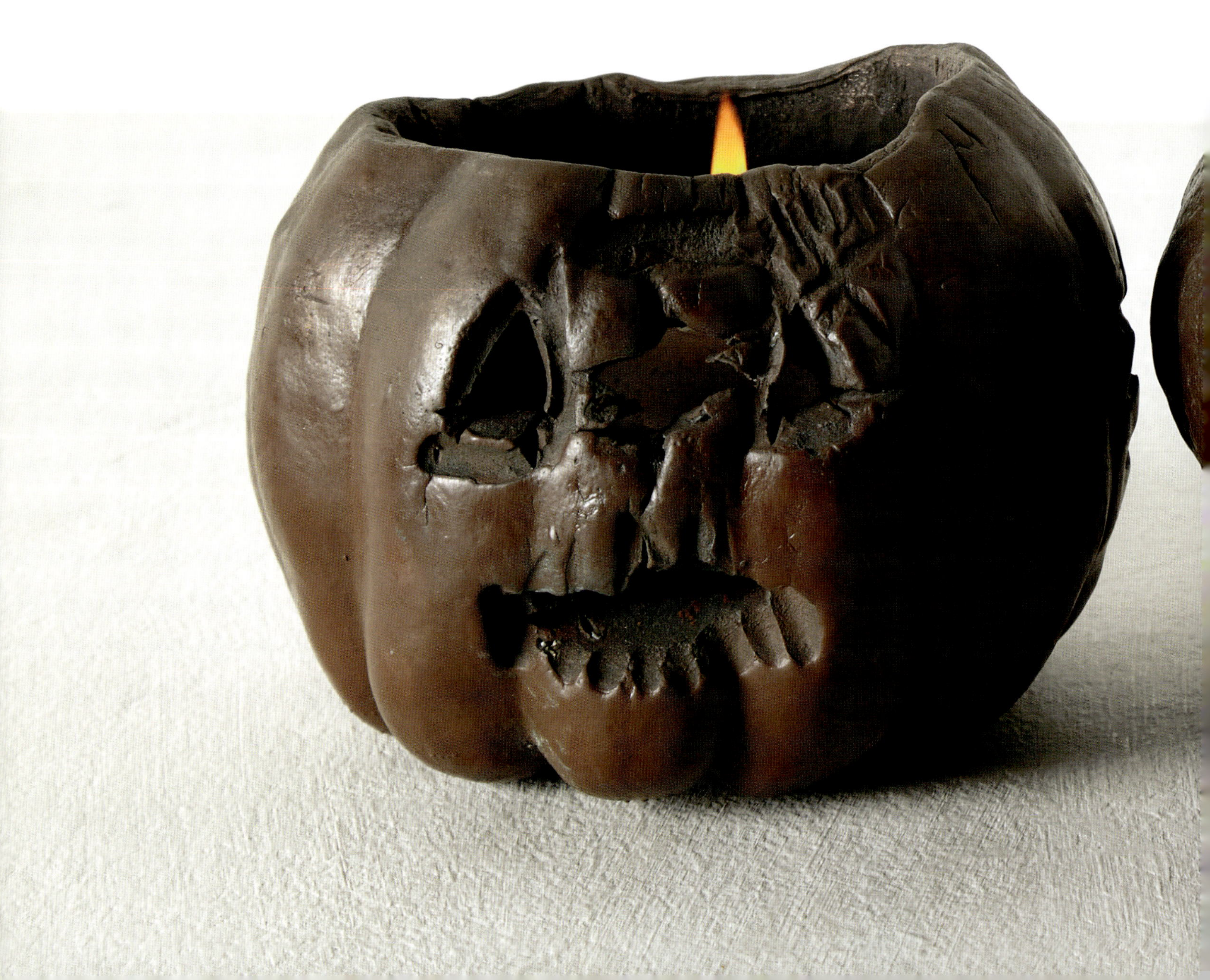

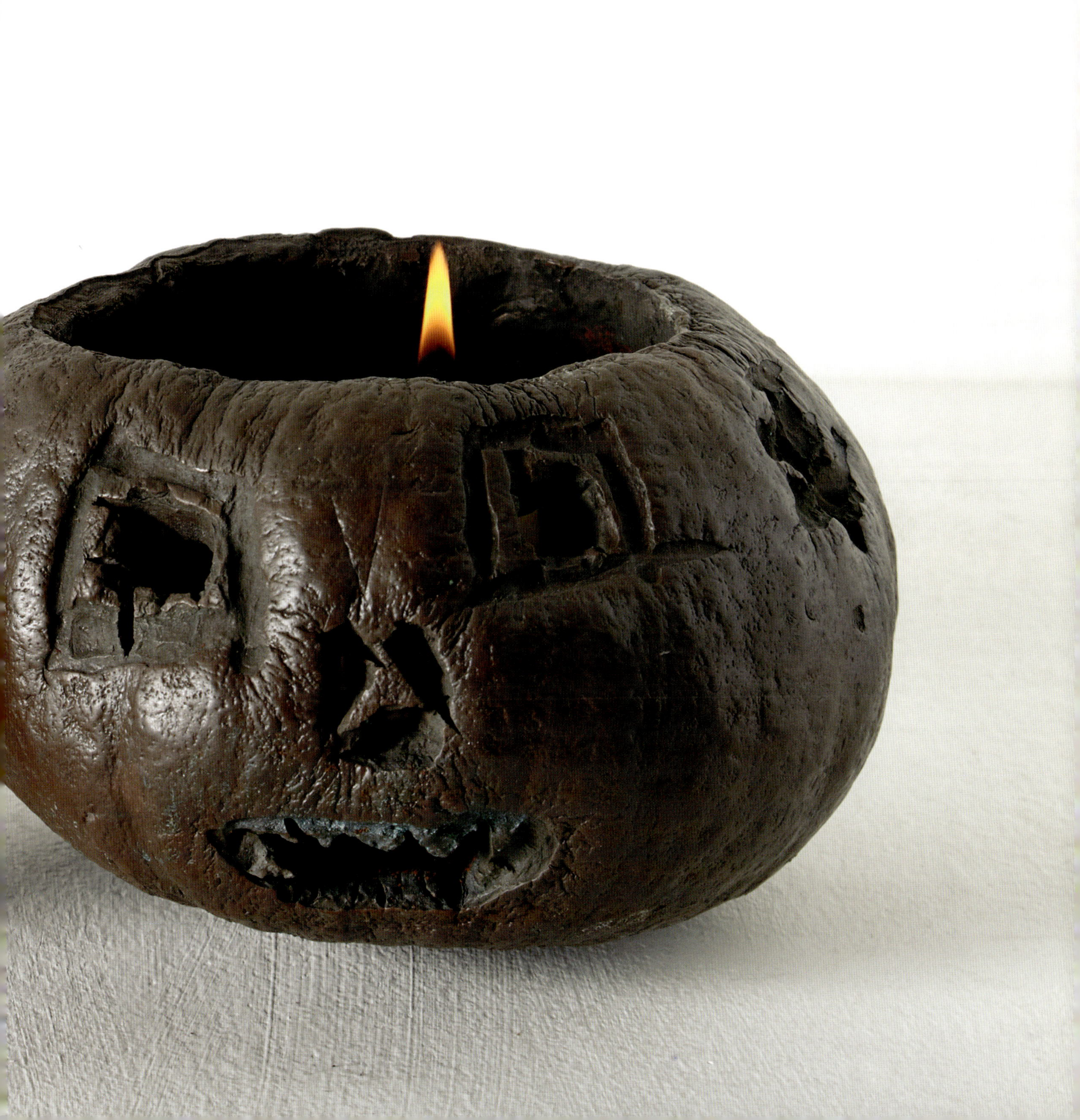

'Most casting processes are difficult and irritating. Particularly if you are after perfection. They are sometimes satisfying in the end, but are mostly frustrating. The rules are very strict. I sometimes think that being successful in the studio involves being either very good or very bad at these processes, and nothing in between. I tell students that when casting, they should imagine a blueberry muffin. The choice is either to cast into something with as much control as possible, like the bottom part of the muffin, which has carefully picked up the pattern of the paper case; or else to lose it a bit, like the top of the muffin. The "Dark Lights" are the latter. They follow a rare process that is elegant and satisfying. A carrier bag is filled with newspaper, dipped in latex, and then covered in fibreglass. You pull the filling out of a hole in the bottom; the latex is a perfect release and pulls out with a satisfying pop. There is little control over any of this process, but the results are just right.'

Dark Light 2003
Resin, pigment, fibreglass, copper and pipe,
130 × 50 × 8 cm

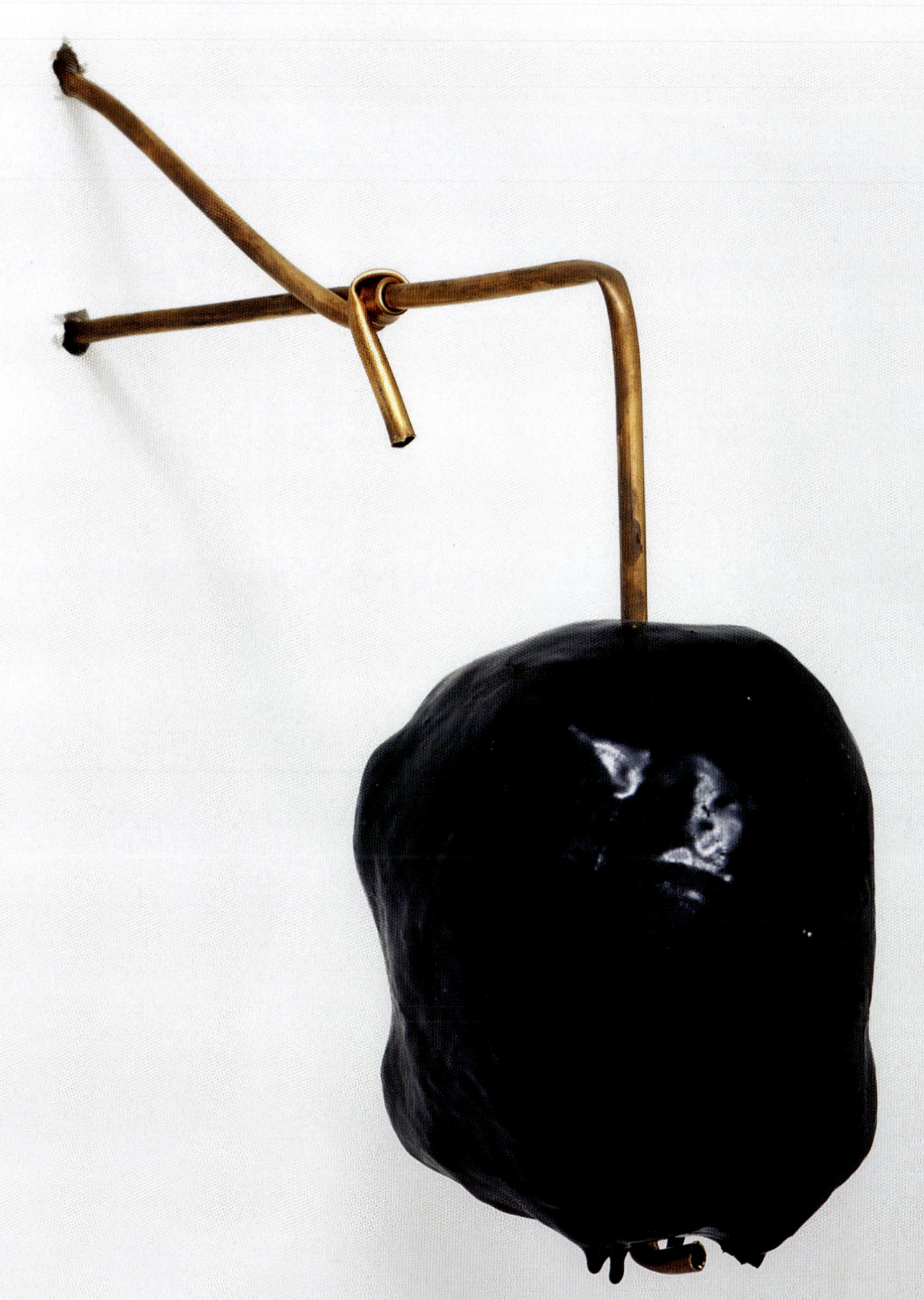

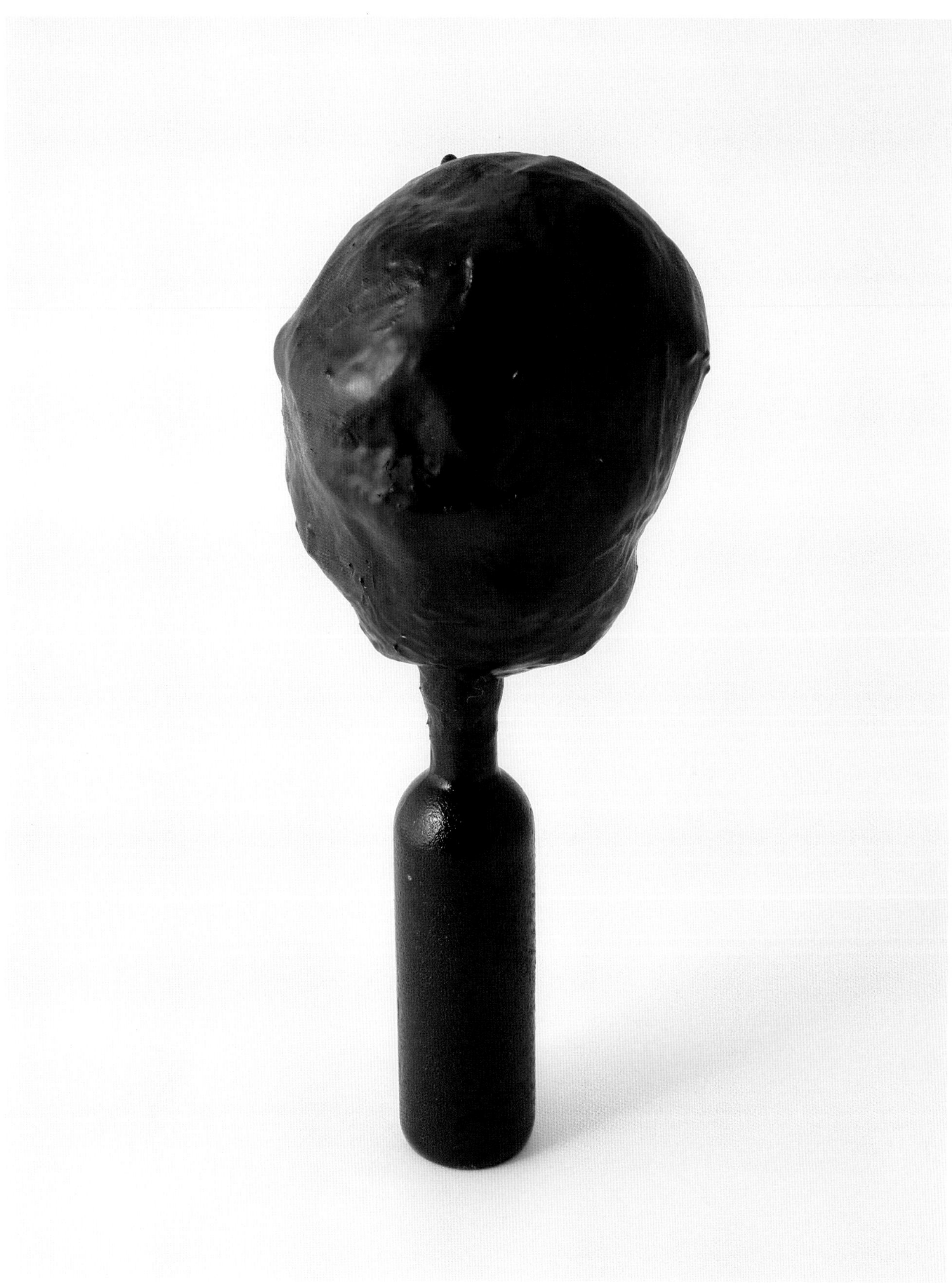

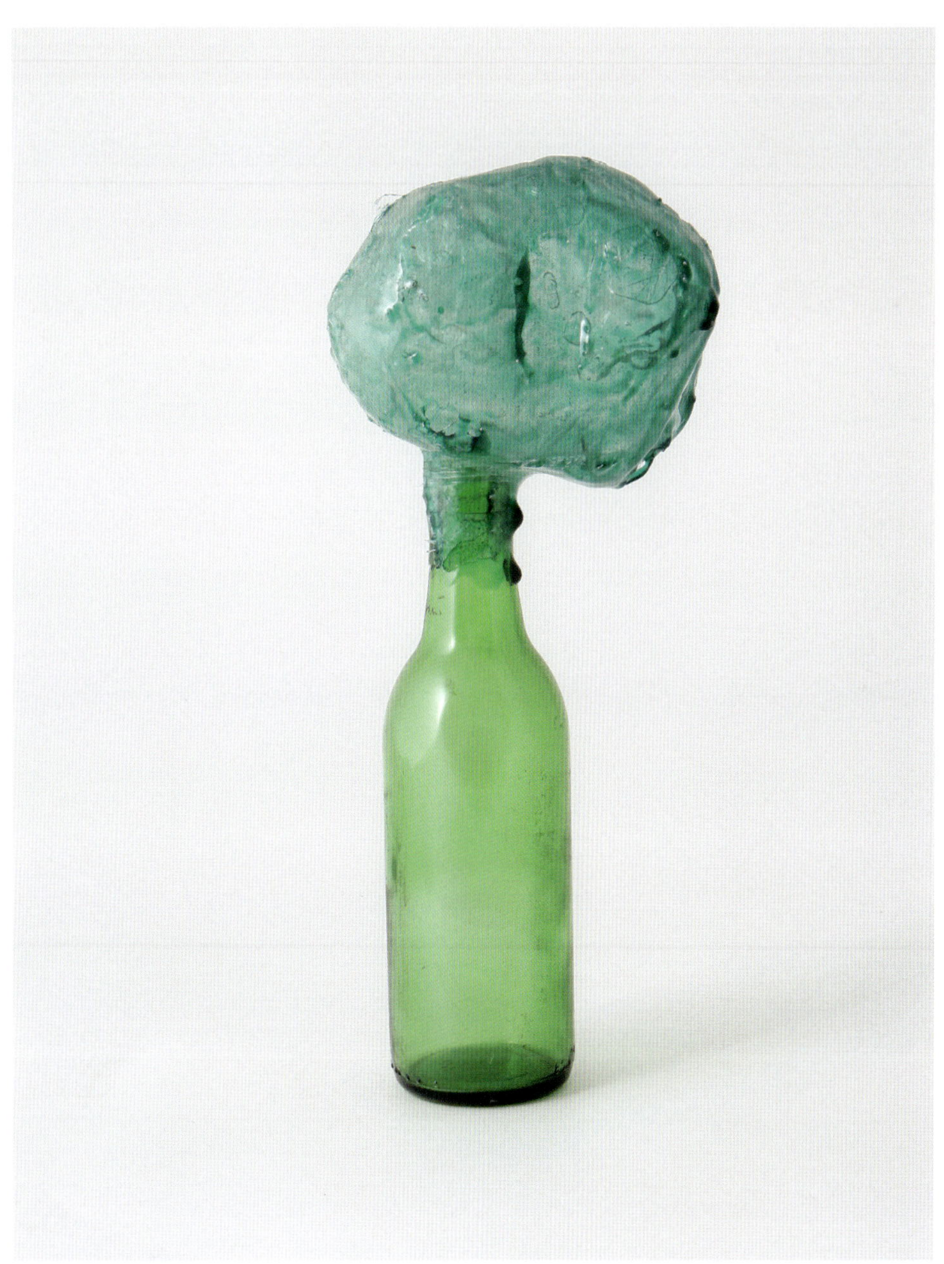

above
Green Bottle With 2003
Resin, pigment, fibreglass
and empty wine bottle,
30 × 11 × 10 cm

opposite
Black Tower 2003
Resin, pigment, fibreglass
and empty wine bottle,
35 × 14 × 11 cm

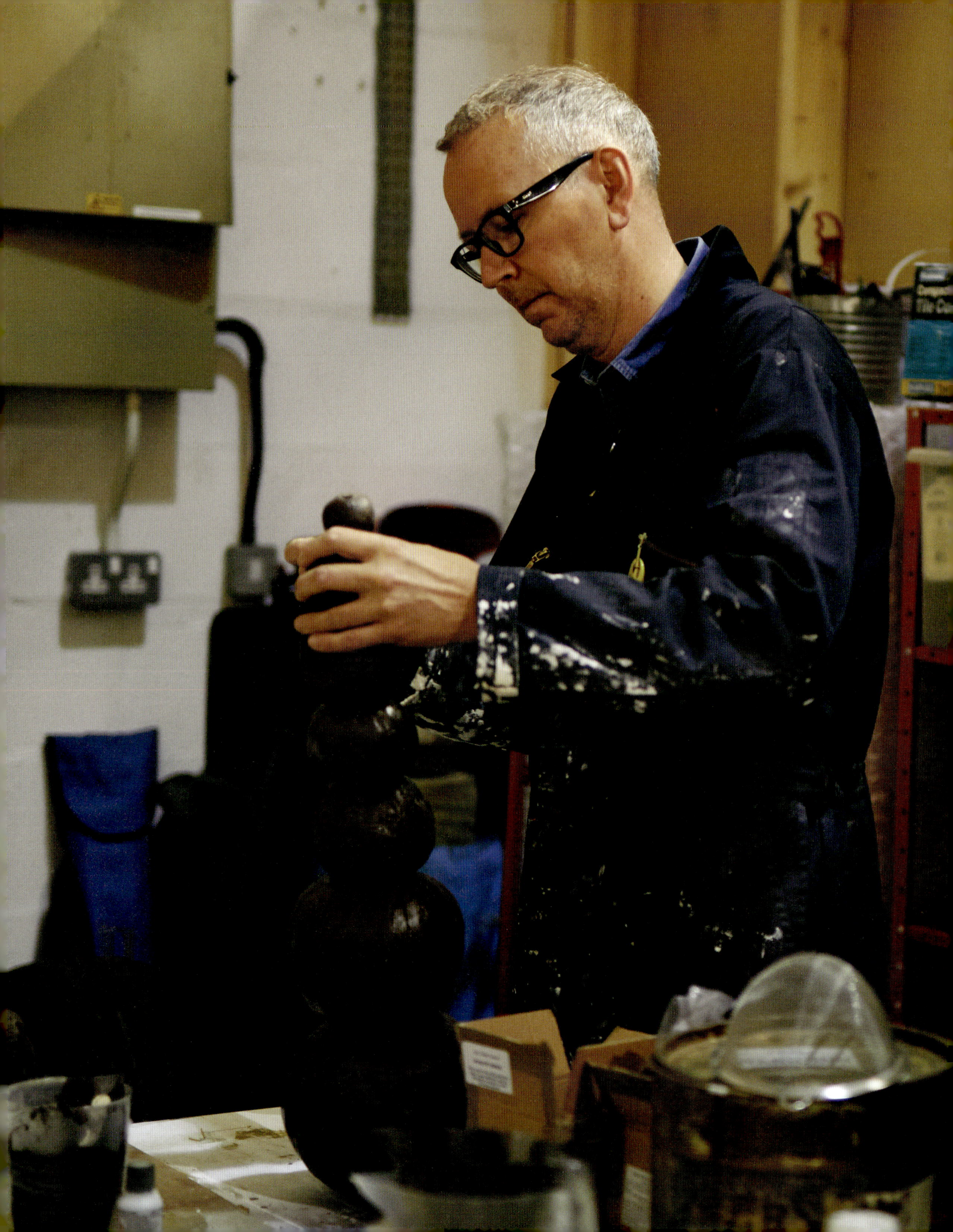

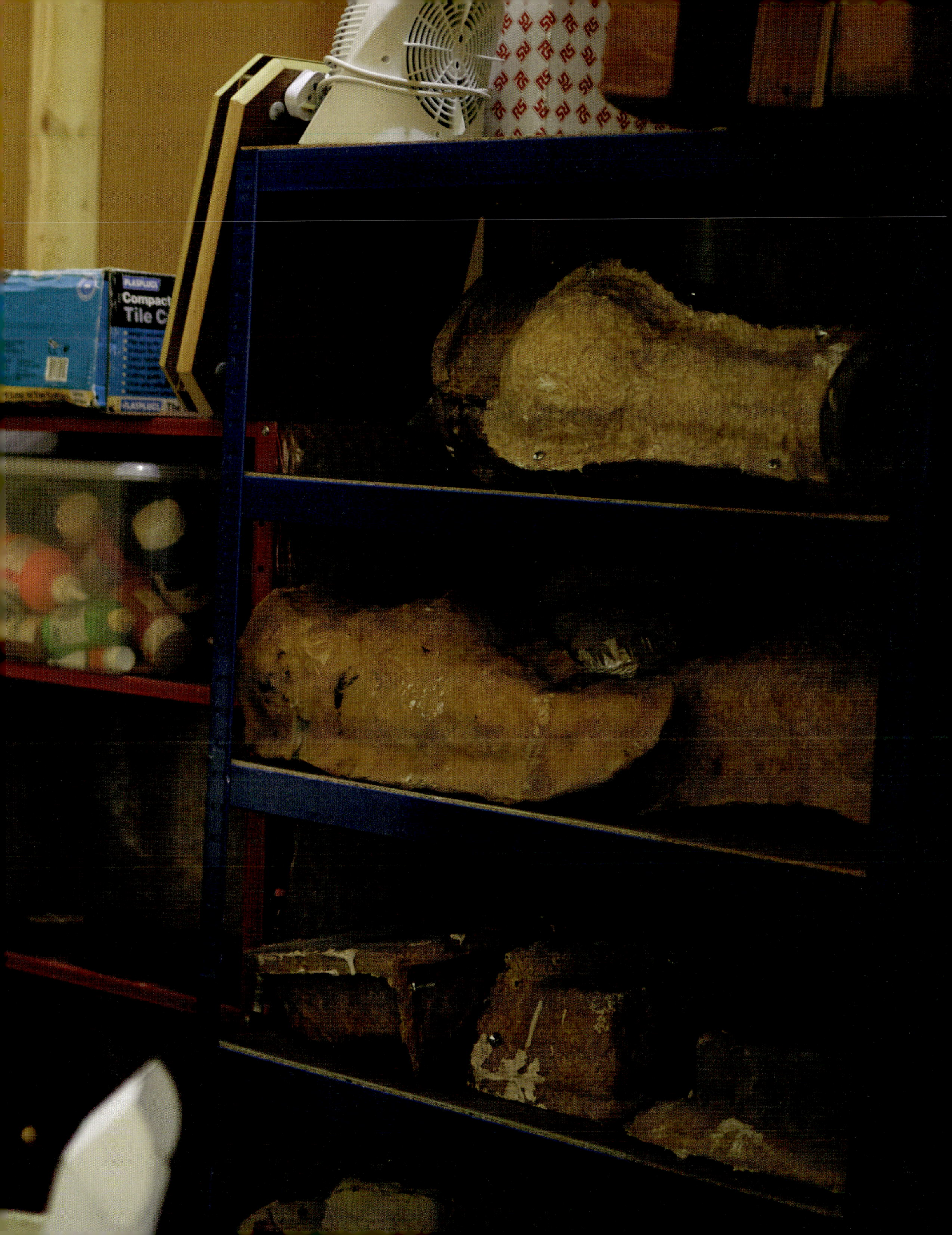
Compact
Tile

Sing Me To Sleep 2000
Resin, marble powder, metal
bolts and water,
12 × 30 × 49 cm

Stationary Mobiles 2004
Plastic rulers, Bic pens,
Sellotape and rope,
dimensions variable.
Installed at Laing Art Gallery,
Newcastle, 2005.

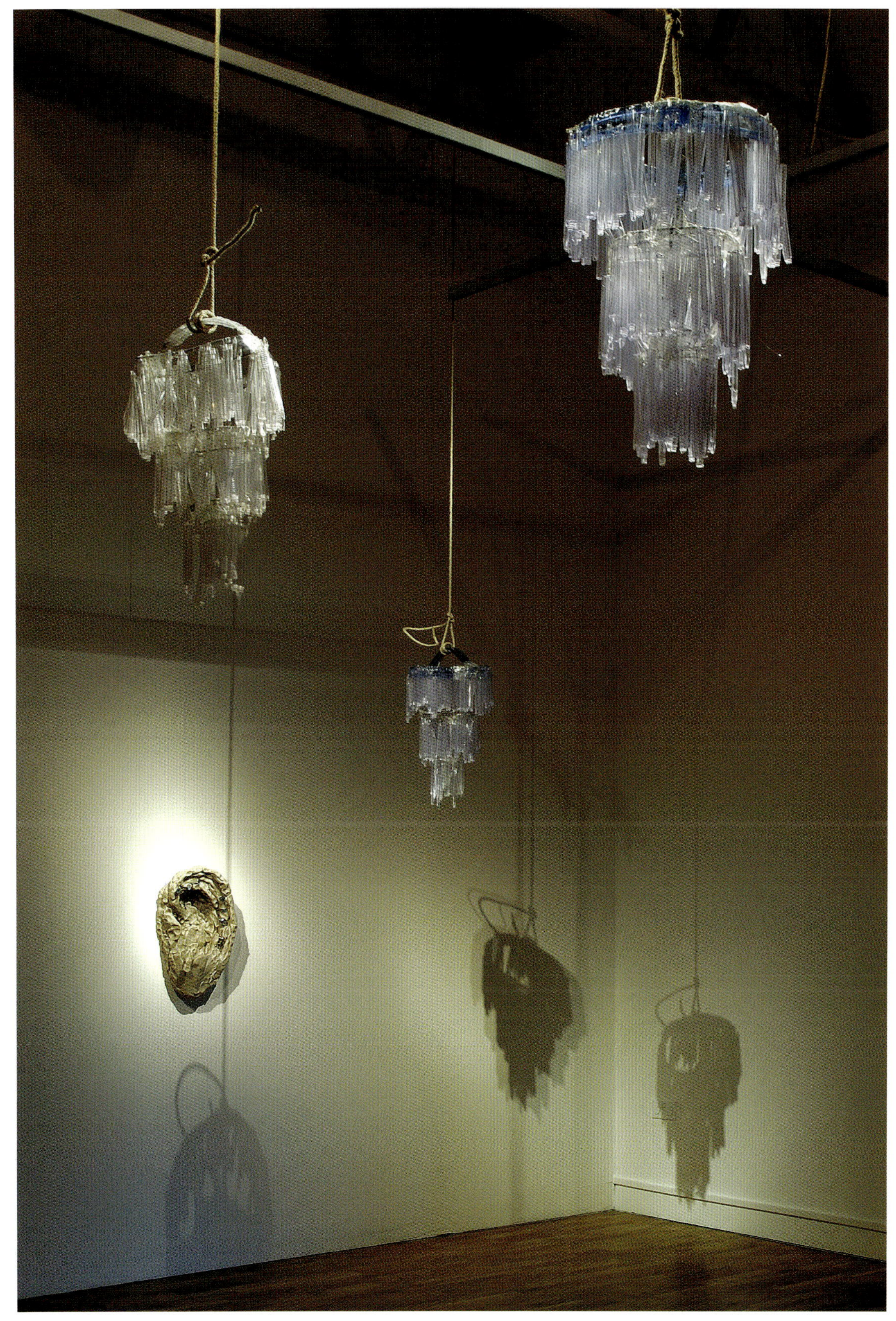

'When I was growing up, the first sculpture I remember seeing was a large marble horse's head by John Gibson in Birmingham Art Gallery. It wasn't so much the sculpture that struck me, but the fact that there was always crisp packets or sweet wrappers poked in the horse's nostril. The bright colours were very vivid against the white marble. This small act of creative vandalism seemed to finish the work. It updated it and placed it in the present. When I made *Boneless* for the Laing Art Gallery in Newcastle, a large reclining figure constructed from bin bags full of old work, I put crisp bags into the eyes. Visitors to the show kept on taking the bags out of the sculpture and throwing them away, thinking they'd been placed there by naughty schoolchildren. It was me.'

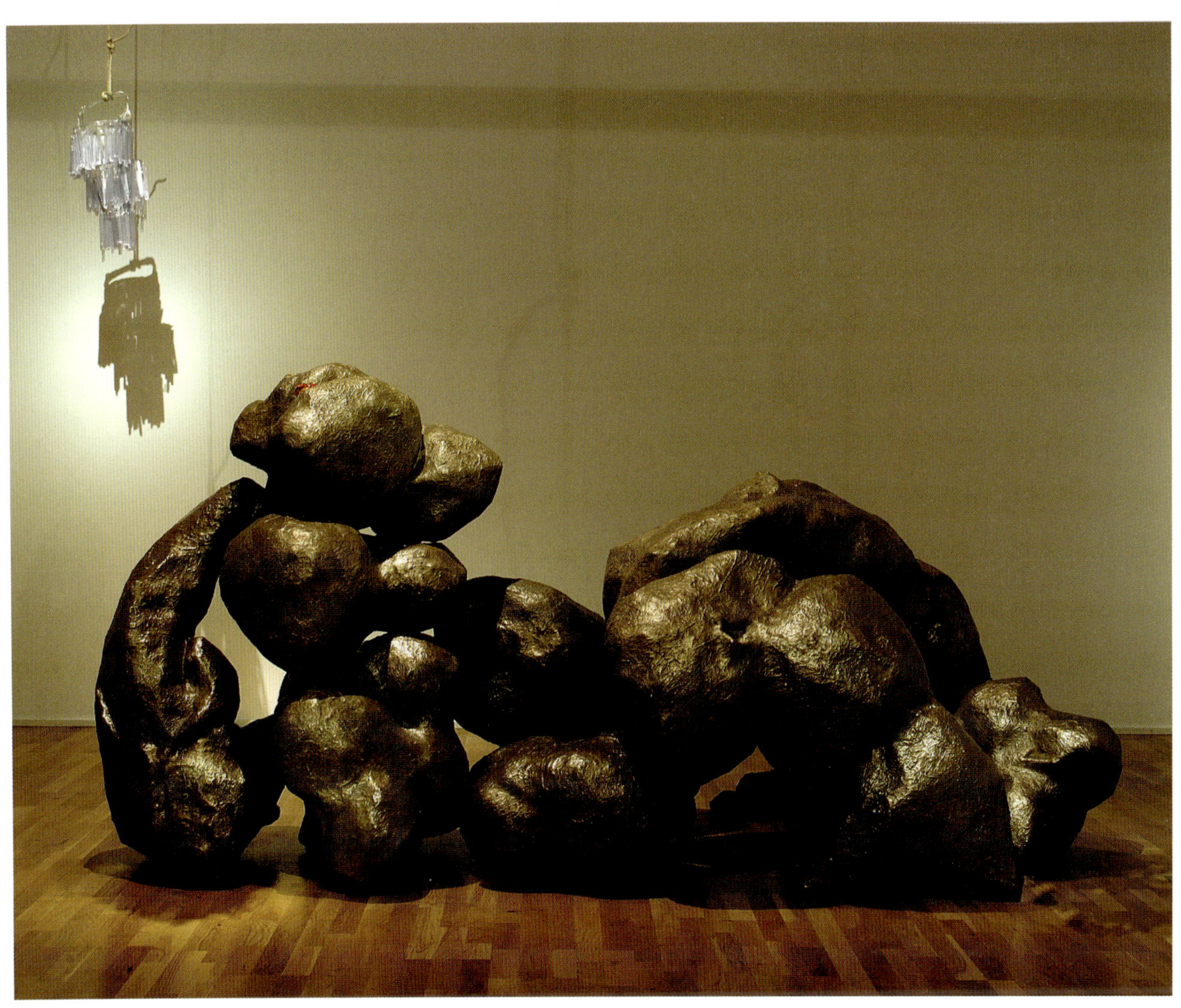

Boneless 2005
Resin, fibreglass, bronze,
and bags of old sculpture,
dimensions variable.
Installed at Laing Art Gallery,
Newcastle, 2005.

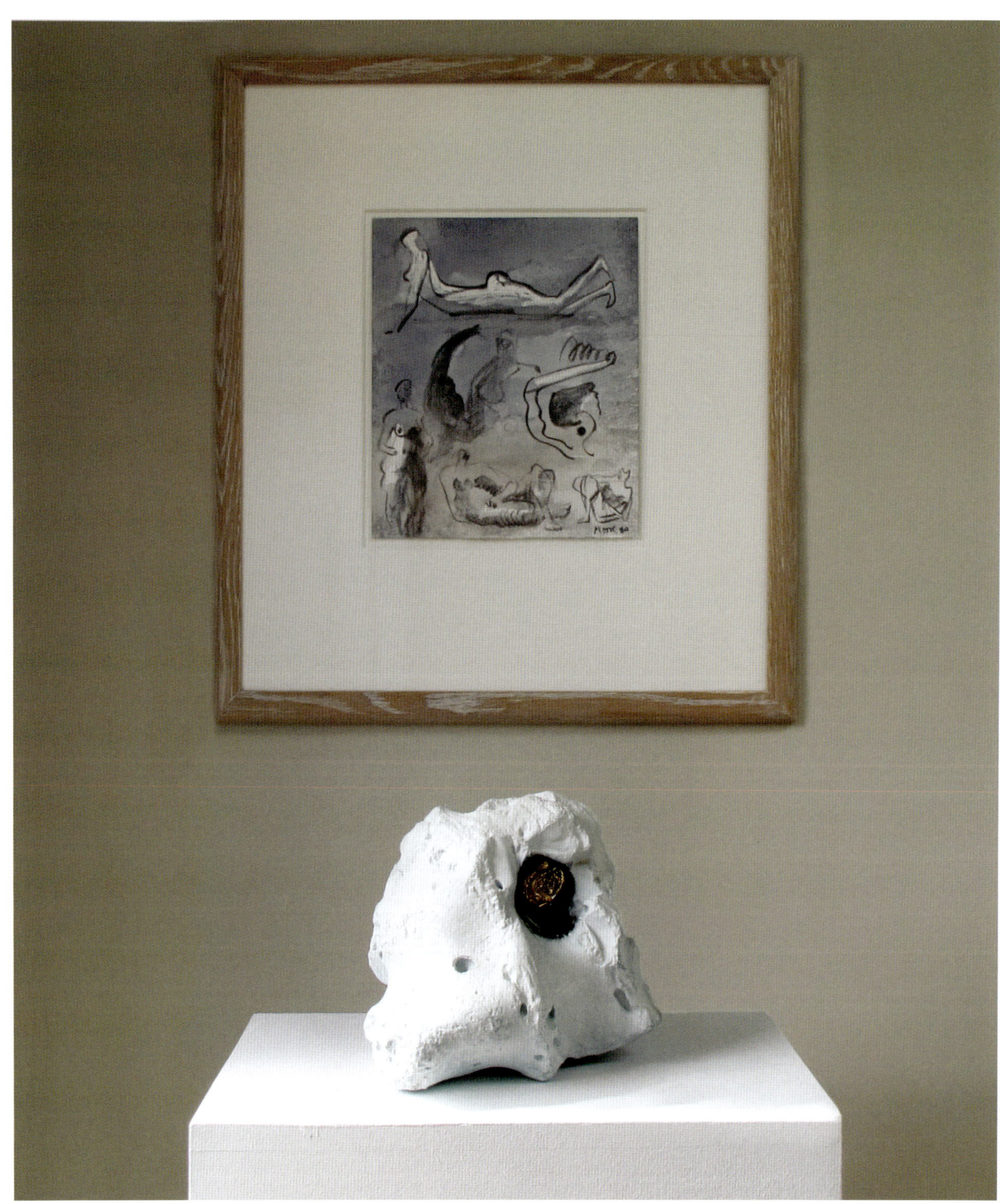

Stonut 2008
Bronze and crisp bag, 21 × 20 × 14 cm.
Installed with Henry Moore at
New Art Centre, Roche Court, Wiltshire.

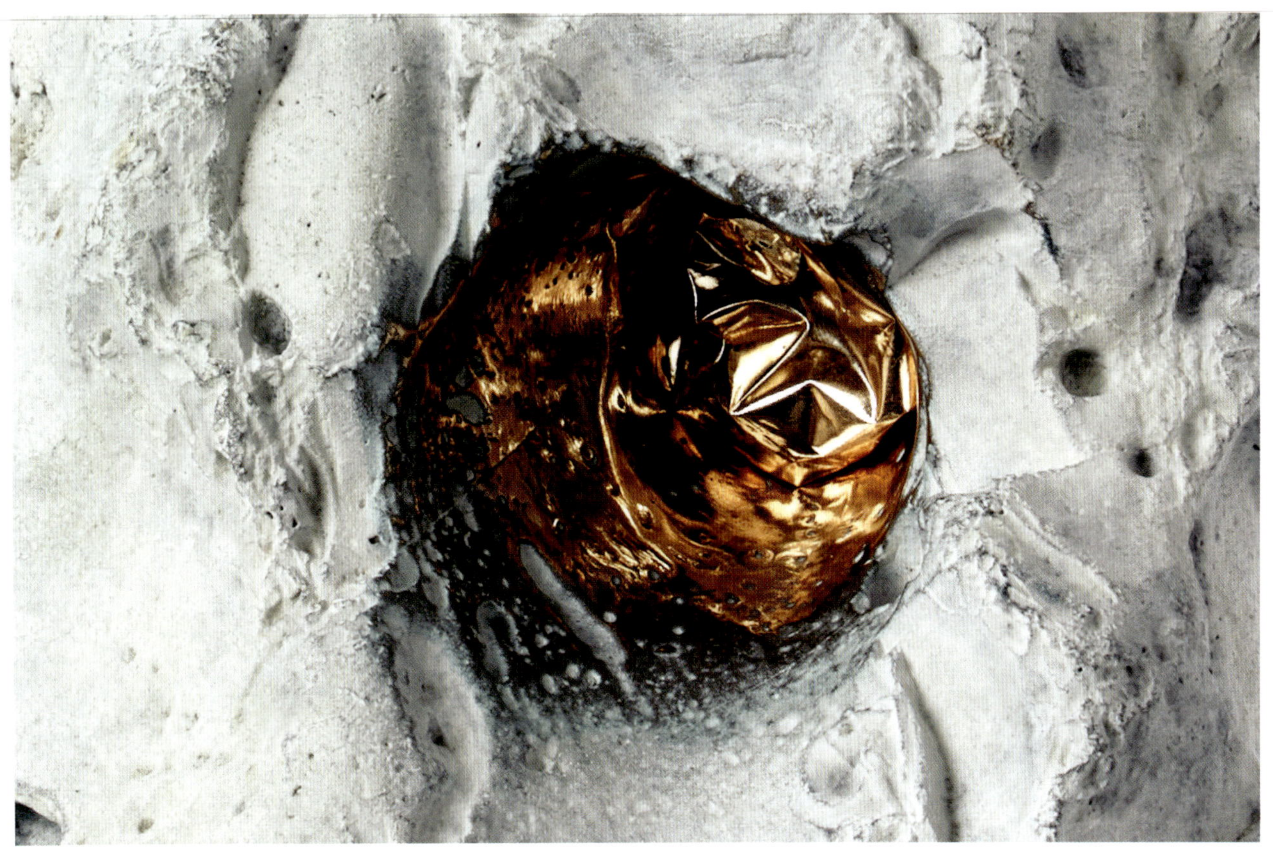

'A few years later, I had this theory that polished bronze was exactly the same colour as the foil of a McCoy's crisp packet. I had a large flint in the studio with a hole in the centre that I had cast in bronze. I polished a small sunburst around the hole and poked in a crisp packet. It was a perfect match and a very pleasing coincidence. It allowed me to start thinking about the possibilities of bronze as a material and led onto a whole series of works. Until that point, I'd just thought that bronze was cynical.'

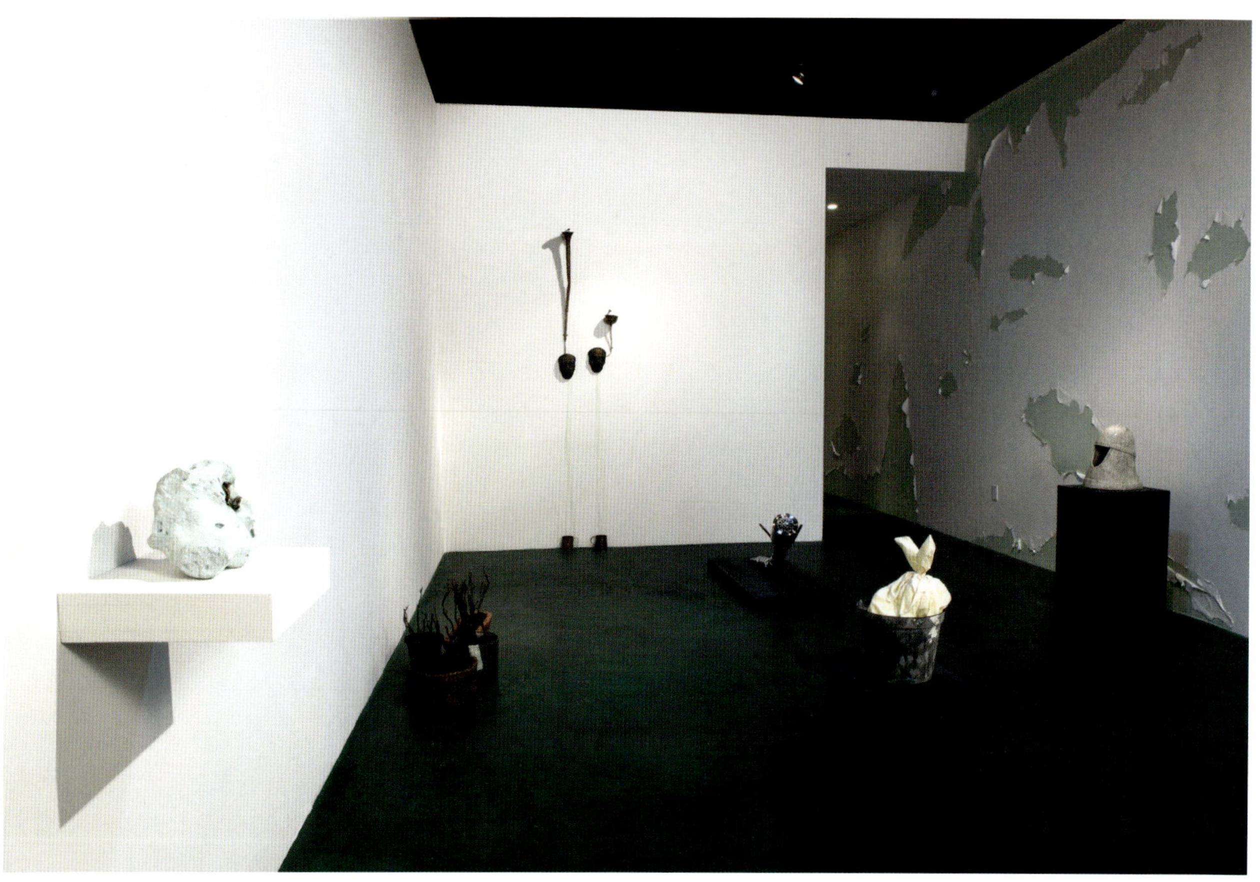

above, opposite and following spreads
'Des Hughes and Richard Hughes' 2008
Michael Benevento Gallery, Los Angeles

Magic Flute 2008
Chrome-plated tin cans and twig,
78 × 160 × 160 cm

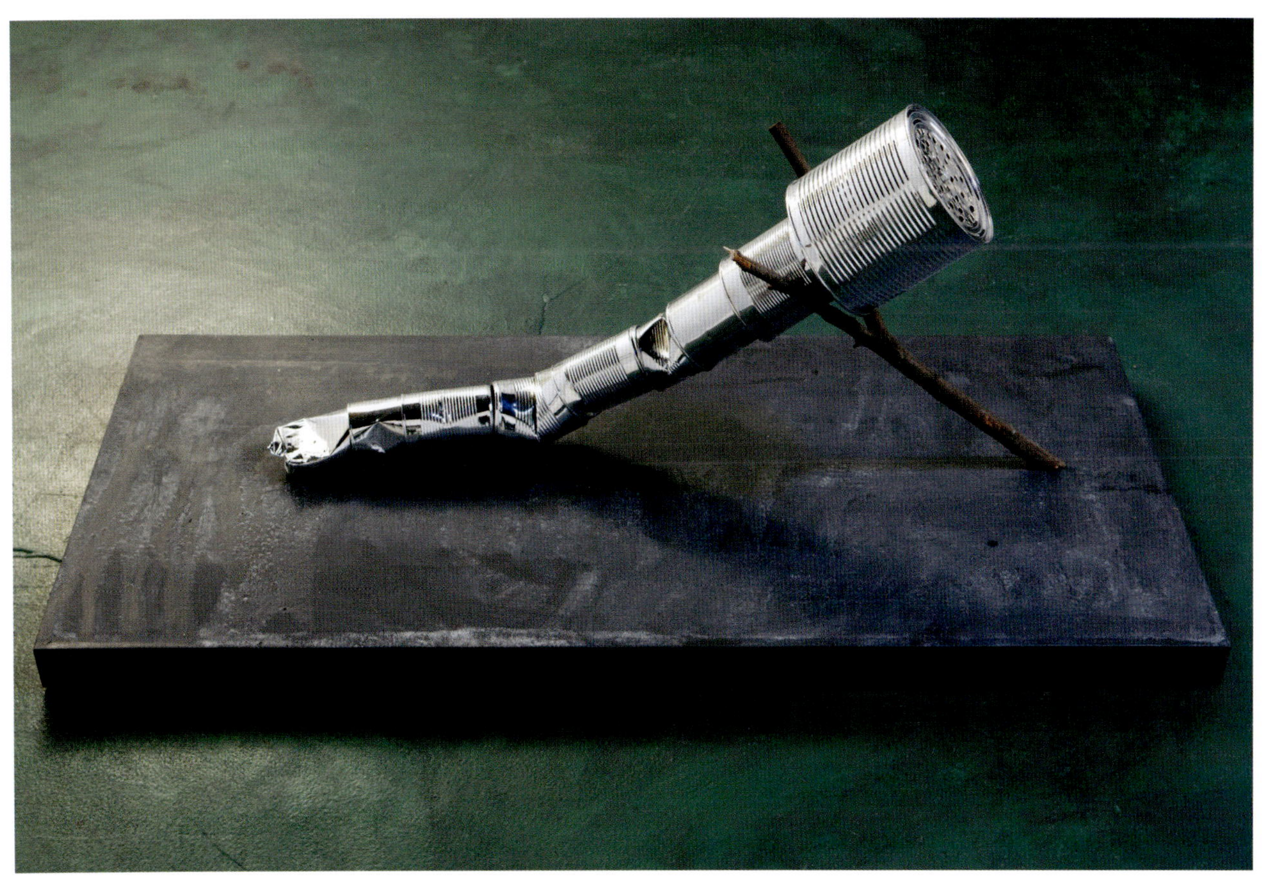

The Lovely Faces 2008
Resin, copper powder, copper pipe, funnels, copper horn, water and pump, dimensions variable

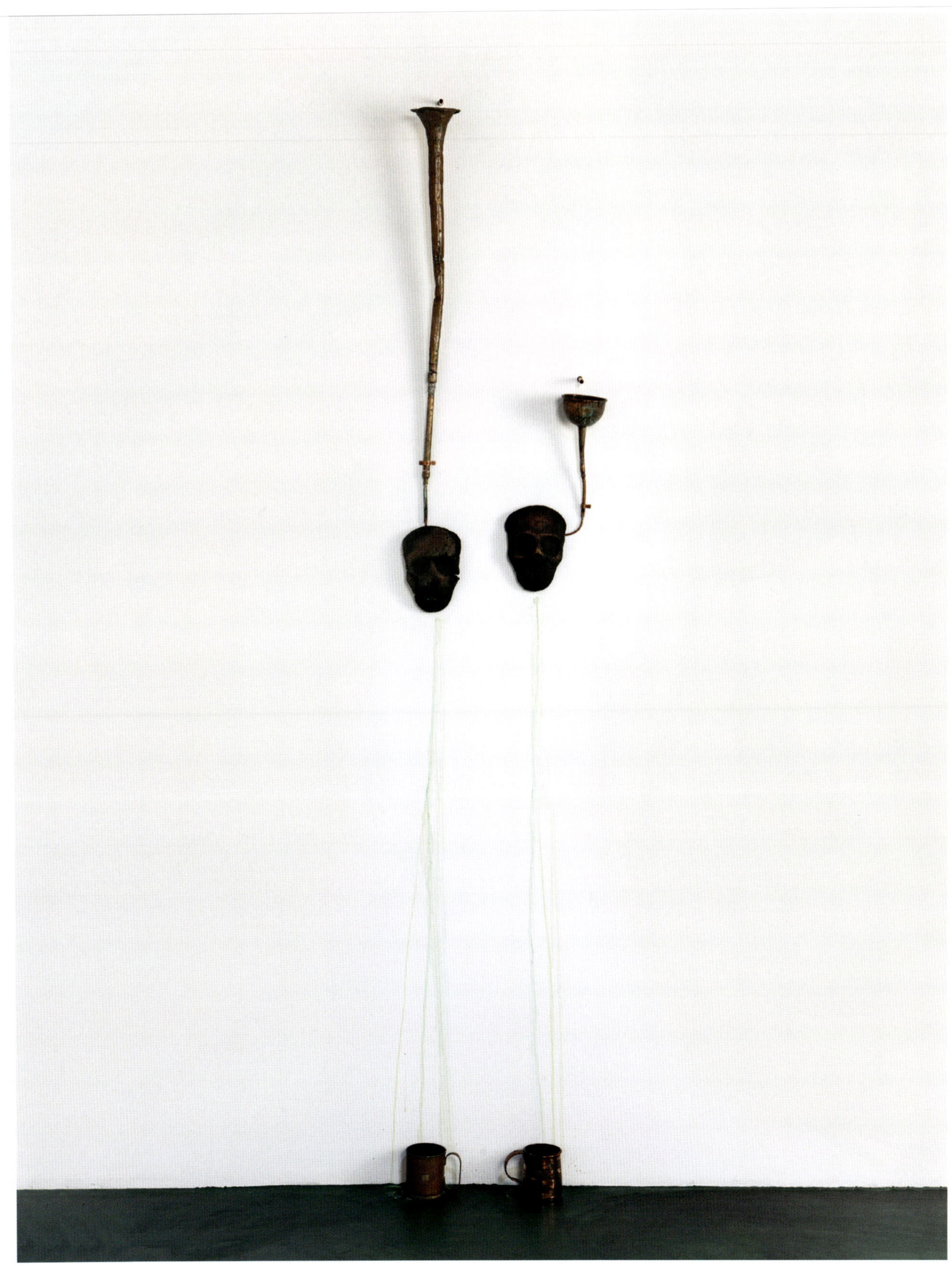

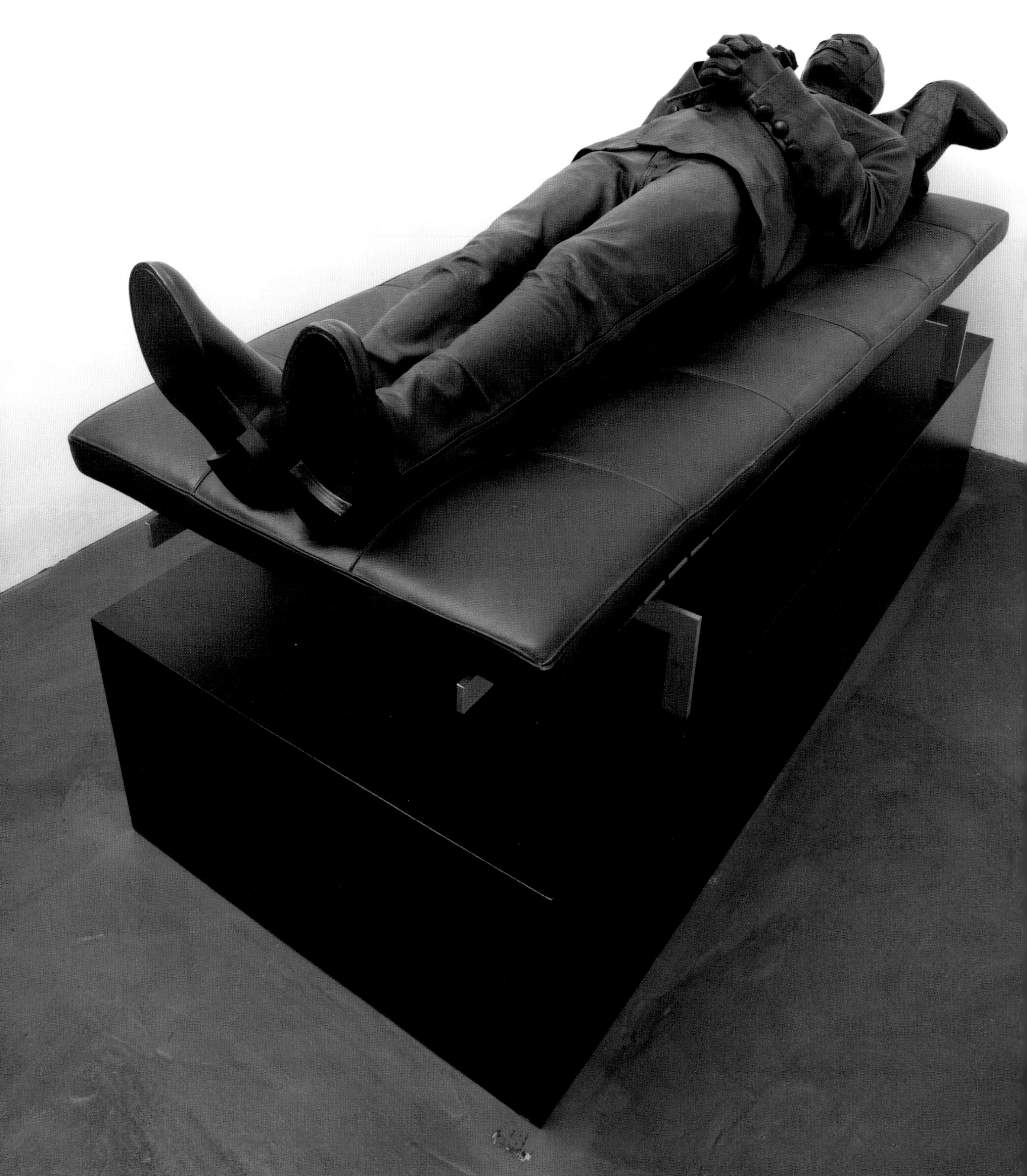

... **the Terrible** 2008
Leather, mannequin and
Poul Kjaerholm PK80 daybed,
200 × 100 × 60 cm

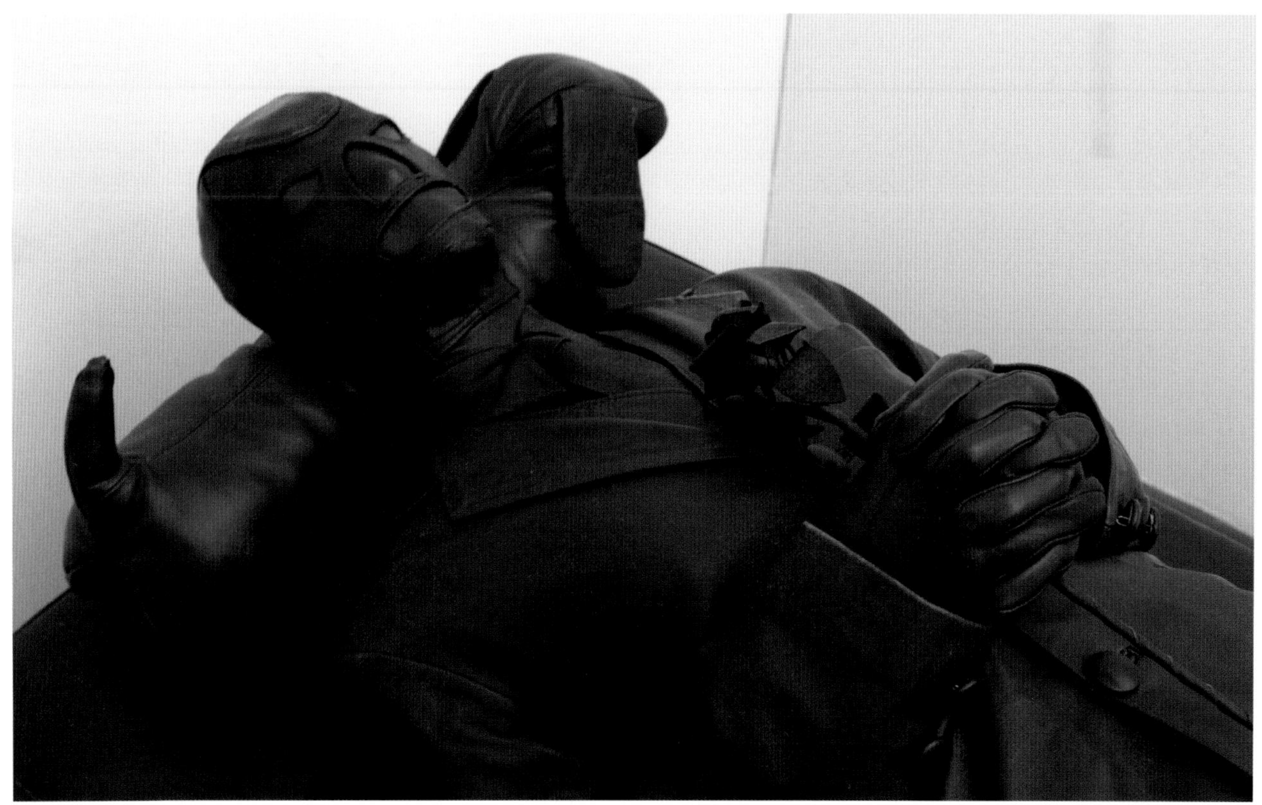

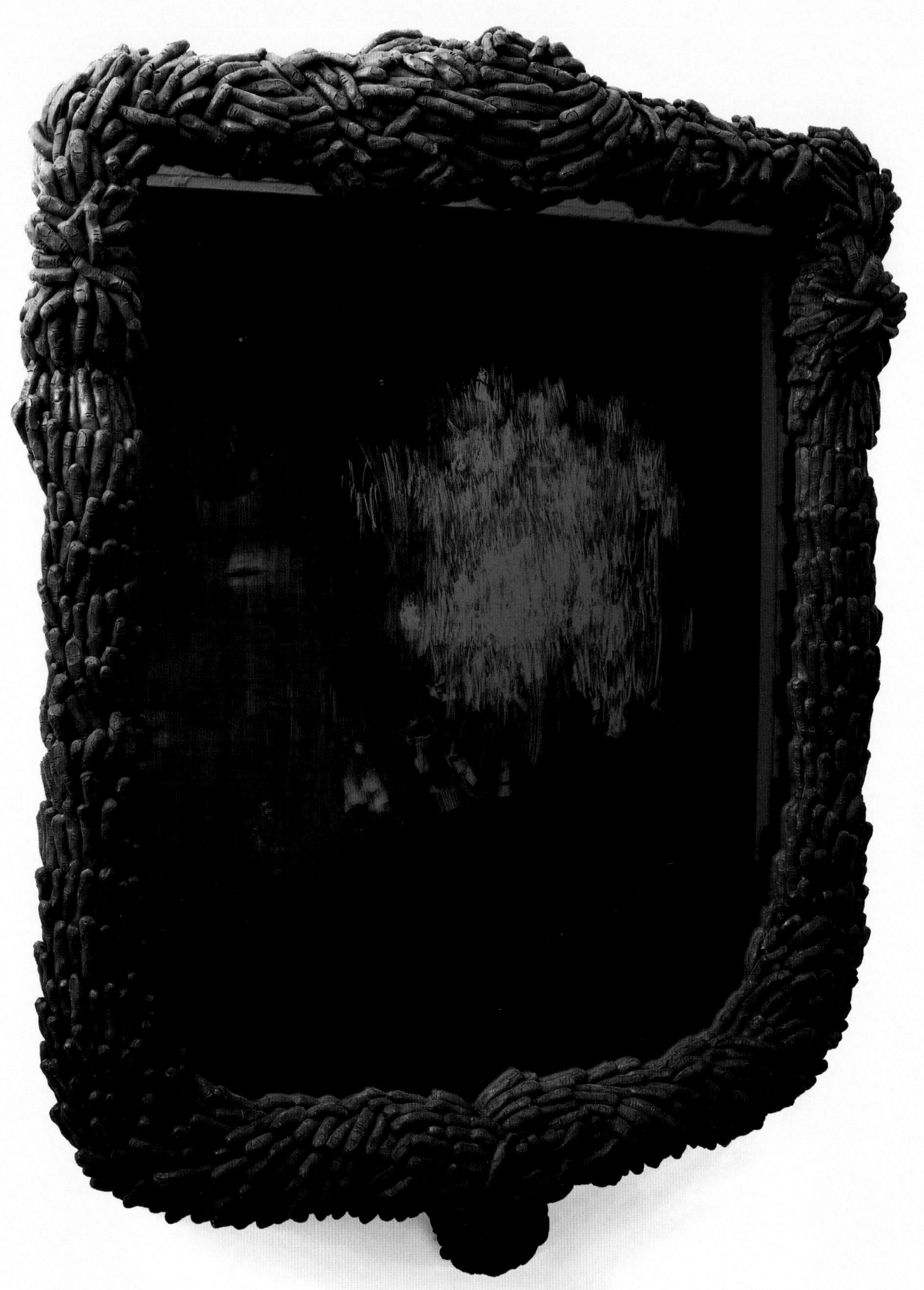

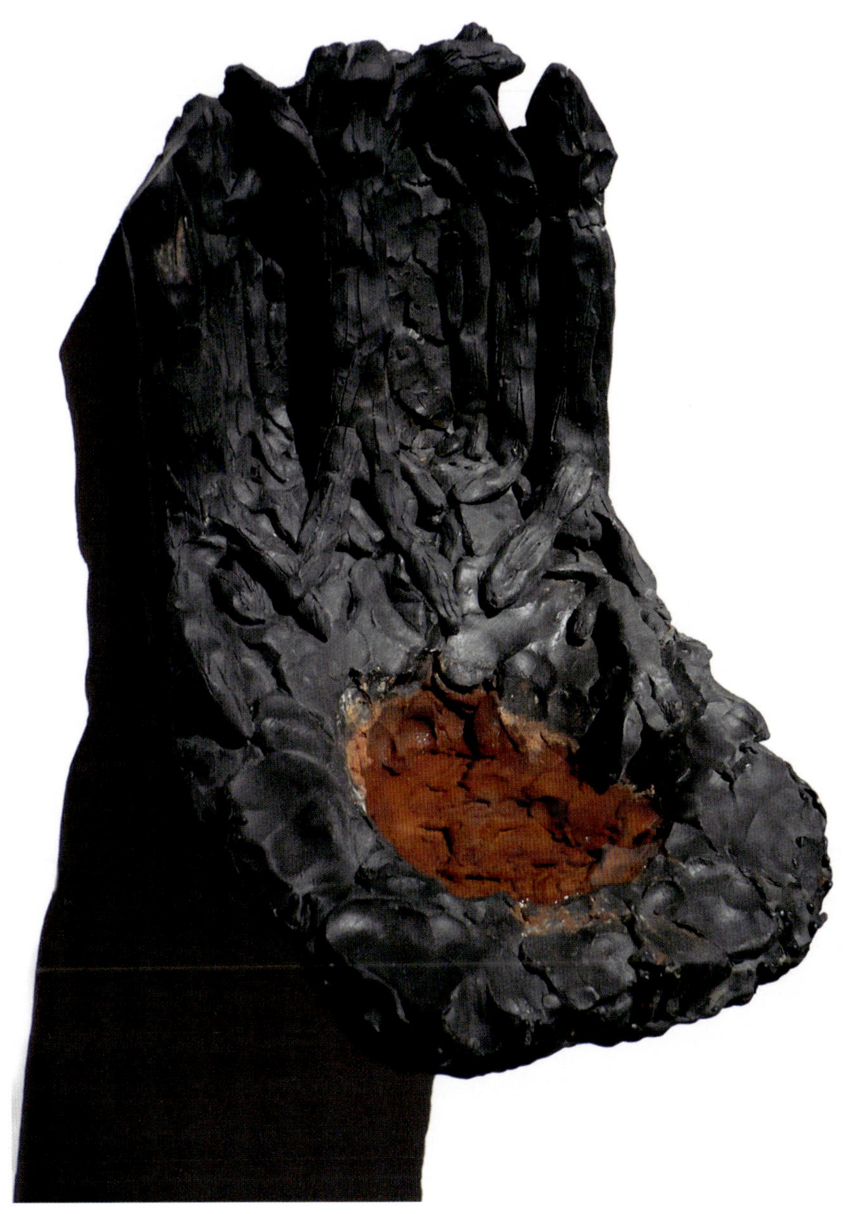

above

Spoilt Water 2005
Resin, iron powder and water,
25 × 19 × 21 cm

opposite

Dark Mirror 2008
Resin, black pigments
and black glass,
130 × 99 × 10 cm

Middle Aged 2006
Resin and marble powder,
50 × 30 × 30 cm

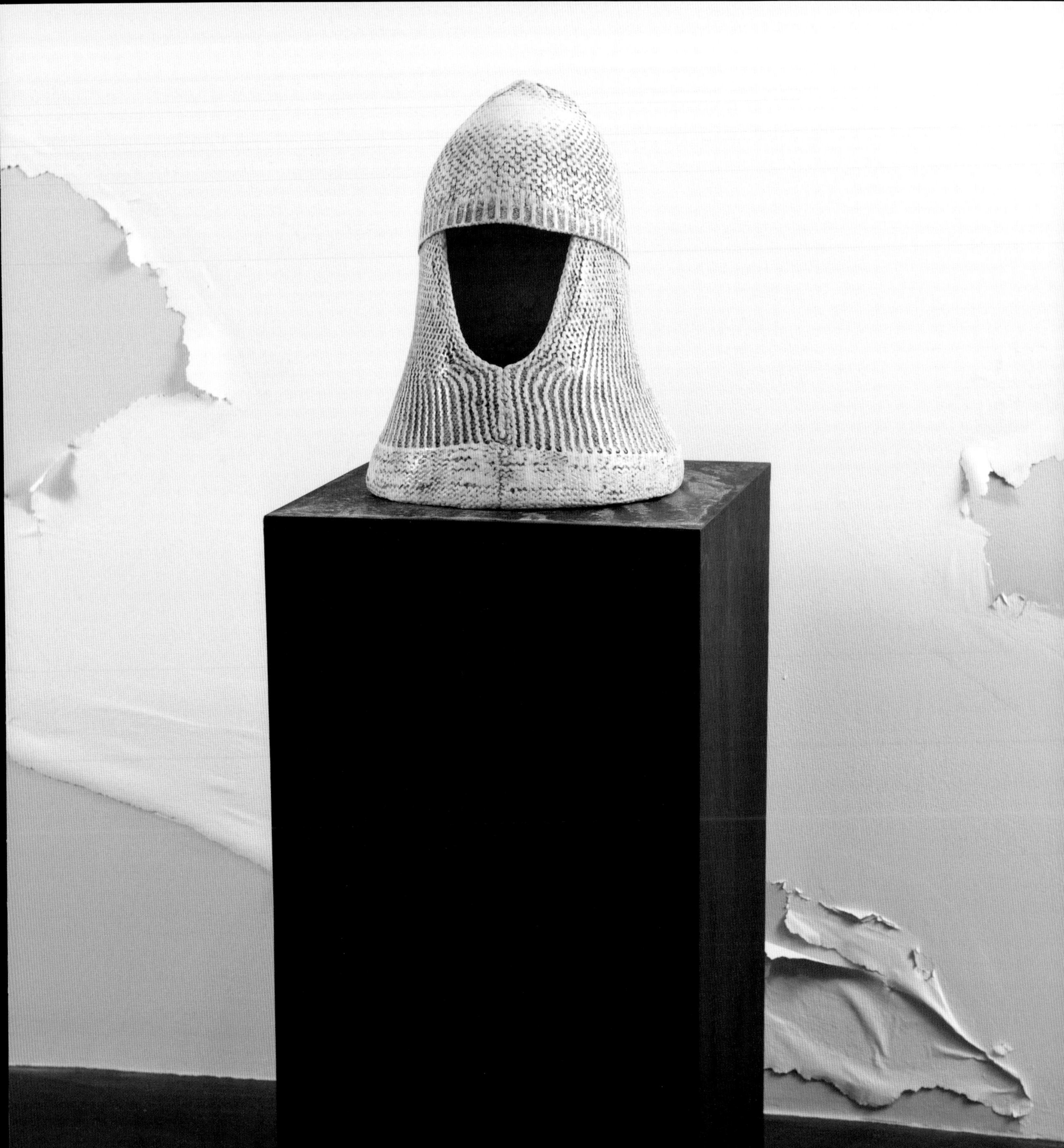

opposite
Each Way 2010
Fibreglass, pigment and glass,
109 × 97 × 8 cm

below
Endless Endless 2010
Fibreglass, resin and iron powder,
450 × 200 × 100 cm.
Installed at Frieze Art Fair,
Frame solo presentation.

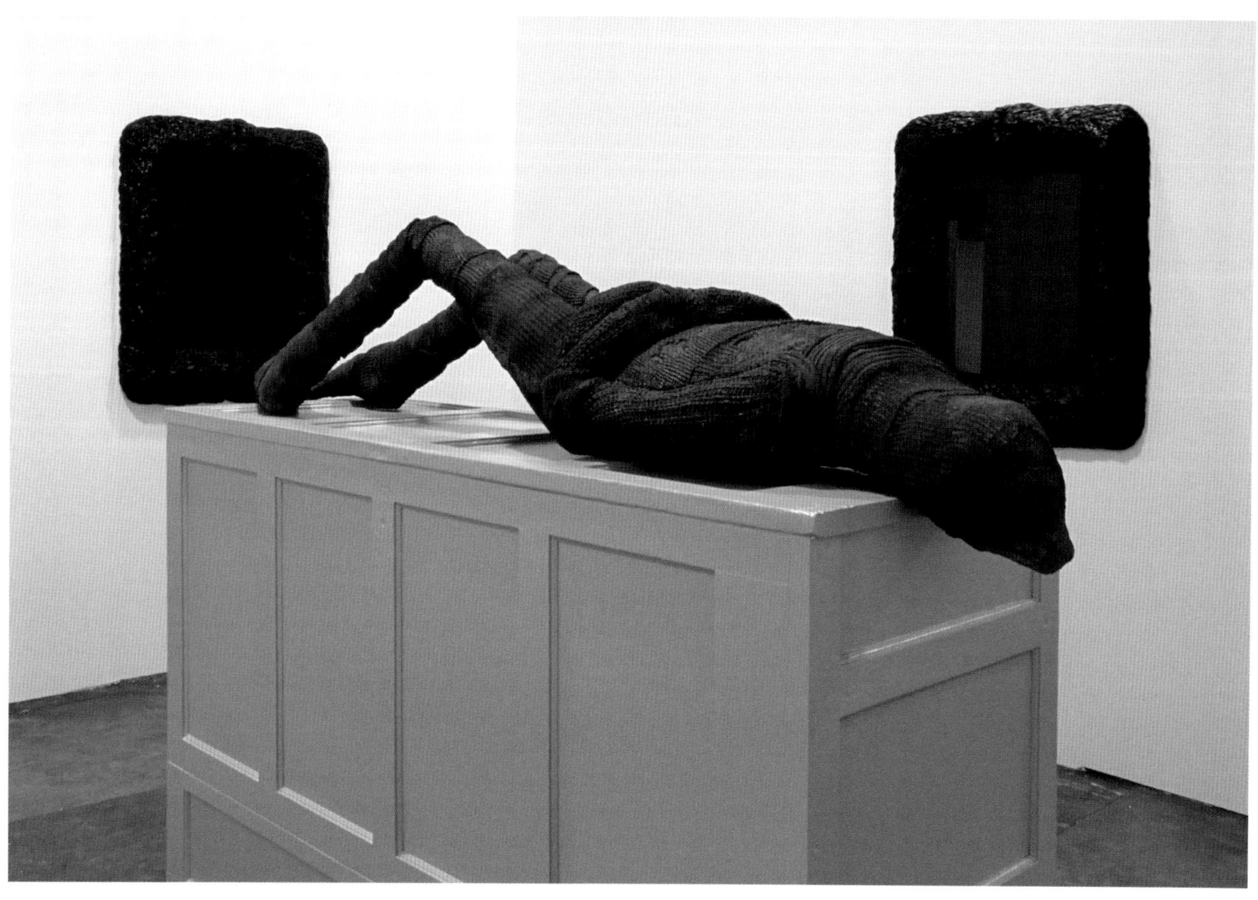

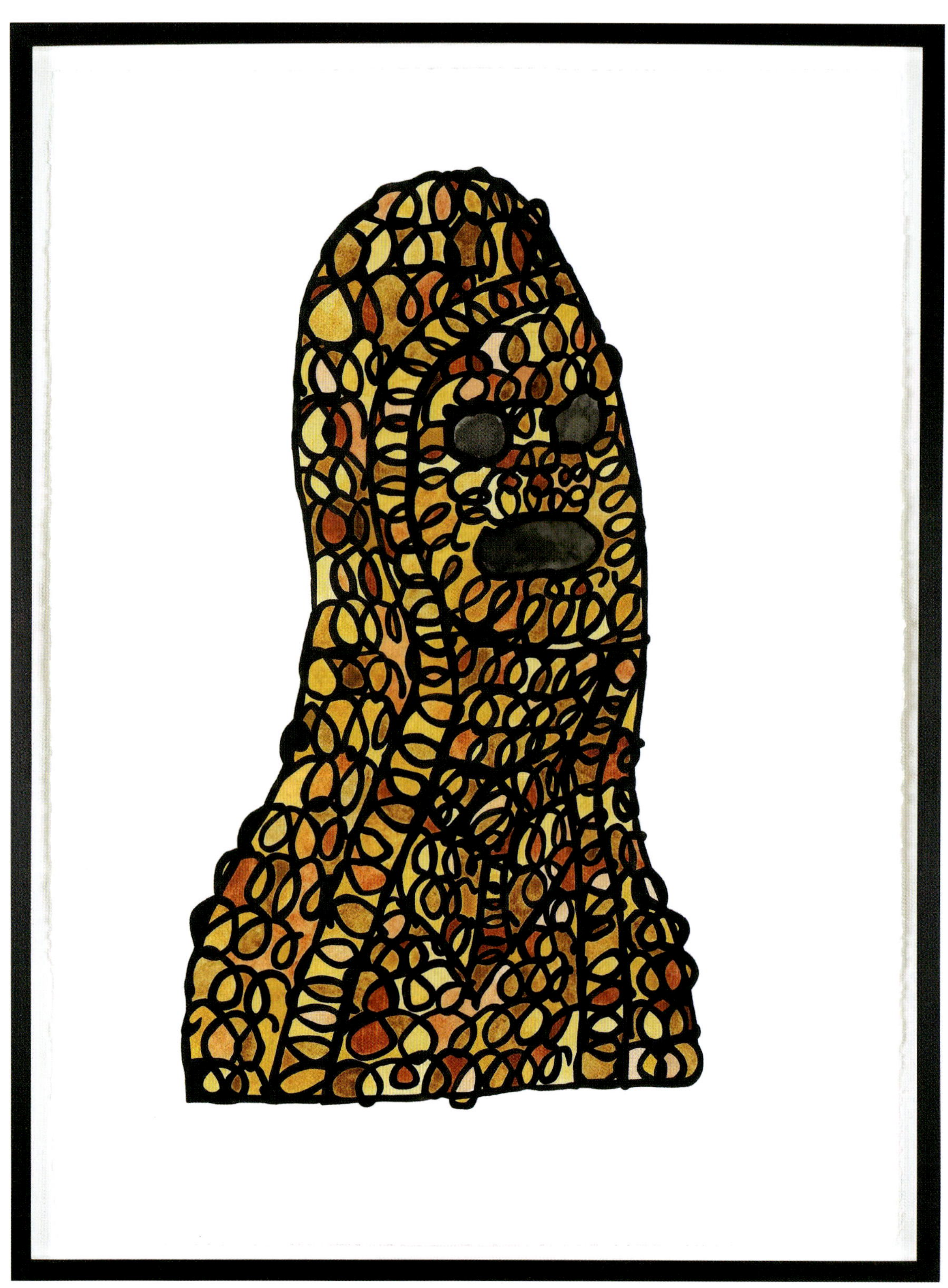

Open Mouth Rusted Hood 2010
Watercolour on paper,
76.7 × 57 cm

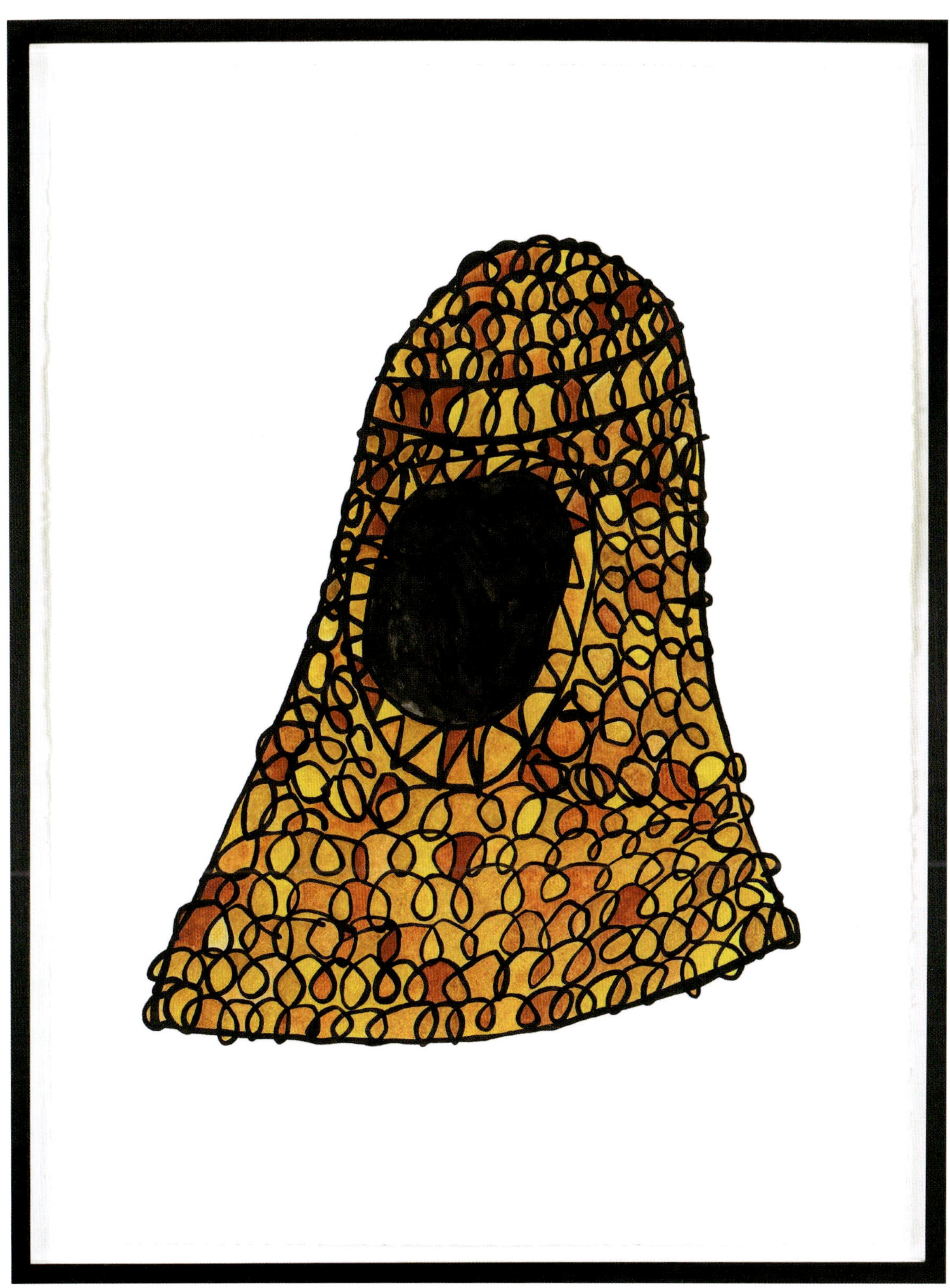

Balaclava Rusted Hood 2010
Watercolour on paper,
76.7 × 57 cm

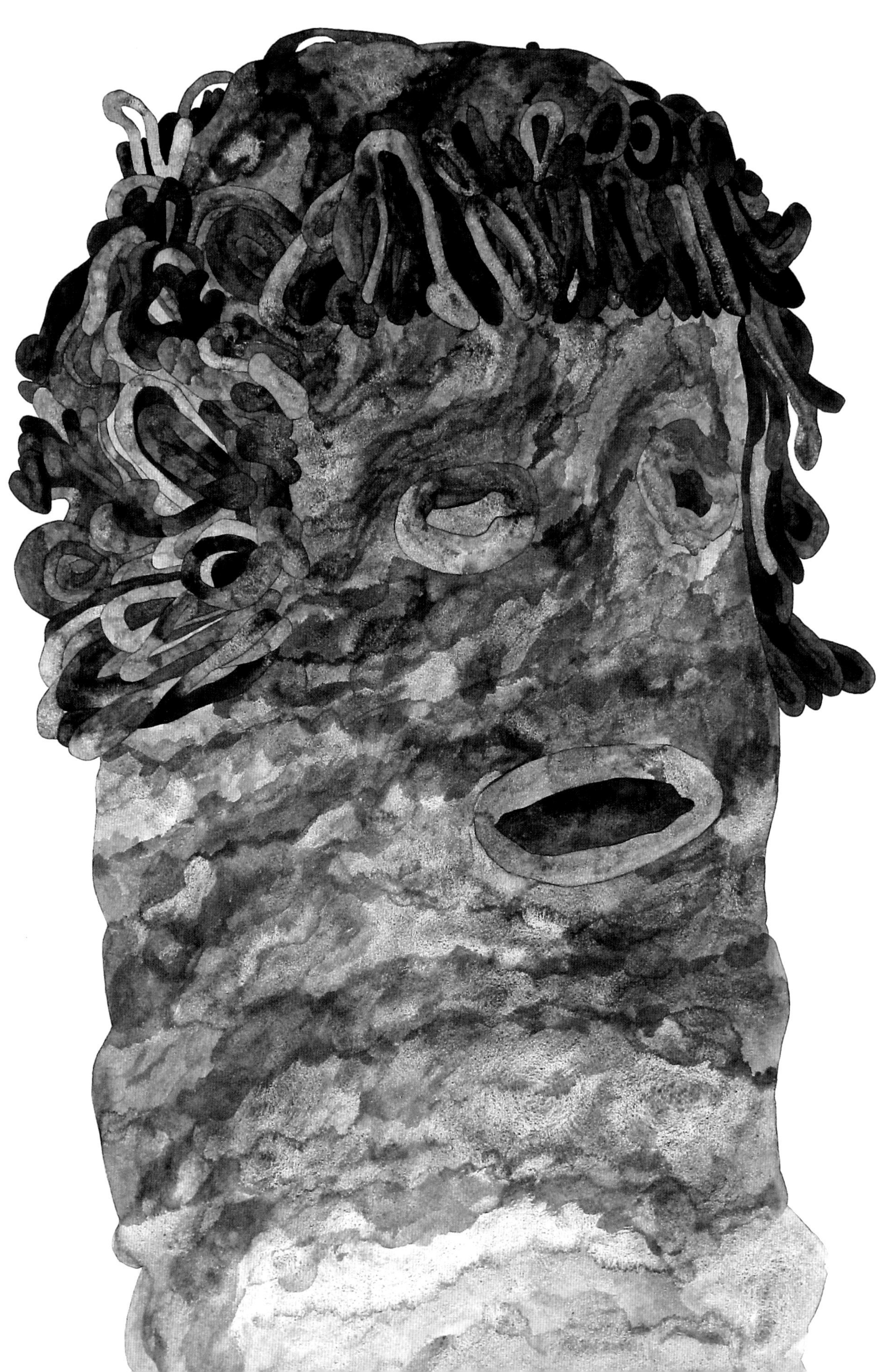

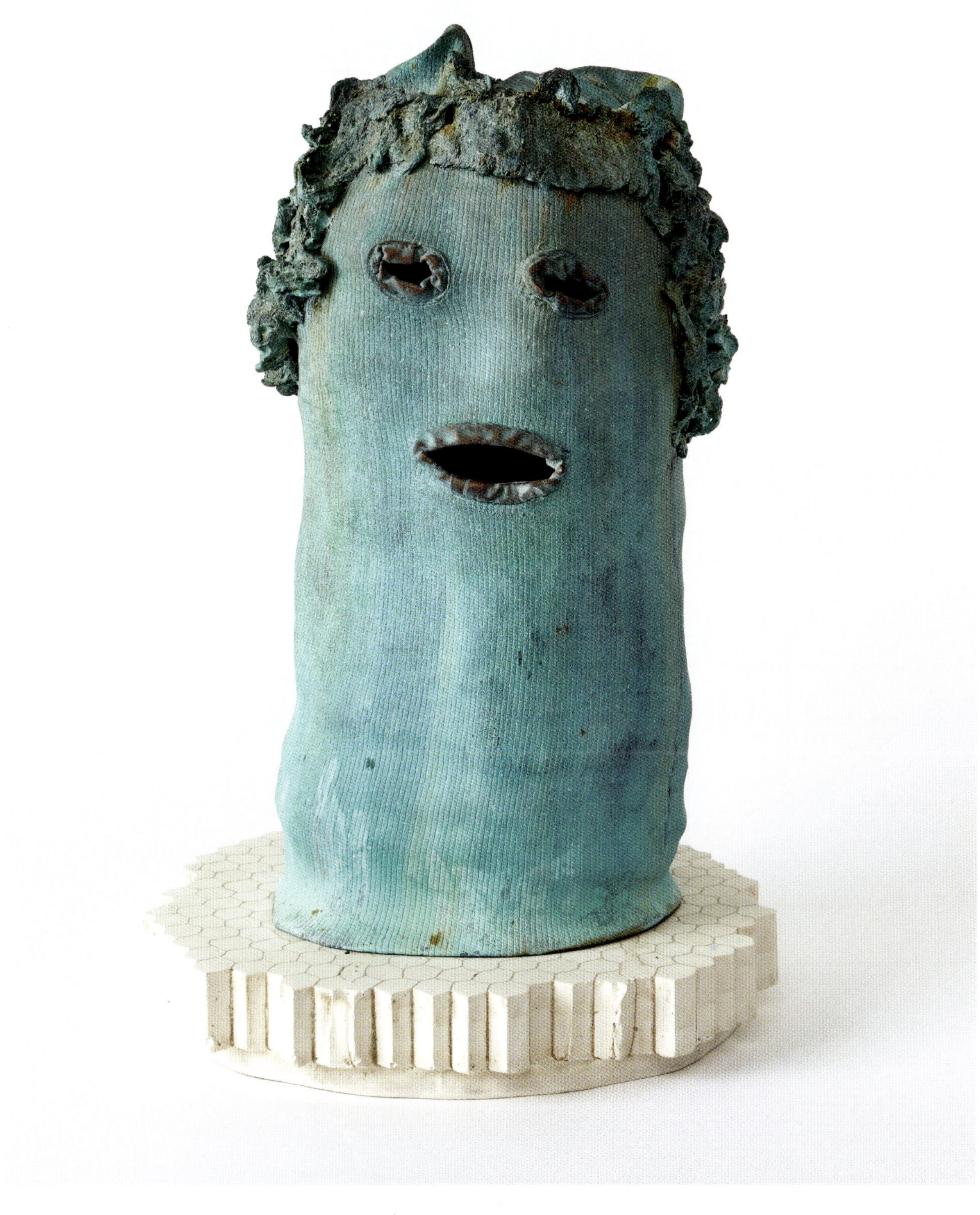

opposite
Watercolour For Small Adult 2012
Watercolour on paper,
76.7 × 57 cm

above
Small Adult 2014
Resin, copper powder and plaster,
39 × 25 × 24 cm

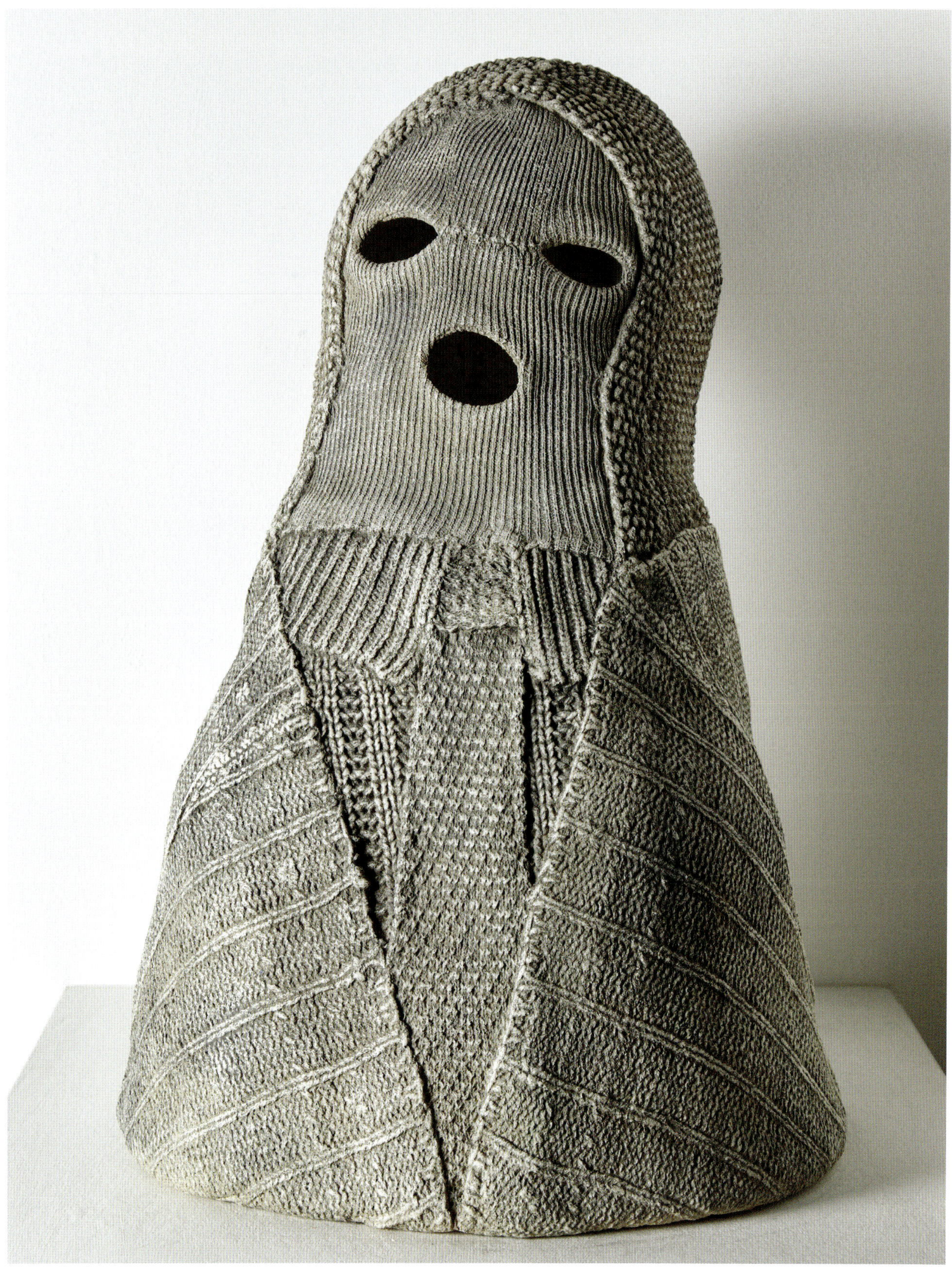

Thousand Metre Stare 2016

Resin and marble powder,

53 × 25 × 27 cm

'The first hoods came about after I was shown the process of adding metal powders to resin. I was excited by its potential, but had no way to show it off. The technique was particularly useful because I'm colour blind. By oxidizing the surfaces with mild acids, I had a limited palette of colours to work with. I used a particular nasty drain cleaner that contained hydrochloric acid. Not surprisingly, it has disappeared from the shops in recent years. I was curious about how the softness of the wool would be translated into cast iron and weighty rusted chain mail. I could make something in an afternoon that looked like it had been under the sea for years. Similarly, the hoods made with marble powder are so dirty after being ground off and finished with wire wool that they look like they have suffered years of heavy traffic. I think all artists have a particular "reach" in their work. The scale of these hoods is about my limit, in cast works at least. Their size is decided largely by what I can lift easily on my own.'

Damp Folds 2008
Resin and marble powder,
80 × 40 × 40 cm

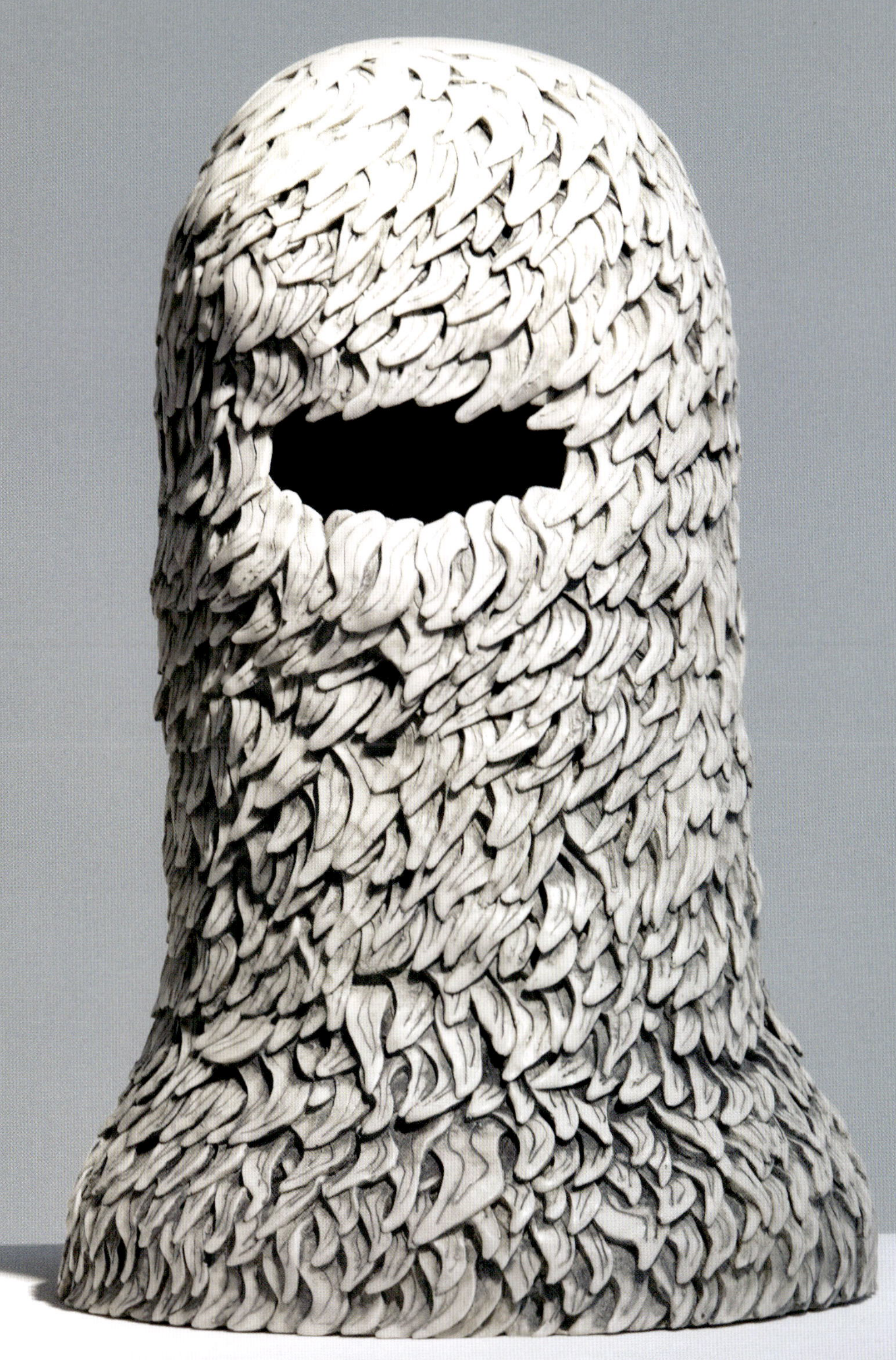

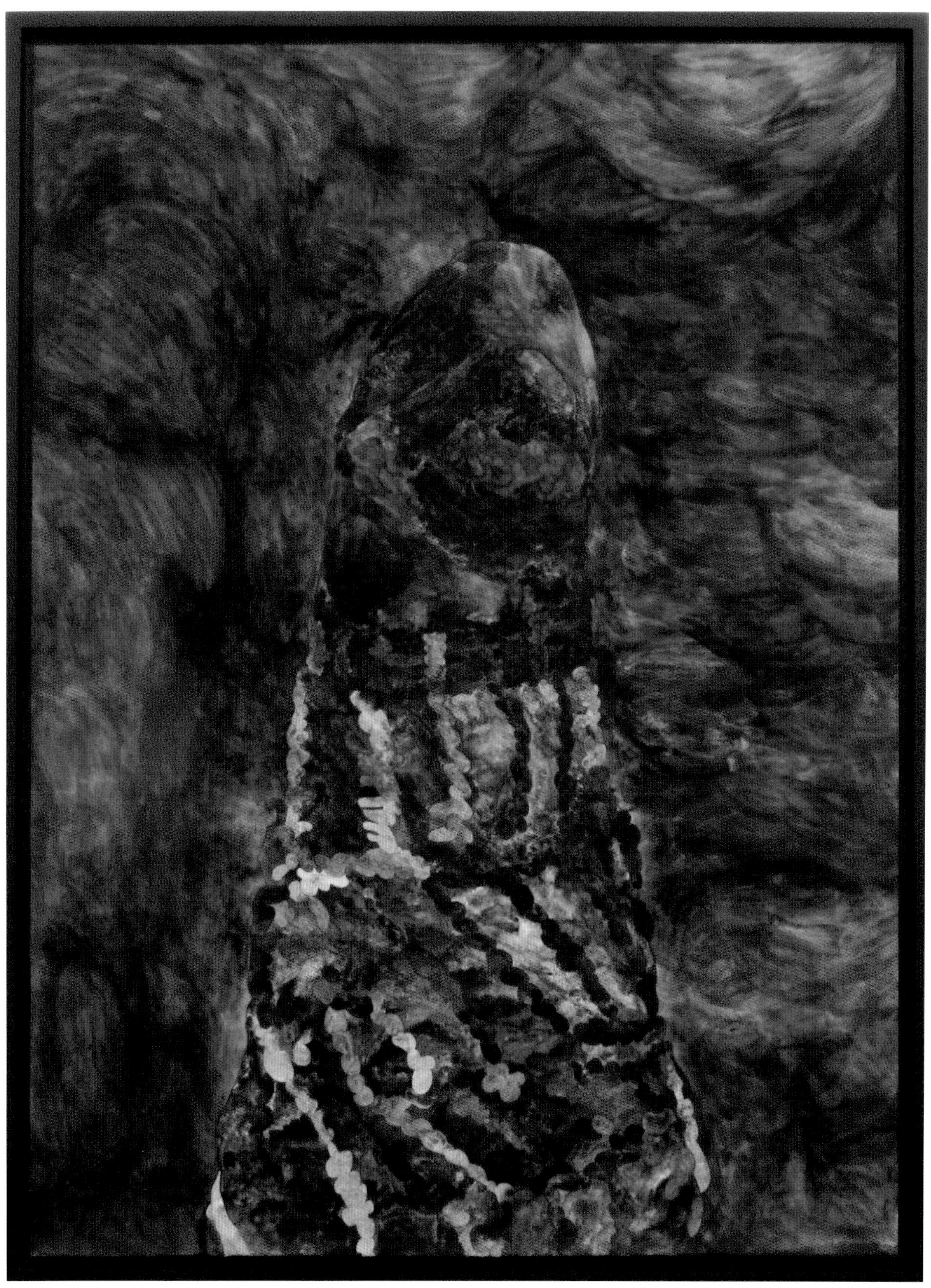

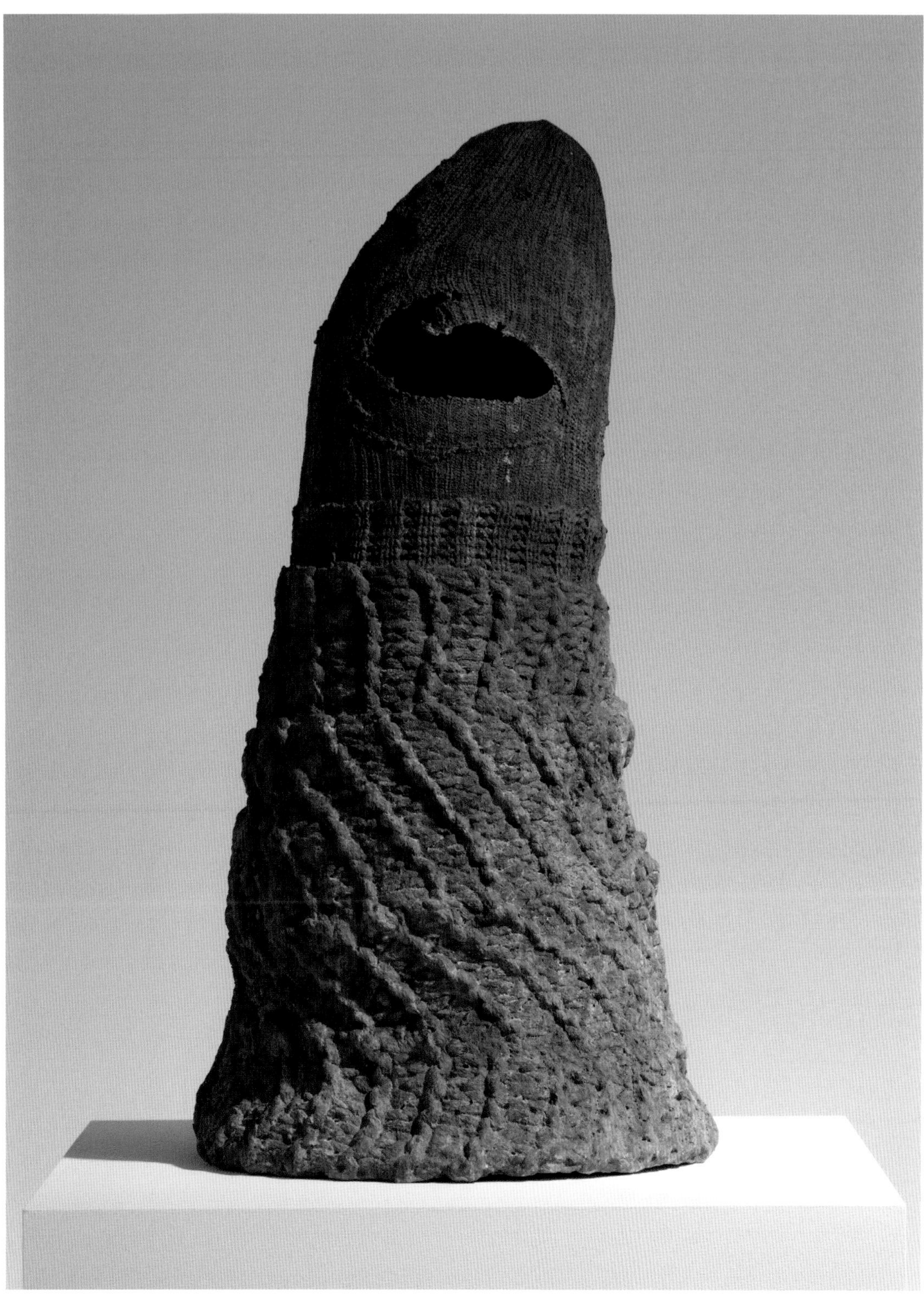

opposite

Watercolour for The Grind 2010

Watercolour on paper,

76.7 × 57 cm

above

The Grind Is So Ungrateful 2010

Resin, copper powder and iron powder,

68 × 40 × 40 cm

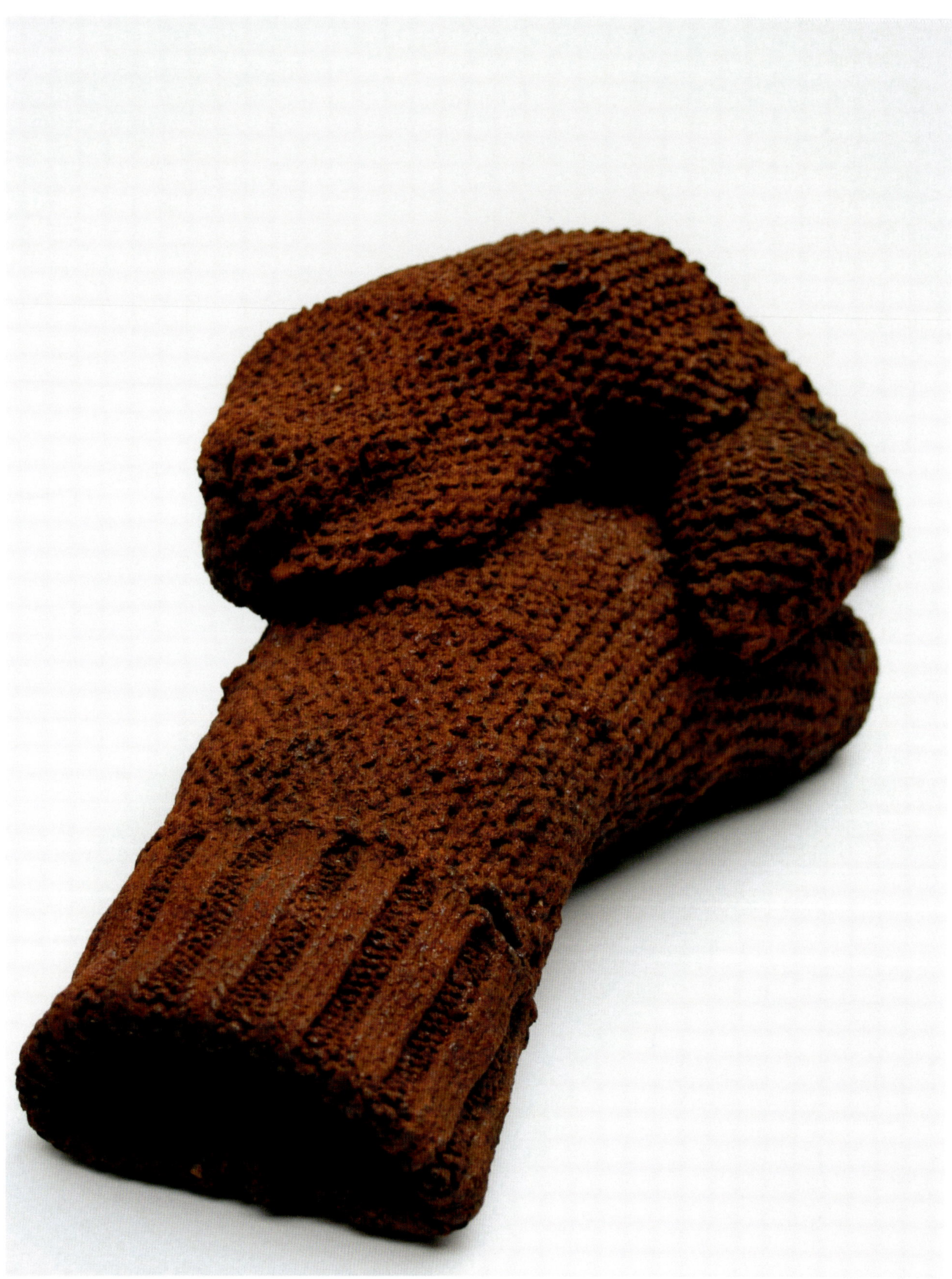

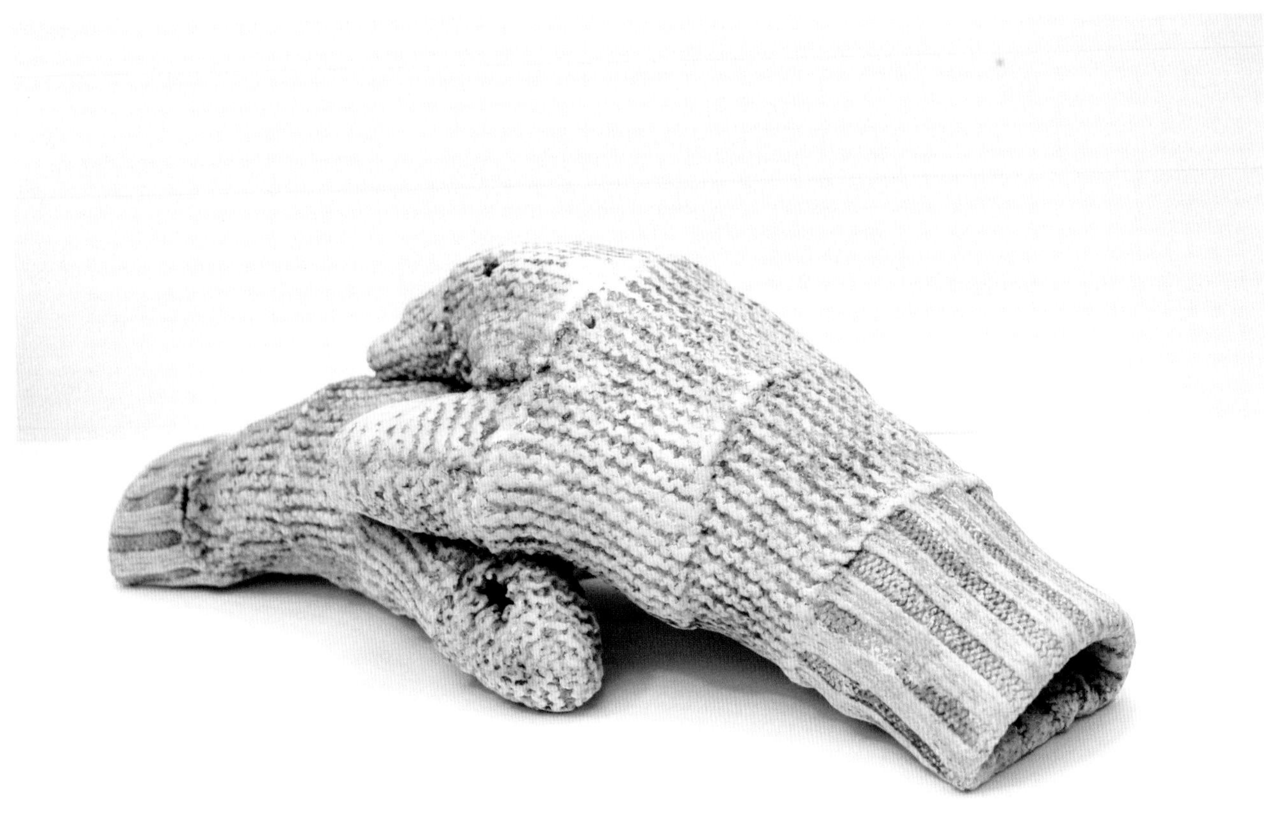

above

Friends of the Friendless 2010

Resin and marble powder,

6.5 × 43 × 18 cm

opposite

Friends of the Friendless (Rusty) 2010

Resin and iron powder,

6.5 × 43 × 18 cm

Do You Think Of Me Often 2011

Bronze, 64 × 83 × 54 cm

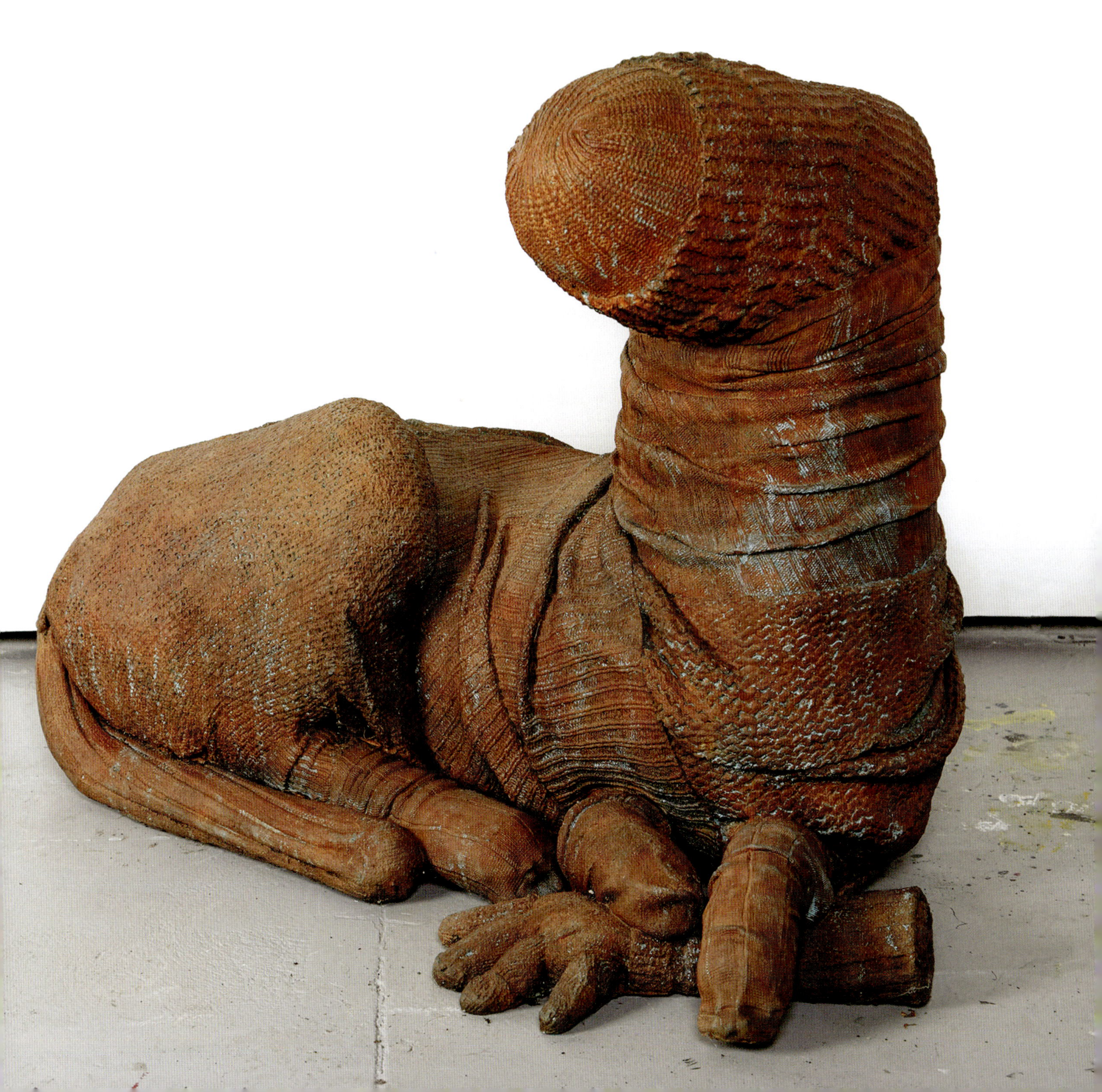

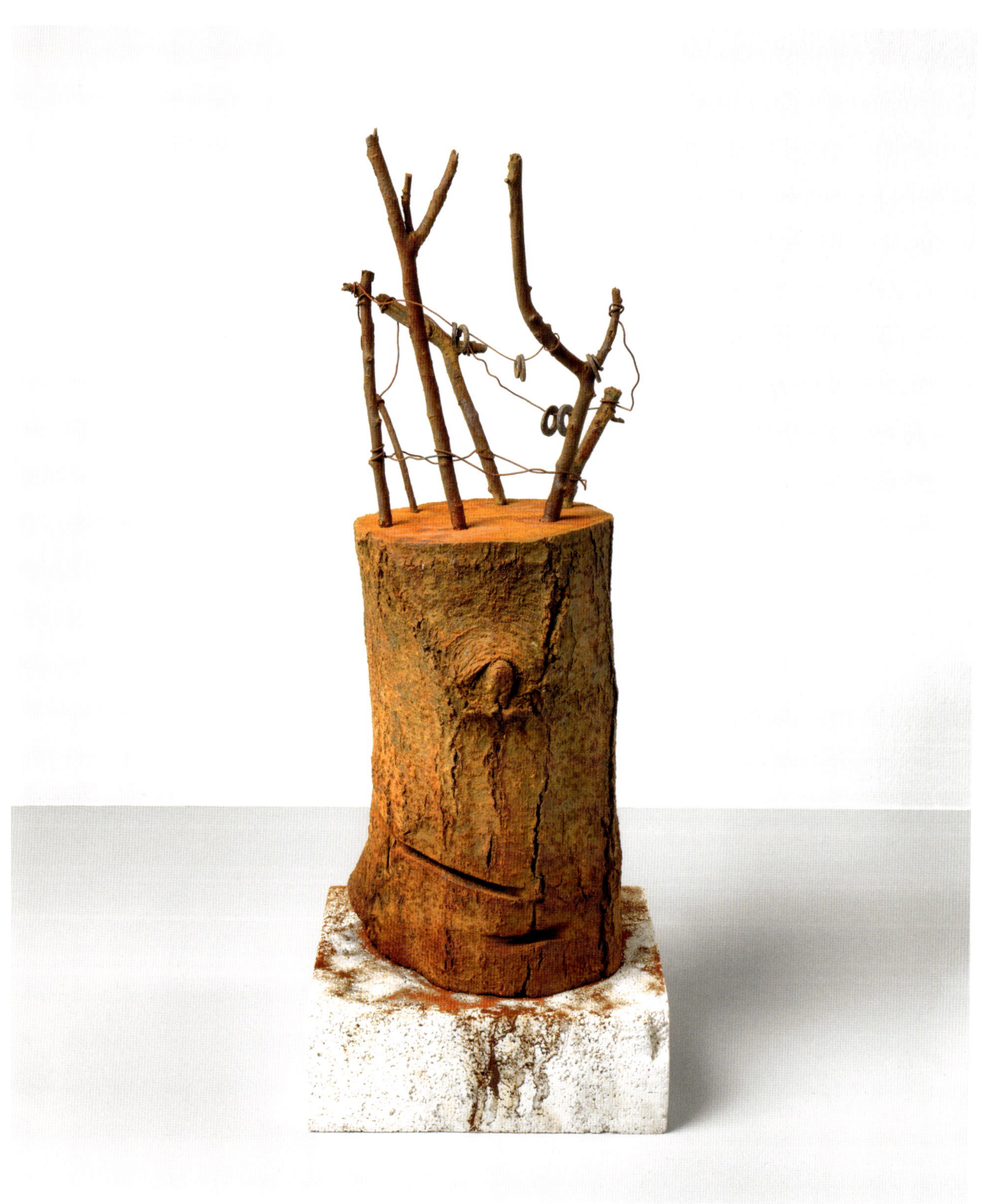

Sweet Heart 2013
Resin, iron powder, steel and plaster,
55 × 20 × 20 cm

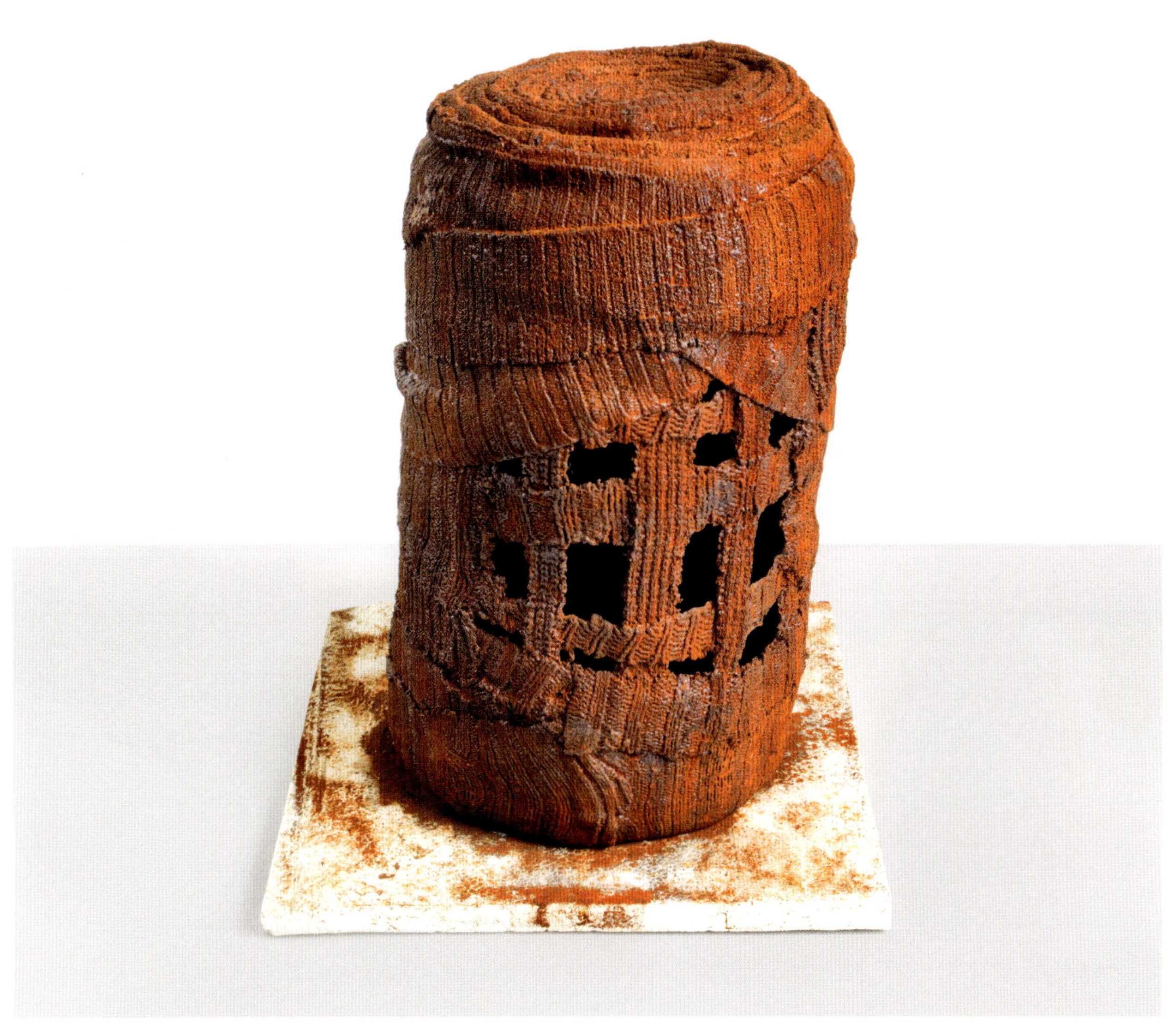

Don't Interrupt The Sorrow 2013
Resin, iron powder and plaster,
55 × 20 × 20 cm

Rust Never Sleeps 2013
Fibreglass, wool, resin and iron powder,
199 × 216 × 83 cm

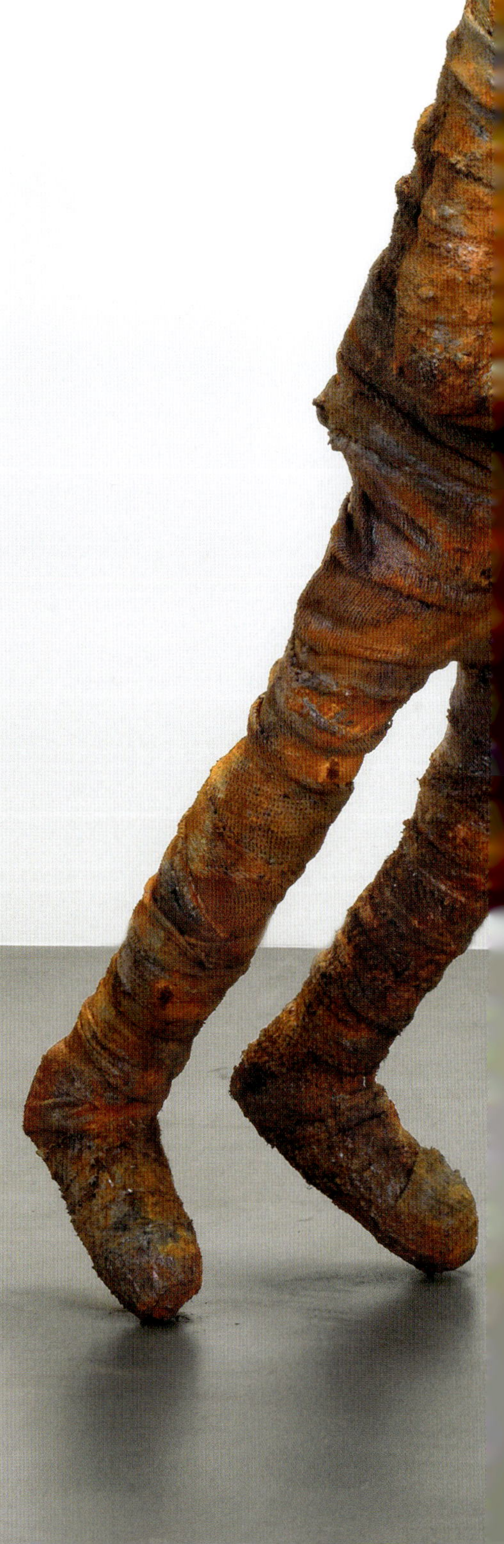

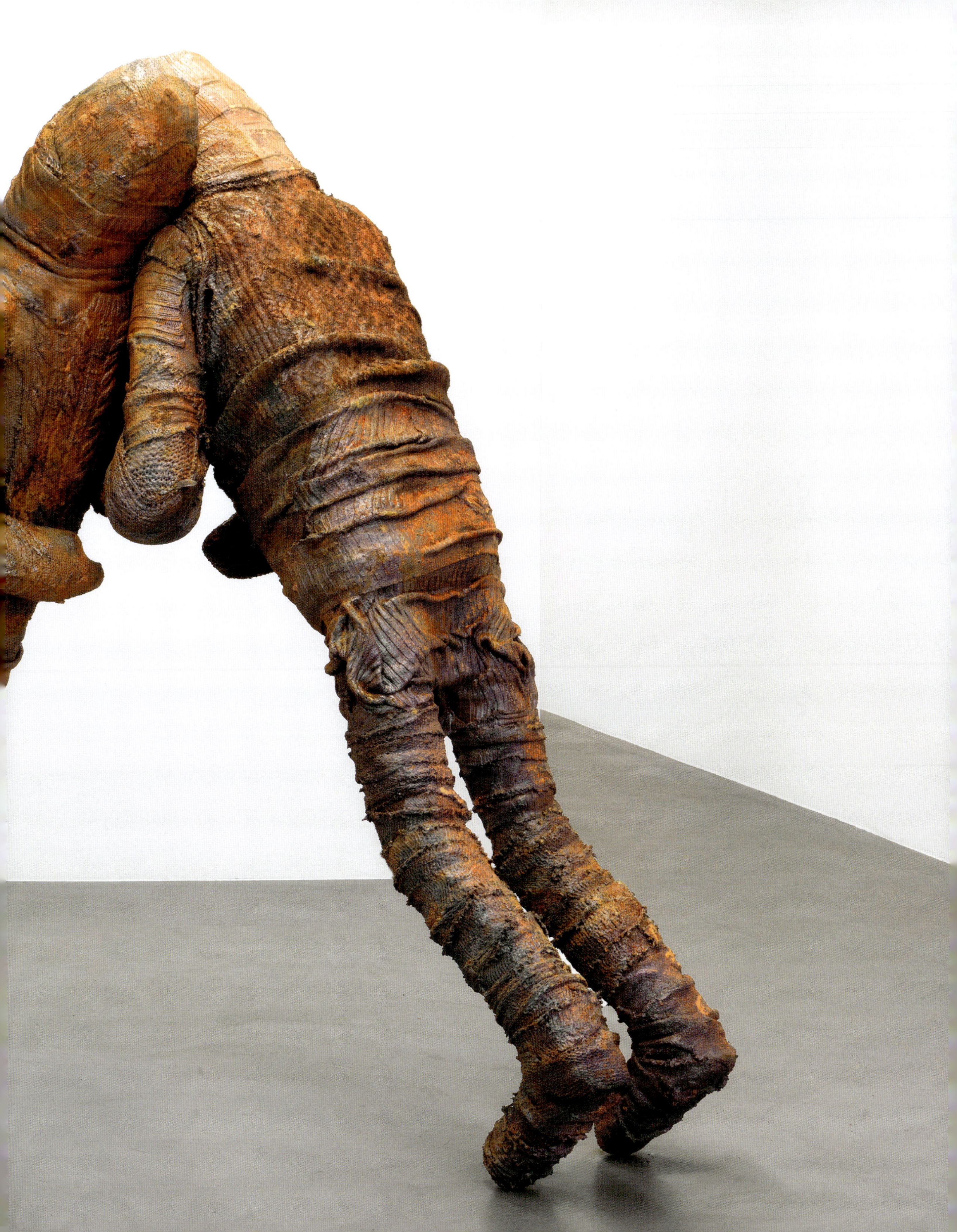

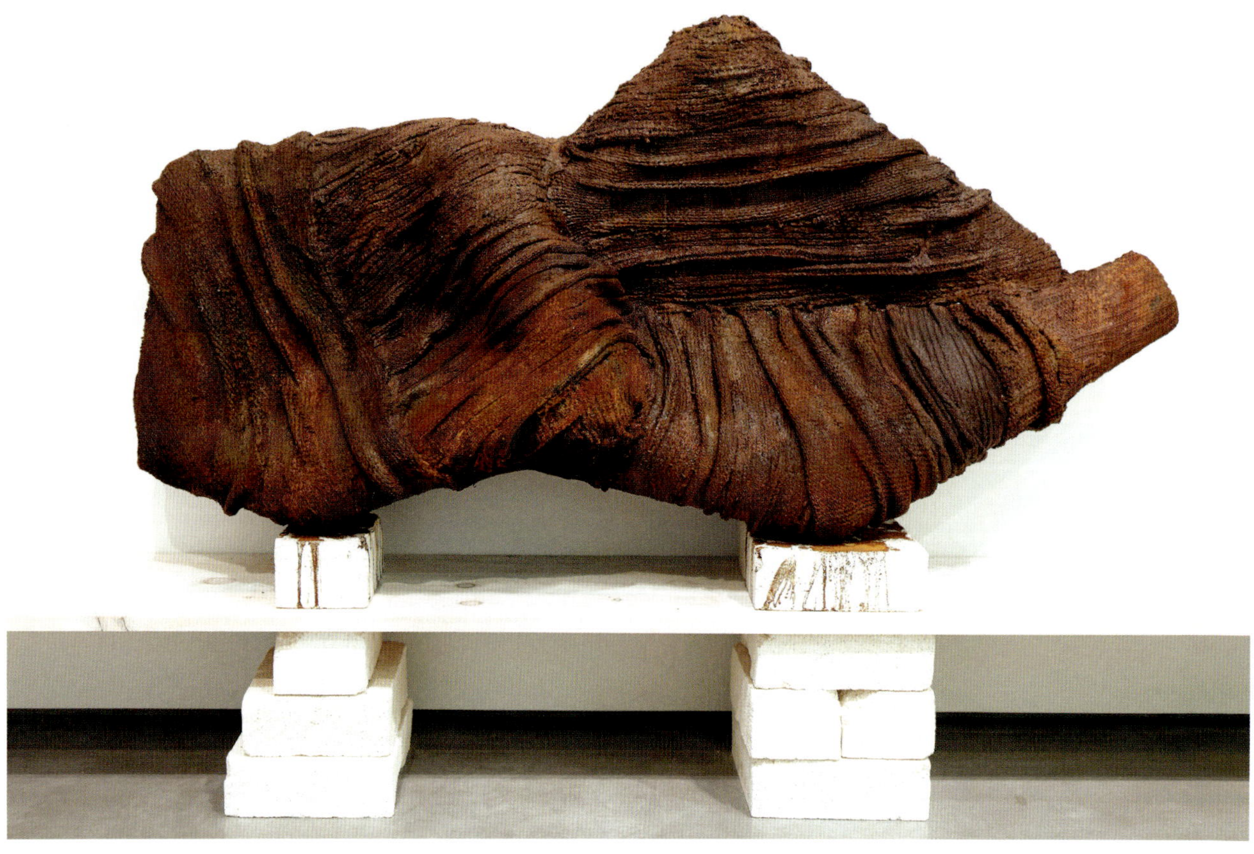

Jumper 2013
Fibreglass, wool, resin, iron powder and plaster,
81 × 160 × 37 cm

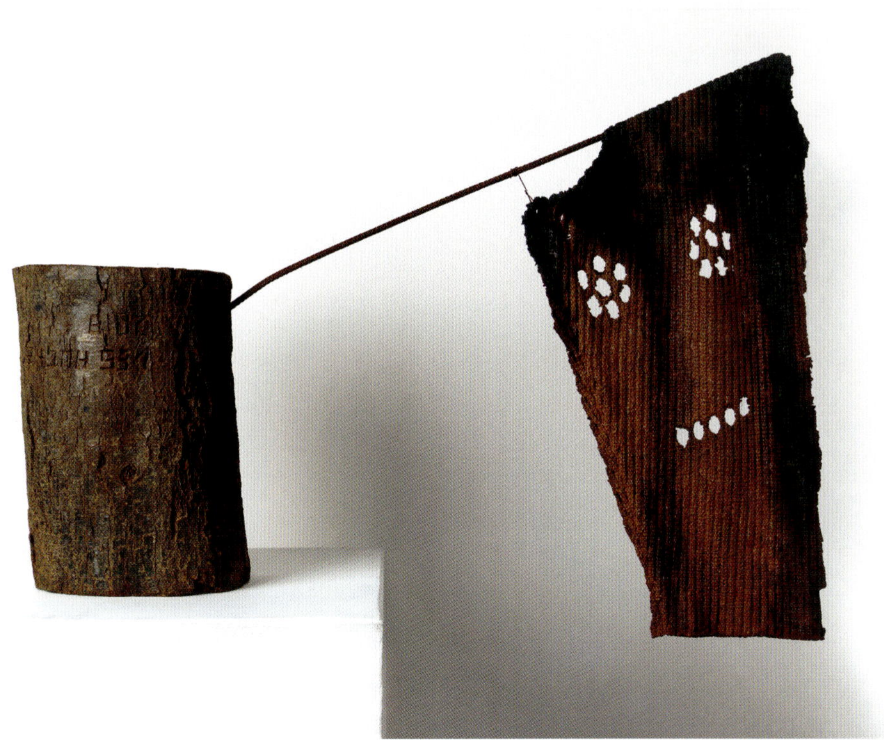

Pterodactyl 2013
Resin, iron powder and rebar,
56 × 78 × 17 cm

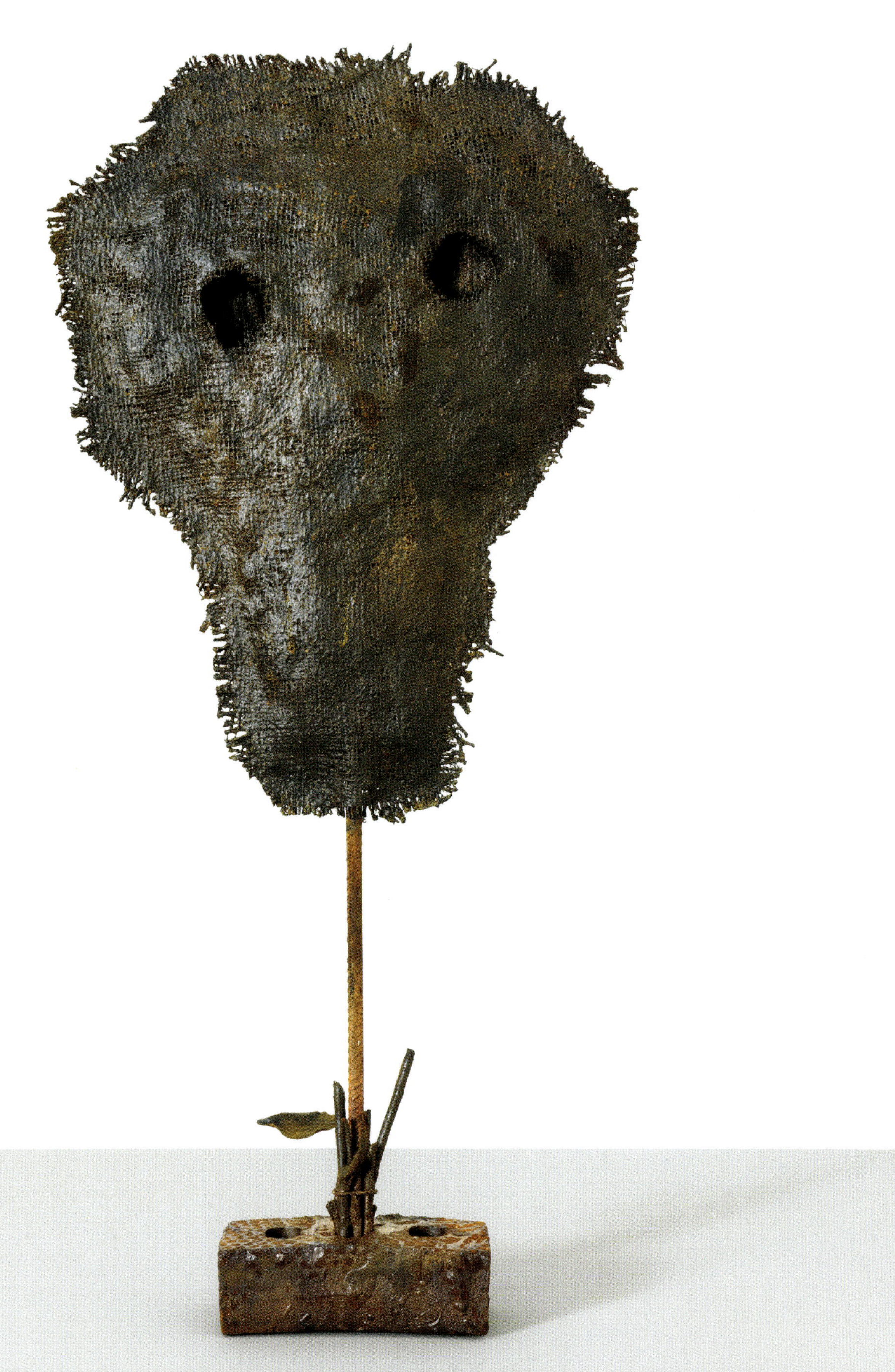

opposite and right

Stink Eye 2013

Resin, iron powder, scrim and rebar,

55 × 20 × 20 cm

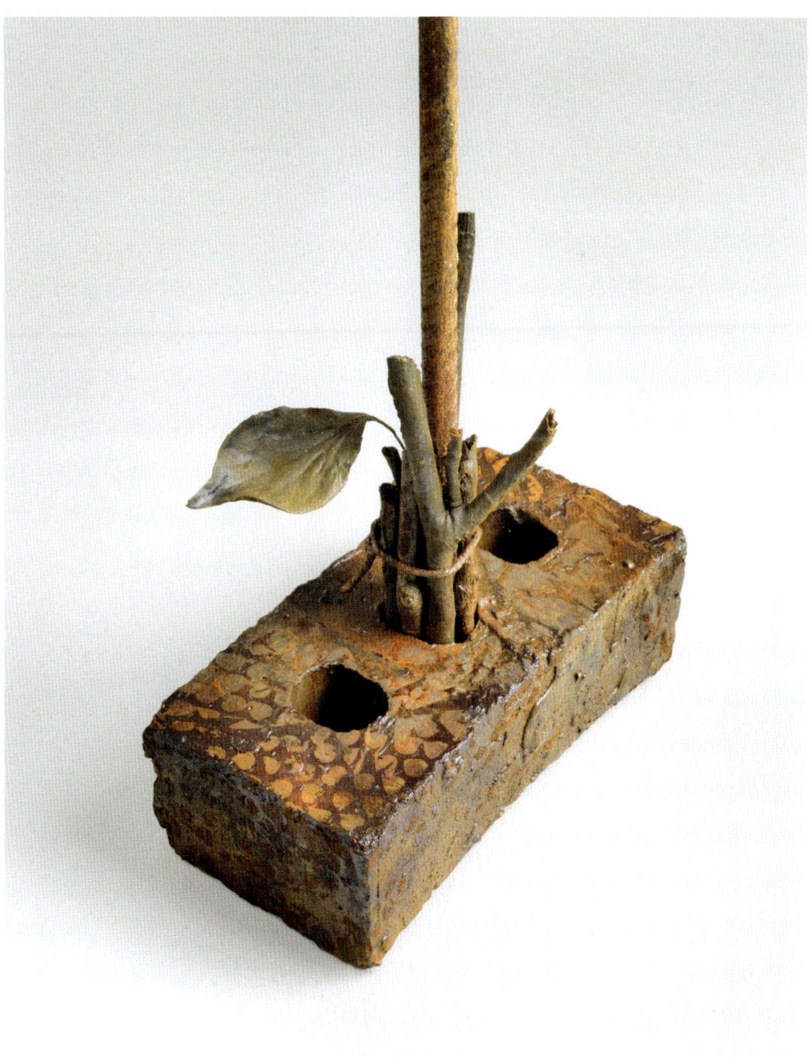

'Baler twine is what holds the countryside together, from fences and trailers to trousers. It's easy to spot because of its bright colours, and it becomes impossible not to notice after a while. I'd made a cast of a knitted hood that I wanted to lie on its side to show the fretwork of frayed wool along its edge, but I needed to disguise the blind inside surface where the fibreglass had been laid up, so I filled it with dirty baler twine. When I laid it on the floor, it looked like innards hanging out of a chopped-off head or a failed firework lying on the floor. All razzle and no dazzle. When I showed the work in Berlin in 2013, the opening was very quiet at first, just me and a man and his dog. When the dog got a whiff of the baler twine, it went berserk and started to pull the sculpture apart looking for rats.'

Razzle 2013
Resin, iron powder and baler twine,
25 × 110 × 35 cm

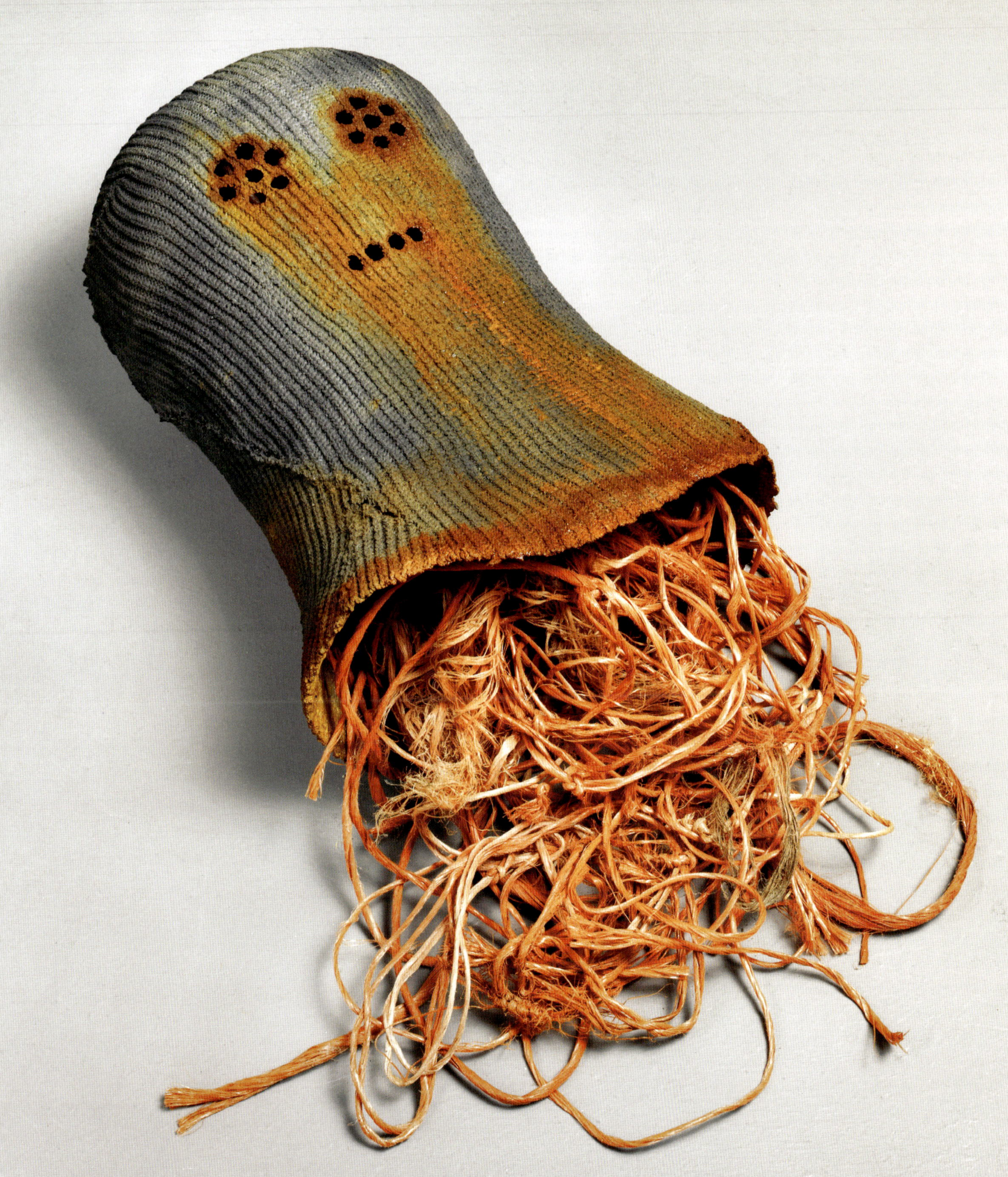

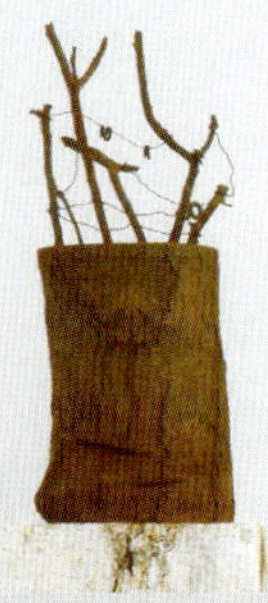
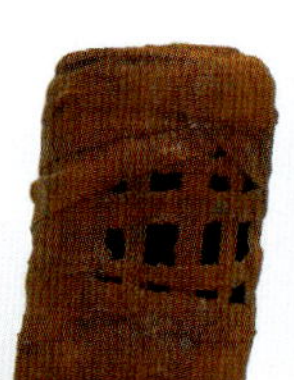

'Rust Never Sleeps' 2013
Buchmann Galerie, Berlin

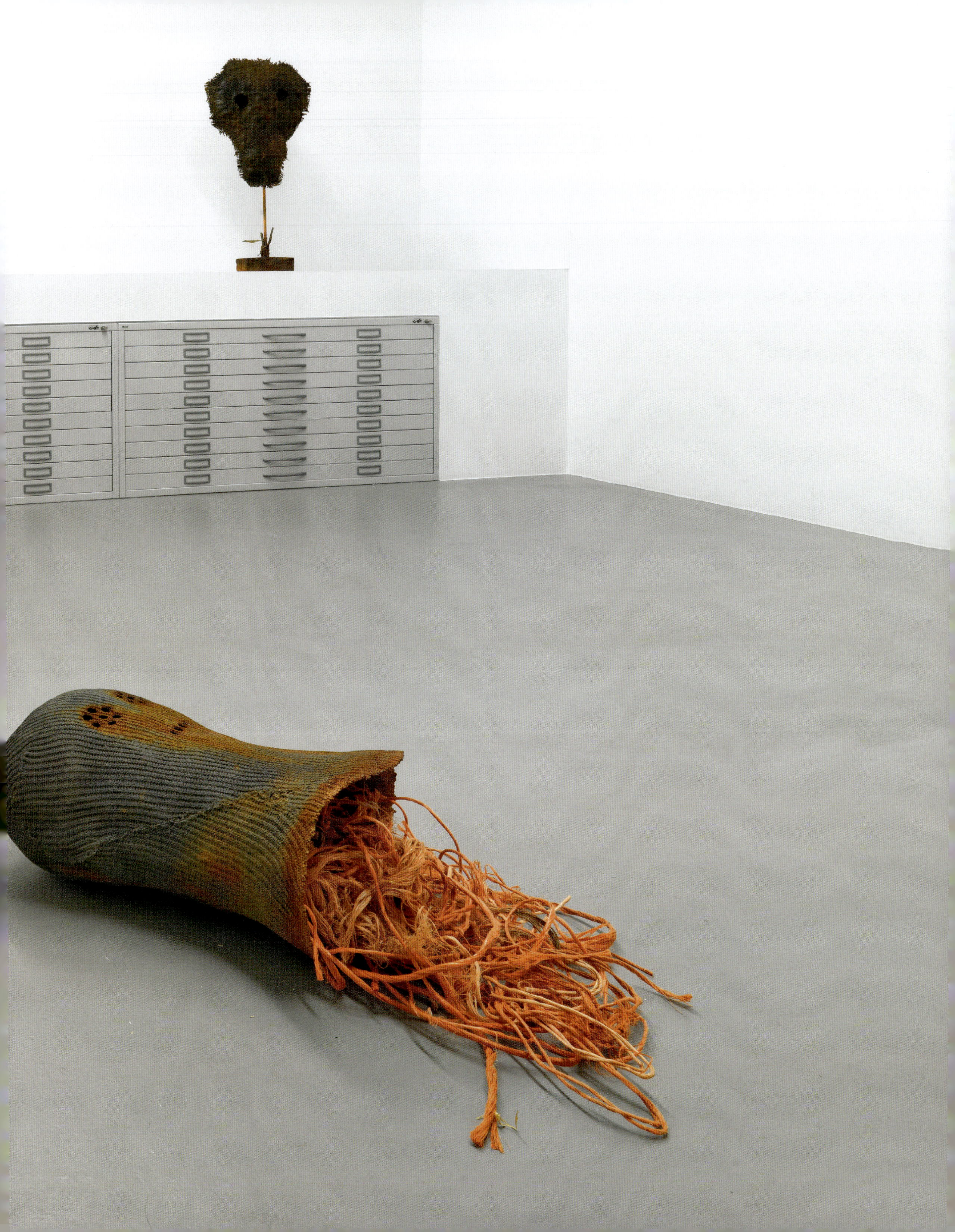

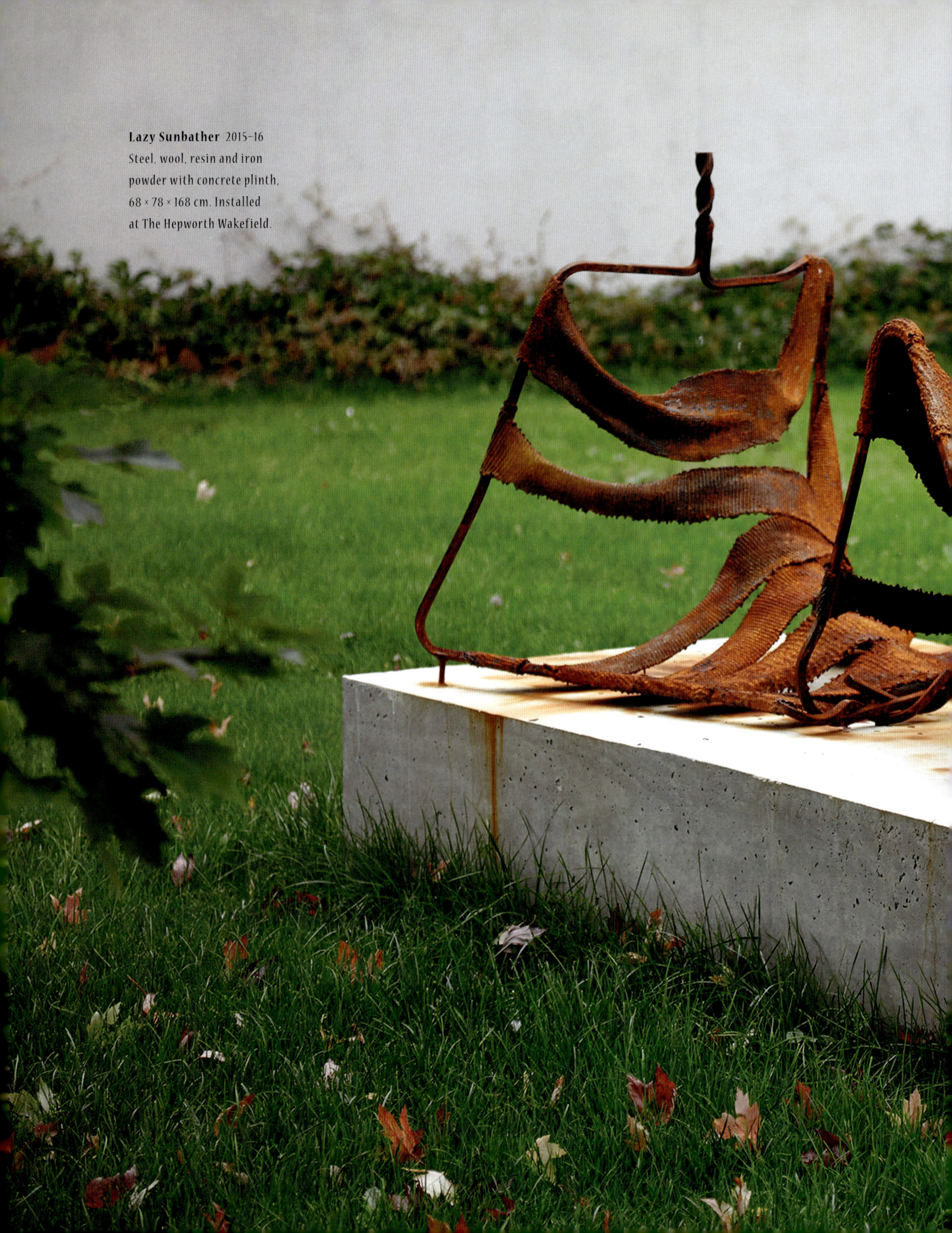

Lazy Sunbather 2015–16
Steel, wool, resin and iron powder with concrete plinth, 68 × 78 × 168 cm. Installed at The Hepworth Wakefield.

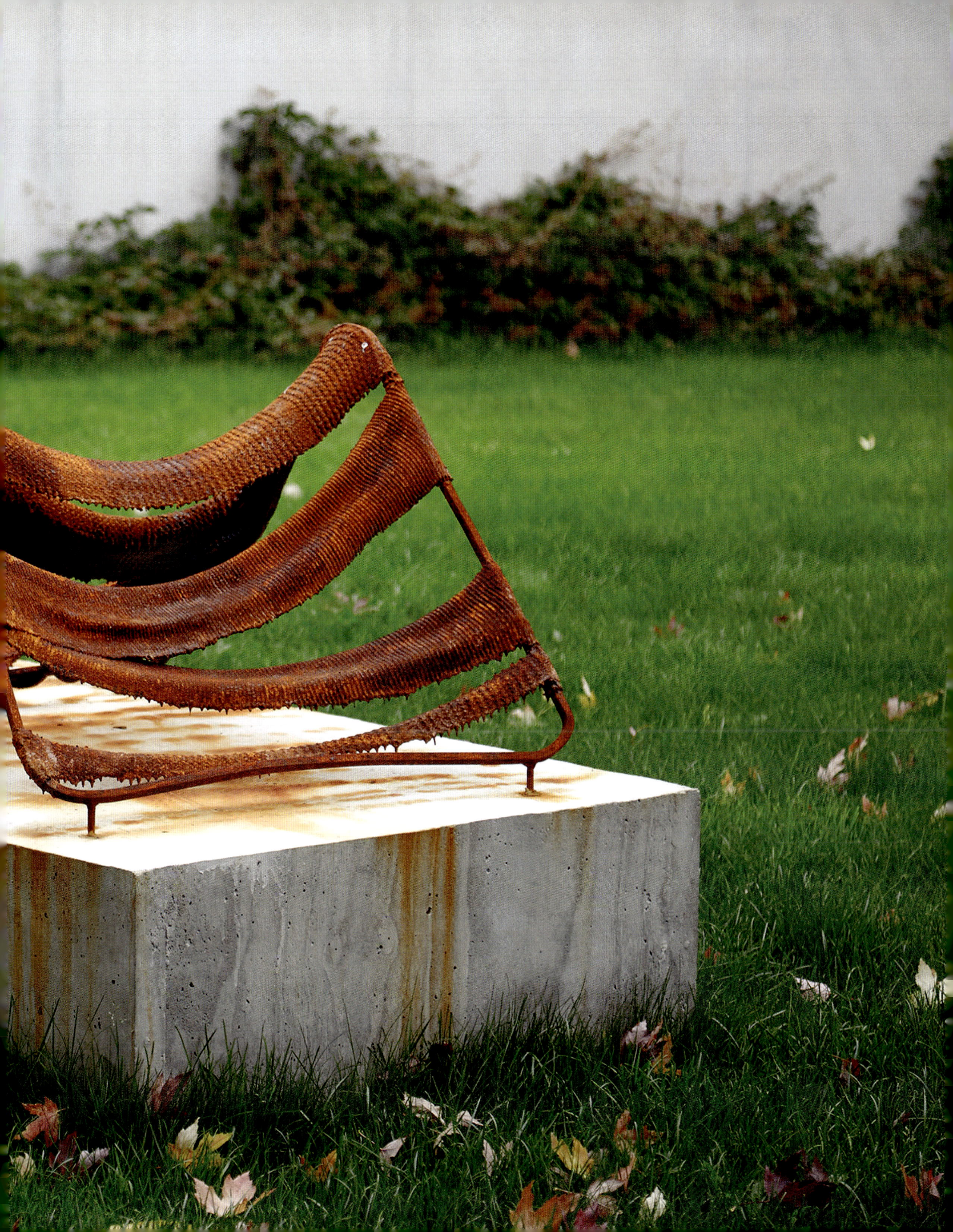

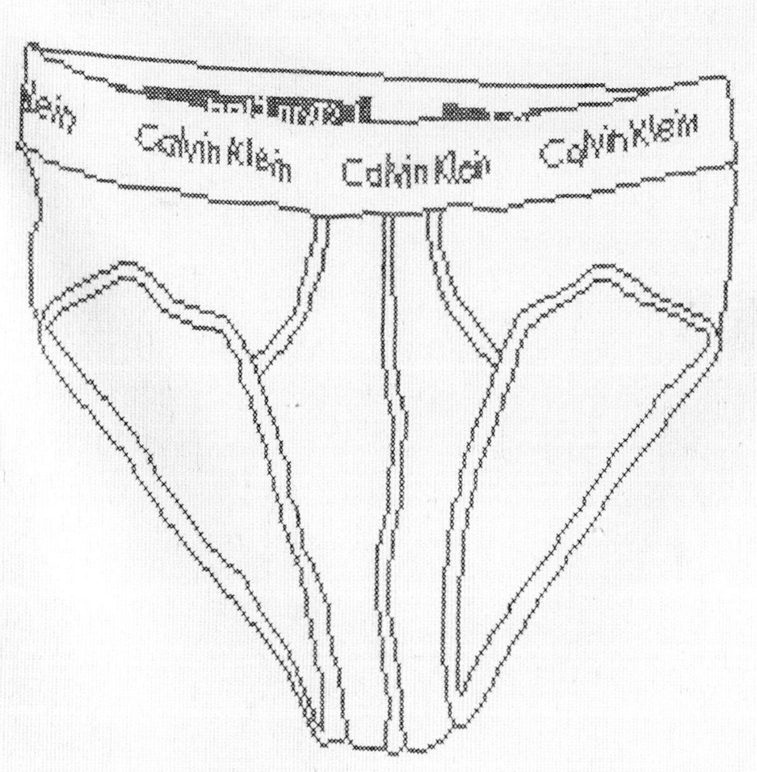
Calvin Klein
Calvin Klein
Calvin Klein

Opus Anglicanum

Stephen Feeke

Latin for 'English work', the phrase *opus anglicanum* was first coined in the thirteenth century to describe the highly prized and luxurious religious embroideries made in England from silk and gold and silver thread.[1] My allusion here to the celebrated period of skilled artistic production is obviously intended to be ludic, irreverent even, considering the deliberately artless appearance of Des Hughes's cross-stitch works in comparison to the craftsmanship of medieval masterpieces.[2]

Textiles have appeared occasionally in Hughes's work over the past five years or so, a small but particularly potent aspect of his oeuvre. While time-consuming, his embroidering looks spontaneous, like a hastily handwritten scrawl. His cross-stitch is self-taught and has a distinctly amateur appearance; raw edges and wonky lines of text give his own samplers a homespun quality. Craft without craftsmanship. However, Hughes is an artist who is serious about exploring parodic and ironic forms. He is actually highly skilled at needlepoint, so that on close inspection, one sees a definite precision to his tiny stitches, and the analogy to an earlier kind of embroidery is therefore entirely appropriate. Moreover, it is the contradictory nature of the artist's work that also makes it seem so peculiarly English.

Another aspect that gives these works their English flavour is Hughes's deliberate use of humour. A pair of Calvin Klein underpants, for example, is rendered on a linen fragment; its title (of course!) is *Loin Cloth*. A blank sheet of paper from an exercise book recalls the horror of lessons and exams (*p. 148*); memories from school are a great inspiration for the artist. It is somehow typical of him to make a sampler with no text at all.

1 My thanks to Des Hughes and Clare Woods for helpful discussions about cross stitch and to Dr Stacy Boldrick for her comments on the first draft of this text.

2 See C. Browne, G. Davies, M. A. Michael, *English Medieval Embroidery: Opus Anglicanum*, London: Victoria and Albert Museum, 2017, exh. cat.

Loin Cloth 2017
Cotton silk cross-stitch on linen, 80 × 80 cm

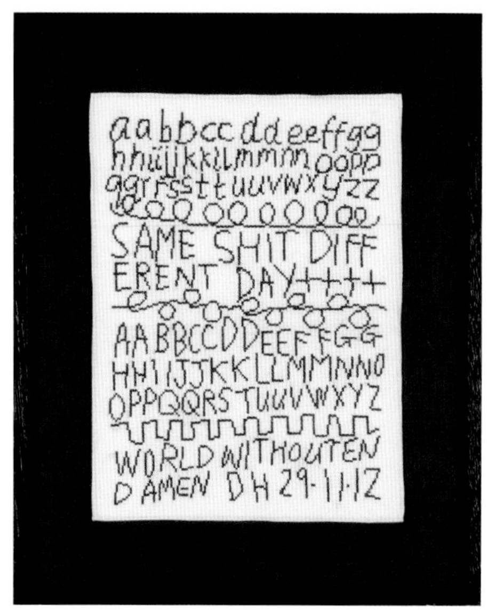

Same Shit, Different Day 2012
Cotton silk cross-stitch on linen,
32 × 24 cm

'I definitely think there is something ridiculous about what I do and that the objects have aspirations beyond their modest means. I also make sure that there is an element of failure so that the original material and any attempt at a transformation both exist at the same time. I'm also obsessed by us and our bizarre habits. Reginald Perrin is a big influence.'[3]

Cross-stitch has indeed become a bizarre habit for Hughes. There he sits by the fire at home, long-legged and beslippered, an absurd nana-like sight surrounded by his sewing kit, including the indispensable quick unpick and the increasingly necessary illuminated magnifier. He enjoys the close proximity of making, being totally absorbed by the object emerging in his lap. He is also a man unconcerned with what we might now consider the gender-specific overtones of needlework. Nor is he an artist unduly worried about using craft techniques. Today, when so many boundaries have been subverted – in life and in art – it seems unnecessary to be too concerned with stereotypes, labels and hierarchies. Indeed, it is probably more interesting to experiment with them and look at the points at which different – and even opposite – concerns and disciplines intersect and to have no concern for contentious or pejorative terms. And this seems to be the ground that Hughes prefers to occupy: anti-heroic, happily eccentric and using non-art processes and materials.

The first examples of Hughes's embroidery have the graphic quality of concrete poetry: laid out on white linen fabric, the shaky black text creates loose typographical effects. On occasion, in *Turn Turn Turn* for example, the verbal significance of the words is almost lost in the complexity of the design. While the maxim *Same Shit, Different Day* is obscured by the loopy letters of the alphabet in a sampler; the suggestion is that the repetition of learning by rote at school – or indeed other tedious, mundane acts – is the 'shit' to which the work refers. And in *No*, an untidy list of don'ts is reminiscent

3 Des Hughes quoted in S. Feeke and S. Raikes, *Undone: Making and Unmaking in Contemporary Art*, Leeds: Henry Moore Institute, 2011, exh. cat., p. 44.

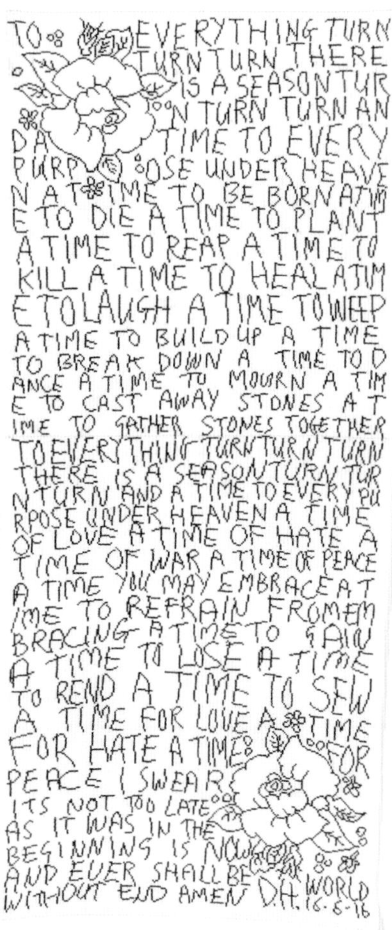

Turn Turn Turn 2016
Cotton silk cross-stitch on linen,
90 × 40 cm

of a 1970s swimming-pool safety sign and warns against dirty fighting (*p. 142*); it reads almost like the commandments, and even concludes with a resounding 'Amen'.

In later examples, Hughes has reused textiles found in junk stores and second-hand shops. These hark back to the peculiar custom for domestic textiles that began in the nineteenth century, and gave rise to doilies, antimacassars and tray liners, bizarrely still used at the time of the artist's youth. Apparently indispensable at the time, such decorative items now seem pretty pointless along with the outmoded sense of gentility they offered interiors, especially, it seems, at teatime. *I Thought I'd Climbed a Mountain* (*p. 146*) is suitably anachronistic. In it, the crinolined lady looks up to some distinctly cartoonish mountains that Hughes has added to a found tray liner; to underline the incongruity of the object, and of her, he has included the adage 'over the hill'.

Hughes has long possessed a fascination with the material world of objects and a collector's magpie mentality – which, like belief systems applied to objects, is one of obsession involving a constant and systematic gathering. The textiles he finds, slightly yellowed by age and occasionally tea-stained, are manipulated, partly unpicked and partly enhanced with modern text. Often, his additions are taken from lyrics and song titles, which he also collects to reuse as titles for his own work at a later date. Hence the title of The Stone Roses song 'I Want to Be Adored' is reconfigured at the heart of a floral border on a tray liner (*p. 145*). Hughes's additions contrast markedly with the sewing skills of the original maker, yet the plaintive words seem all the more poignant and pathetic surrounded by the prettiness of the embroidered flowers. Likewise, lyrics from 'Reel Around the Fountain' by The Smiths reappear in *I Dreamt About You Last Night and I Fell Out of Bed Twice* (*p. 144*) and a line from 'That Joke Isn't Funny Anymore' forms the new sentiment at the centre of a sampler for *I've Seen it Appear in Other People's Lives*.

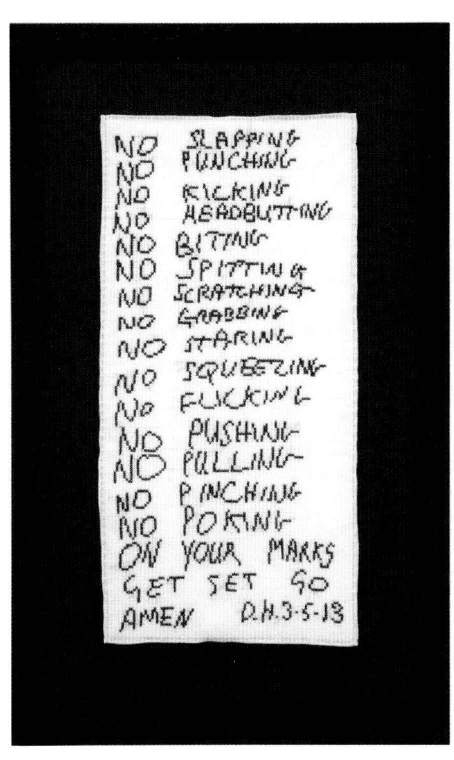

No 2013
Cotton silk cross-stitch on linen,
35 × 17 cm

Morrissey's words also appear in *Yes, I Am Blind*, in which an extant embroidered flower ejaculates from Hughes's cross-stitch penis; an innocent handkerchief is relabelled as a wank rag, the graffiti-like additions adding a layer of toilet humour that is both puerile and sophisticated. It is a fine line, after all, that Hughes has chosen to thread.

'I'm looking for a state of balance and would feel the need to remove anything that isn't essential. Each component needs to justify itself.... I'm also looking for transparency, in that the works are explicit about what they are and how and why they have been put together – anything else feels like trickery or being dishonest. I find it incredibly satisfying when the work feels inevitable.'[4]

Yes, I Am Blind 2017
Cotton silk cross-stitch on linen,
35 × 35 cm

4 Ibid.

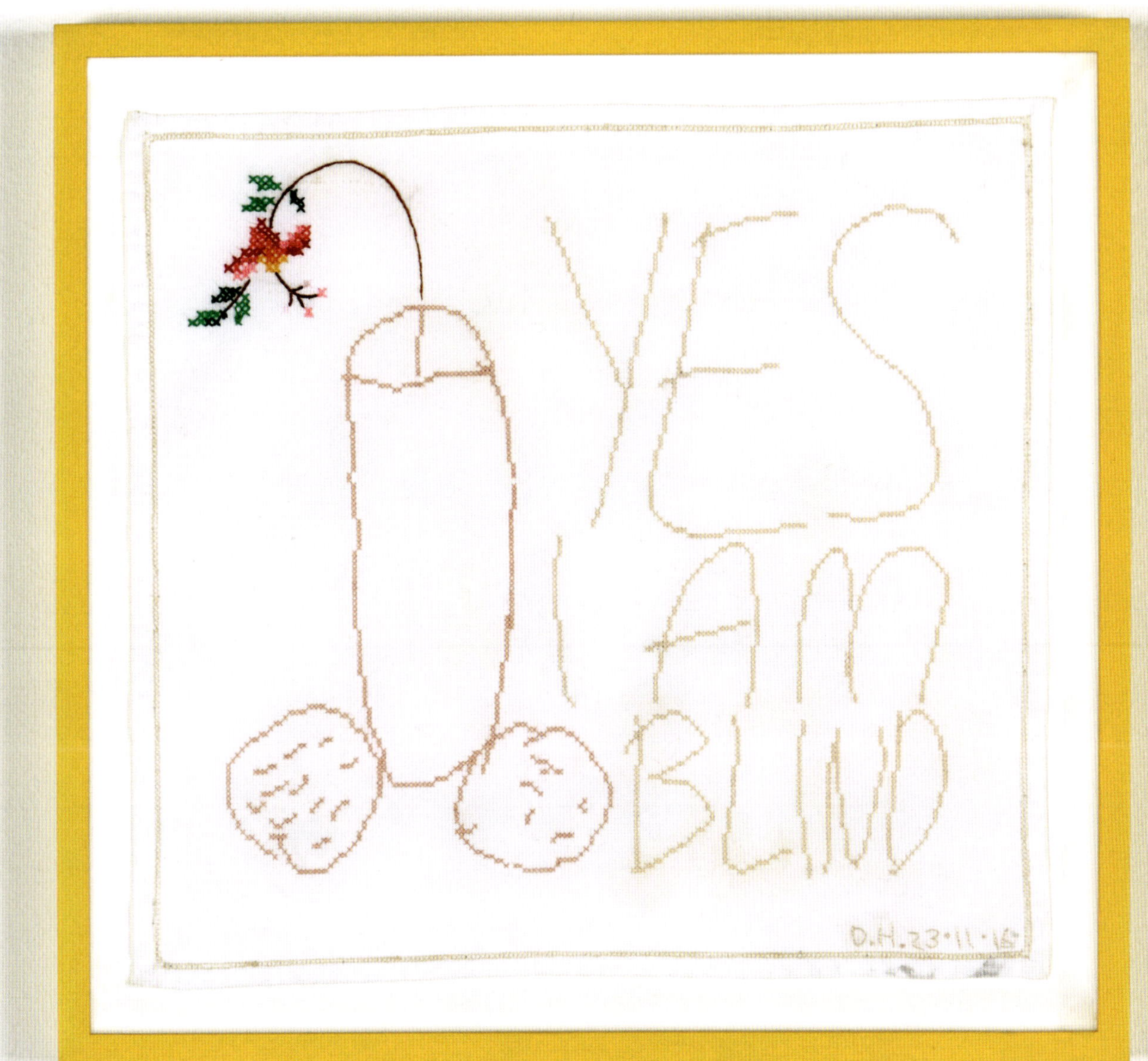
YES
I AM
BLIND
D.H. 23·11·16

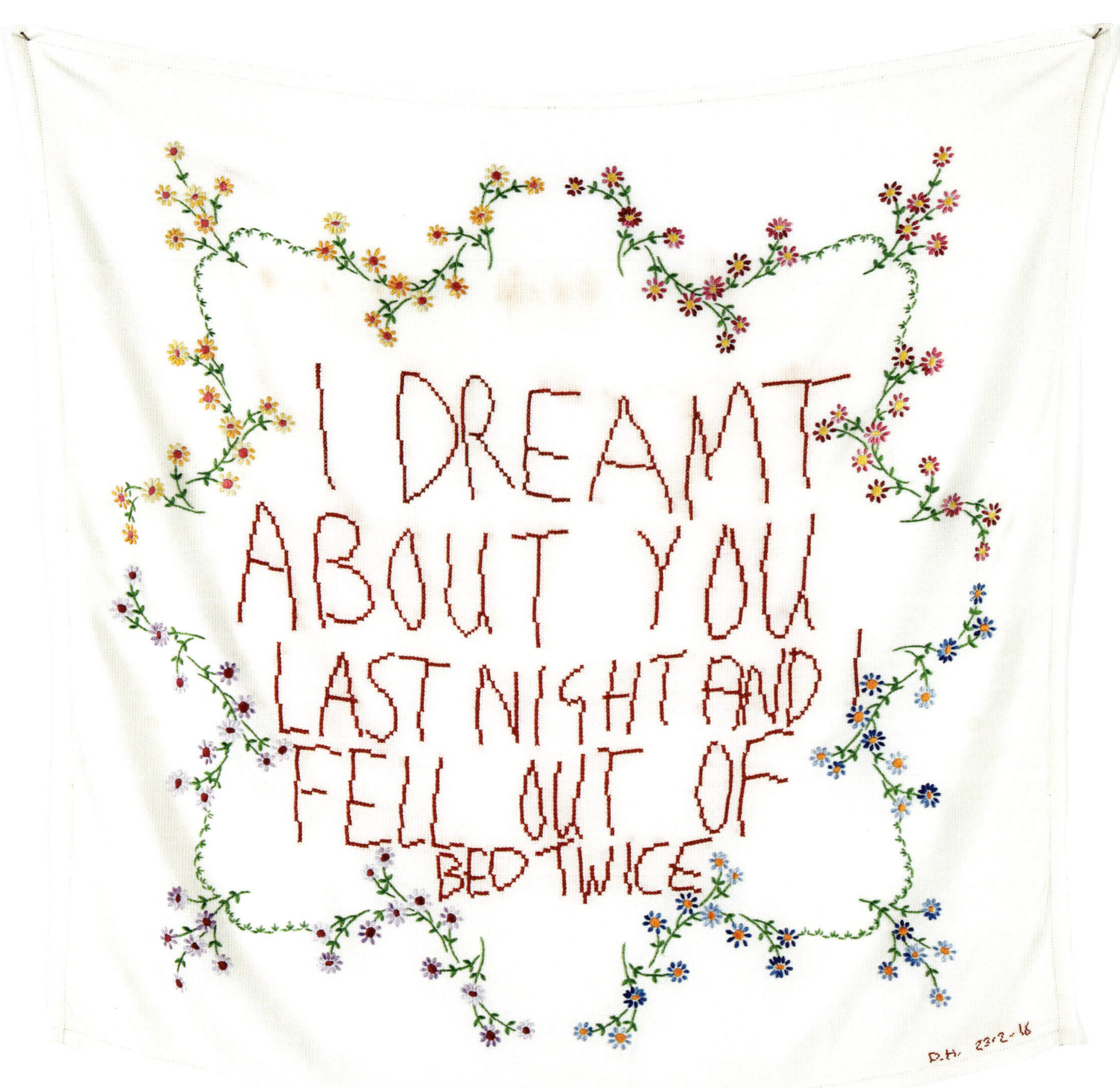
I DREAMT
ABOUT YOU
LAST NIGHT AND I
FELL OUT OF
BED TWICE
D.H. 23-2-16

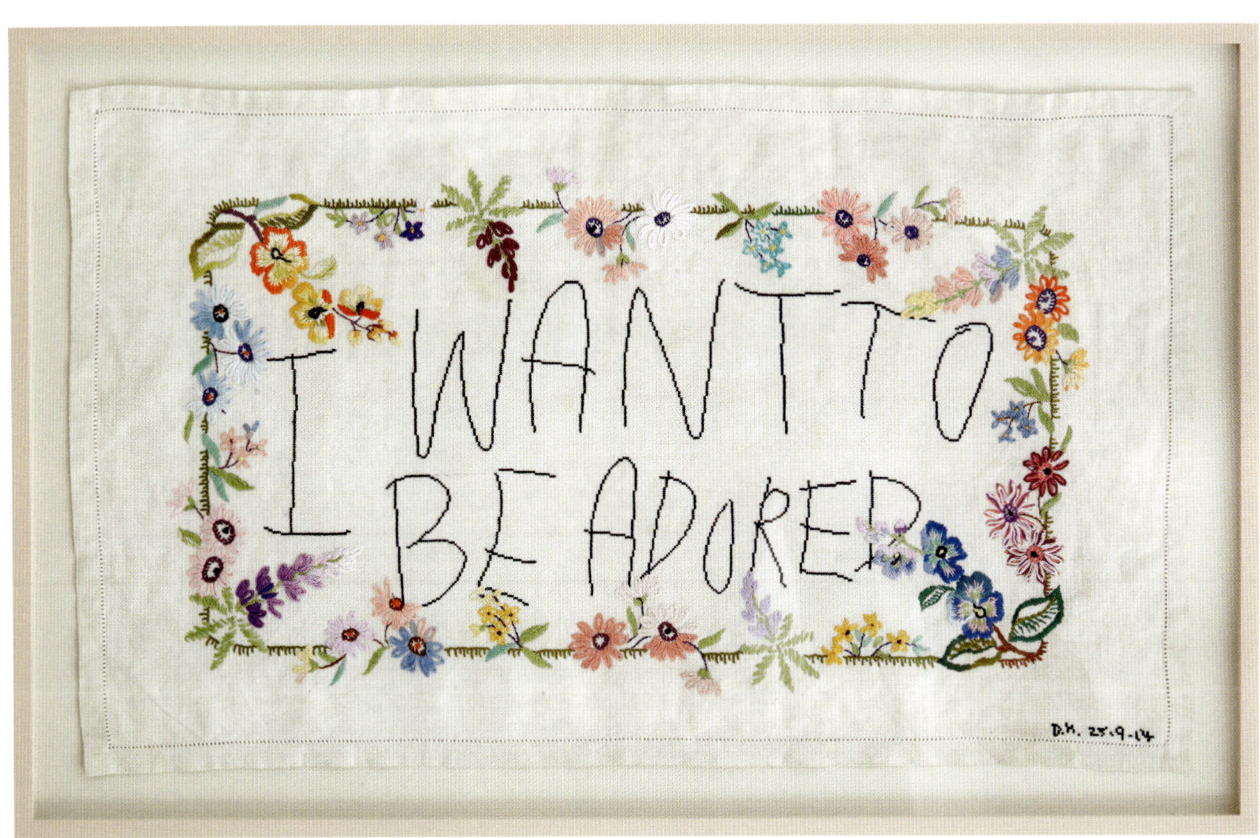

above

I Want To Be Adored 2014
Antique embroidery with cotton silk
cross-stitch on linen,
33 × 58 cm

opposite

I Dreamt About You Last Night 2016
Antique embroidery with cotton silk
cross-stitch on linen,
87 × 82 cm

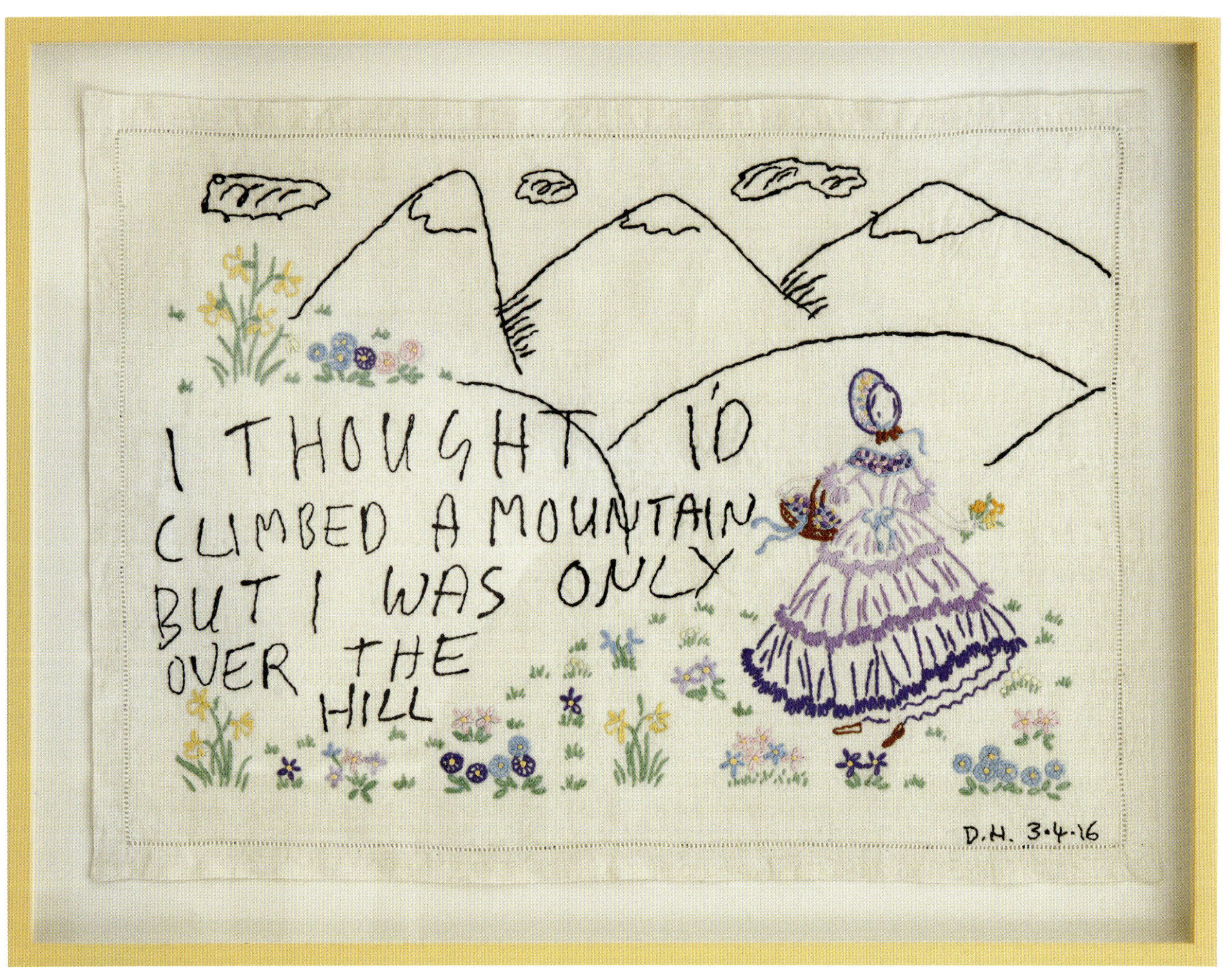

I Thought I'd Climbed A Mountain 2016
Antique embroidery with cotton silk stitch
on linen, 33 × 47 cm

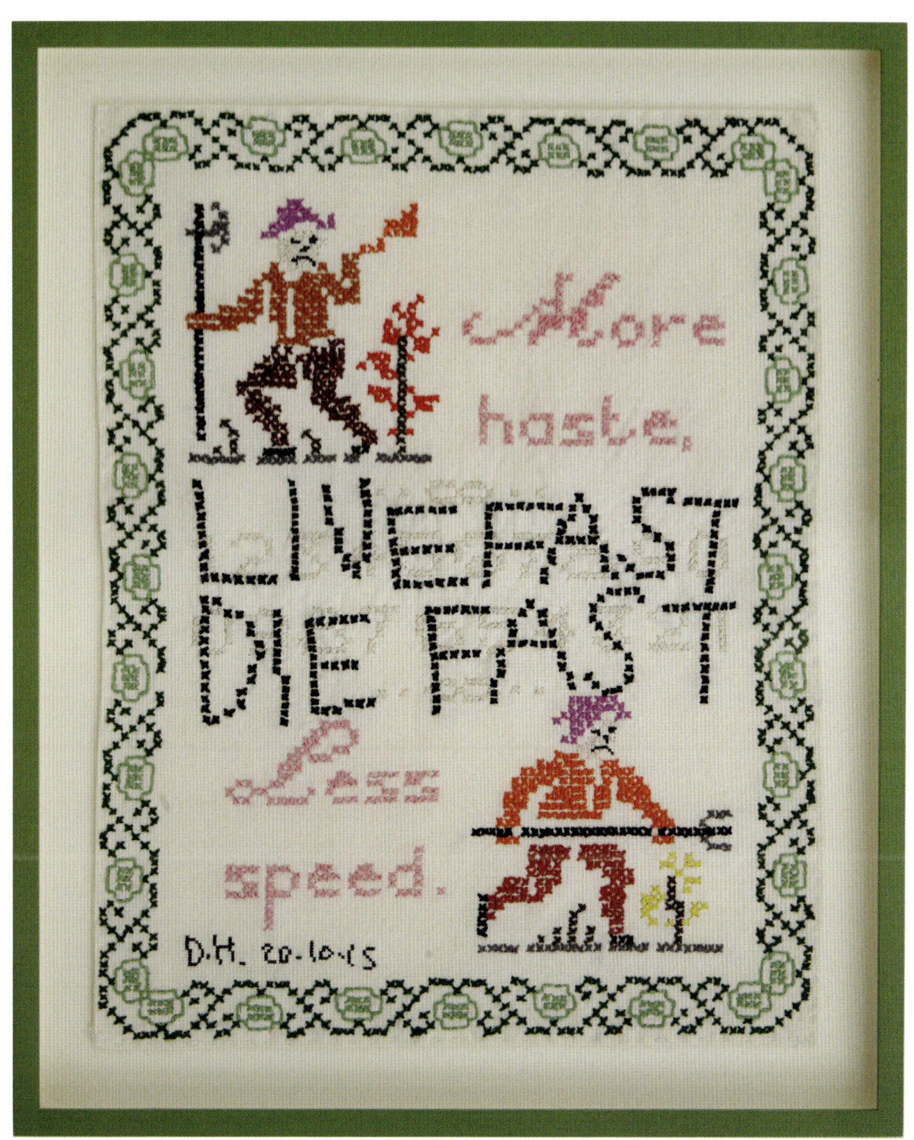

Live Fast Die Fast 2015
Antique embroidery with cotton
silk cross-stitch on linen,
38 × 28 cm

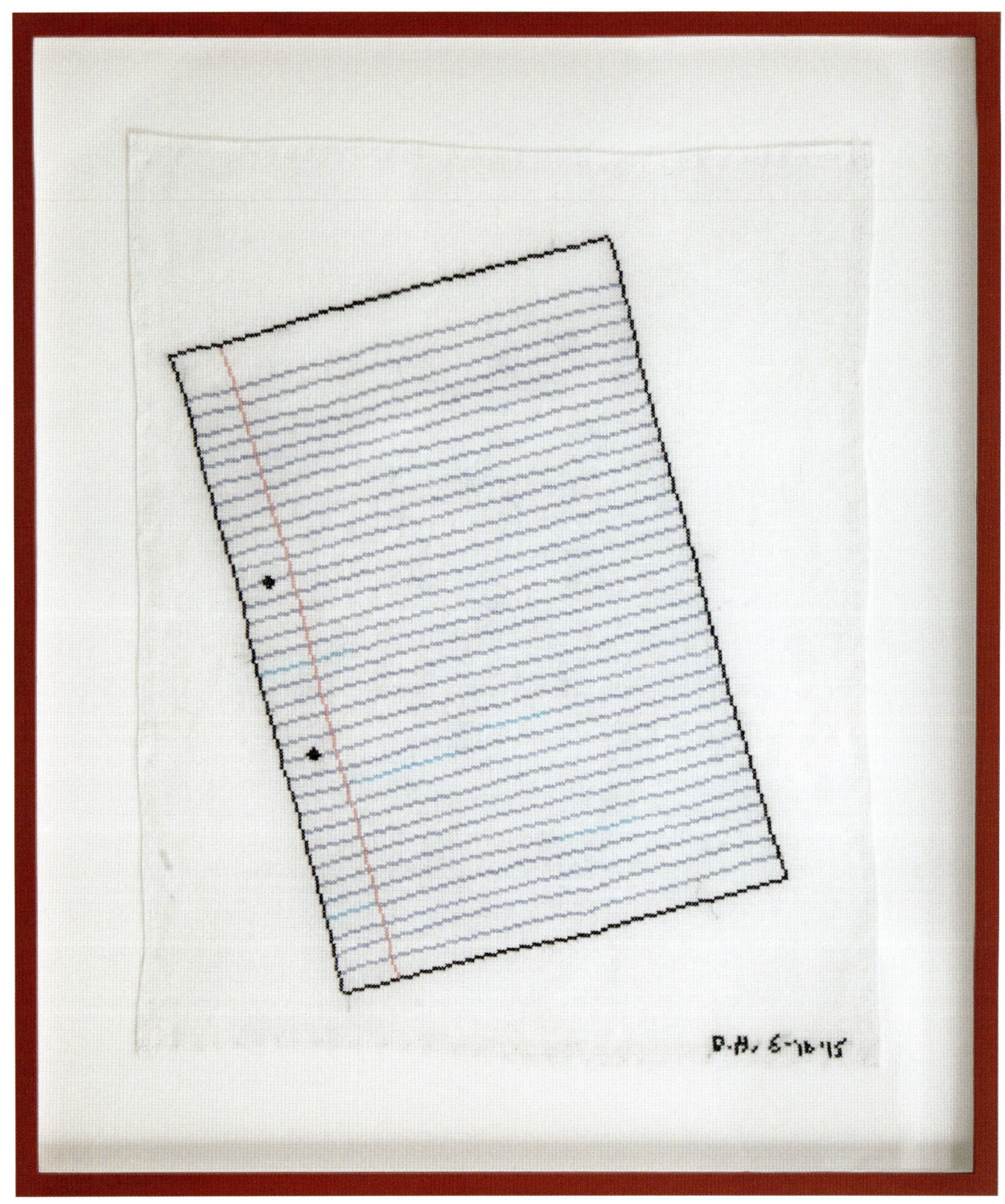

Slowness 2015
Cotton silk cross-stitch on linen,
39 × 35 cm

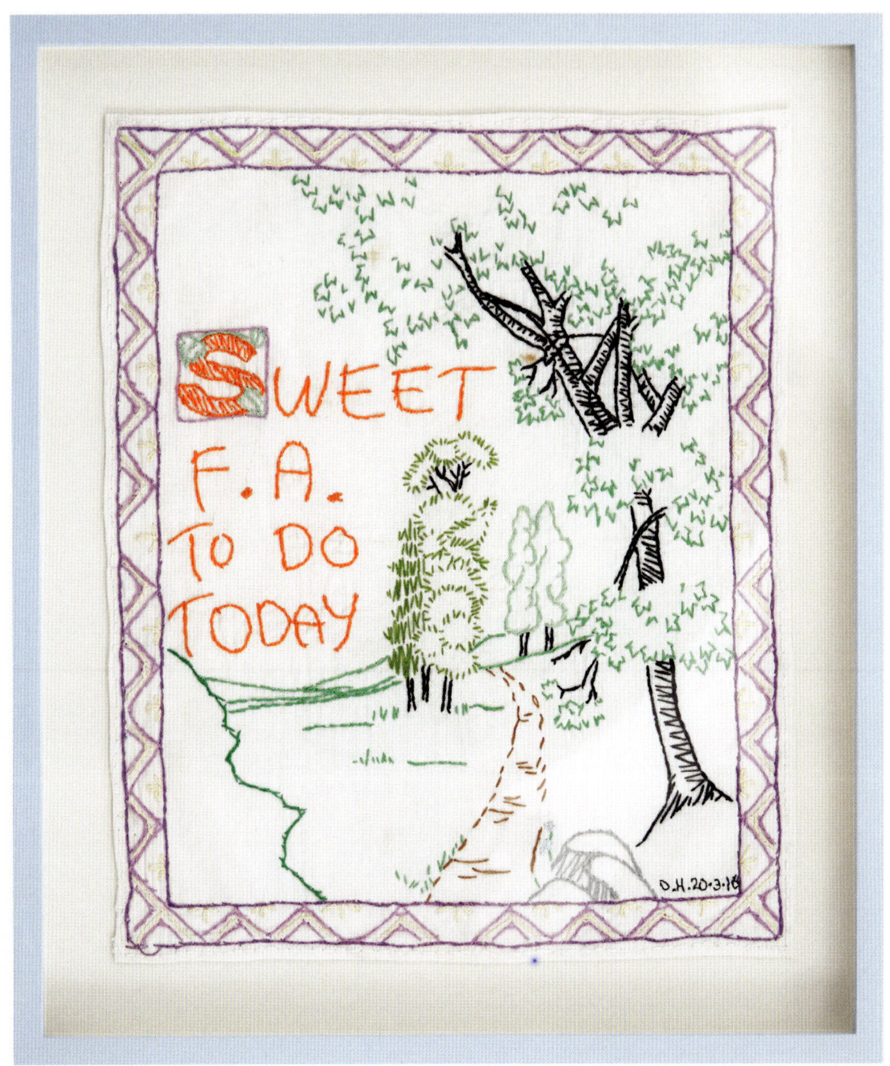

Sweet FA 2016
Antique embroidery with cotton
silk stitch on linen,
31 × 25 cm

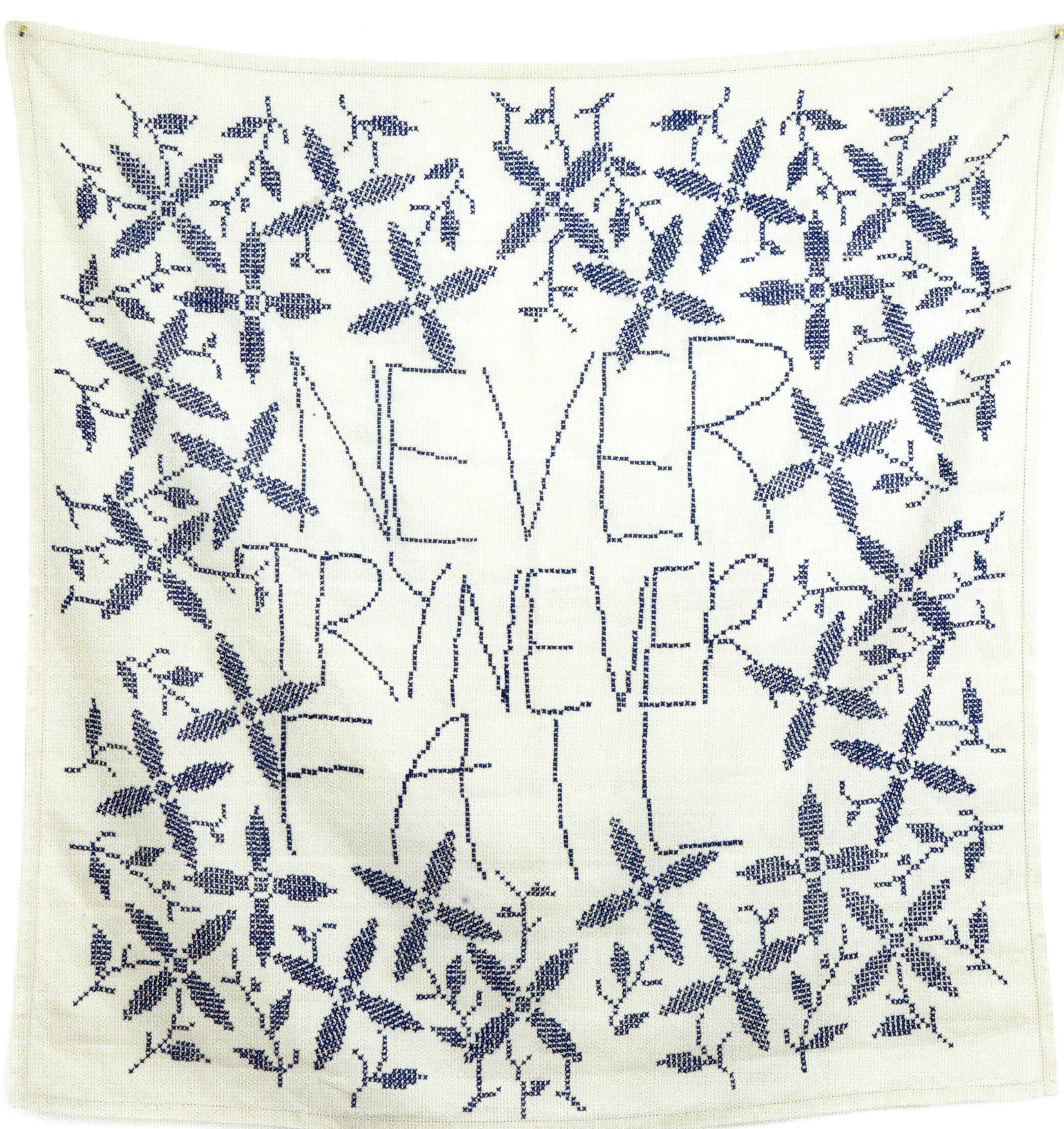
NEVER
TRY NEVER
FAIL

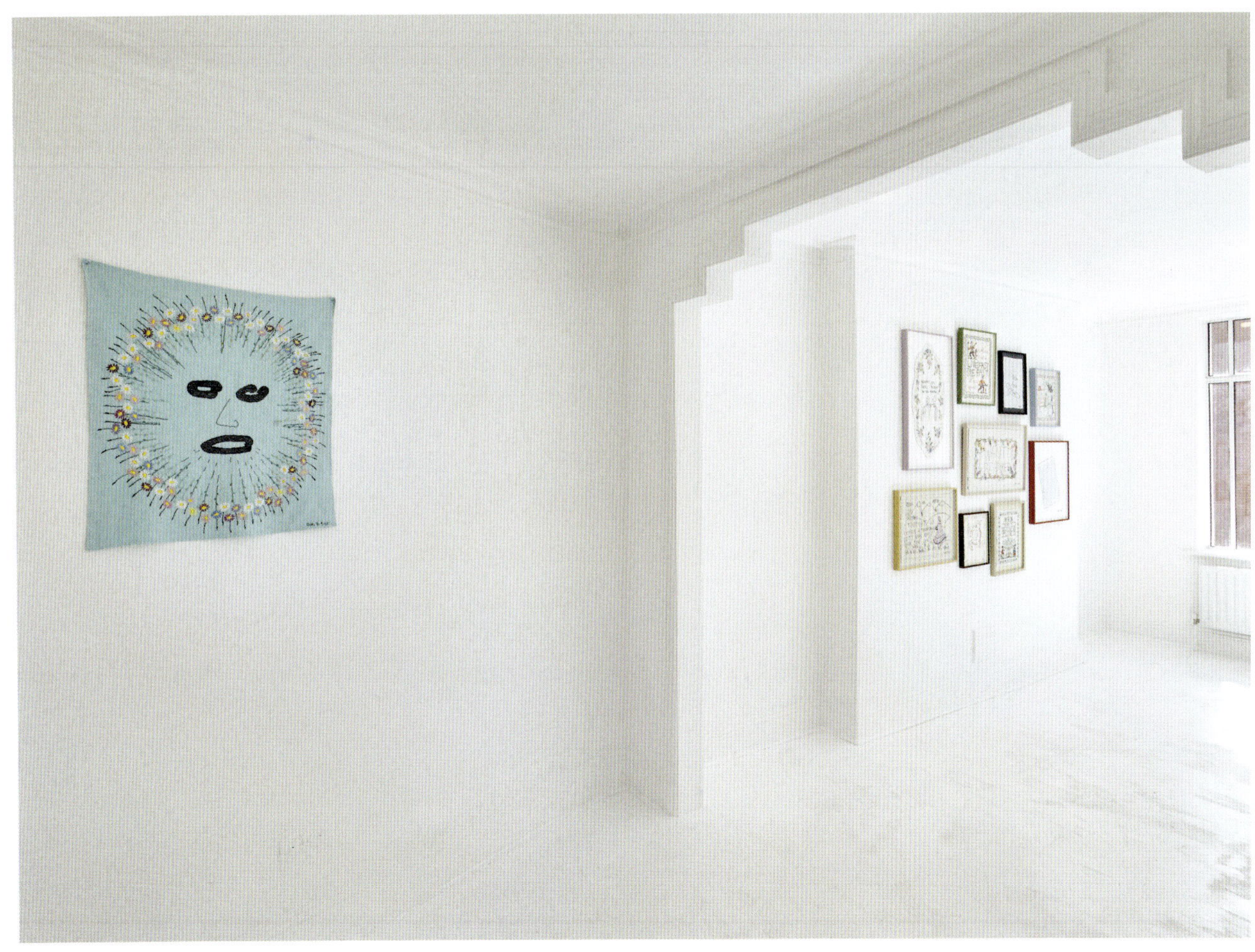

above
'Des Hughes: XXX' 2016
Bruce Haines Mayfair, London

opposite
Never Try Never Fail 2015
Antique embroidery with cotton
silk cross-stitch on linen,
85 × 85 cm

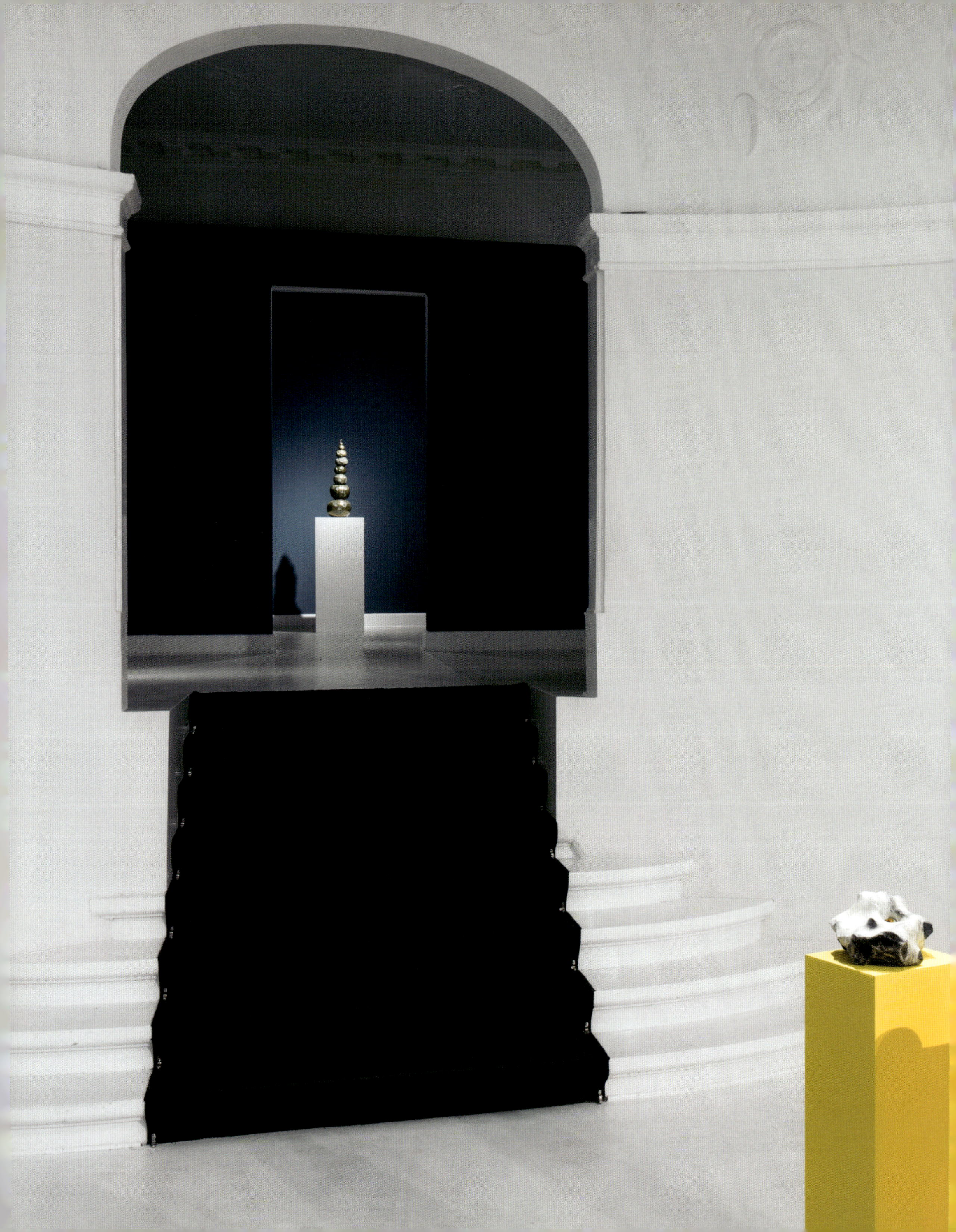

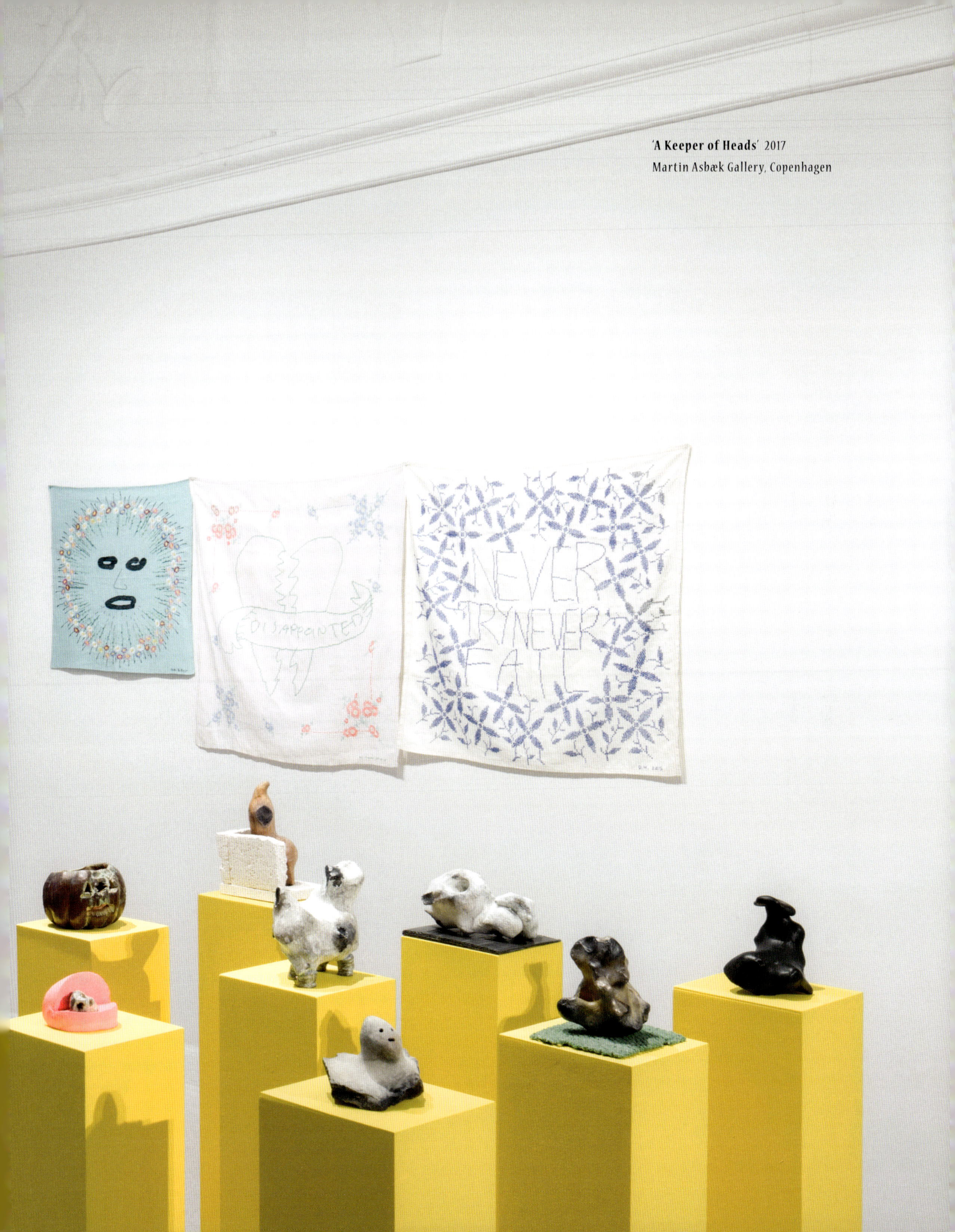

'A Keeper of Heads' 2017
Martin Asbæk Gallery, Copenhagen

Soft Fruit 2007

Bronze and nylon string,

9 × 12 × 8 cm

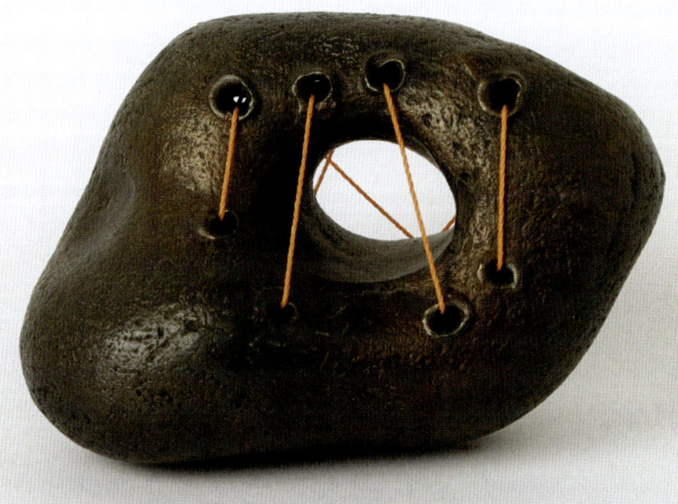

Infirm 2012
Bronze,
9 × 12 × 9 cm

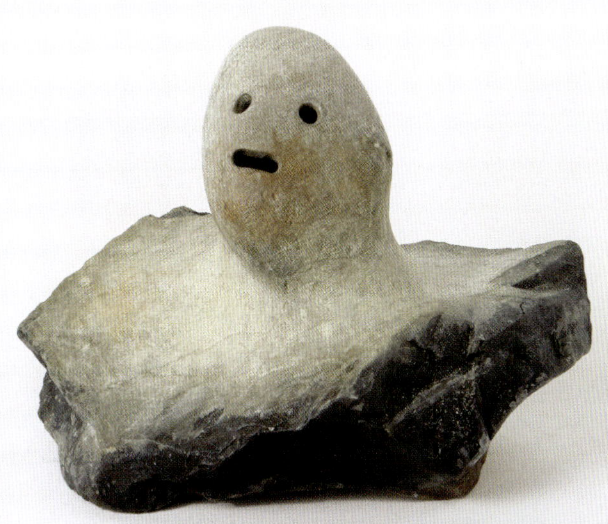

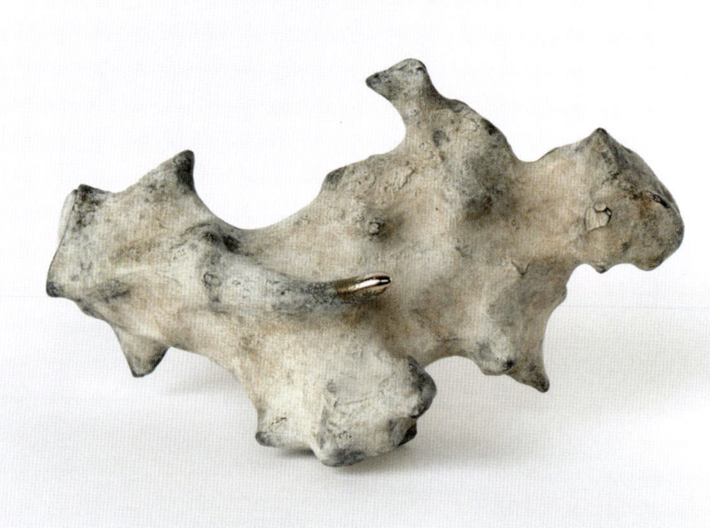

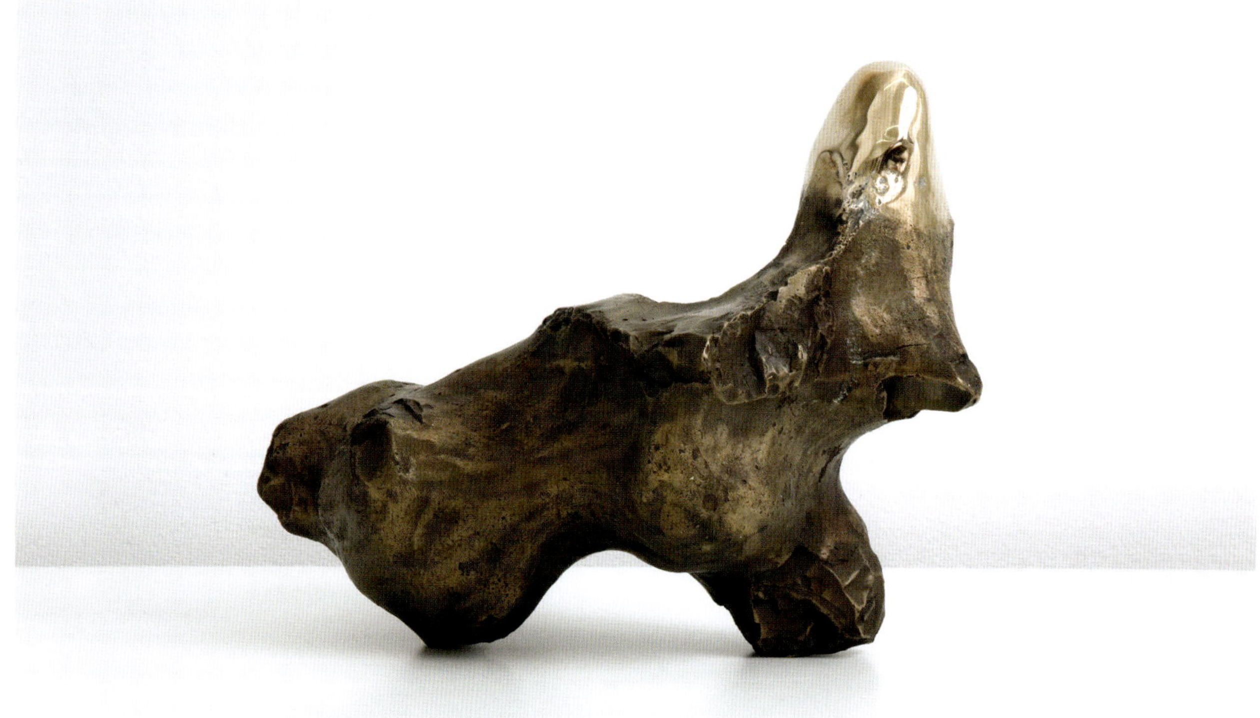

top
Wink 2012
Bronze,
12 × 12 × 12 cm

bottom
Norfolk Flint (with Prominence) 2007
Bronze,
20 × 27 × 16 cm

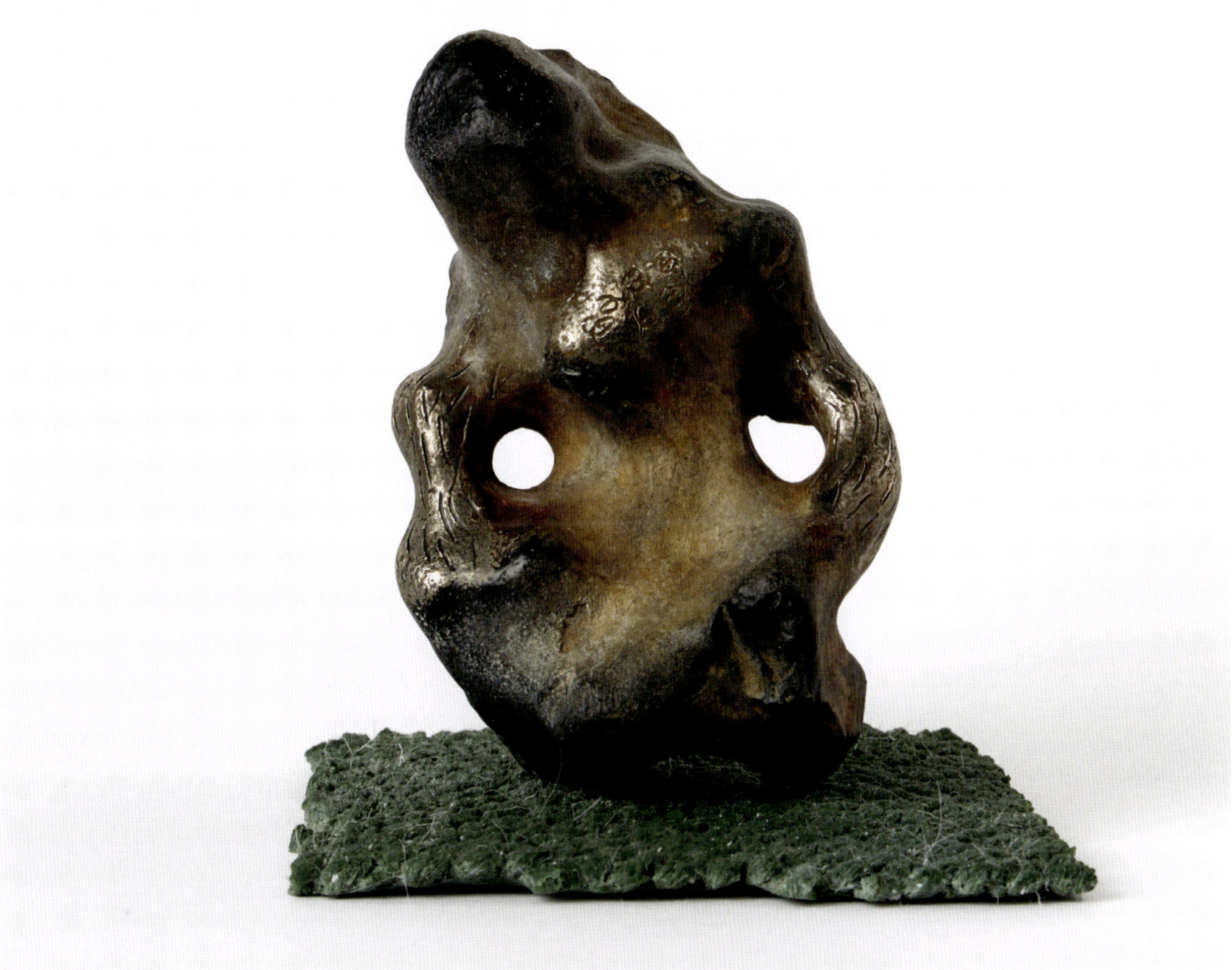

Three Hairs 2015
Bronze, resin and pigment,
14 × 8 × 10 cm

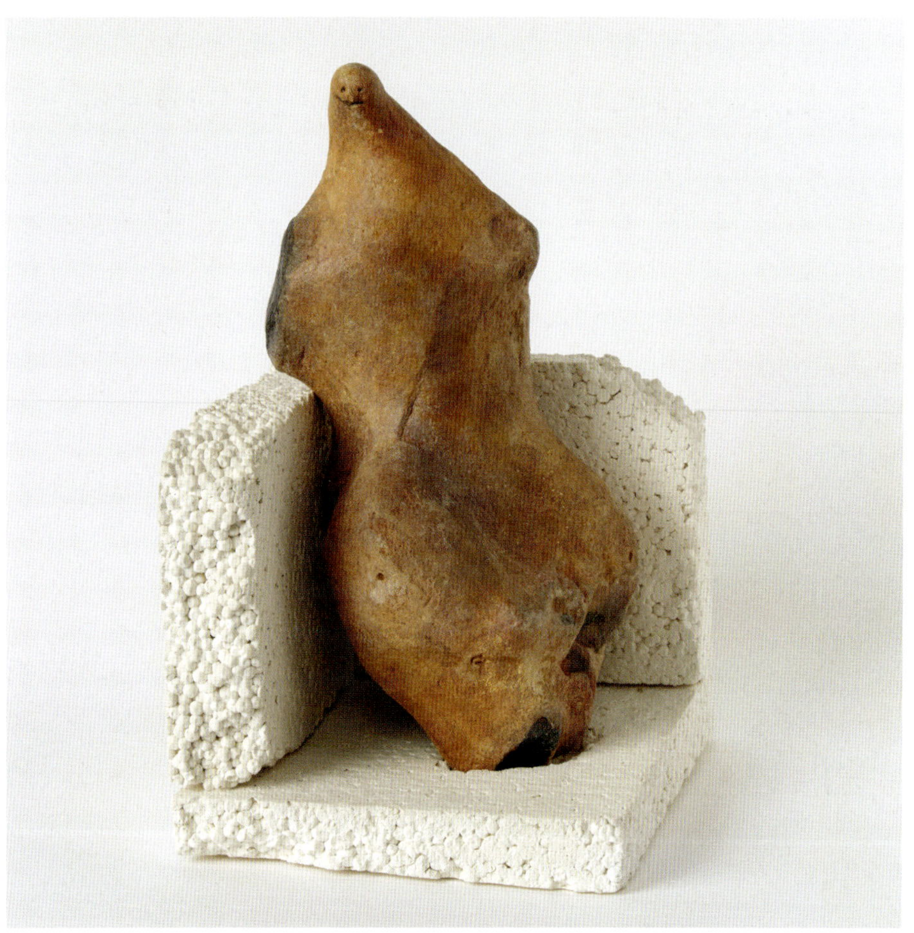

Man Walks Into A Bar 2015
Bronze and plaster,
18 × 12 × 13 cm

The Hermit 2012
Bronze and glass marble,
10 × 18 × 15 cm

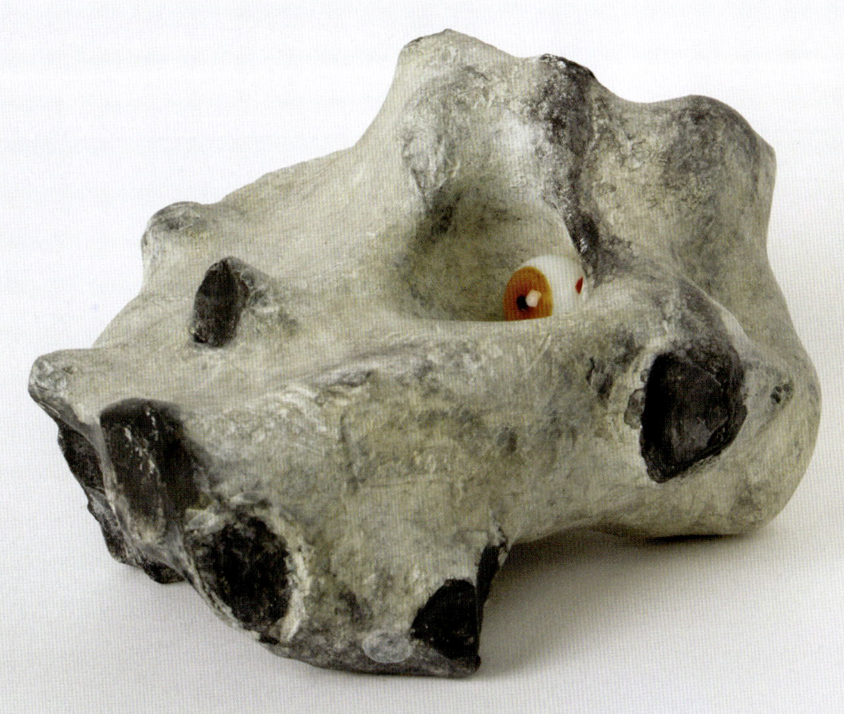

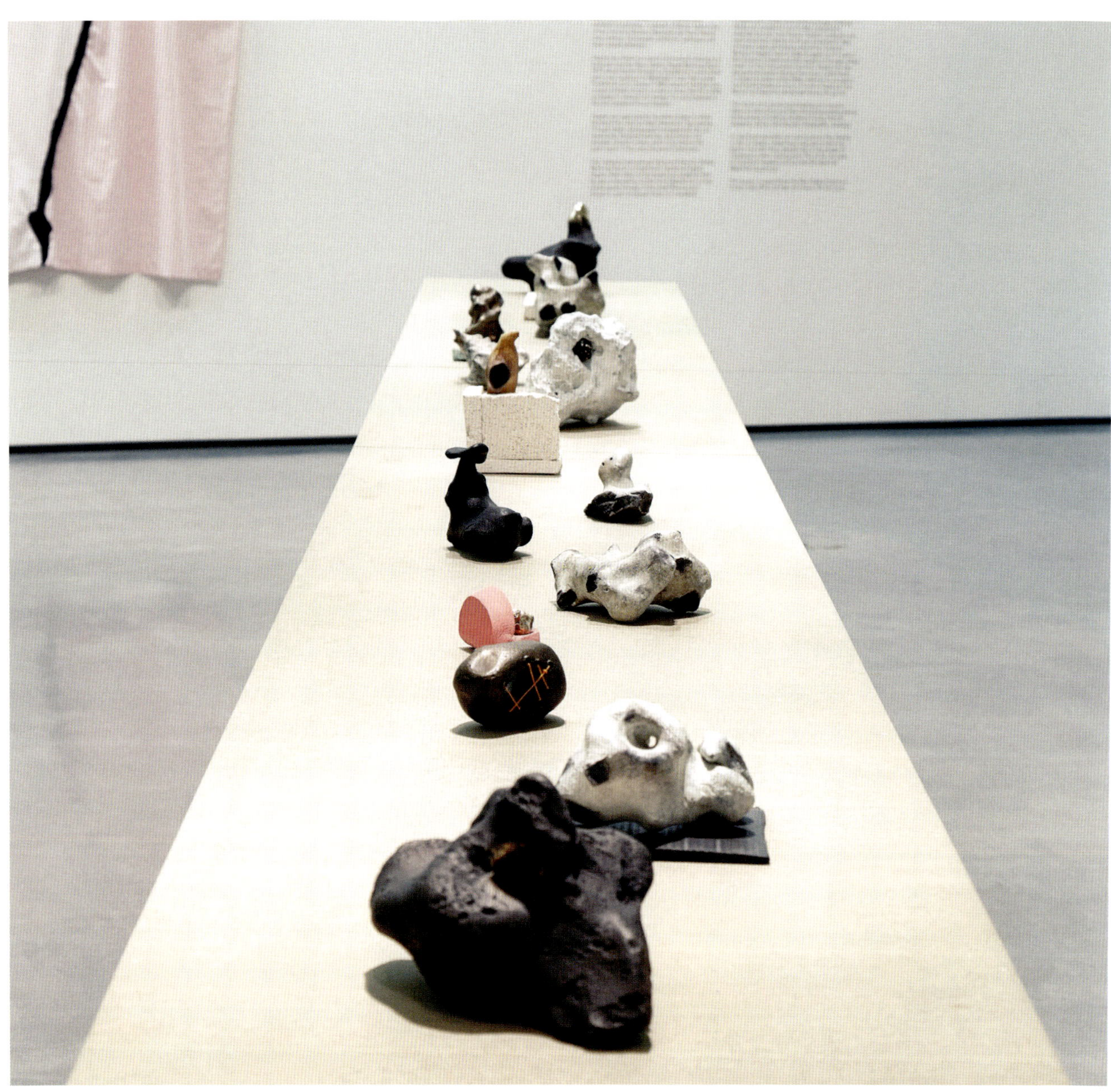

'Stretch Out and Wait' 2015
The Hepworth Wakefield

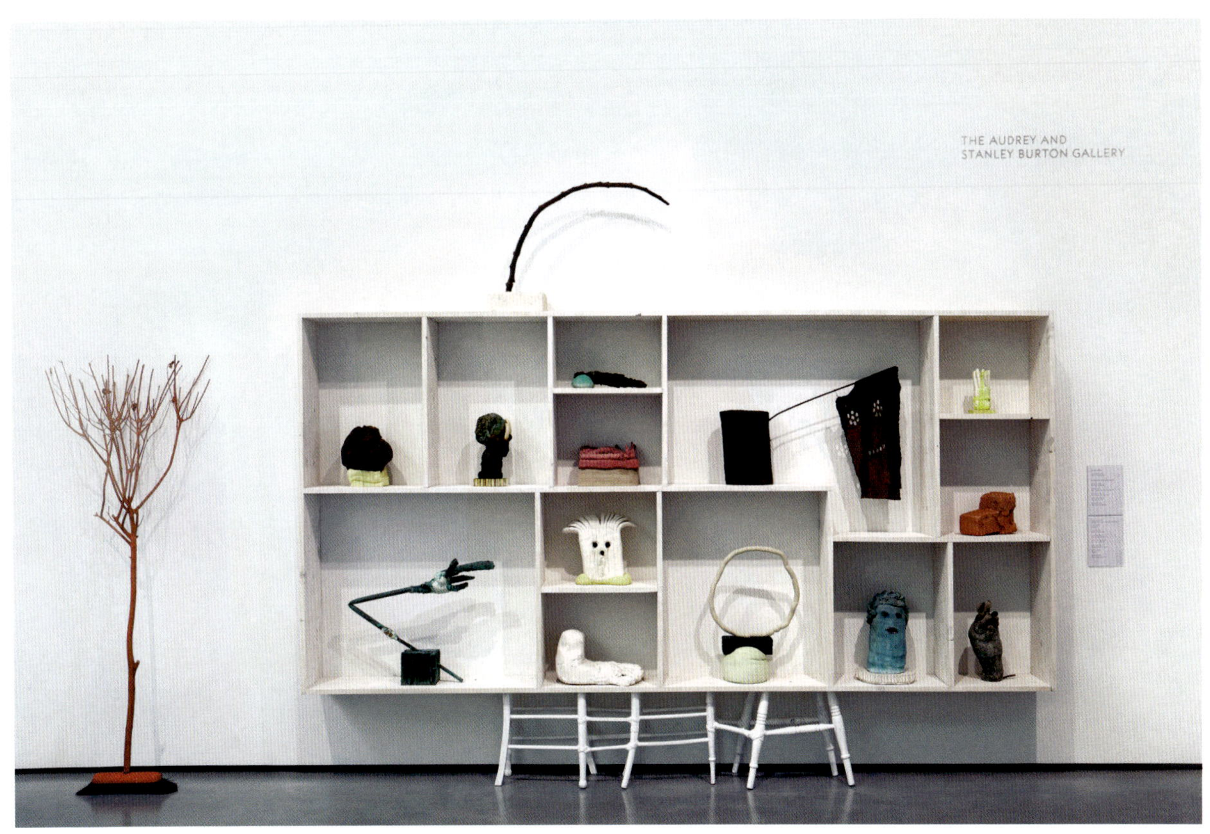
THE AUDREY AND
STANLEY BURTON GALLERY

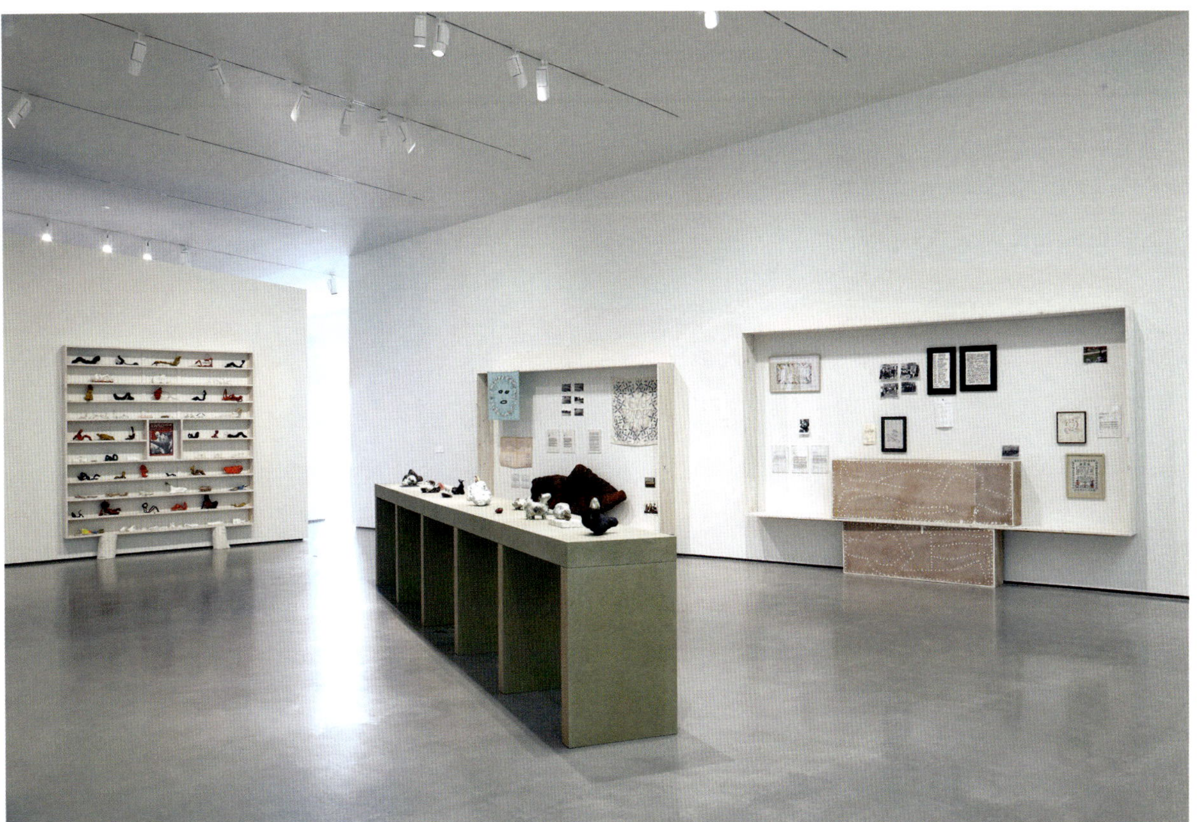

Tree Brush 1993
Tree branch, broom head and gloss paint,
180 × 80 × 60 cm

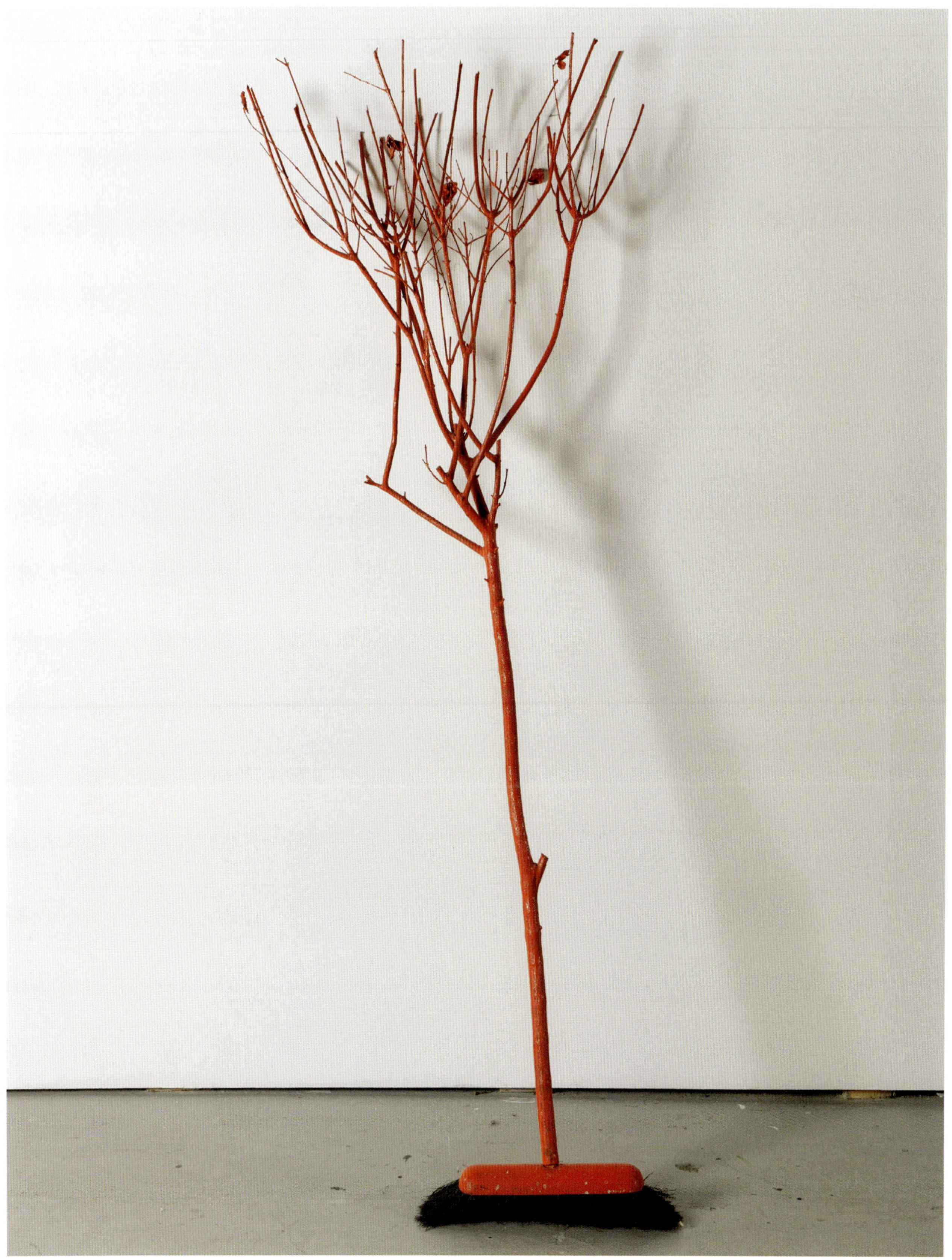

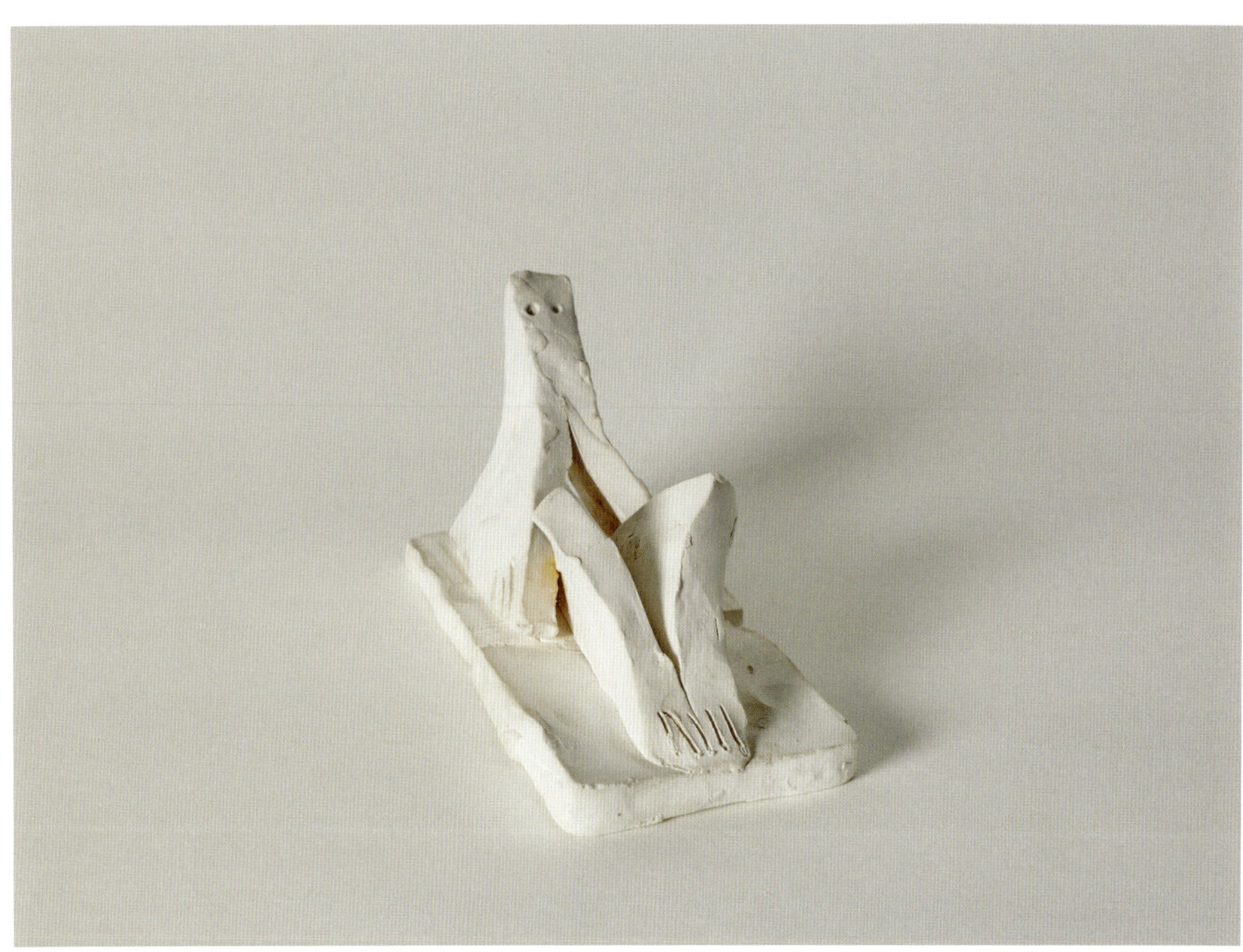

Small Sliced Reclining Figure 2015
Plaster,
9 × 16 × 8 cm

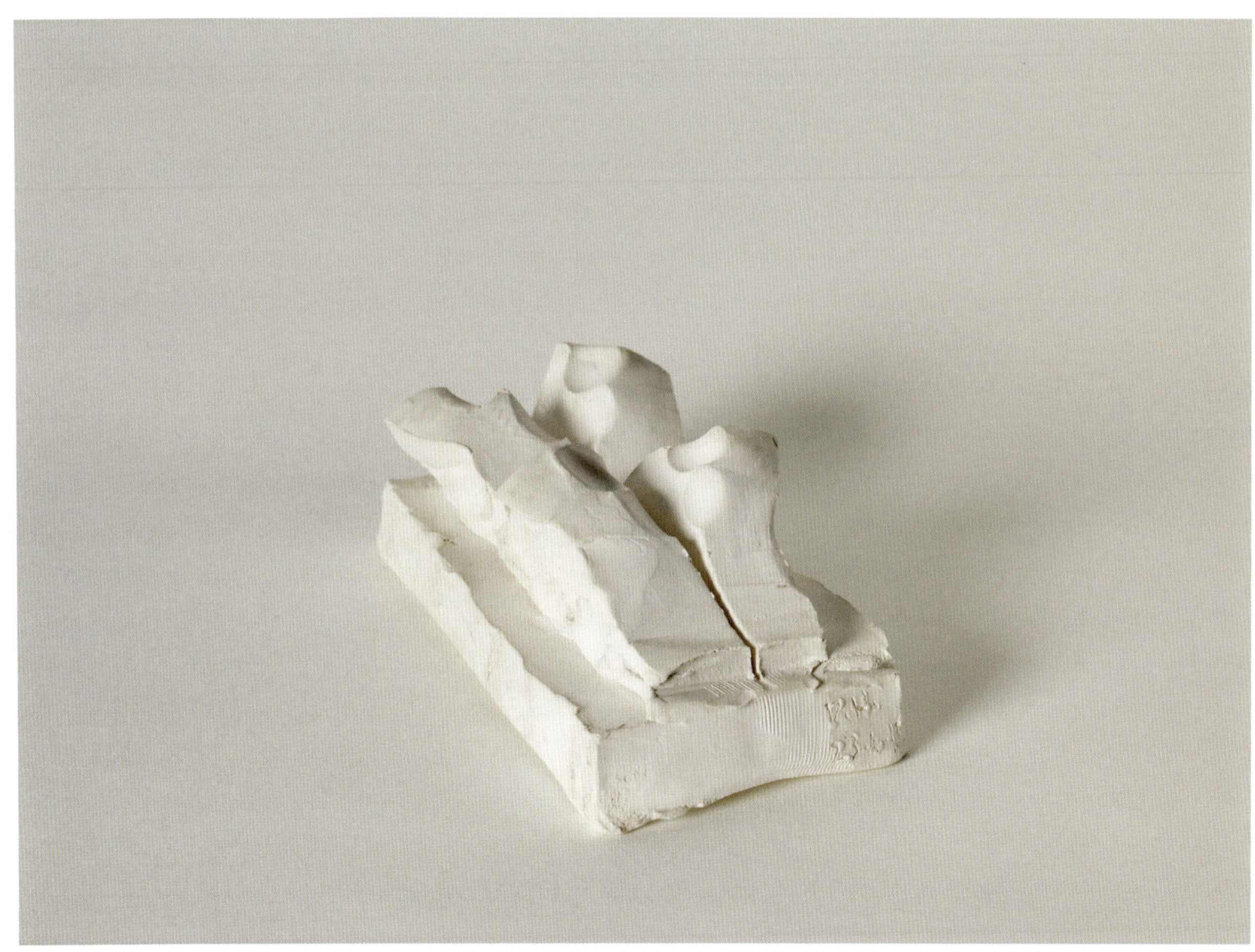

Small Parted Reclining Figure 2015
Plaster,
6 × 18 × 9 cm

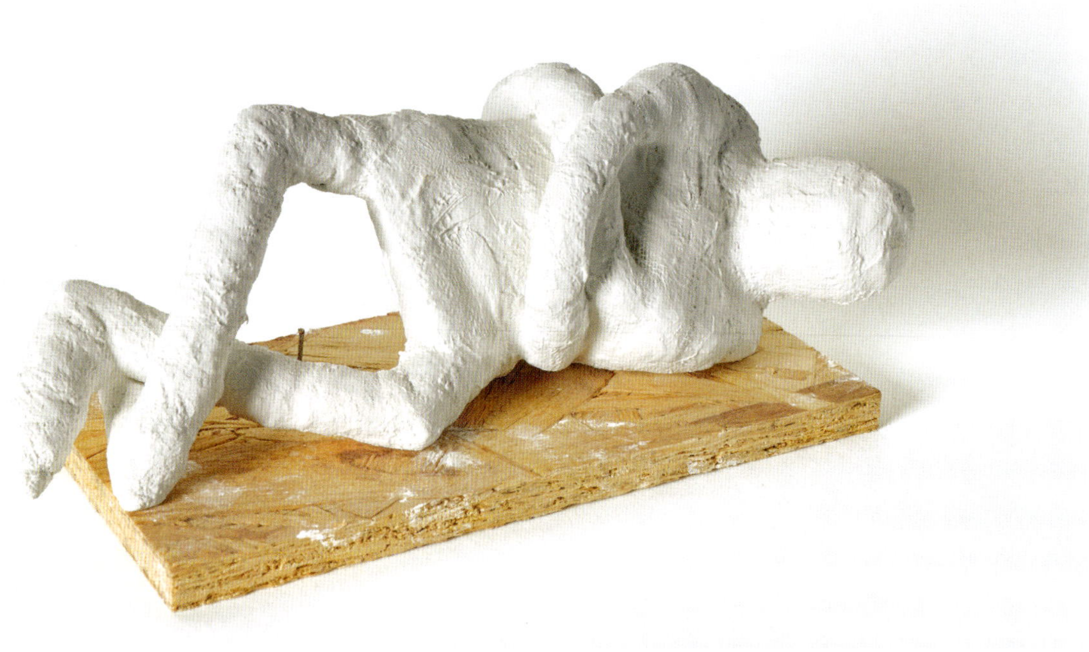

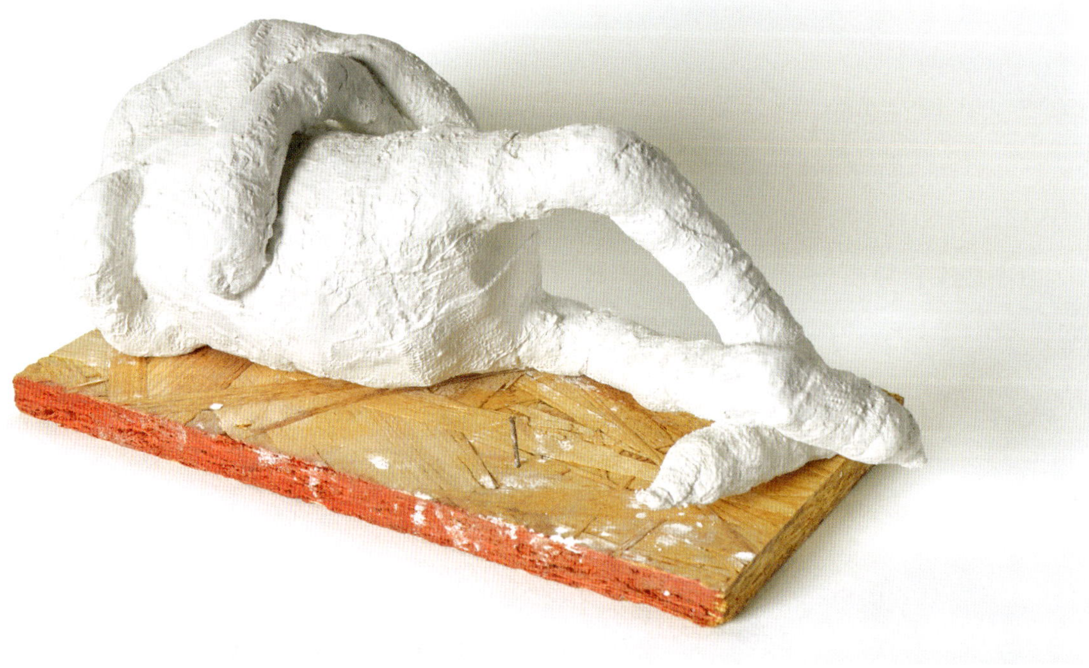

above
Learn To Love Yourself 2010
Plaster bandage, cardboard
and sterling board,
19 × 12 × 7 cm

opposite
Small Abdabs 2003
Plaster bandage
and wood,
each 9 × 5 × 5 cm

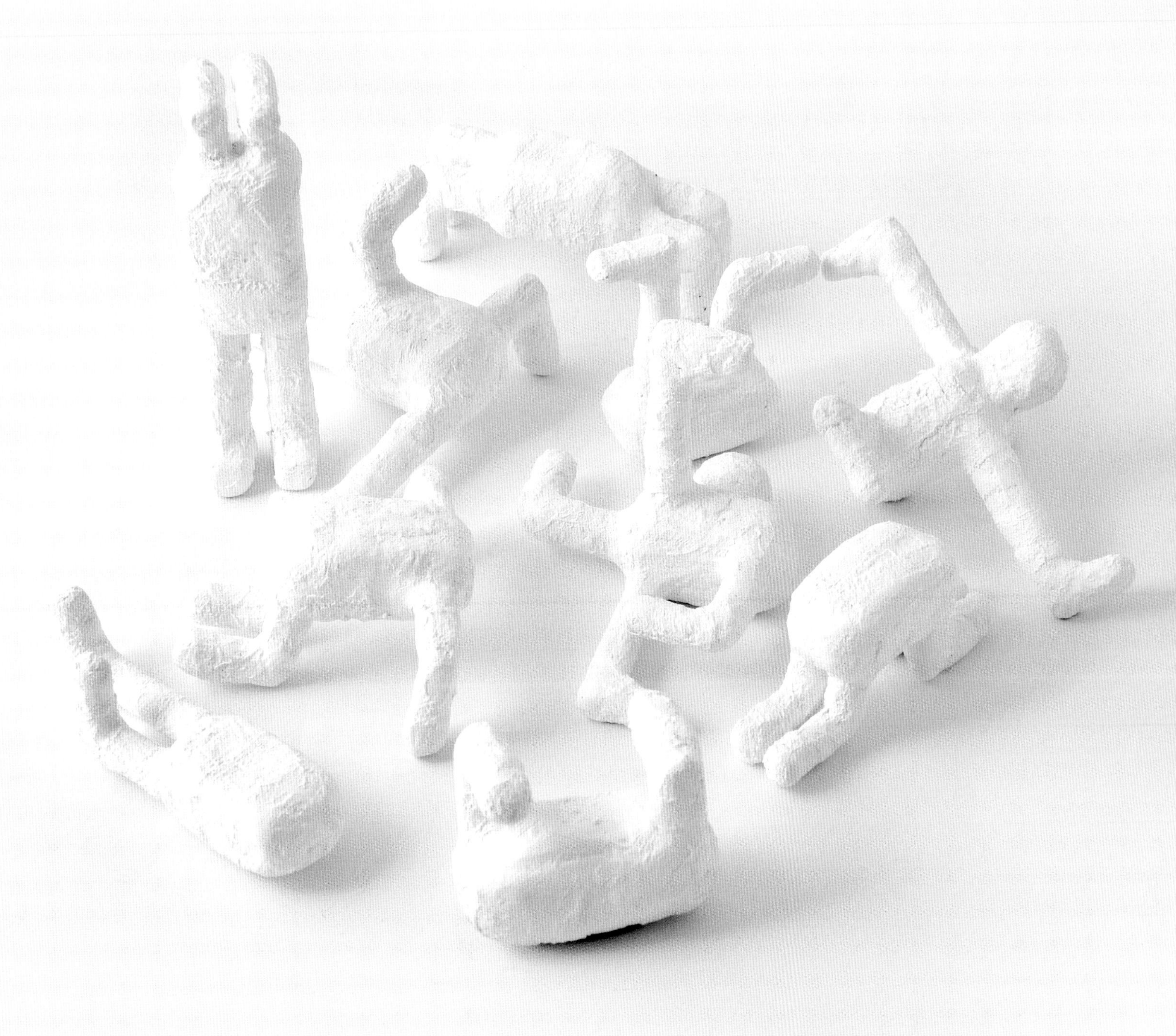

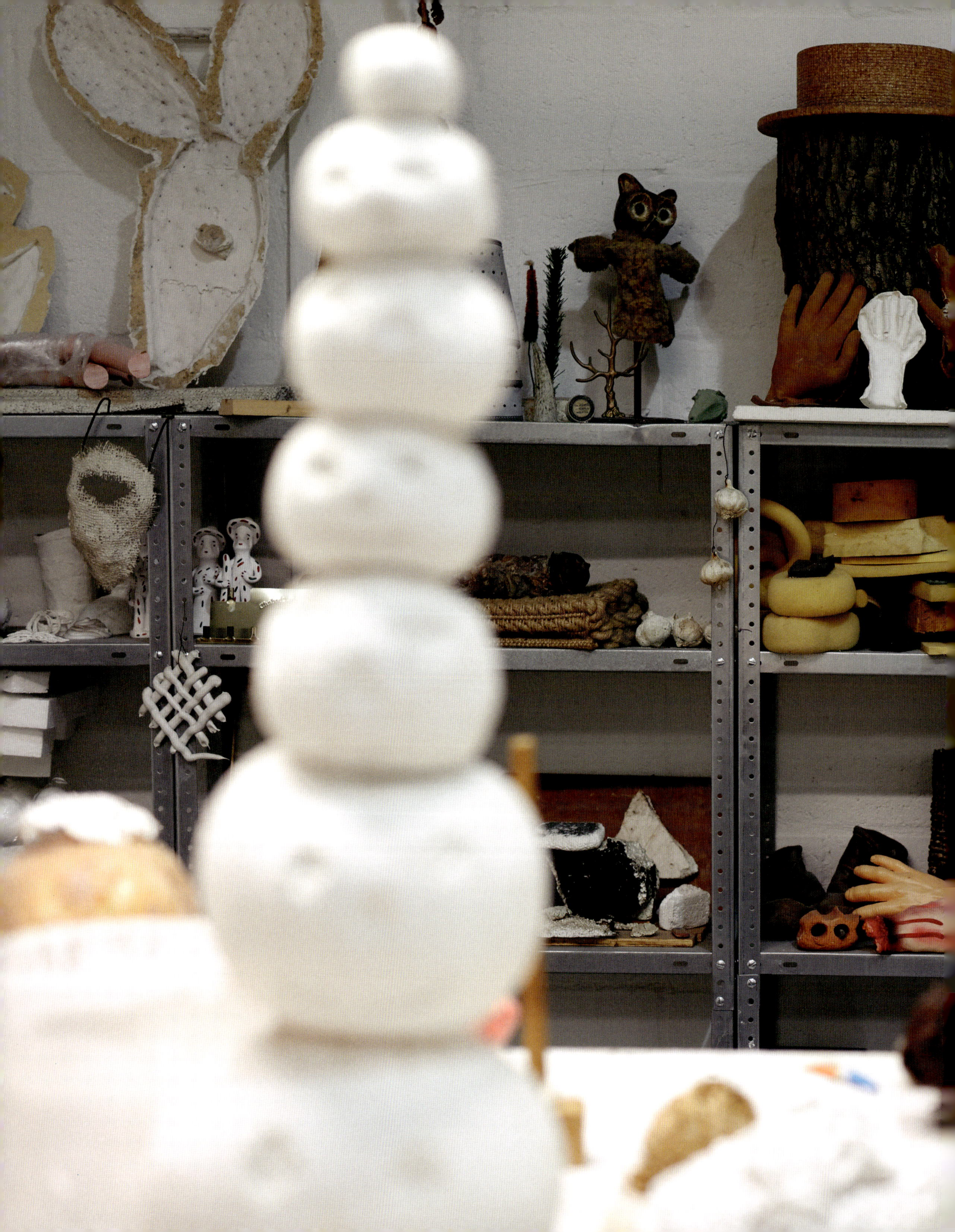

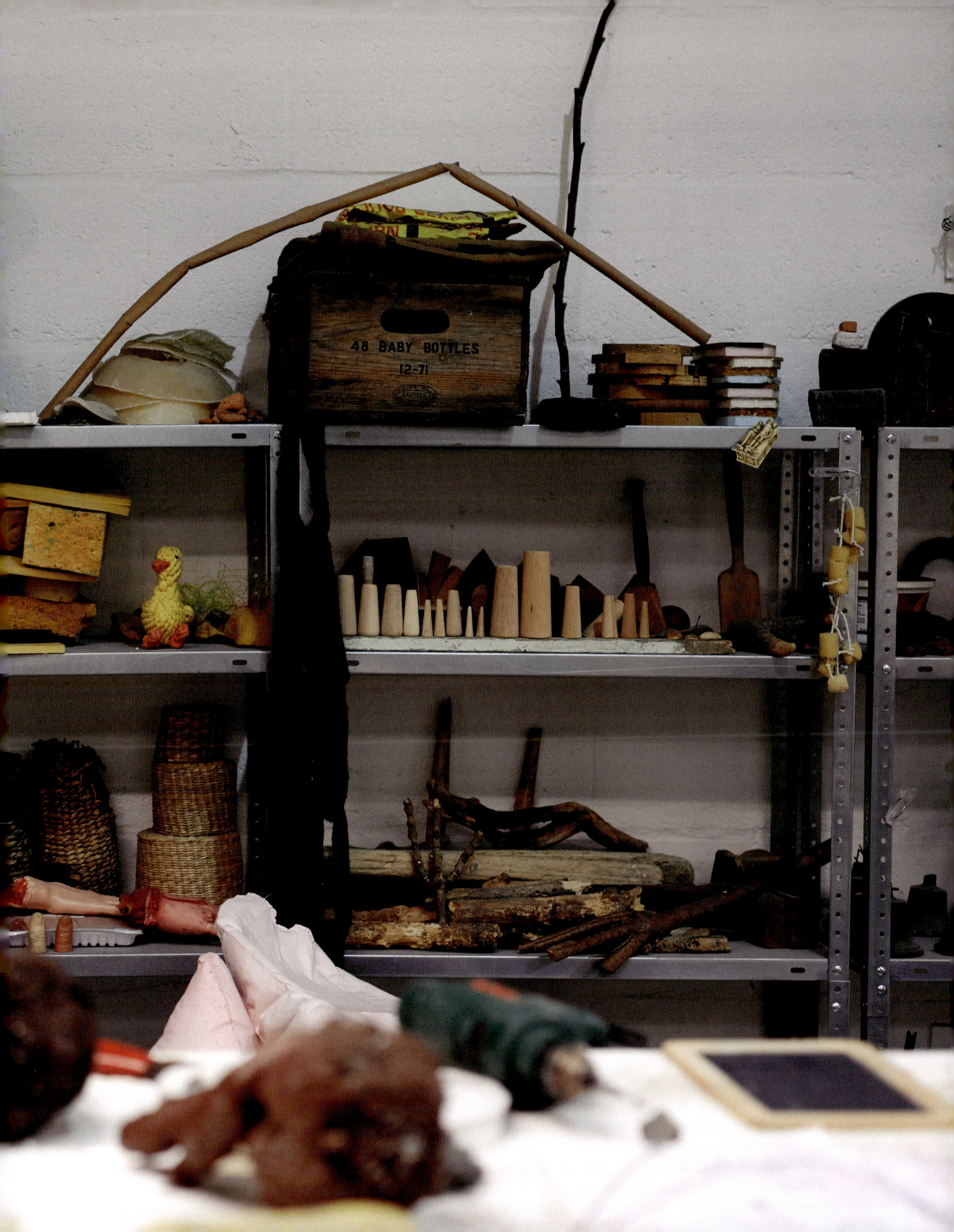
48 BABY BOTTLES
12-71

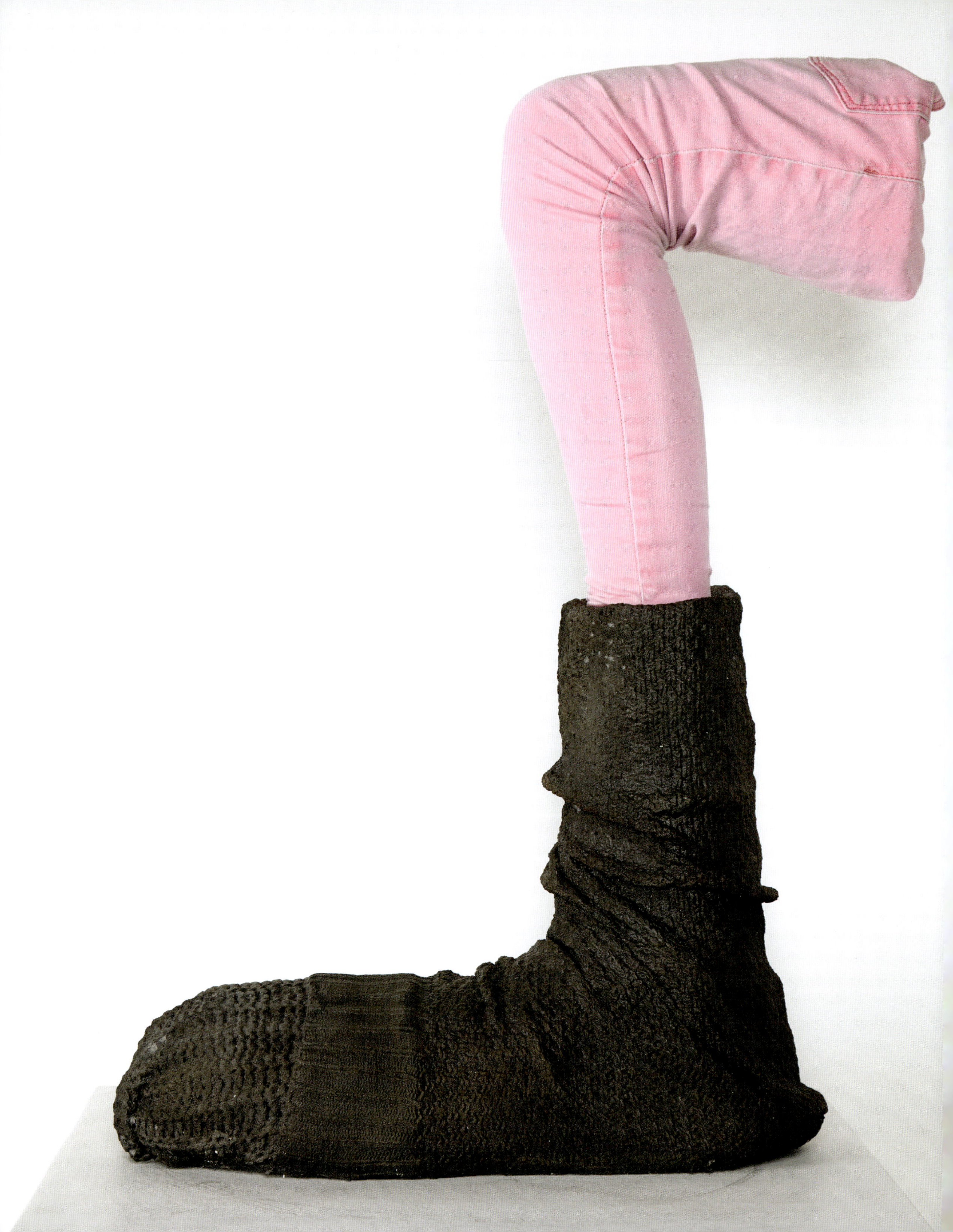

Logic to the Lack

Harry Thorne

'He felt as if the limbs did not fit each other.'[1]

'so-called ... all that together ... imagine!... whole body like gone ... just the mouth ... lips ... cheeks ... jaws ... never – ...what?'[2]

'Ruin is [...] this memory open like an eye, or like the hole in a bone socket that lets you see without showing you anything at all, anything of the all.'[3]

Severed limbs and the silver screen go hand in bloodied hand. *The Beast with Five Fingers* (1946); *The Crawling Hand* (1963); *And Now the Screaming Starts* (1973); *The Thing* (1982); *Re-Animator* (1985); *Severed Ties* (1992). In *Dr Terror's House of Horrors* (1965), Christopher Lee assumes the role of pompous art critic Franklyn Marsh, who victimizes, dismembers via vehicular assault, and pushes the painter Eric Landor (Michael Gough) to the point of suicide, only to be tormented by the merciless digits of the artist's reanimated hand. In taking that hand, Marsh stripped Landor of his craft; the hand returns and claims the same from the critic: his vision, which causes another car crash and the loss of another life. An eye for a hand leaves the whole world blind – or dead at the wheel.

Why is absence of the body, signified by its partial presence, such potent terrain for horror? Why is the 'phantom' limb a greater source of anxiety than a fully formed beast? Some options: there is the Freudian sensation of the 'uncanny', which manifests (or re-emerges) upon being confronted by an amalgamation of the familiar and the eerie. Freud found this in Wilhelm Hauff's *The Story of the Severed Hand* (1827); my livelier example is the scuttling 'Thing' in *The Addams Family*.

1 Paul F. Schilder recounting the effects of mescal intoxication upon E. Forster in 1917, in *The Image and Appearance of the Human Body*, 1999.

2 Samuel Beckett, *Not I*, 1972.

3 Jacques Derrida, *Memoirs of the Blind: The Self-Portrait and Other Ruins*, 1990.

Face Like A Foot 2016
Resin, iron powder, expanding foam and cotton, 70 × 44 × 18 cm

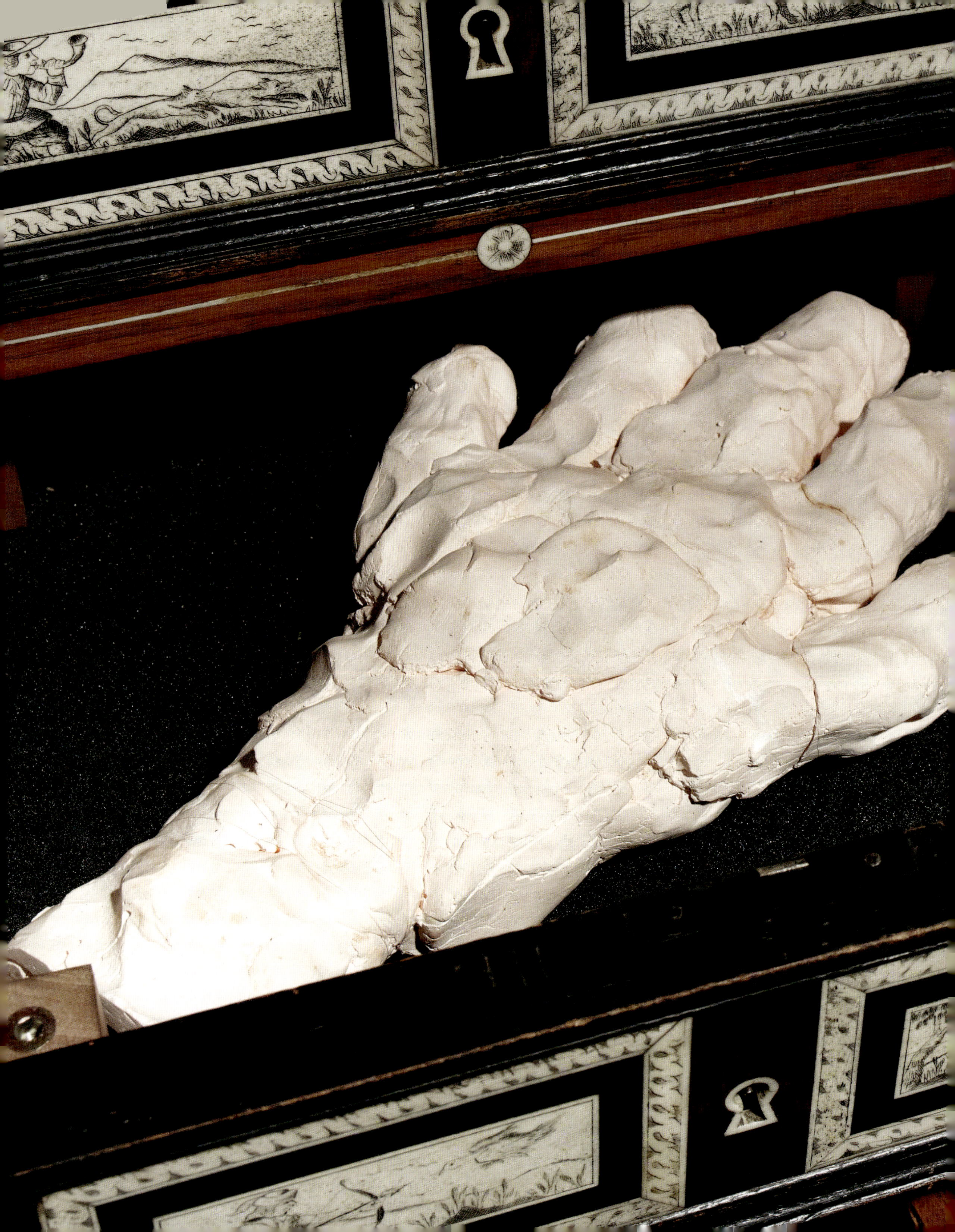

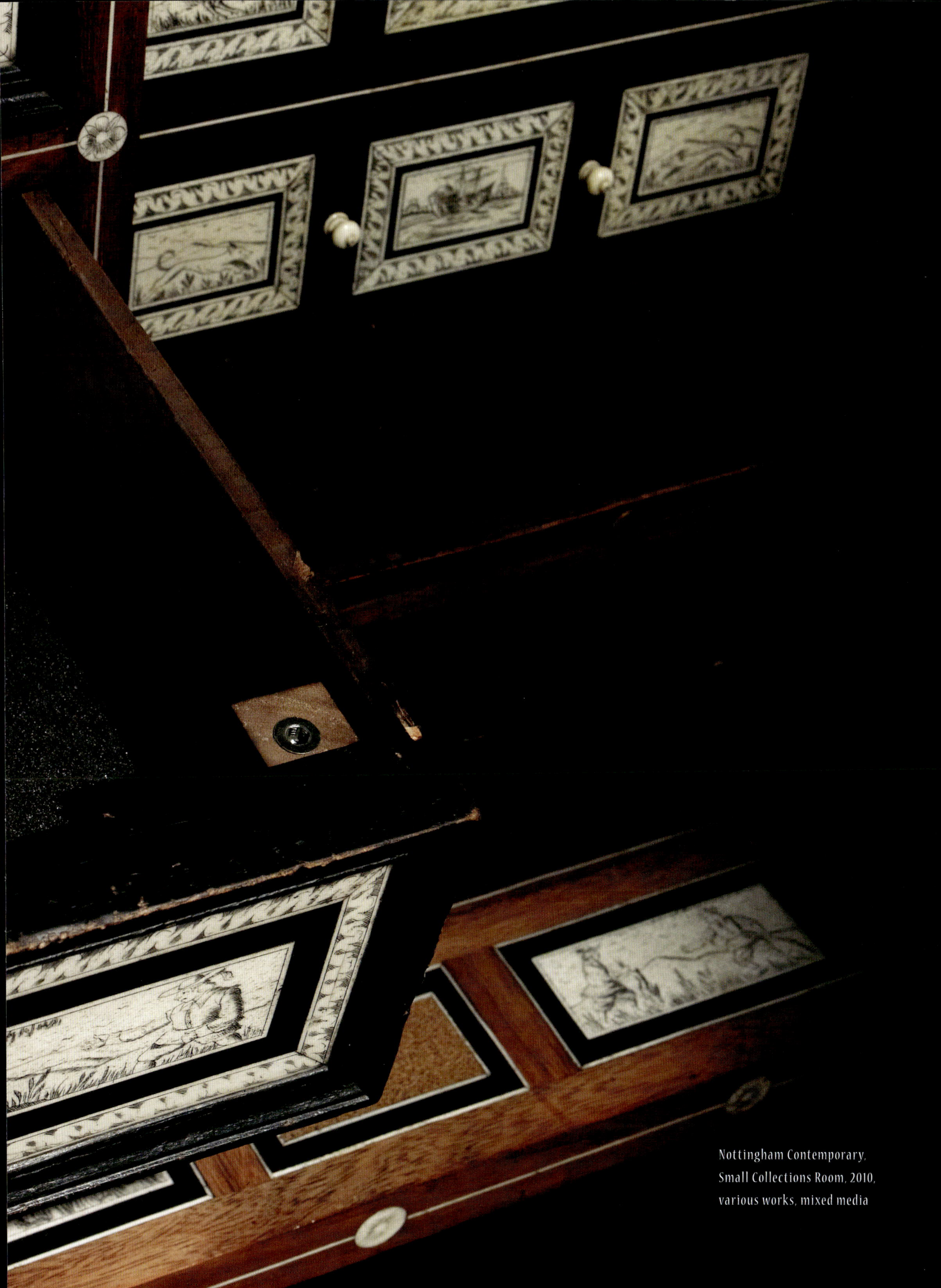

Nottingham Contemporary,
Small Collections Room, 2010,
various works, mixed media

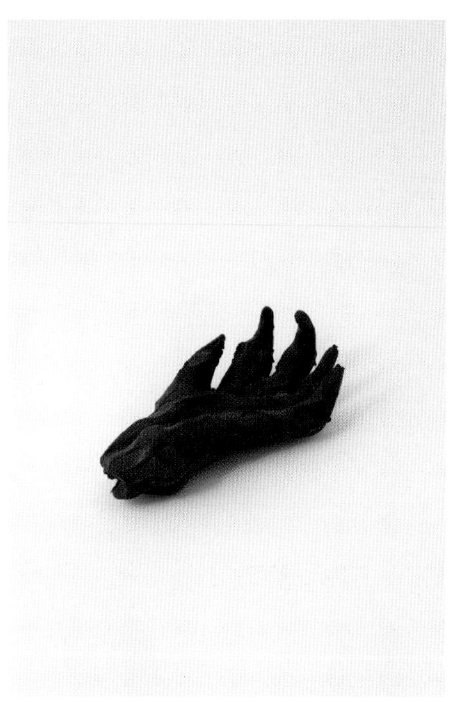

Monkey's Paw 1999
Latex and pigment,
2.5 × 15 × 5 cm

Then there is the dread of latent retribution. Why would a once-known, once-trusted limb reanimate and seek vengeance were it not for an injustice of sorts? Or could it be the heralding of a relapse to something that has been psychologically, by way of physically, banished. Matthew 5:30 reads: 'And if your right hand causes you to sin, cut it off.' Something once seen as a risk to the corpus, and promptly amputated, now returns, indicating that the cut was far from clean. That the rot has not stopped. That 'sin' persists.

The slight suggestion of evil, as opposed to the depiction of evil *complété*, plays upon a scepticism that lingers deep within each of us – residue of the survival instinct. When we see an unabridged version of a beast, a bogieman, a Brando in *The Island of Dr Moreau* (1996), we are able to comprehend, process and place said ghoul within a wider context. As a result, the creeper lacks the agency that it once had to terrorize. But place afront a fragment and you deny us the possibility of completion. Because with rupture comes lack, and with lack comes an absence waiting to be filled – by ghouls and gremlins that no longer crawl from directors' notebooks but from the dusty bookshelves of our minds. Like children walking in the woods, a hint will suffice to convince us that something macabre is lurking in the shadows.

This creative potential of absence (for grizzly imaginings are imaginings all the same) has long been adopted for means more generative than those of our scaremongering Hollywood producers. Take iconoclasts, hell-bent on tearing it all out of shape. What does fracture mean to them? It means to debase, destruct, debunk, yes, but it also represents a clearing of space for construction – propagation via a pulling down. To fold in Linda Nochlin in *The Body in Pieces* (1994): the 'lost state of fecundity and totality' must inevitably be 'displaced into the past or the future; nostalgia or Utopia are the alternatives offered.' We can lament lost wholeness if we must, but what is fragmentation of the customary but an

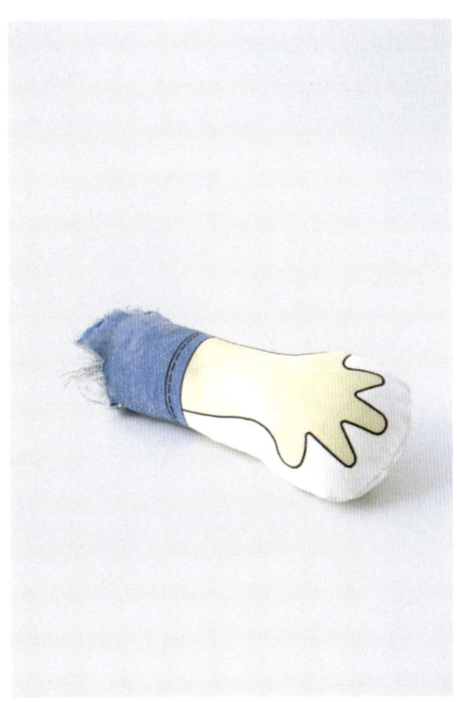

Chewed Up Hand 2000
Found object,
2 × 15 × 50 cm

unveiling of malcontent? And what is an unveiling of malcontent but a heralding of change?

Visual art has witnessed various mutations of the dismembered body stagger through its halls. 'Classical' artists invoked rupture, the body shattered, to remind of the inevitability of decay; in the eighteenth century, it was an ideologically charged call to reduce, refigure and rebuild; for the modernists, it became an emblem of both the psychological fissures of the postwar period and the hapless figure forced through, mangled by, the machines of industrialization. To lift an oft-quoted aphorism of Friedrich Schlegel: 'Many works of the ancients have become fragments. Many works of the moderns are fragmented at the time of their origin.' And to paraphrase a lesser-quoted belief of Georges Bataille: 'humanism' is an idealized concept that we should neglect as we push towards '*l'informe*' (formless), as through liberation from accepted notions of form, we might push towards anything else.

A revered troupe of surrealists (Miró, Morise, Ray, Tanguy, et al) once looked to give form to formlessness via the game *cadavre exquis*, 'exquisite corpse'. If you have not had the pleasure, allow me: I take a sheet of paper, at the top of which I draw a head. Leaving nothing visible but the two lines demarcating the walls of the neck, I fold the sheet, and pass it your way. You take the torso, fold, pass, and we continue, until we have a monstrous patchwork beast whose head, thorax and abdomen line-up to the tee, but are born in different minds. For Rosalind Krauss, in *Formless: A User's Guide* (1997), this authorial relay represents 'the struggle between eros and death, between chance as the unbridled upsurge of endless possibility and chance as the ultimate version of determination and control'. It is a collaborative challenge to the traditional notions of form – what it is allowed to do, what it can do, when given the space, the time, the licence to breed.

'Licence to breed', to cultivate in near-autonomous fashion, is something that Des Hughes has long-since granted

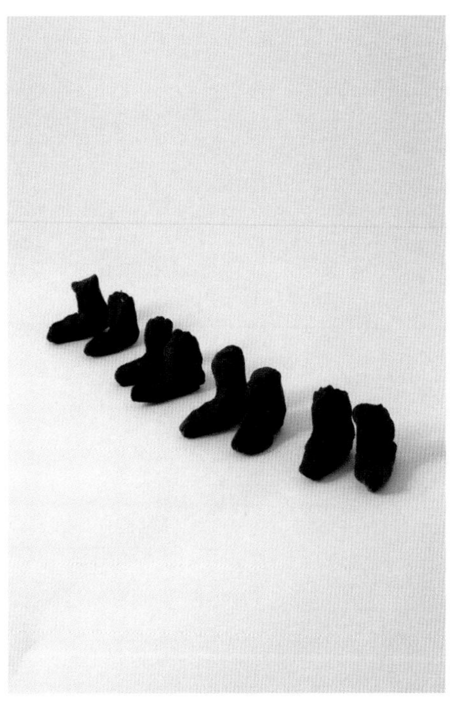

Pixie Boots 2001
Latex and pigment,
each 2.5 × 1 × 2.5 cm

with his broken bodily sculptures. *Monkey's Paw* (1999), the solitary eponymous lying heel and palm up; *Chewed Up Hand* (2000), a human but cartoonish reiteration whose stuffing puffs from the wrist; *Pixie Boots* (2001), four sets of black clay kickers standing, empty, in line. Padding out these orphaned body parts is a sense of anticipation – an expectancy of an arrival that might herald completion. But for now we wait, ruminating on the various beings that might one day fill the open void. *A Big Hand* (2001), for instance, gives us just that: a severed hand of unprimed, unfinished clay, standing on a stumped wrist as if set down to dry. So, shall we create? Perhaps an arm gloops down from the outline of the wrist, widening into a globular, pinkish mass – bell shaped, almost oozing. From the severed pink feet and ankles of *Dogs and Legs* (*p. 203*), which lie in what might be a bed, I see a tangle of limbs, interweaving in figure-of-eights only to resolve in an opposing collection of saccharine stumps and little piggies. Another work from the same year sees an assortment of limbs held within a sphere of tightly wrapped yellow plastic, their respective forms kept clandestine bar two fingertips that, pink again, poke through a seam – either winding themselves to safety or risking escape. Accordingly, the reticence is titled: *Why don't you find out for yourself.*

In Hughes's words, 'It's about taking everything away from the work until it disappears' – leaving the majority of the construction to a second, third, fourth party. This technique of involving, implicating, collaborating with an audience is not employed here to inspire intrigue alone; rather, it is central to the process. Flip through the pages of this book and you will see old friends meet, separate and reconvene: twisted fingers and crooked thumbs; thought-lacking heads. Hughes is less concerned with suturing these parts, offering something mimetic and composed, than he is with mirroring a life that remains relentlessly fragmented and resolutely transformable. Thus the many taxonomies that litter both his work and his

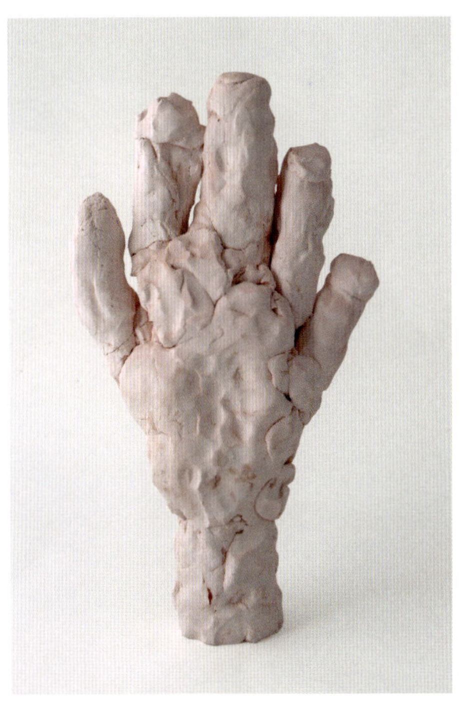

A Big Hand 2001
Plaster and pigment,
35 × 18 × 8 cm

studio. The rudimentary objects organized within these piles are identical in the sense that they each serve the same purpose as those around them – whether hands, feet, funnels, sticks, stones or baskets. But they are each and every one of them different incarnations of their own forms, different imaginings of their own definitions, and in this they pay testament to the near-limitless potential of the present and, in turn, the sheer impossibility of our ever arriving at something truly 'final' – hands, feet, funnels and so on. To draw in Hughes's reaction upon having somewhat atypically reconstructed a broken body: 'It was all *too* closed. [...] And in a way it was quite terrifying.' Rather than strive for this terrifying notion of perfection, which, as in life, will always remain out of reach, one should instead 'let the circumstance decide'. Here: life as process; process as art; art as life. There is logic to the lack.

Following this prioritization of unerring reiteration, of reconfiguration, over faux-unity of form, it is apt that, upon our cognitive completion of these bodies, our avatars (for imaginings are nothing but projections of our own selves)

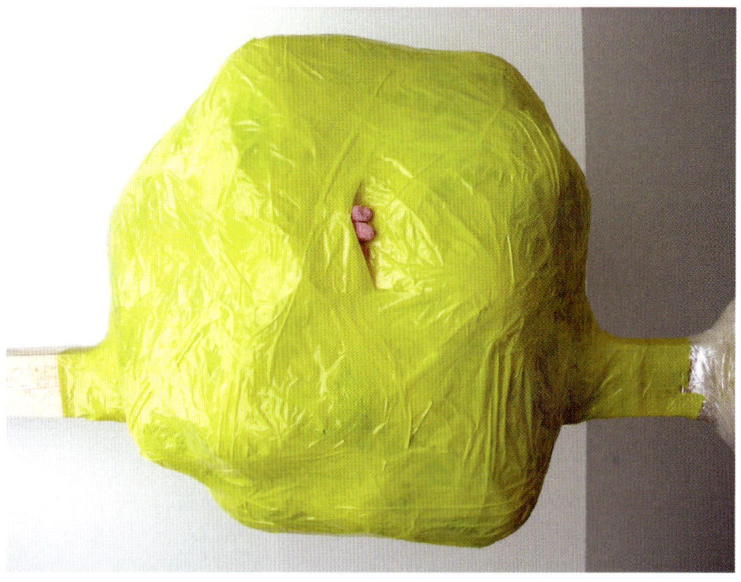

Why Don't You Find Out For Yourself 2003
Mixed media wrapped in parcel tape,
dimensions variable

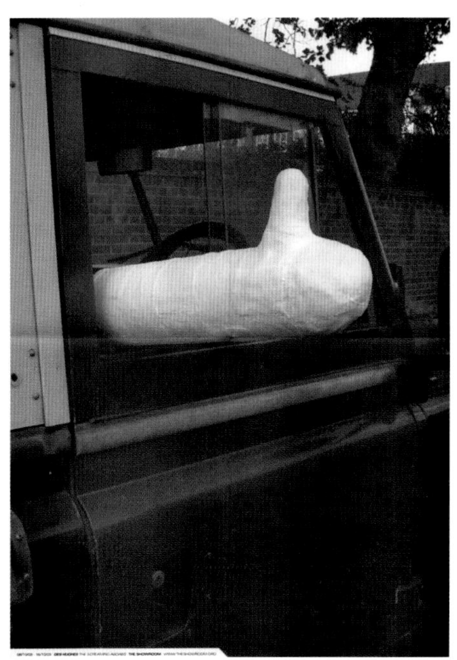

Poster for 'The Screaming Abdabs' solo exhibition at The Showroom, London, 2003

disappear into nothingness, clearing room for other forms to be tried, tested, taken to task, taken apart. Bataille muttered: '[Art] is born of a wound, that does not heal.' And nor is it meant to. Because with the stitching of a wound, with its closing, everything draws to a halt. And nothing ever really draws to a halt, does it? And nothing is ever really defined, is it? Rather, it is constantly reassessed and reworked, and this is what Hughes's absent figures allow for. They are frameworks of possible forms, identities. They are vacant lots upon which one can break down, build up and break down once more. A sprightlier metaphor: they are geckos whose tails are repeatedly lopped to facilitate further (re)growth.

To revisit that title once more: *Why don't you find out for yourself*. Hughes's wanting limbs are a testament to the fact that we will never finish. They are a testament to the fact that we will always have gaps to fill. Here, of course, there is scope for failure (Nochlin's nostalgia), but more astoundingly there is scope for change (her Utopia) – the idea that said filling might herald something far from 'ordinary'. To lift an anonymous quotation that is frequently attributed to the aforementioned surrealists and their aforementioned high jinks: 'the exquisite corpse will drink the new wine'. So get drawing. Connect the lines and see what emerges from the nothingness. See how the new wine tastes.

Phantom Limb 2013
Resin, iron powder and rebar,
68 × 25 × 15 cm

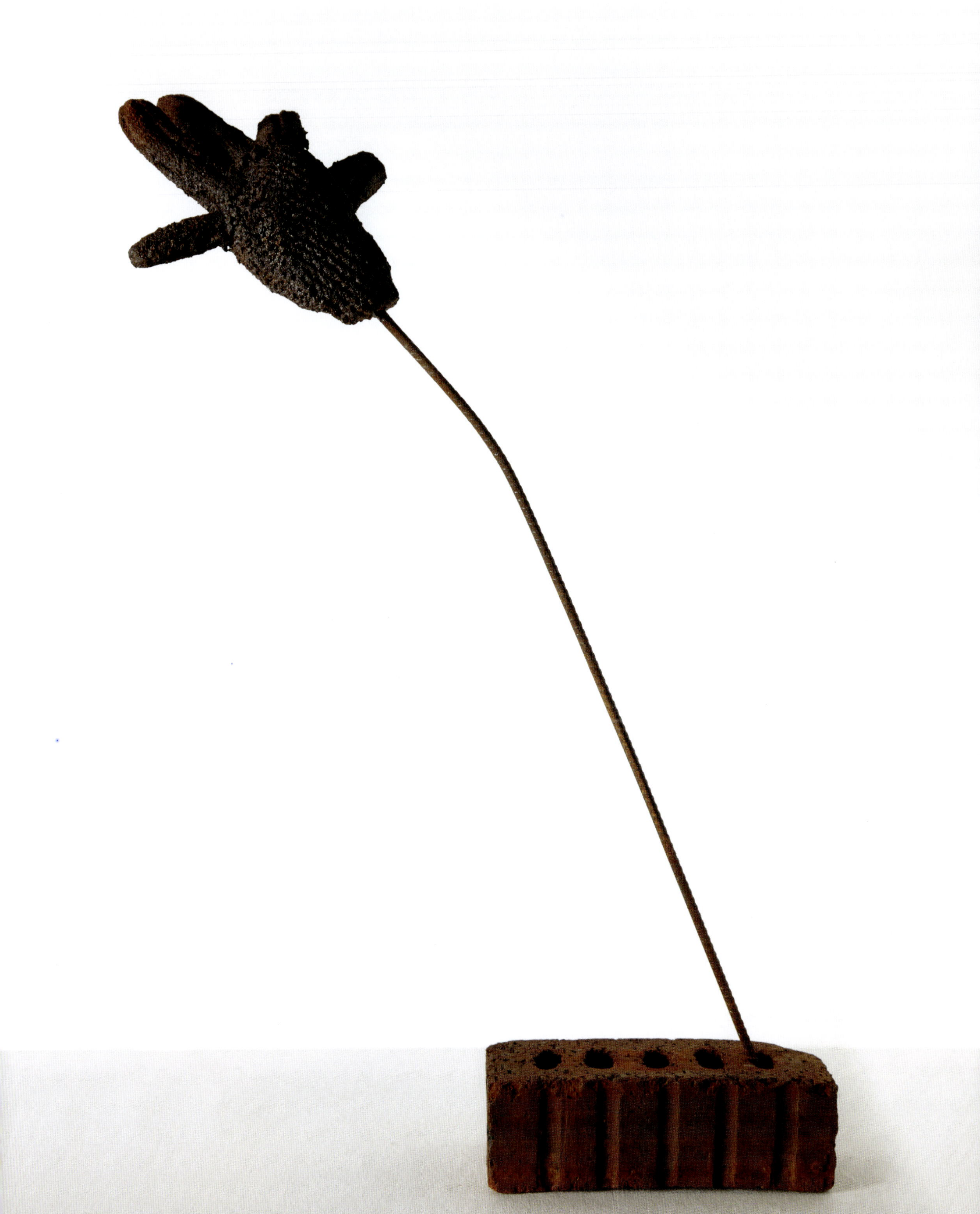

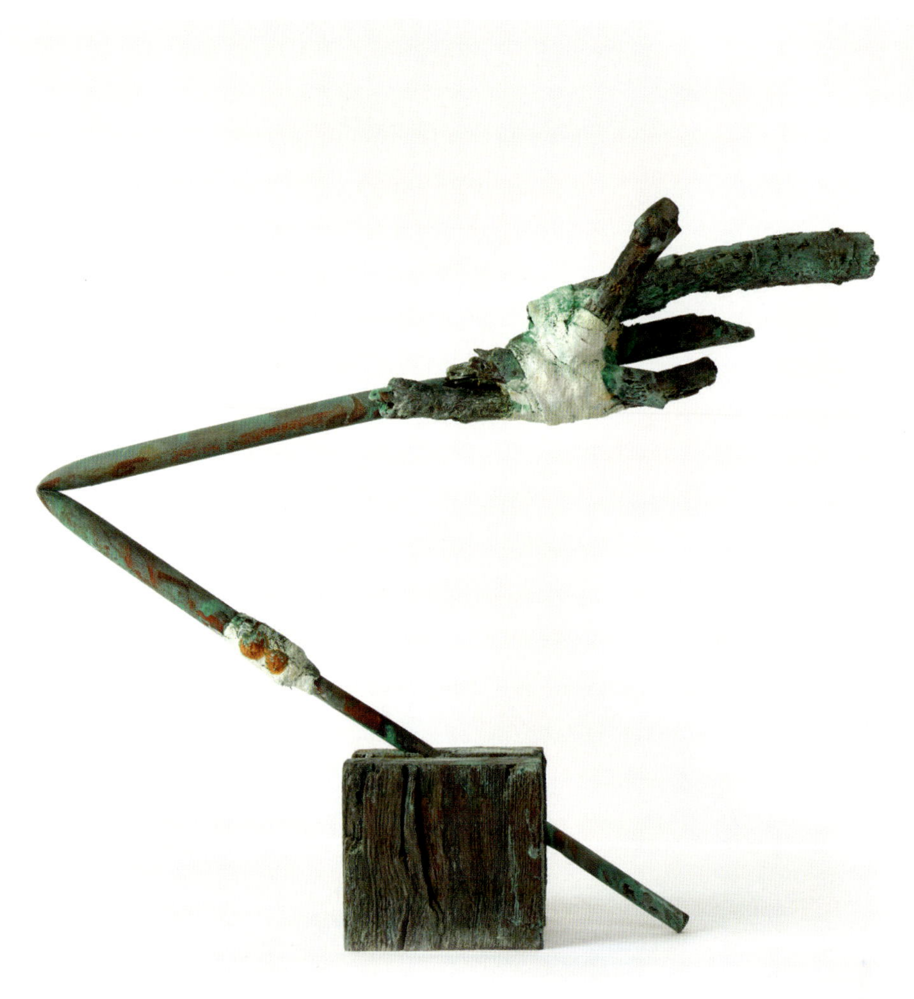

Armature 2013
Resin, copper powder, plaster bandage and copper pipe, 53 × 60 × 20 cm

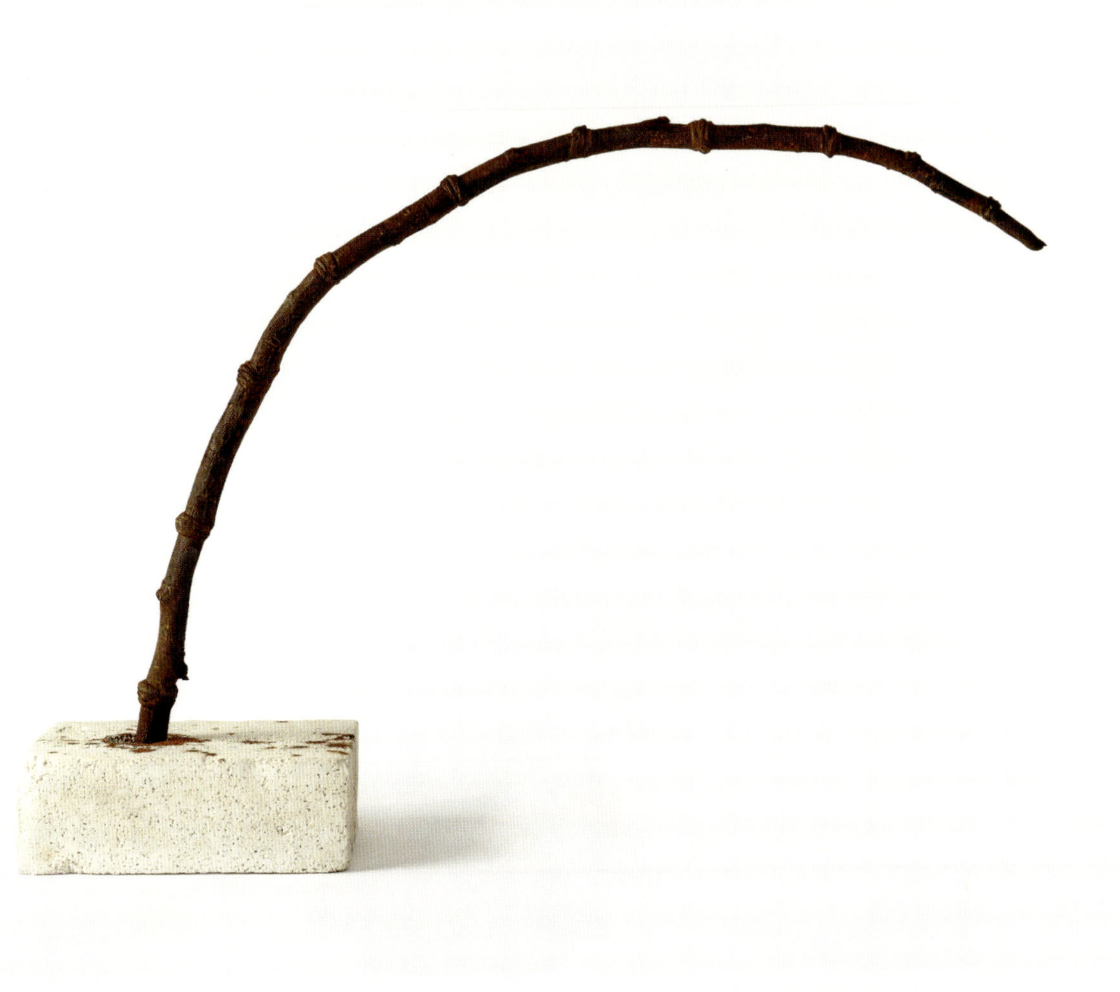

this and following spread
Lively Needle 2013
Resin, iron powder and plaster,
55 × 75 × 22 cm

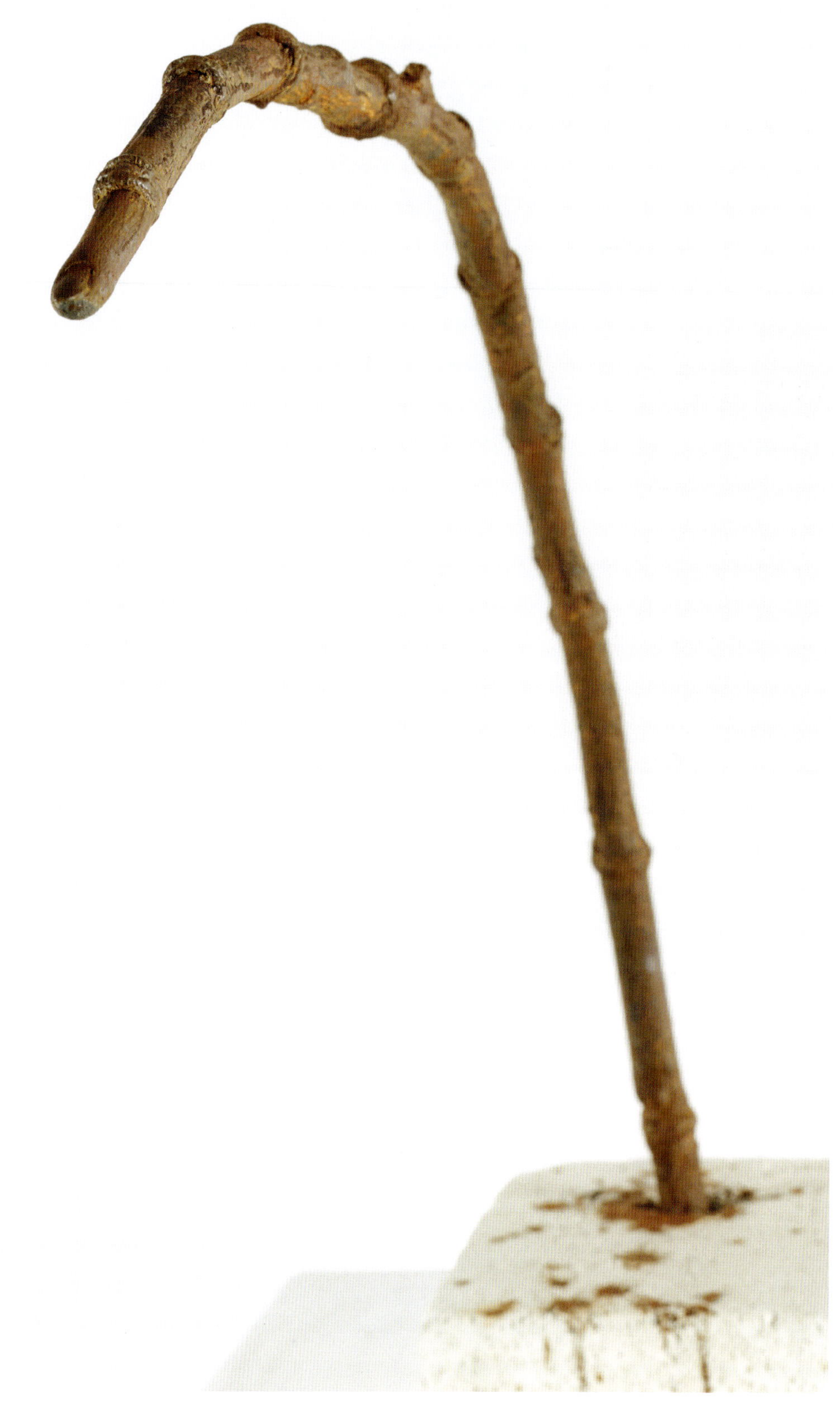

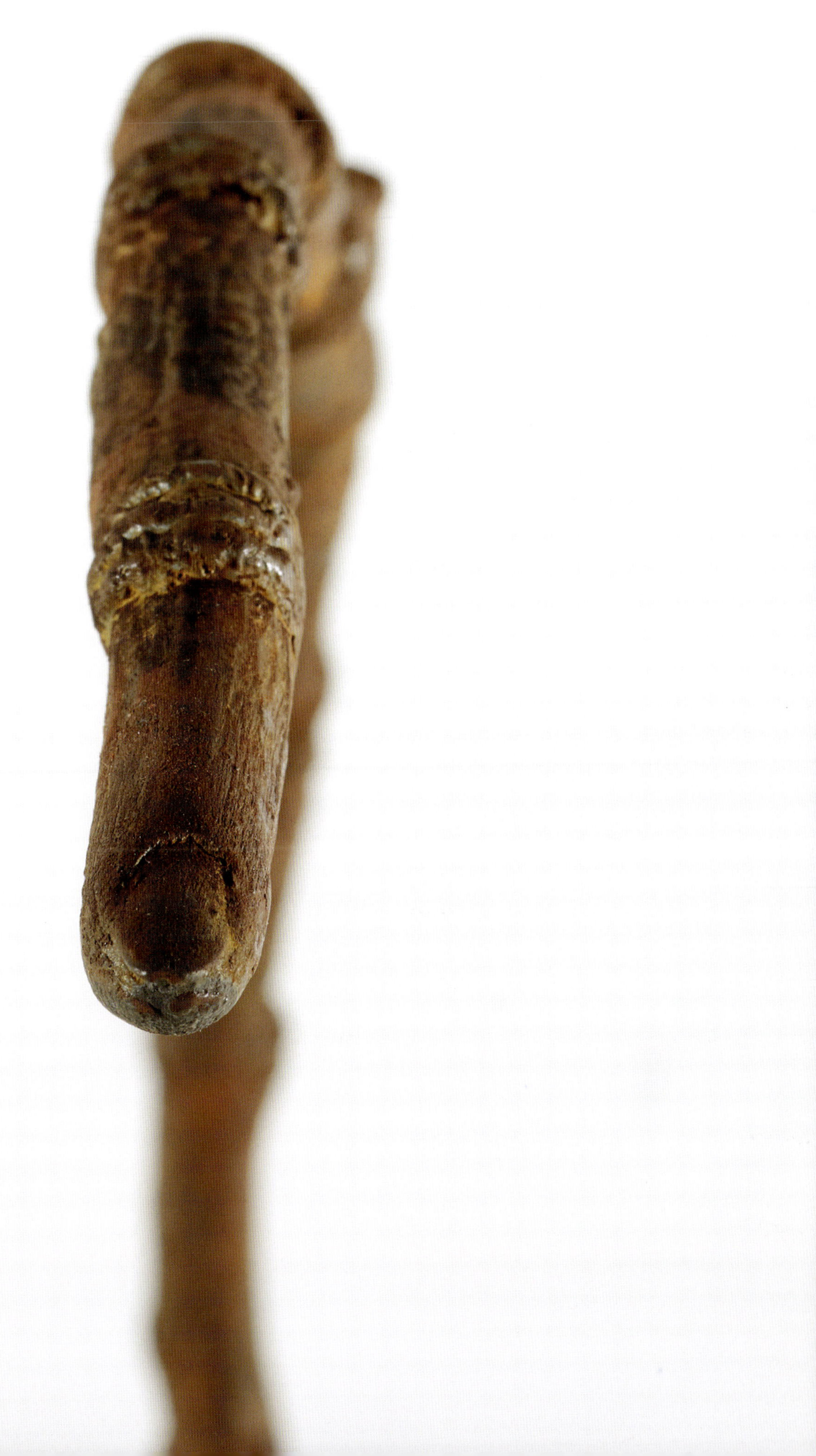

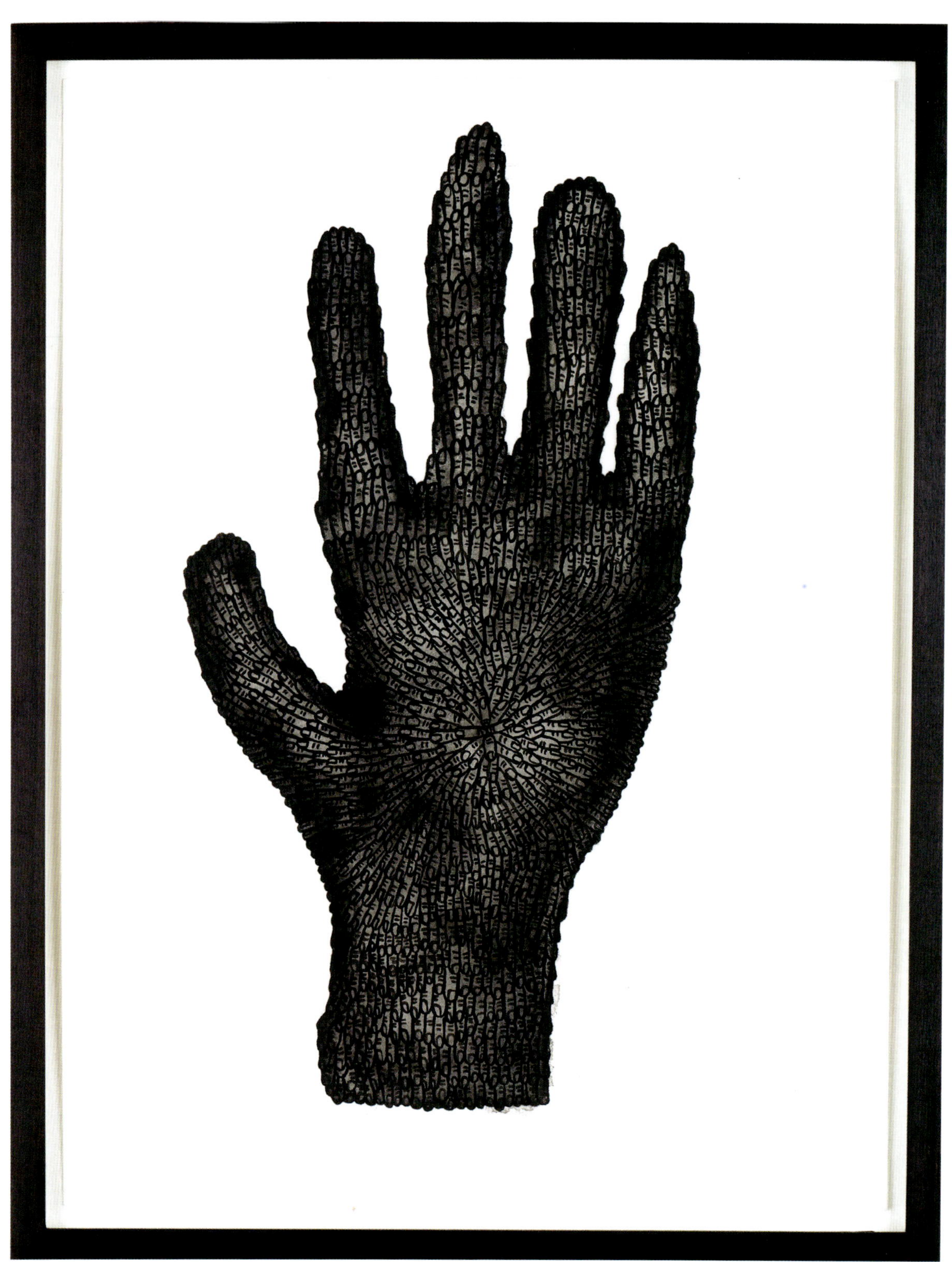

Finger Hand 2010
Watercolour on paper,
28 × 17 cm

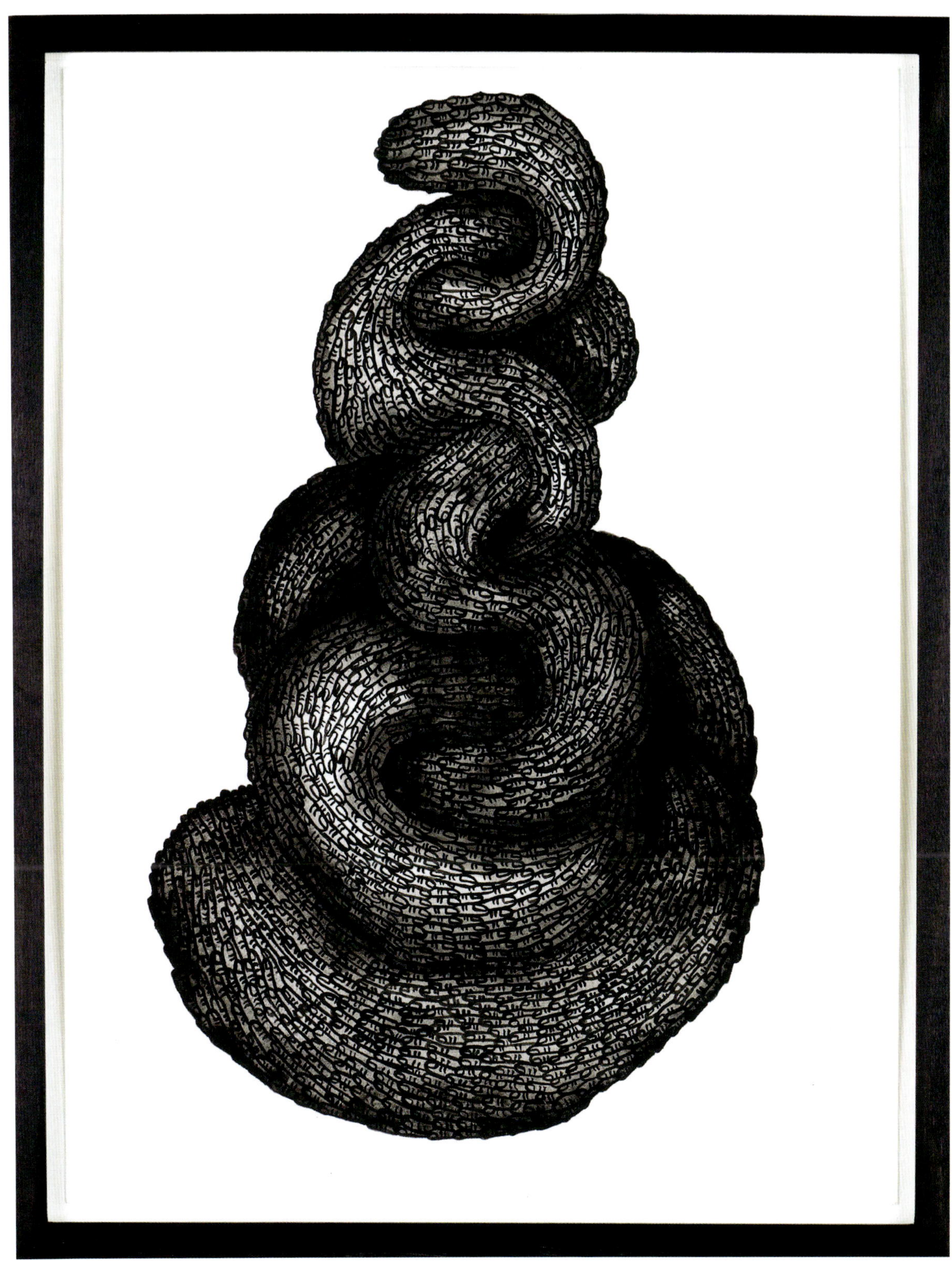

Finger Thing 2010
Watercolour on paper,
28 × 17 cm

Pile of Fingers 2004
Jesmonite and pigment,
each 10 × 1.5 × 1.5 cm

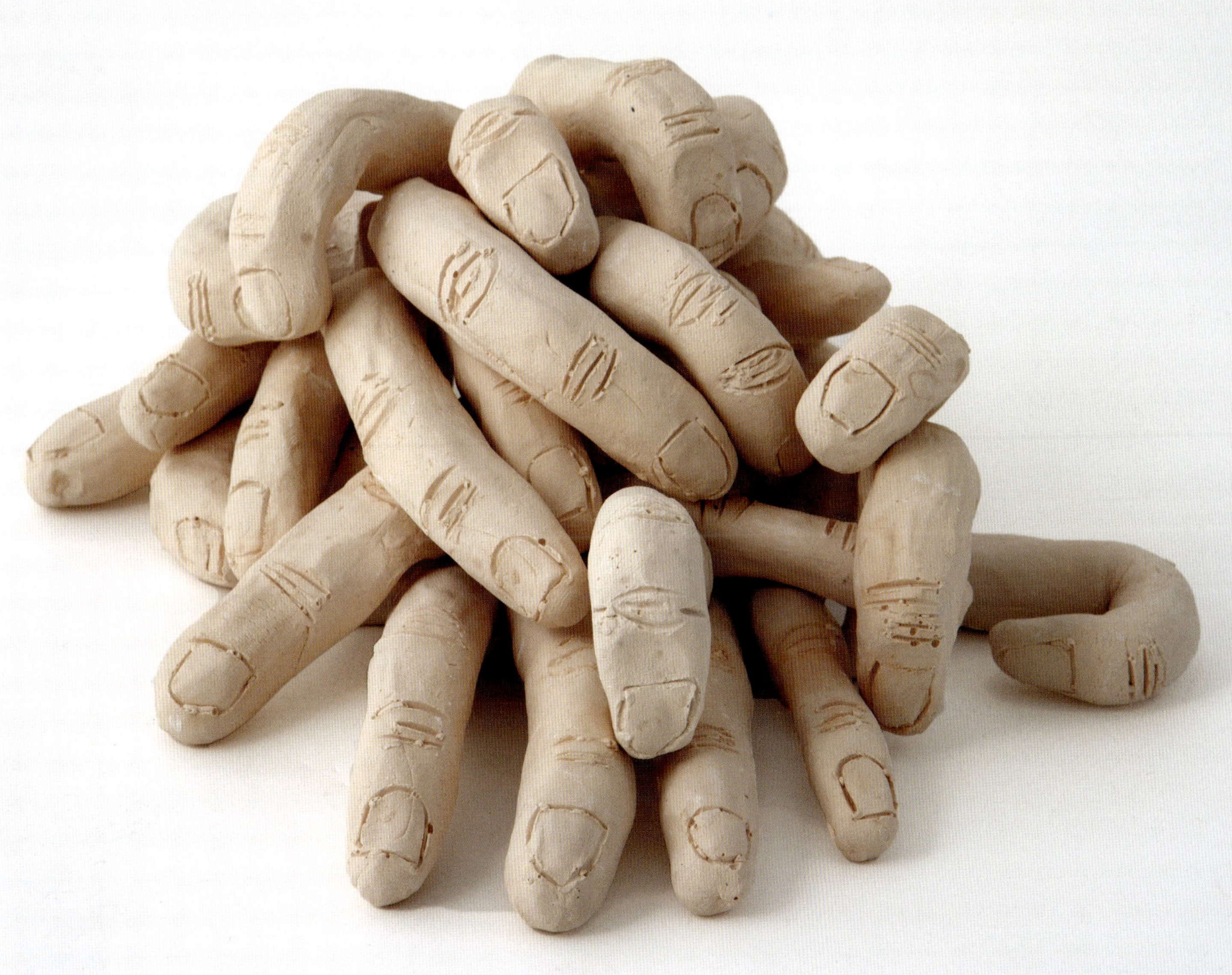

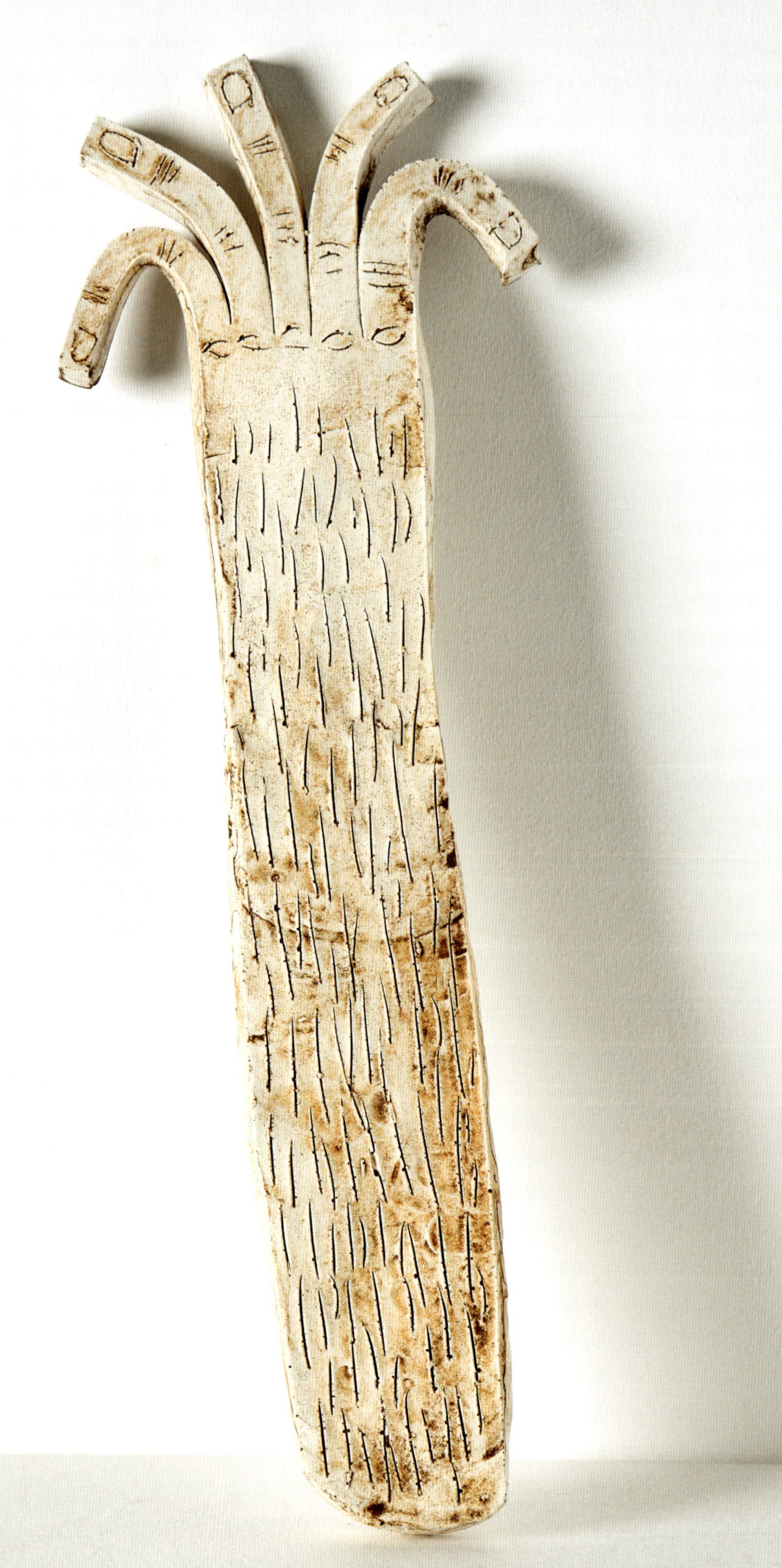

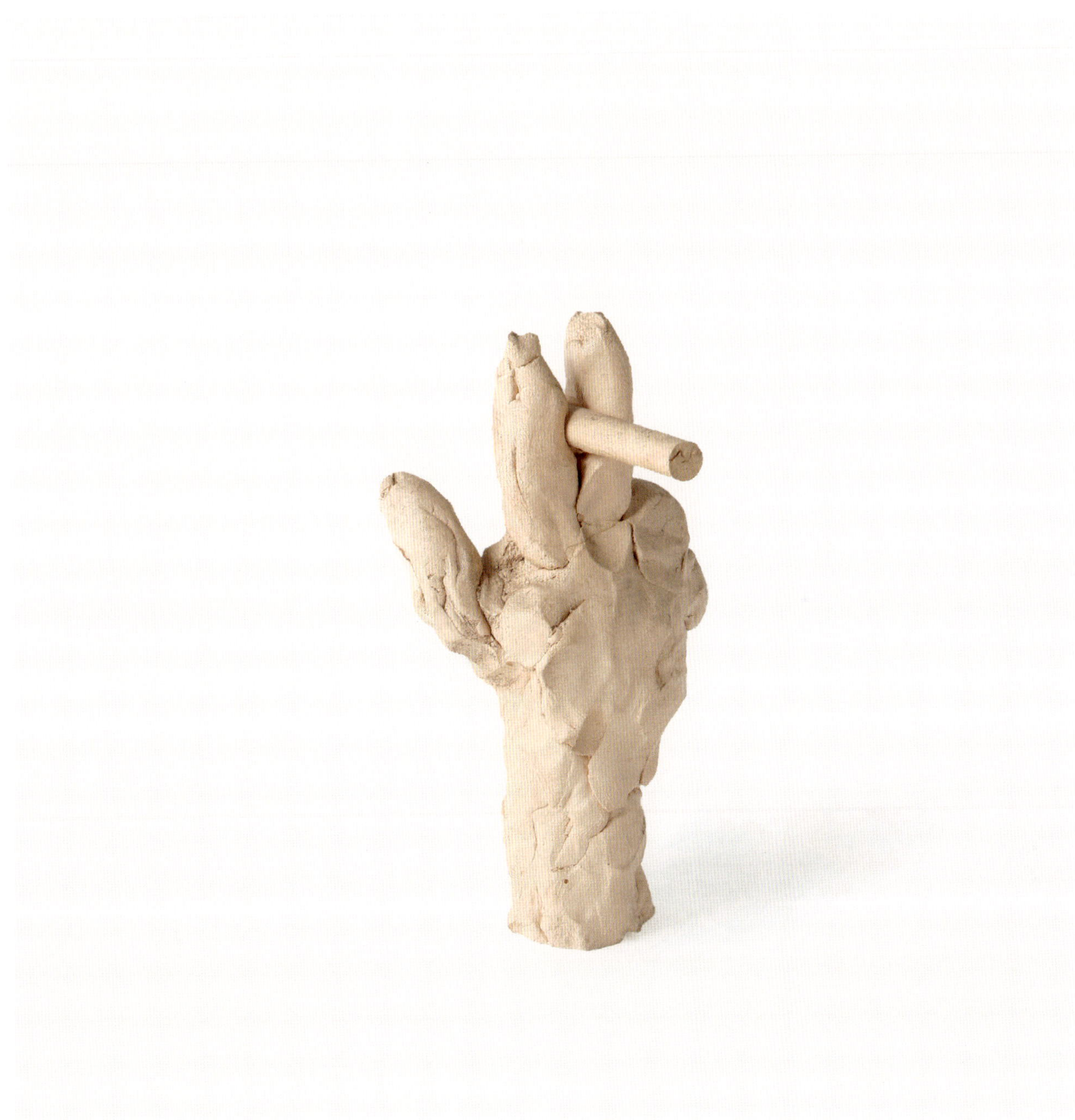

above

Your Smoking Hand 2002
Plaster and pigment,
35 × 18 × 8 cm

opposite

Hairy Hand 2015
Plaster and iron powder,
2 × 52 × 18 cm

'I have always been obsessed by the film *The Wicker Man*. We even had the music played at our wedding. I found out that the Hand of Glory scene was based on the old belief that if one placed a lighted candle in the cut-off left hand of a hanged murderer – one made from the fat of his corpse – it would make anyone present motionless and sleep the "sleep of the dead". I really wanted to try this out and so decided to make one in the studio. But without access to the hand of a murderer, I opted instead for a wax version. I also liked the link to the practice of making plaster casts of artists' hands as an insight into their genius, and the way in which both religious artefacts and art objects are transformed by a particular set of beliefs. The problem with the wax hand was that it was perfect for the first few minutes, exactly as I had intended, but then it started to disappear. As a result, I had to explore many combinations of materials and apparatus just to sustain this effect and make the sculpture permanent.'

Hand of Glory 2007
Candle wax, pigment and string,
30 × 15 × 5 cm

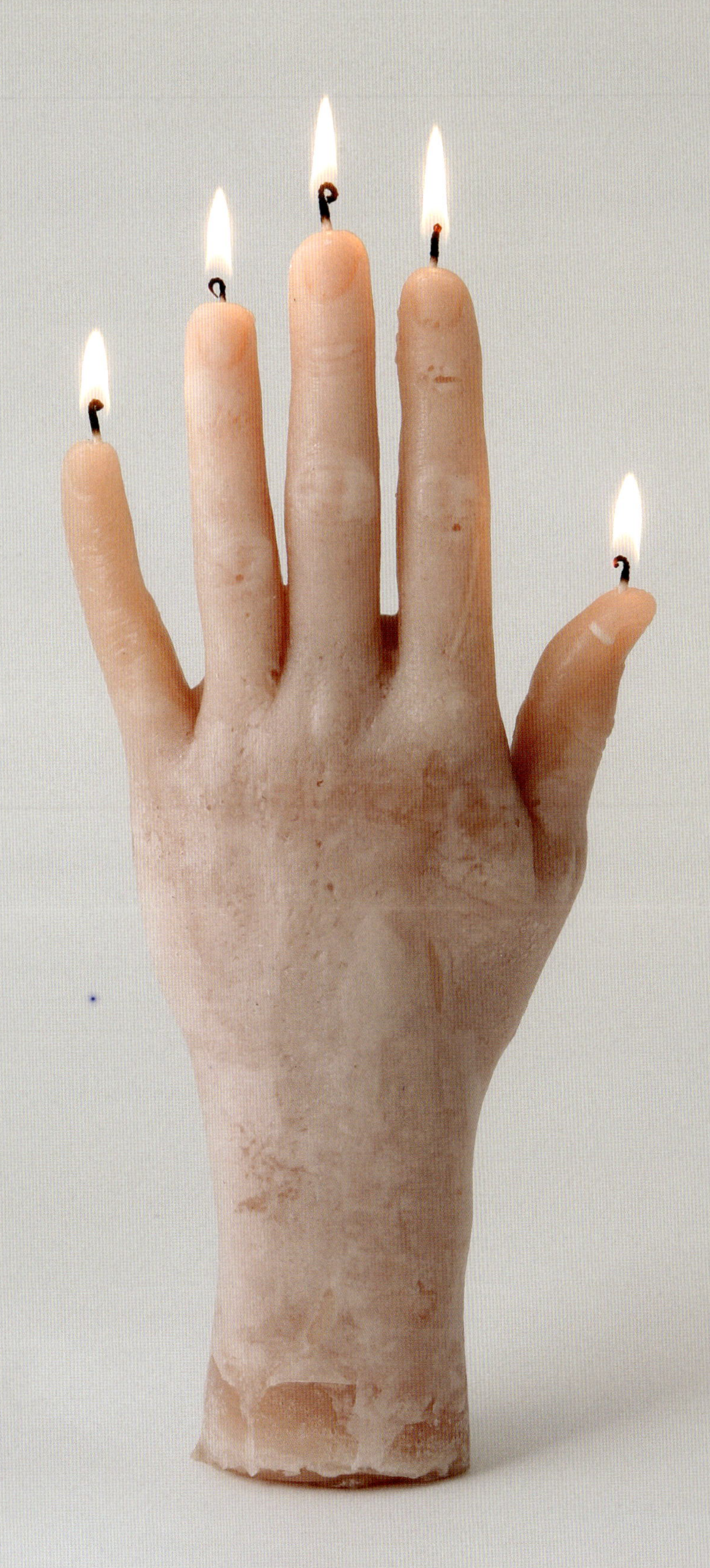

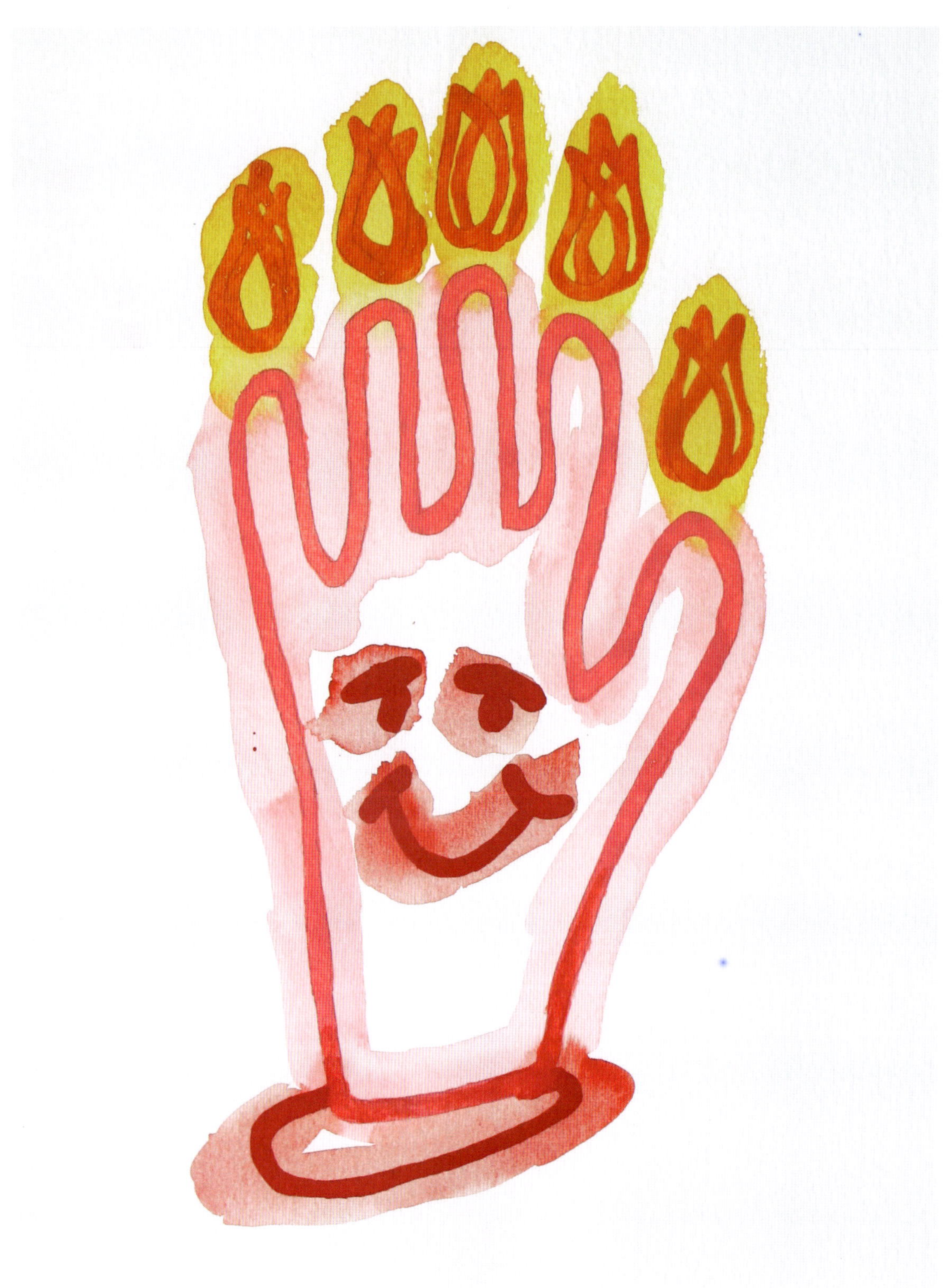

Watercolour For Neon Hand 2012
Watercolour on paper,
40 × 30.5 cm

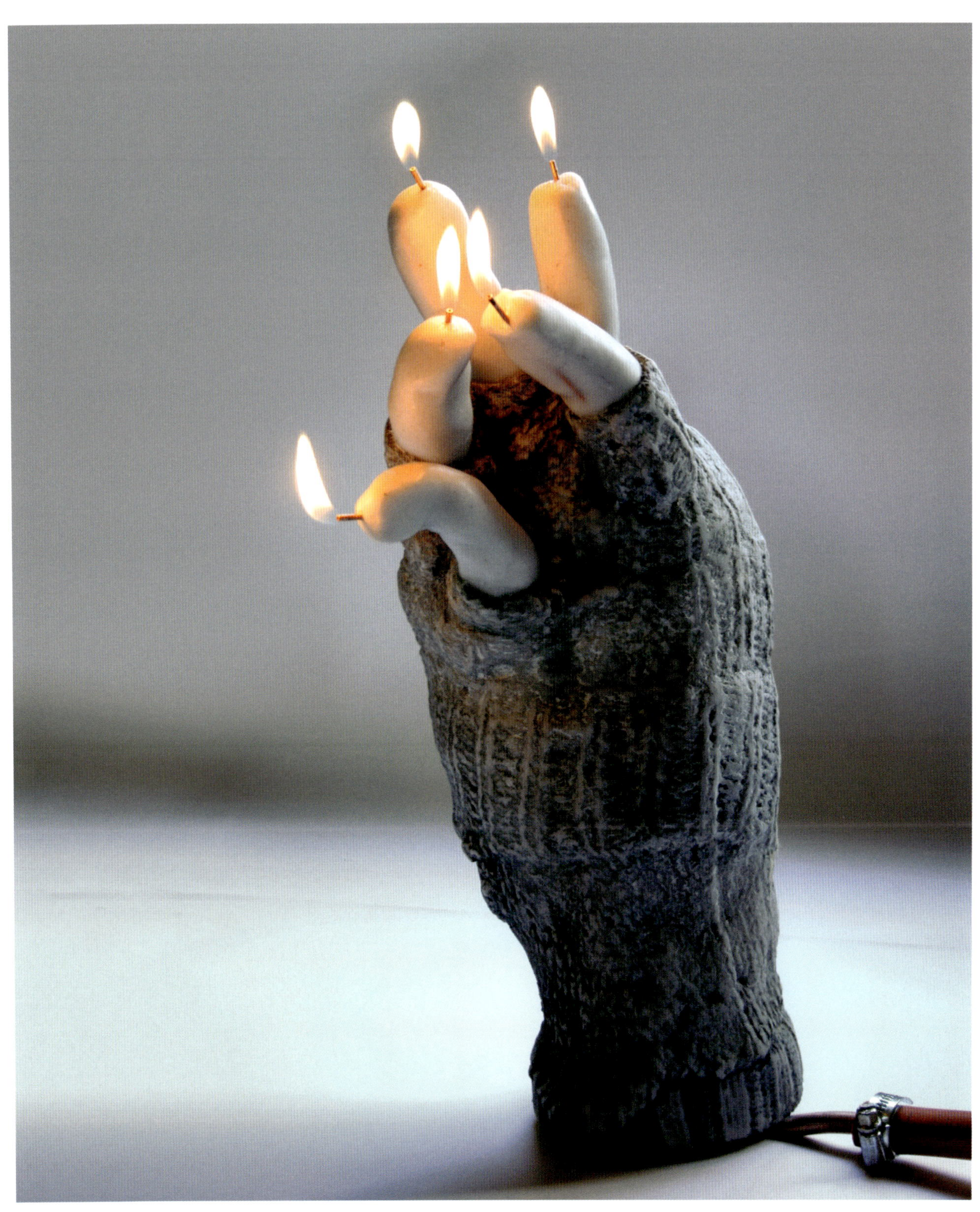

Idiot Fingers 2007
Resin, marble powder, copper pipe and butane canister,
36 × 16 × 14 cm

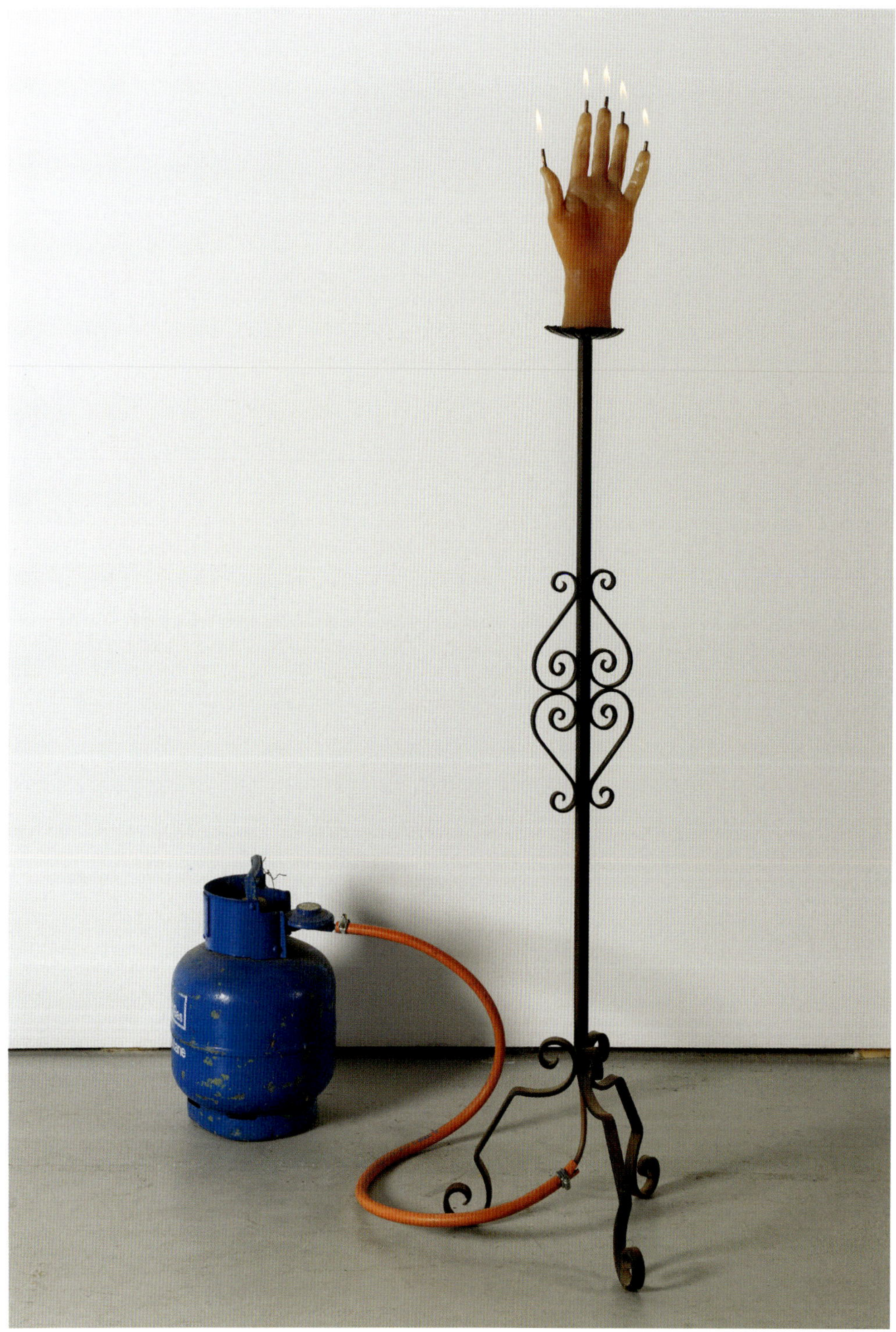

above

Working Model for a Gas-Powered Hand of Glory 2003

Resin, copper pipe, iron stand and butane canister, 147 × 32 × 32 cm

opposite

'Des Hughes' 2007

Ancient & Modern, London

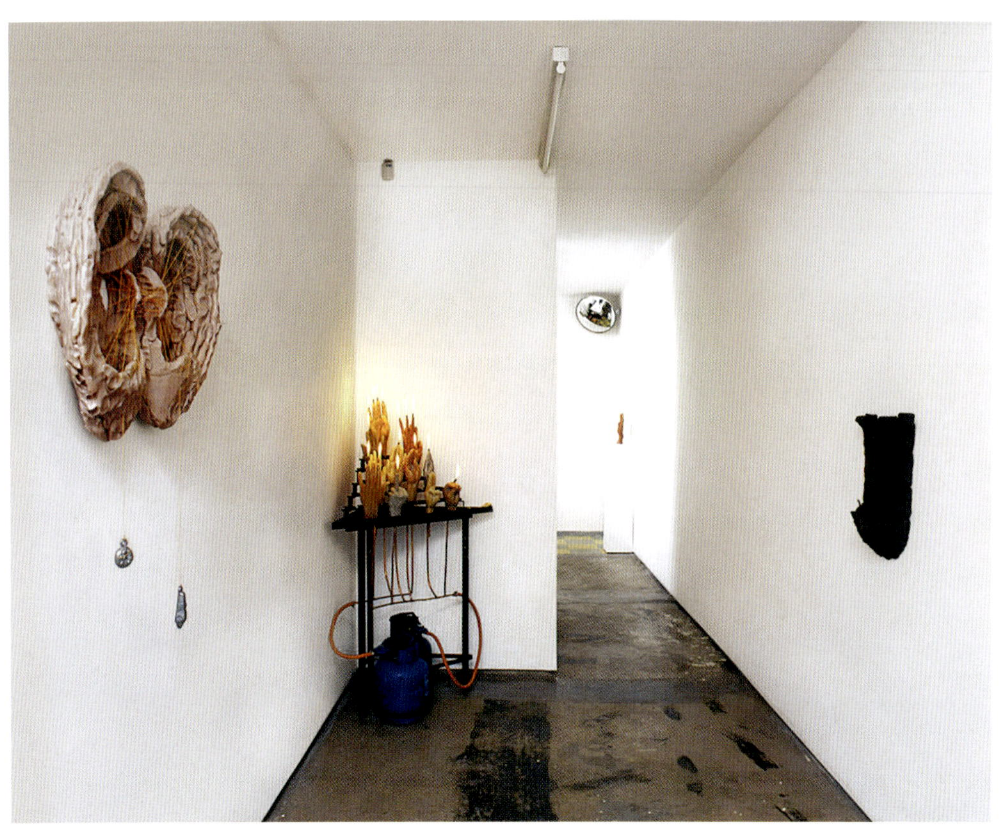

'For this show at Ancient & Modern, I found a triangular votive stand from a church, still with its money box, to use as a base for multiple *Hands of Glory*. I had this theory that for the spell to work, for the burning candle to make those present sleep the "sleep of the dead", it would be largely due to an act of faith on the part of everyone involved (a bit like the act of faith involved in believing in art). The work was connected to two butane canisters, and so actually had the effect of making everyone working in the gallery feel sick and sleepy.'

'I model ears (and hands) in the studio without even thinking about it. It's a kind of mindless doodling when I can't think of anything else to make. On the one hand, it requires a minimum of work before it achieves a likeness, a lazy shorthand; but more importantly, it allows you to indulge in the gestural potential of the material without being too earnest. At college everyone in the sculpture department had lots of piercings in their ears and I thought that this would be a good way to attach these sculptures to the wall. So for years I collected every brass-coloured fixing that I could find. It looks like cheap gold. I also used these fixings in *Middle Ear* to attach string that I then fed through holes to form a criss-cross pattern. The result is like those pictures we used to make in school by wrapping string around nails. It is also a reference to my favourite strung works by Henry Moore and Barbara Hepworth.'

Middle Ear 2007
Resin, marble powder, pigment, nylon string and lead,
13 × 60 × 51 cm

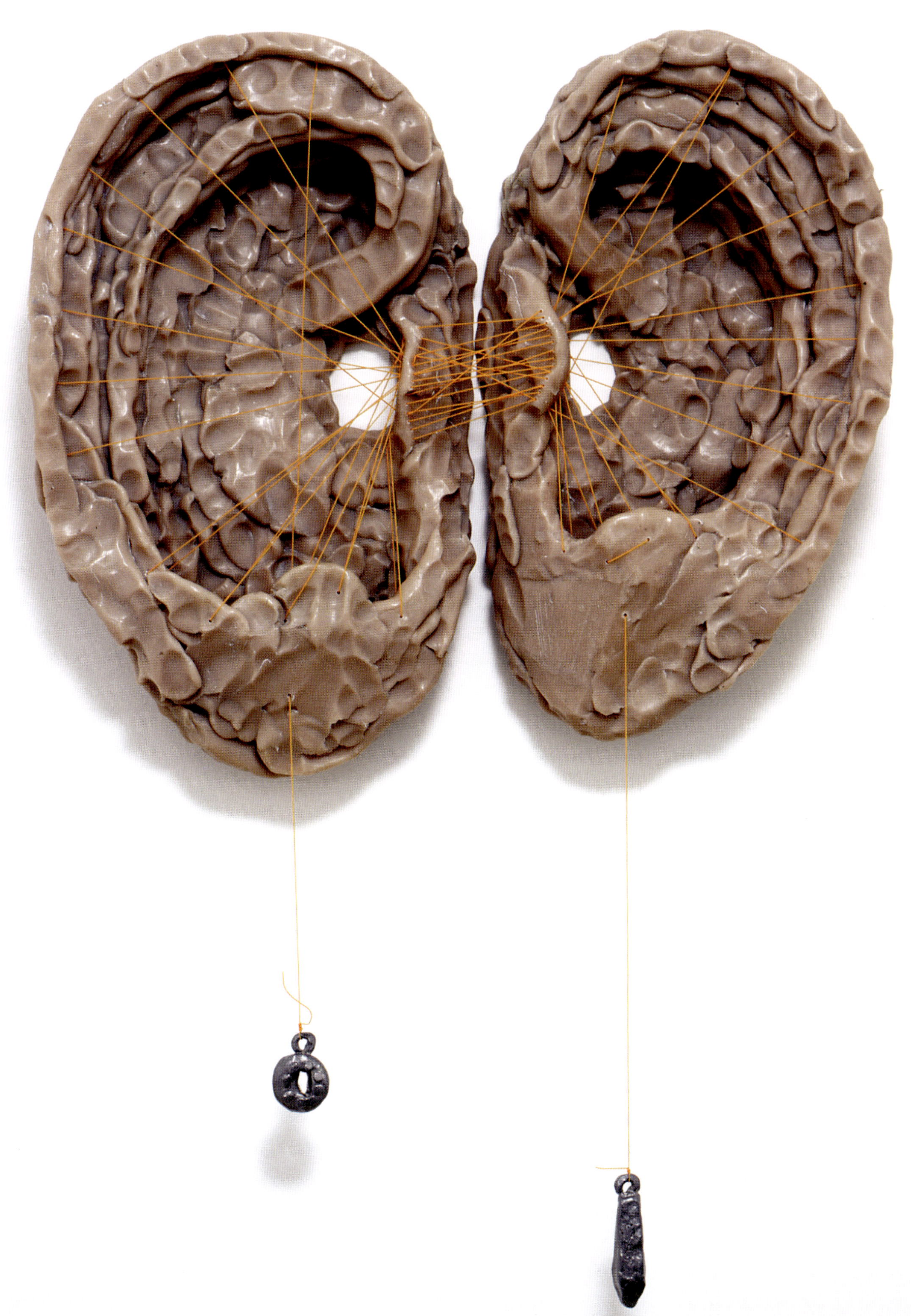

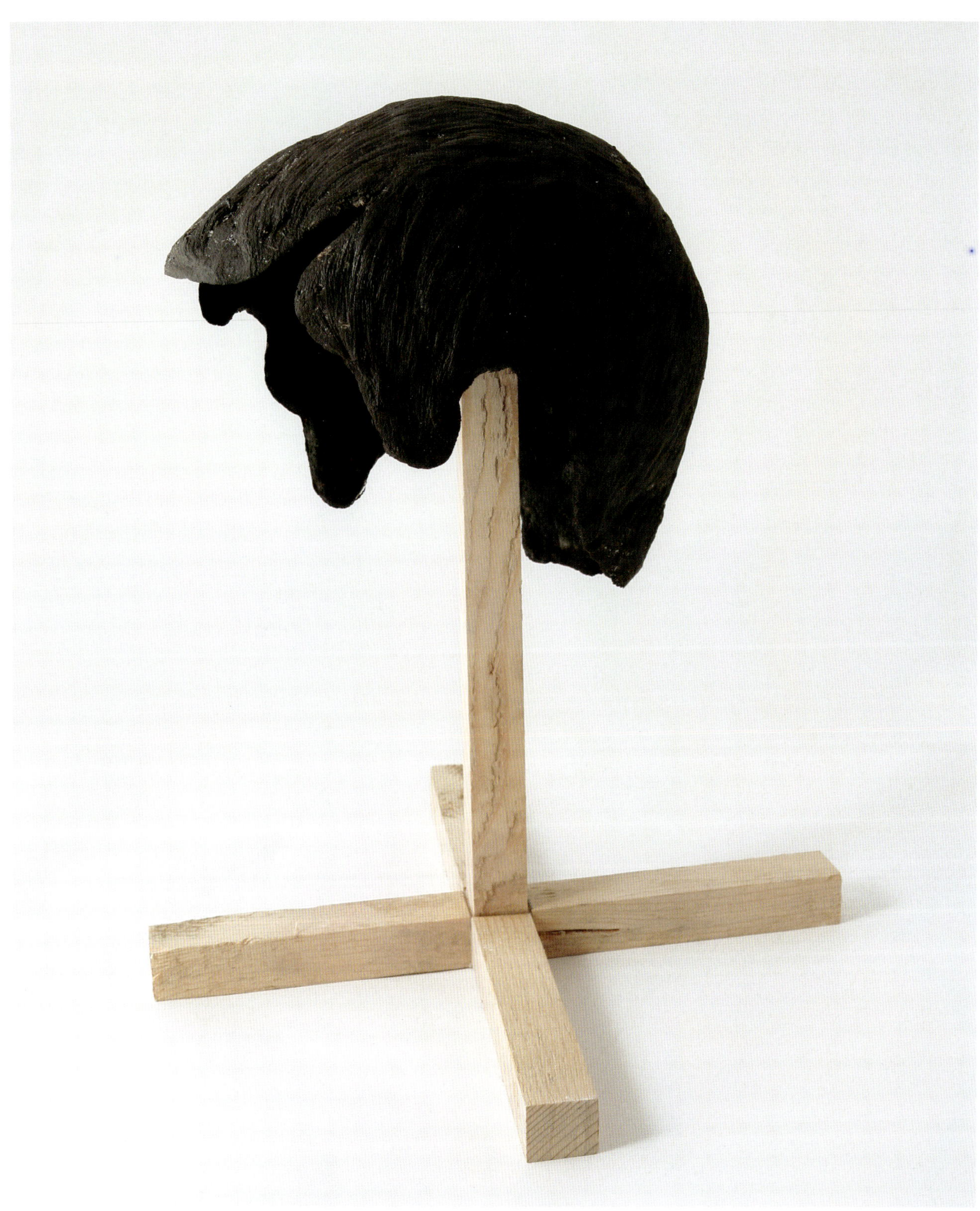

Wig 1995
Latex cast of artist's head
on wooden stand, life-size

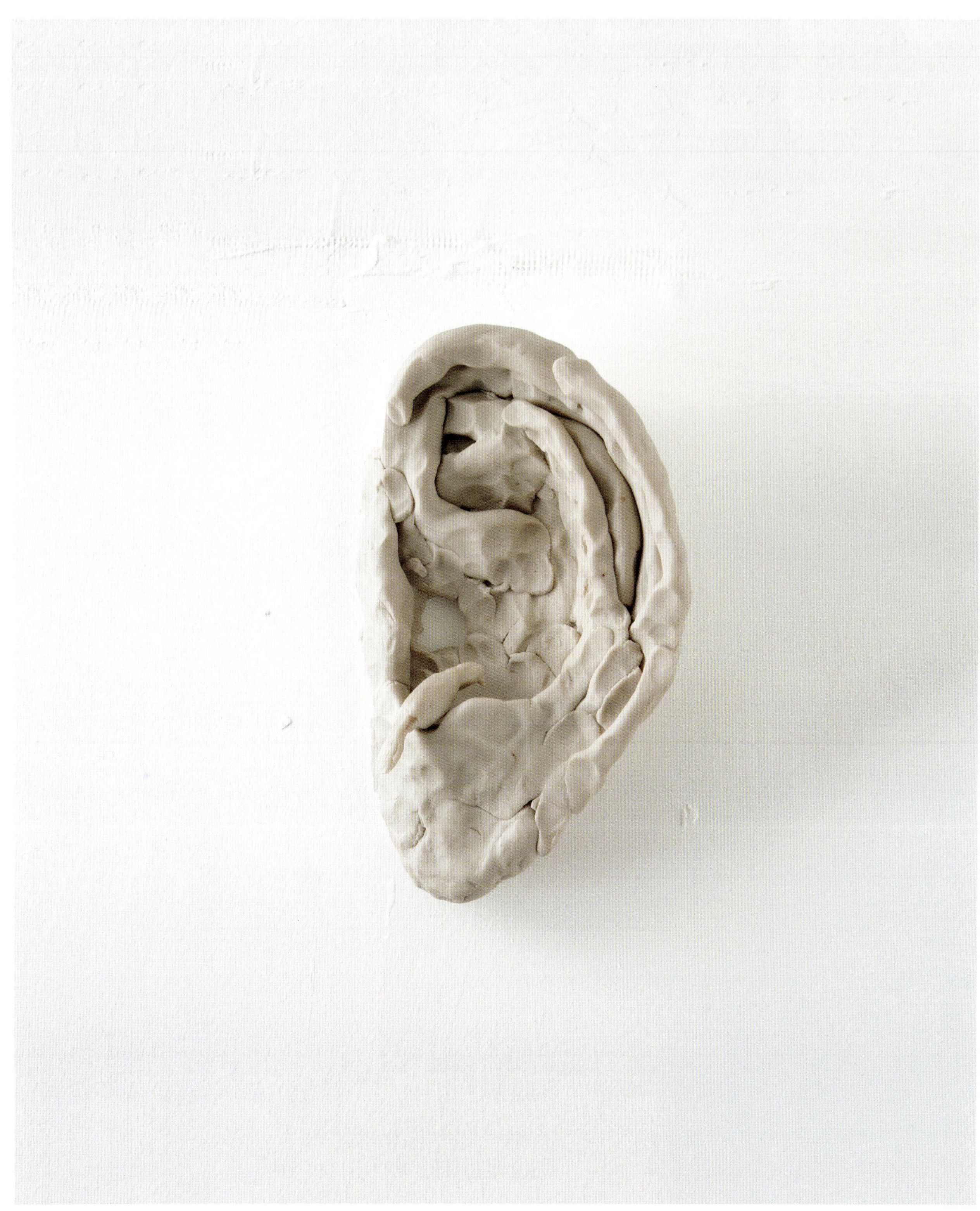

Model for Sing Me To Sleep 2003
Resin, marble powder and water,
26 × 18 × 10 cm

'For one life-size rubber ear, I wanted a chewed stub of a pencil to prop behind it. I had some made with my name printed on them on as a way of signing the work. I only wanted one pencil, but I had to order a thousand, so I was giving them away like promotional gifts for years. I think this work neatly illustrated the idea that a good way to make a sculpture is to keep taking things away until the point where it starts to disappear. But also the crucial emotional relationship that can occur between the various parts, how they justify why each is included. The rubber ear needs the screws that are there to attach the work to the wall, but these also help to suggest that it is a pierced ear, as well as being a convenient place to poke a pencil, which signs it and might help to define it as a sculpture.'

left

Des Hughes Pencils 2003
Pencils, 80 × 180 × 80 cm

opposite

In Just Seven Days I Can Make You A Man 2003
Rubber, pigment, pencil and screws, 10 × 9 × 1 cm

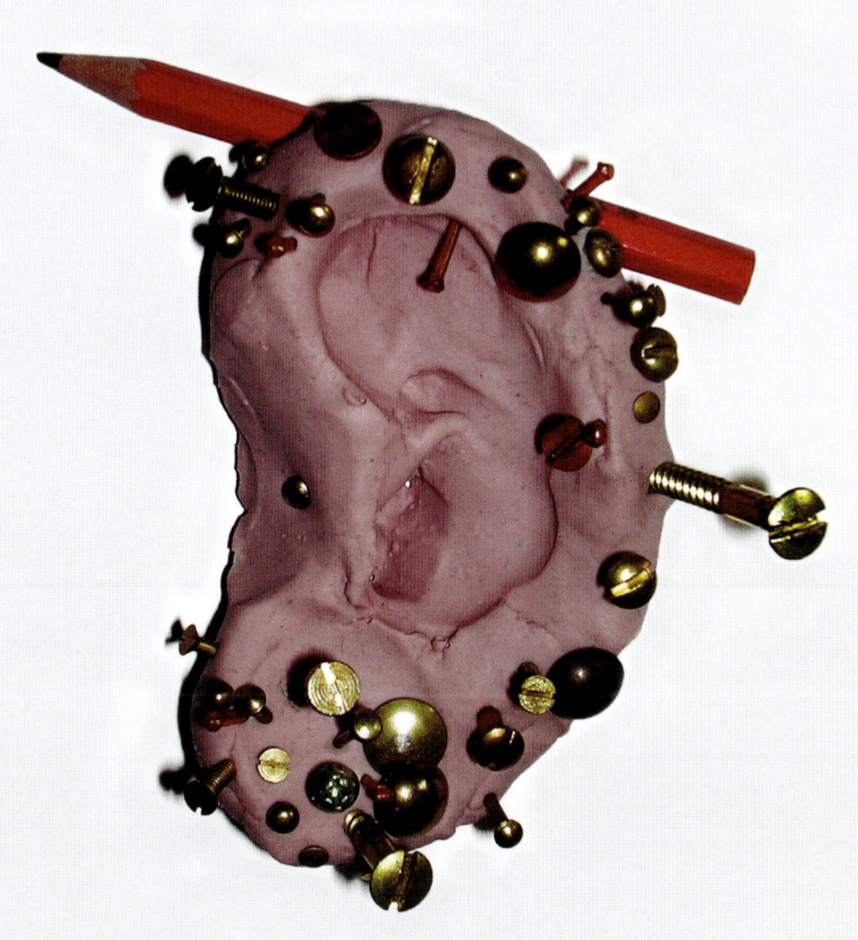

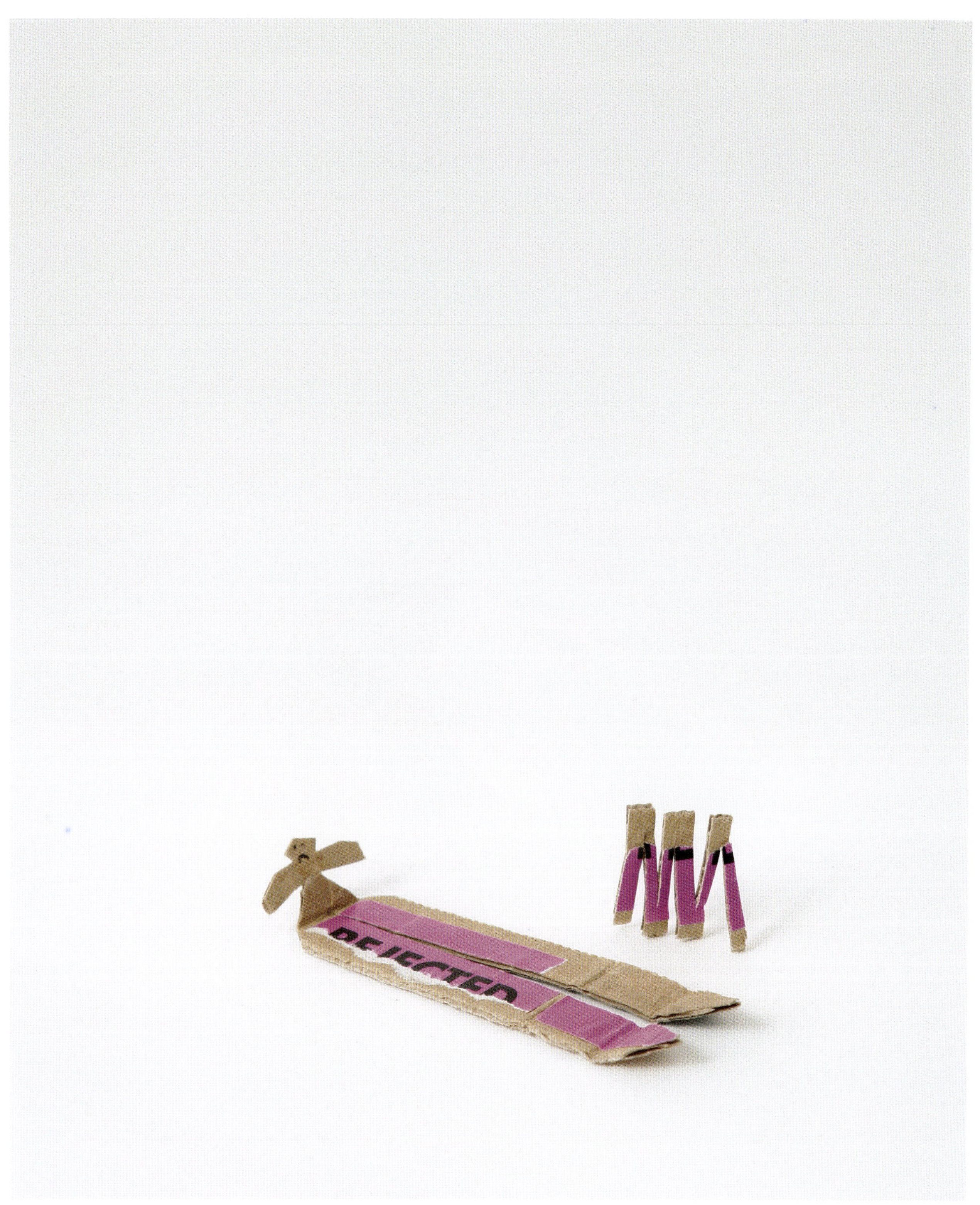

An Industrial Accident 1995
Cardboard, stickers and pen,
2 × 9 × 2 cm

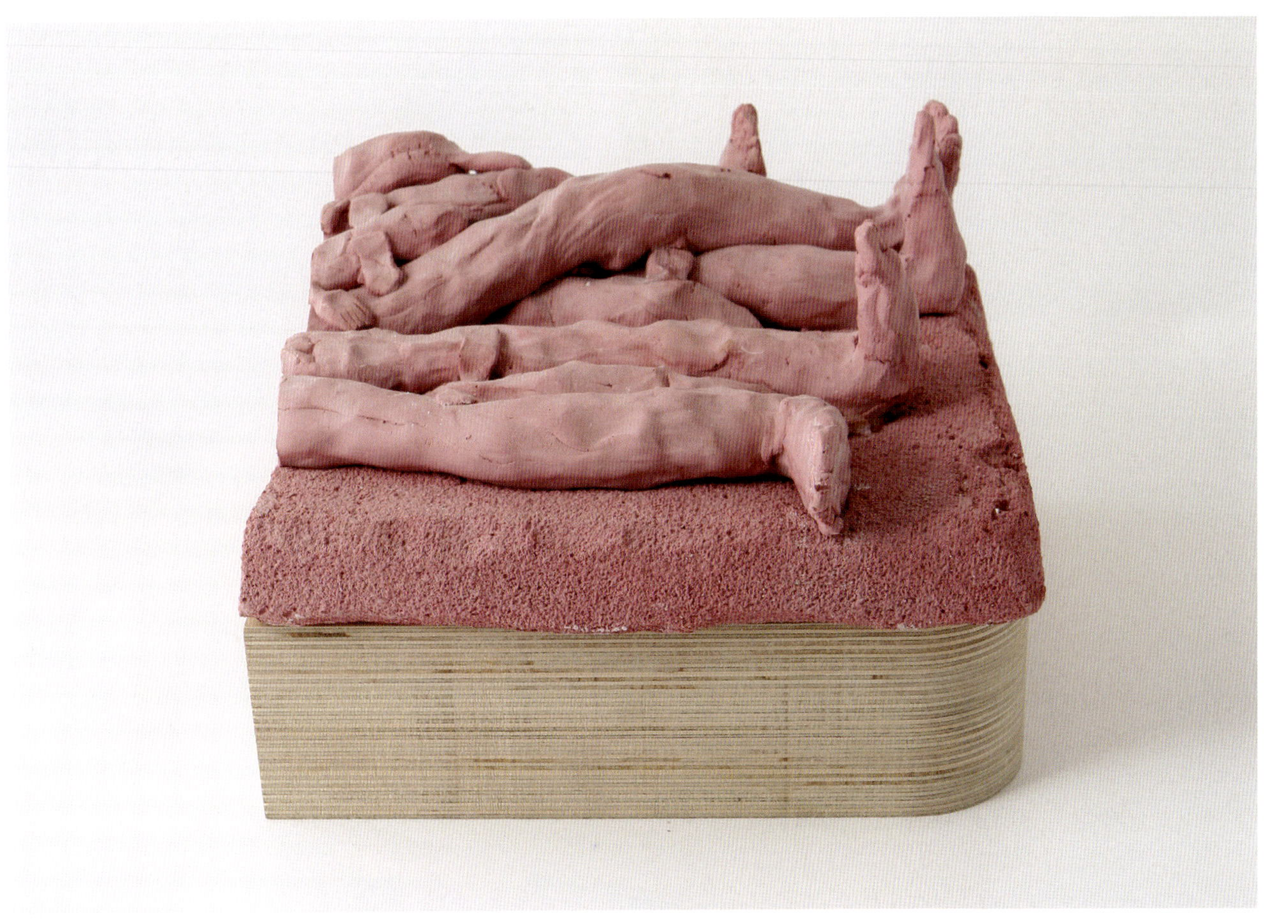

Dogs and Legs 2003
Jesmonite, pigment and wood,
17 × 25 × 23 cm

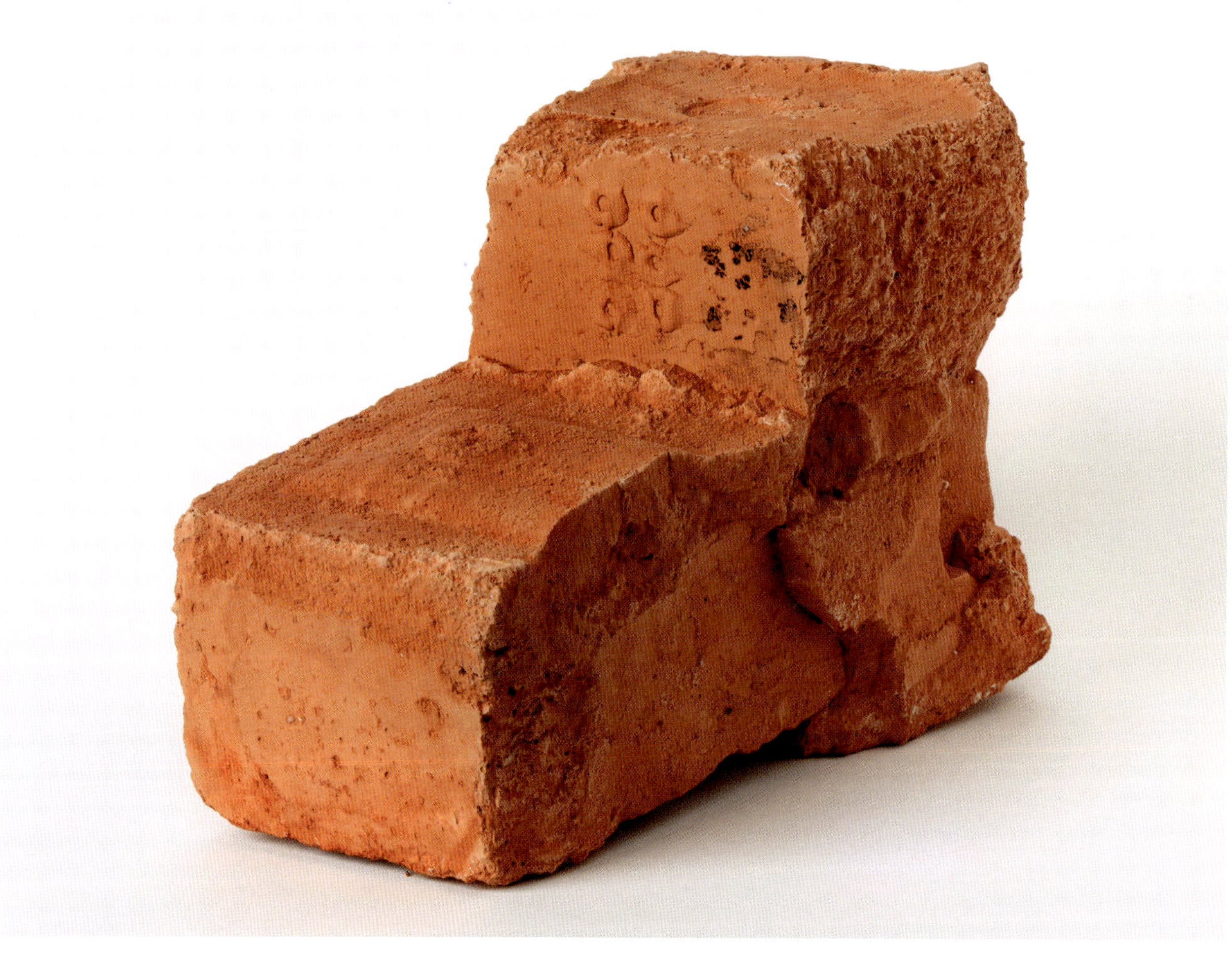

Cherry 2015
Jesmonite and terracotta powder,
18 × 22 × 12 cm

Big Foot 2001
Plaster,
24 × 35 × 19 cm

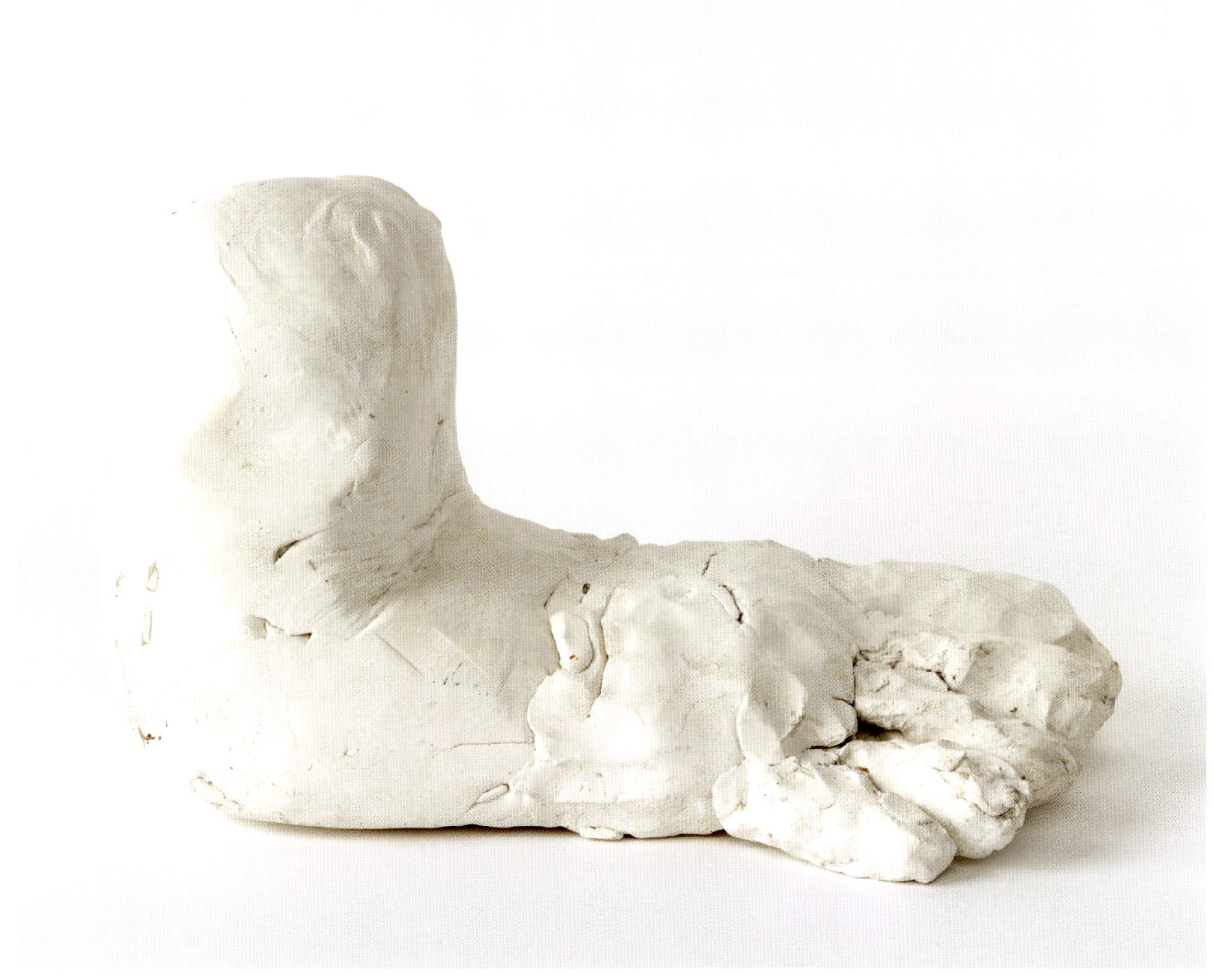

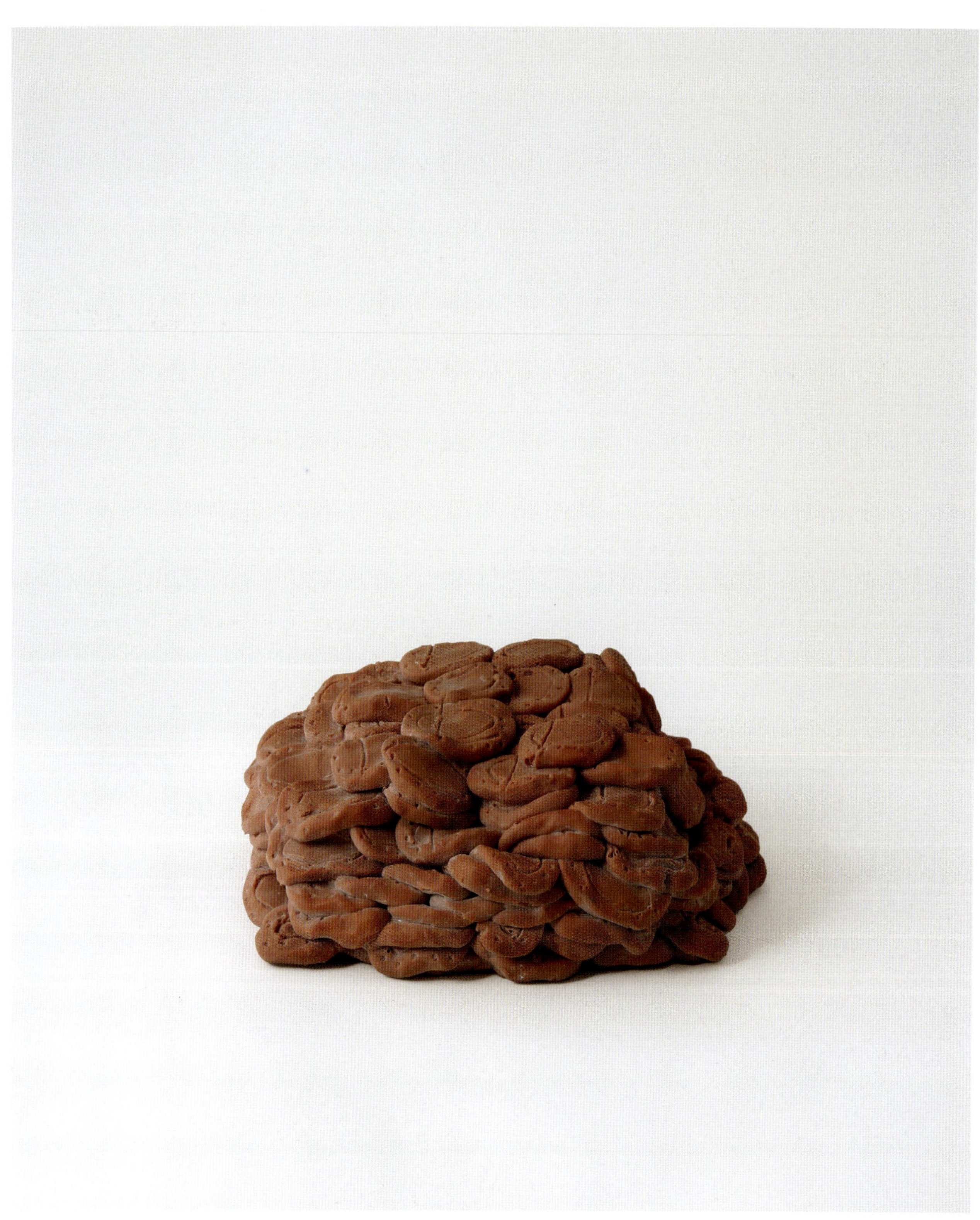

Guston Pile 2000
Latex and pigment,
21 × 10 × 10 cm

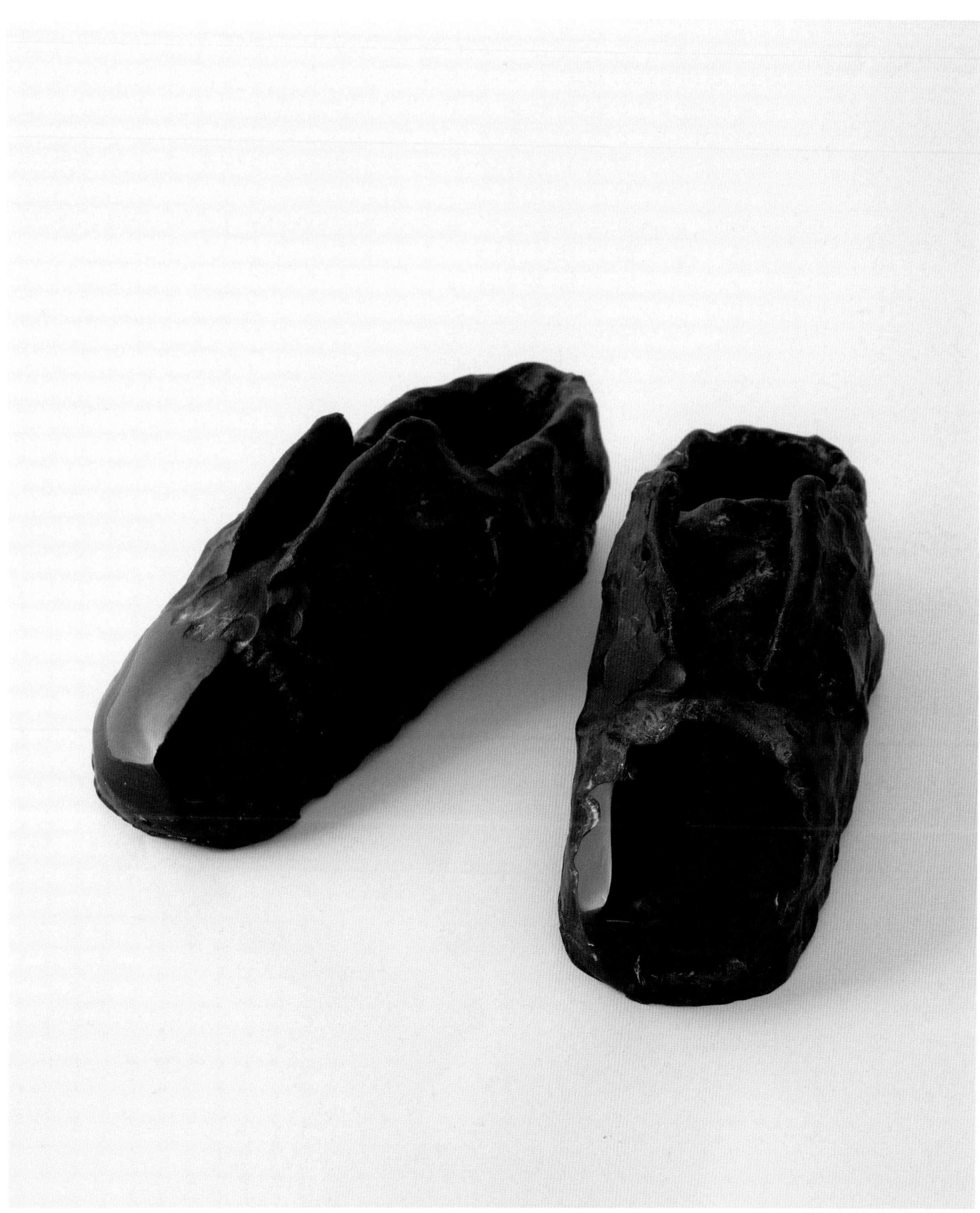

Polished Shoes 2006
Resin and pigment,
9 × 9 × 21 cm

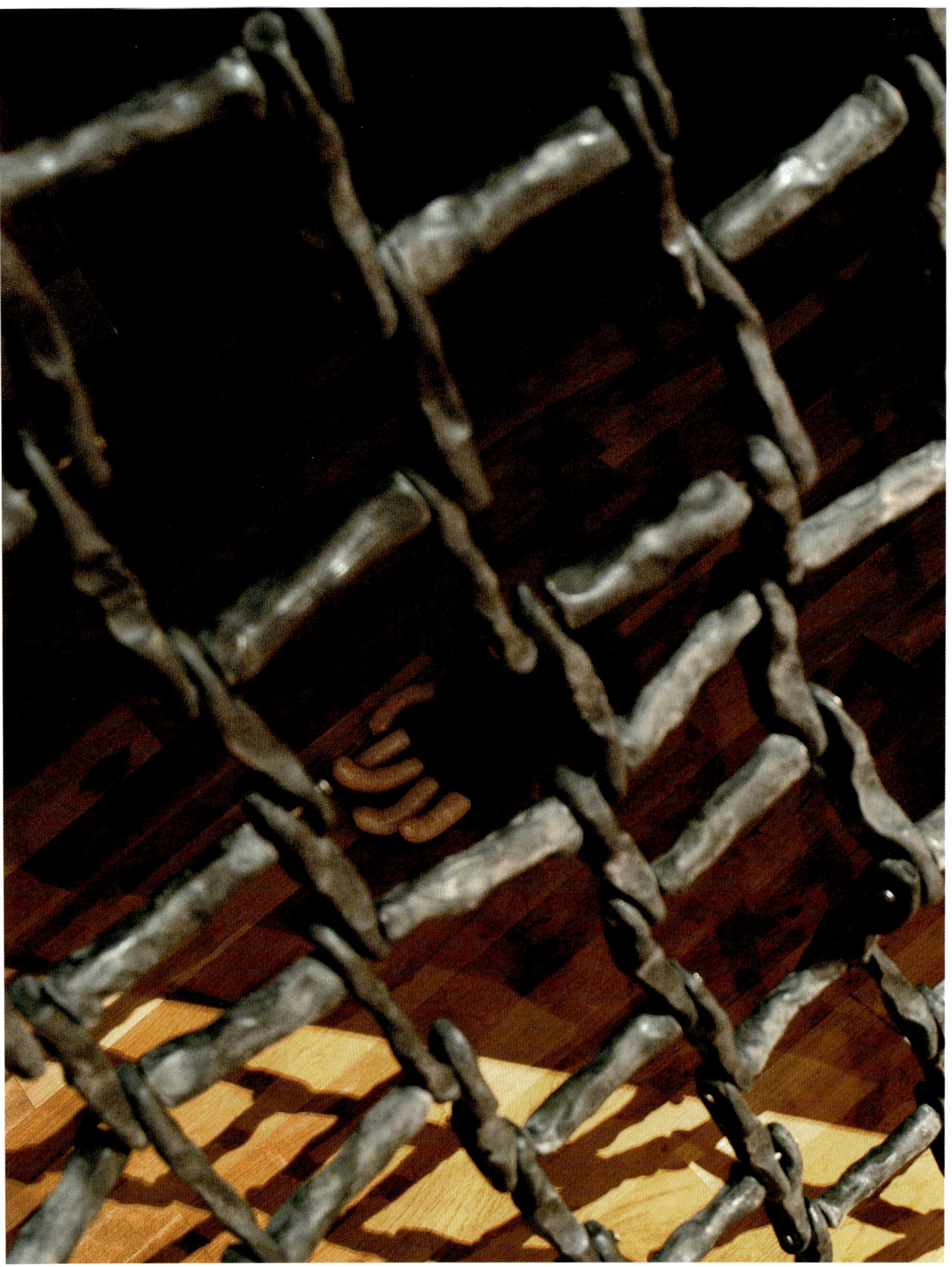

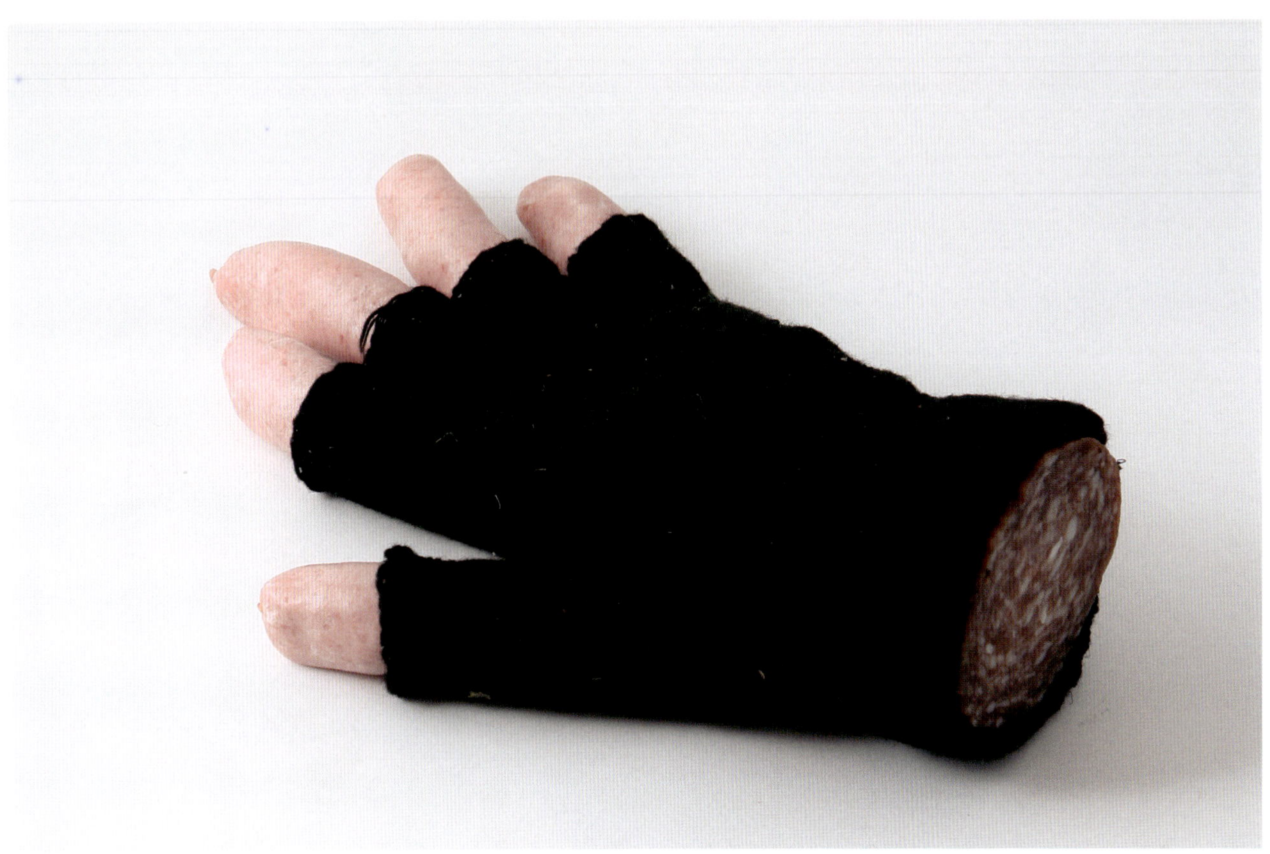

I Haven't Been Feeling Myself Lately 2005
Sausages, salami, fingerless glove and
wire armature, 7 × 23 × 13 cm

'Everyone at some point must have thought that sausages look like fingers. This work is simply that: five sausages and a salami with a wire armature, covered by a fingerless glove. I made it in 2005, when it was fleshy and pink like a piglet. I never tried to preserve it but still have it. It has never gone off and is now dried and shrivelled like something that has been dug up in a peat bog.'

'I had noticed in the supermarket that many dog biscuits were shaped like cartoon bones, so I bought some in every size. When they were arranged in order, they suggested a simple skeleton hand. It seemed inevitable. They didn't make them big enough to continue into an arm or the rest of a body. It wasn't easy, but I stitched them them together and soon I had a pair of hands that could be posed because the fingers moved. But they were far too fragile to handle; maybe biscuits aren't meant to be stitched. Eventually, I found a more durable material, a plaster and sandstone mix, and cast them. At that time, we had dachshunds, who would steal the bones and eat them. I'm not sure if this was testament to the quality of the casting or the stupidity of the dogs.'

Sculpture for Dogs 2007
Jesmonite, sandstone powder and wire,
3 × 1 × 5 cm

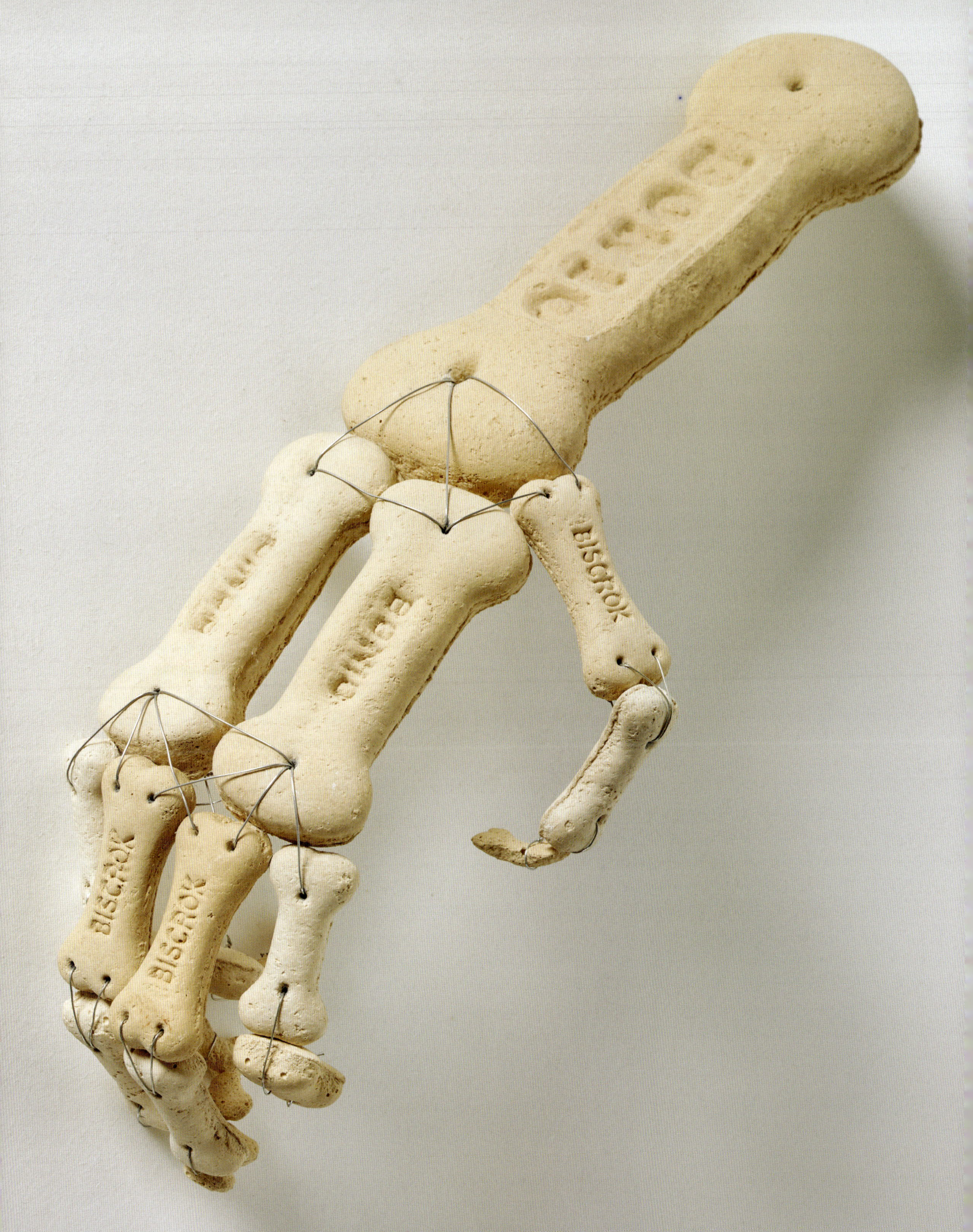
BISCROK
BISCROK
BISCROK
BISCROK

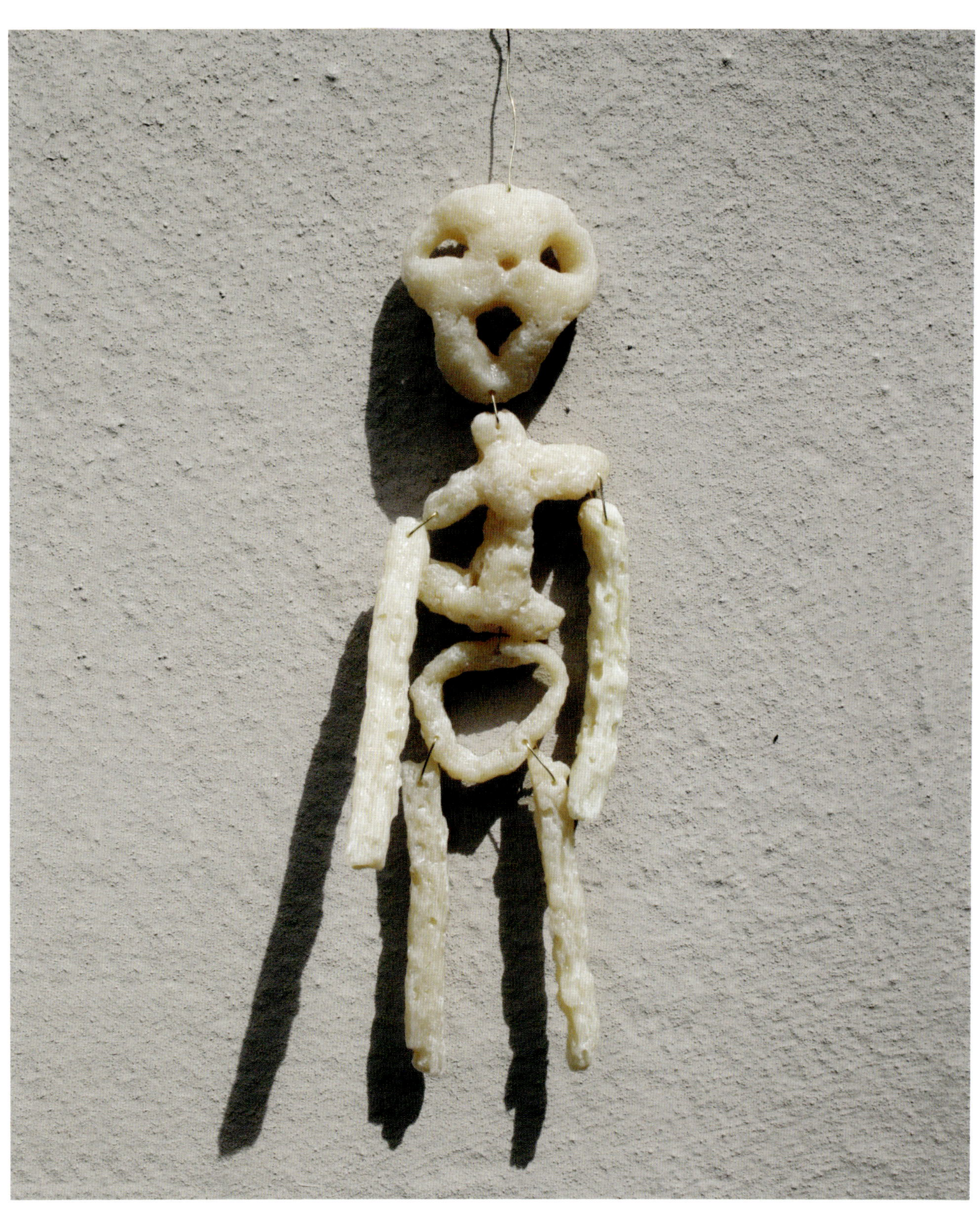

Poppet 2008
Resin, pigment and brass wire,
12 × 5 × 0.5 cm

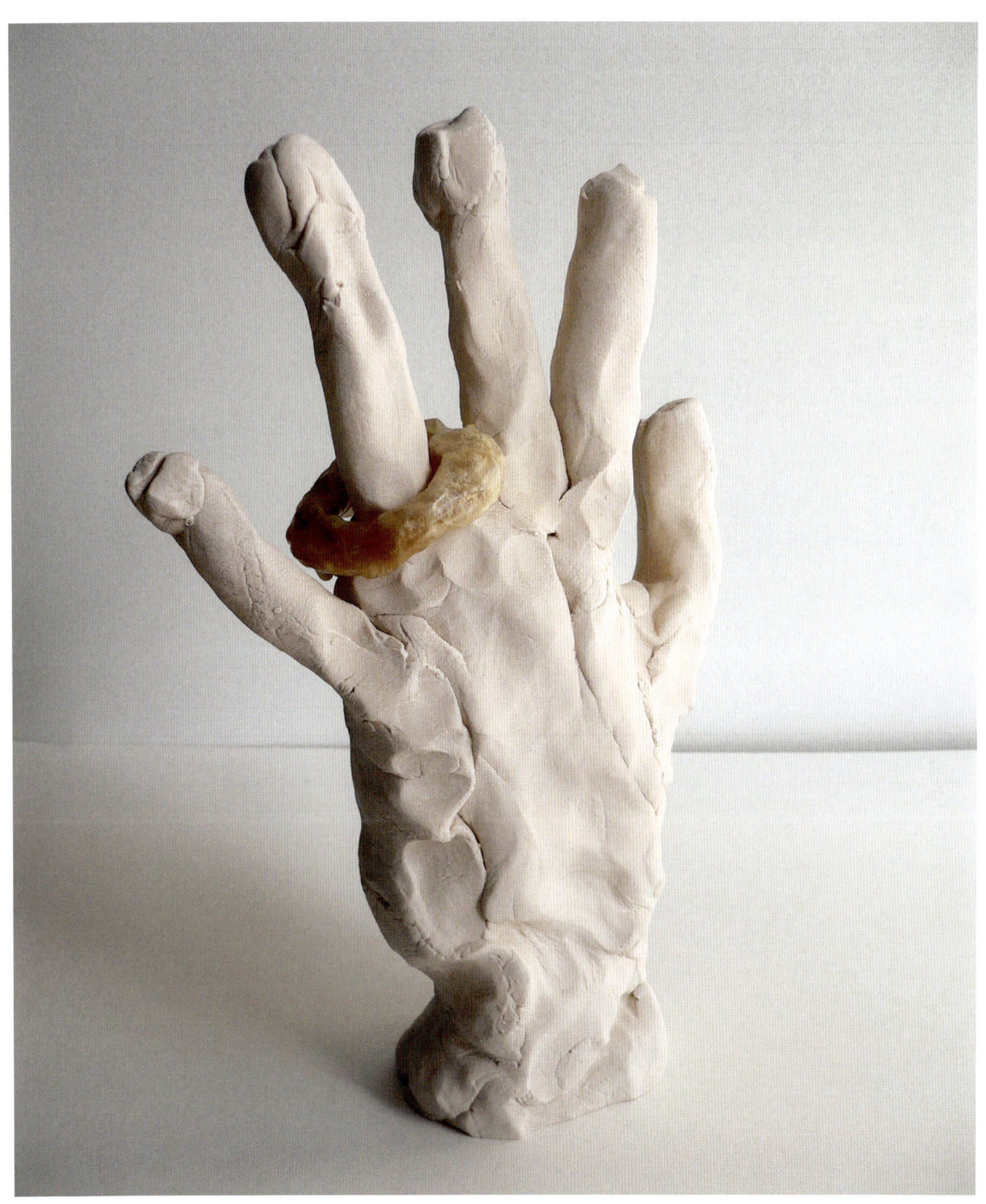

You Got The Ring And I Got The Finger 2005
Resin, marble powder and onion ring,
23 × 15 × 4 cm

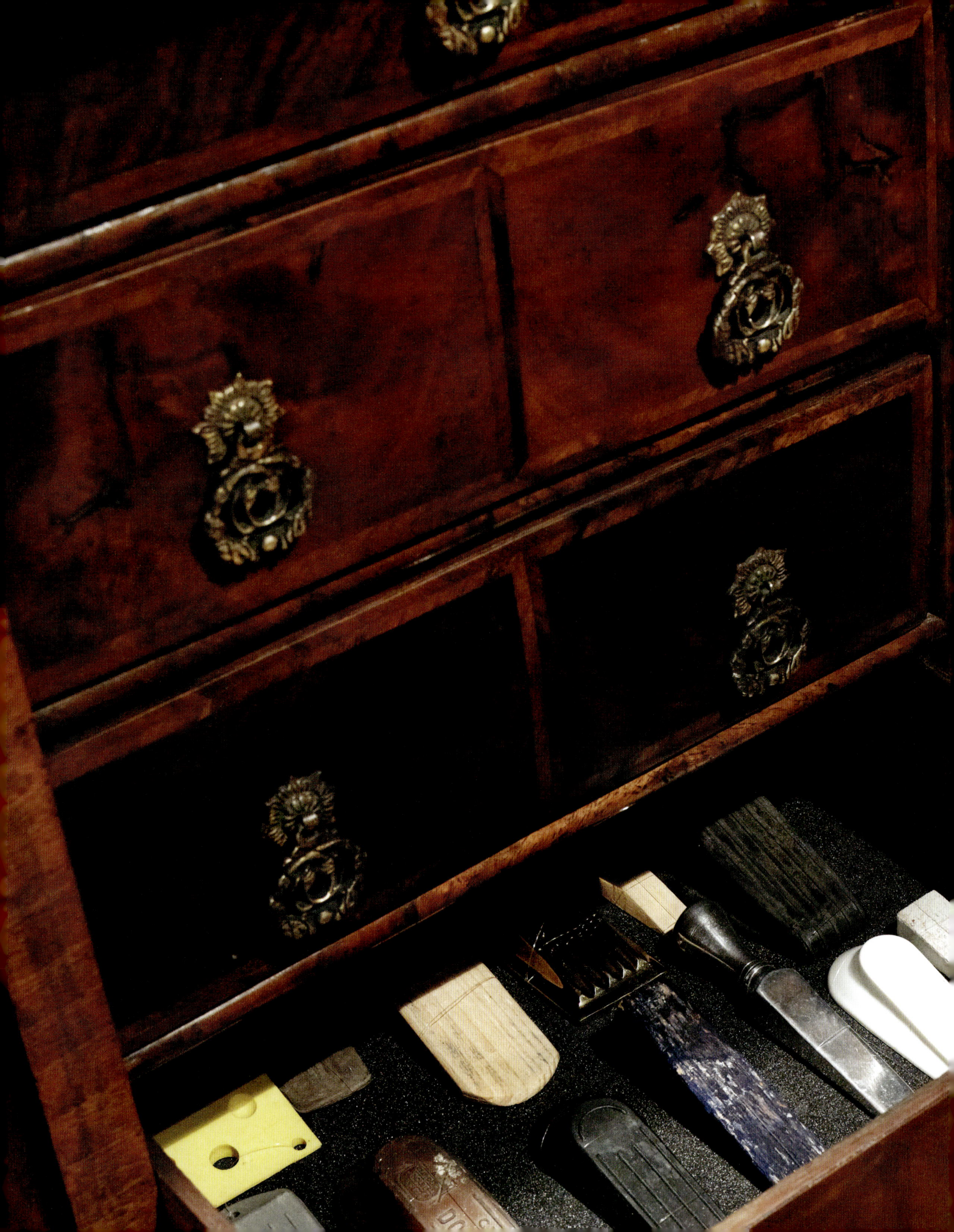

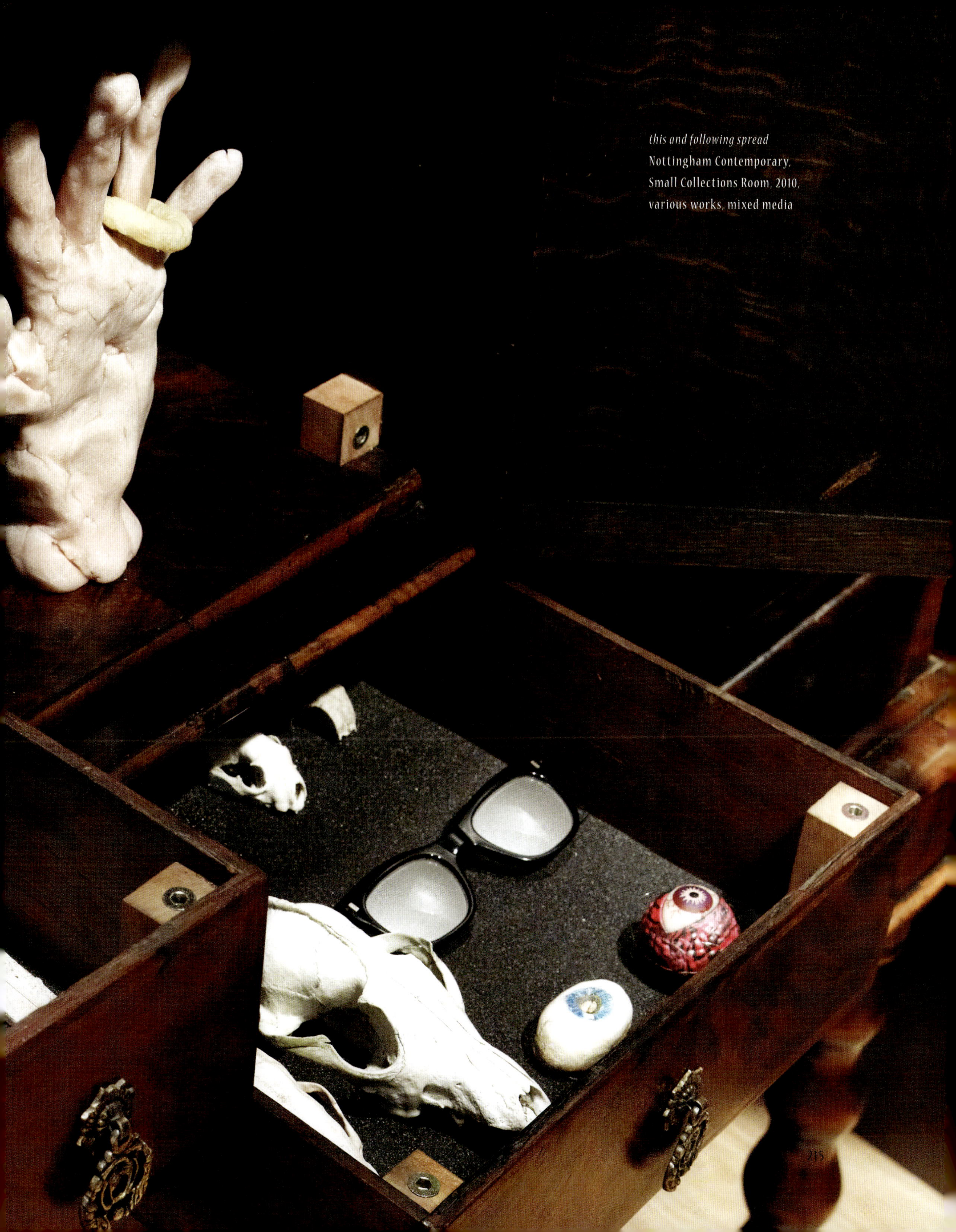

this and following spread
Nottingham Contemporary,
Small Collections Room, 2010,
various works, mixed media

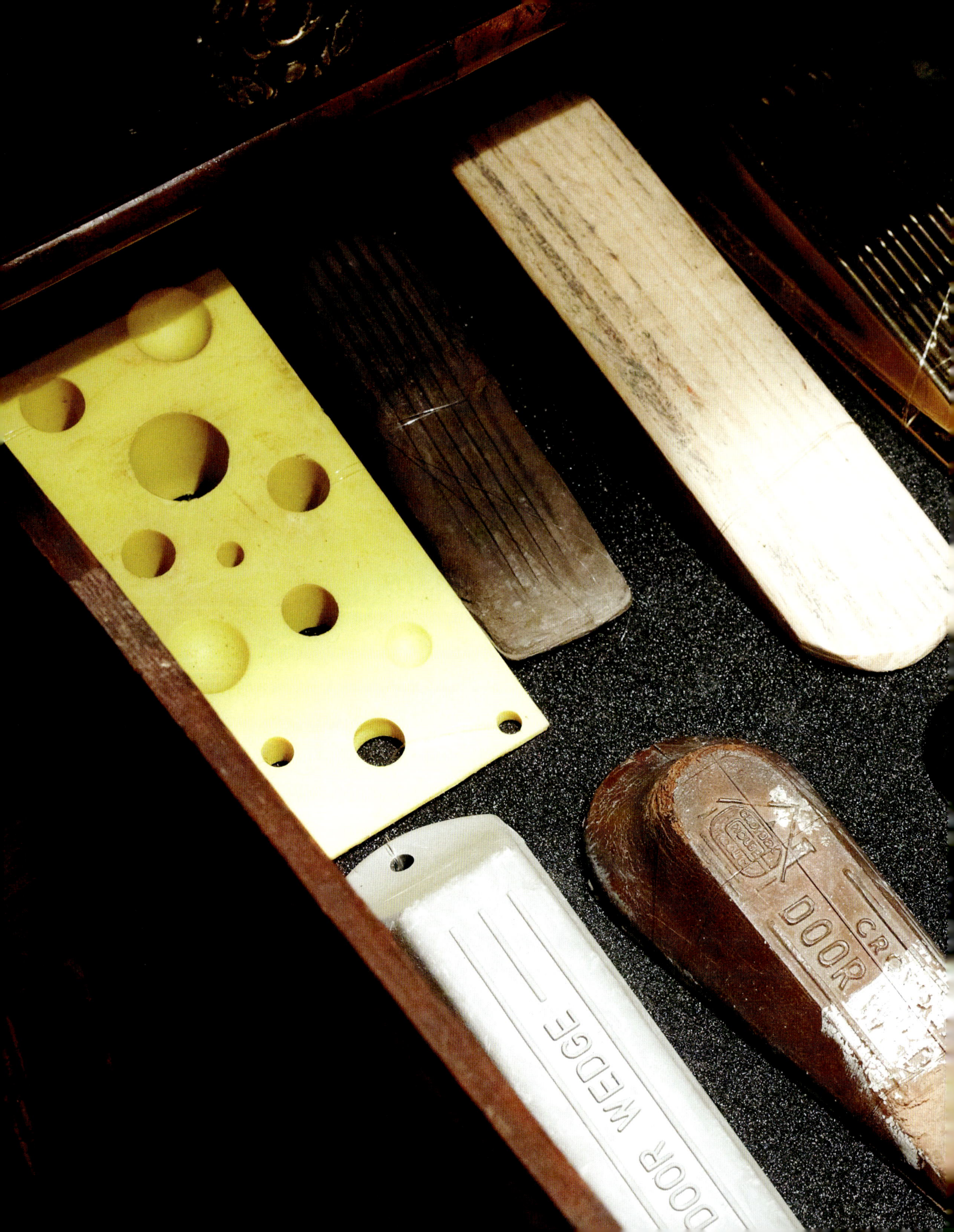
DOOR WEDGE
DOOR

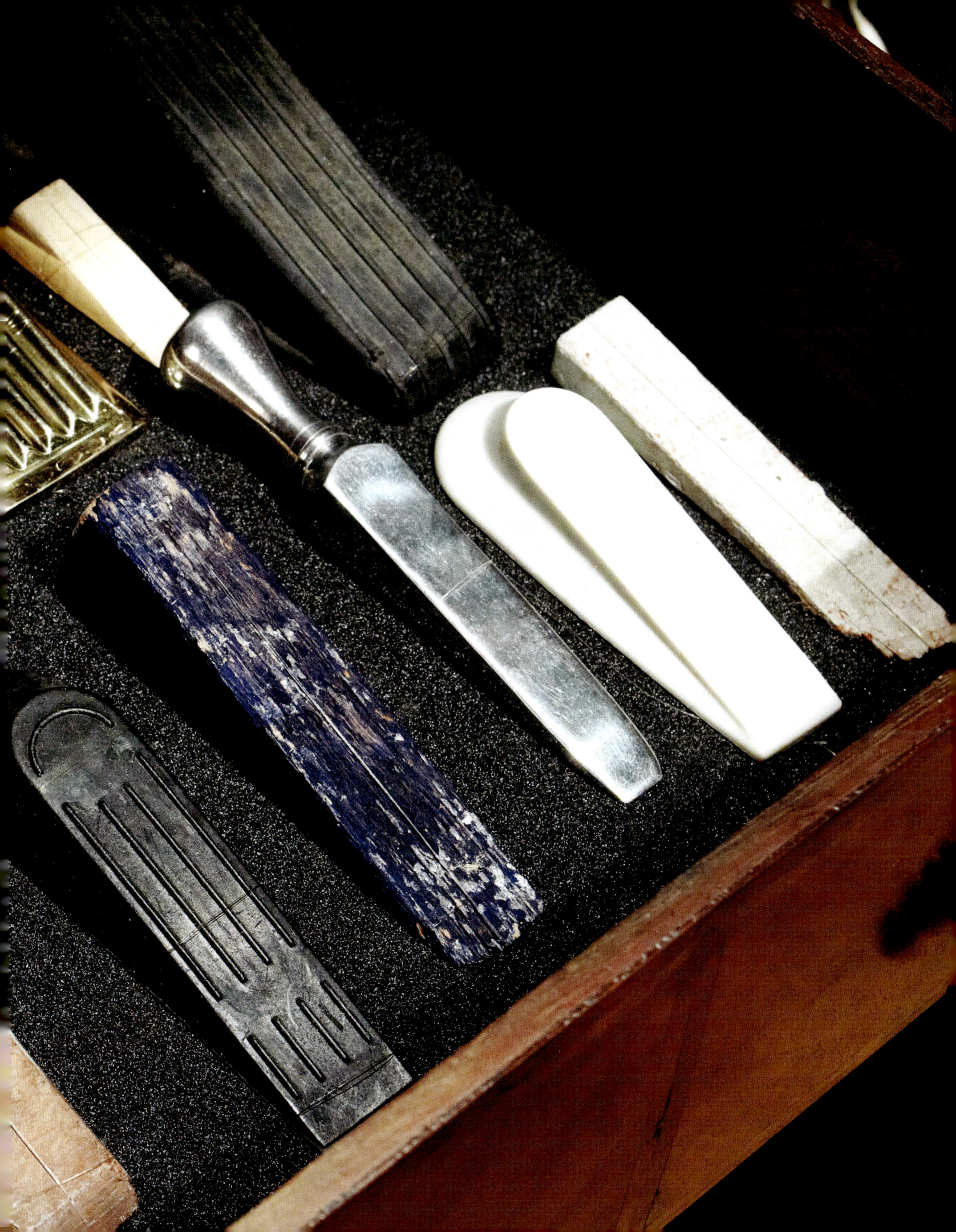

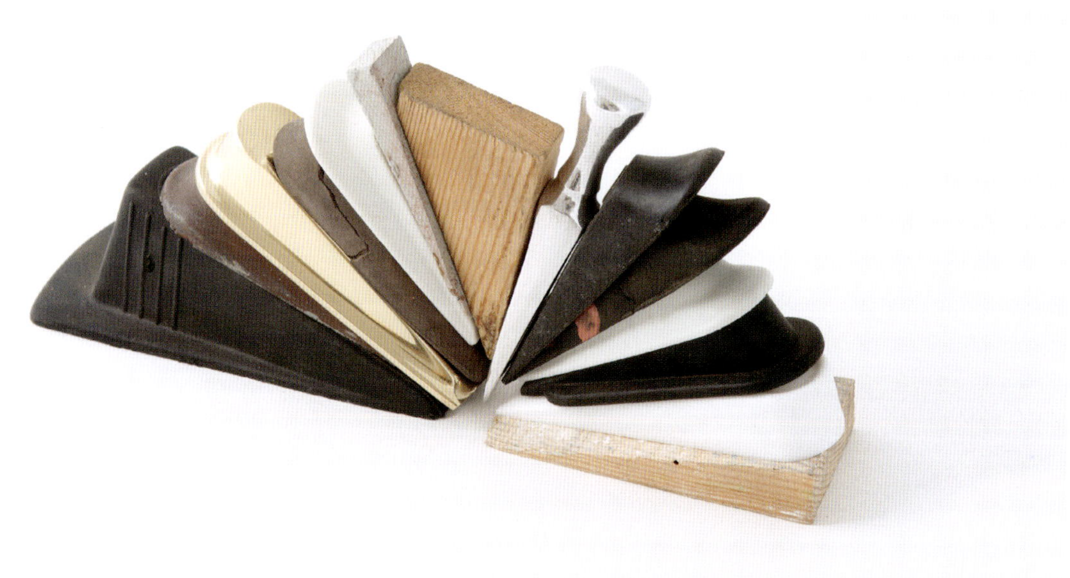

above and opposite
Keystones 2006–7
Appropriated door wedges,
dimensions variable

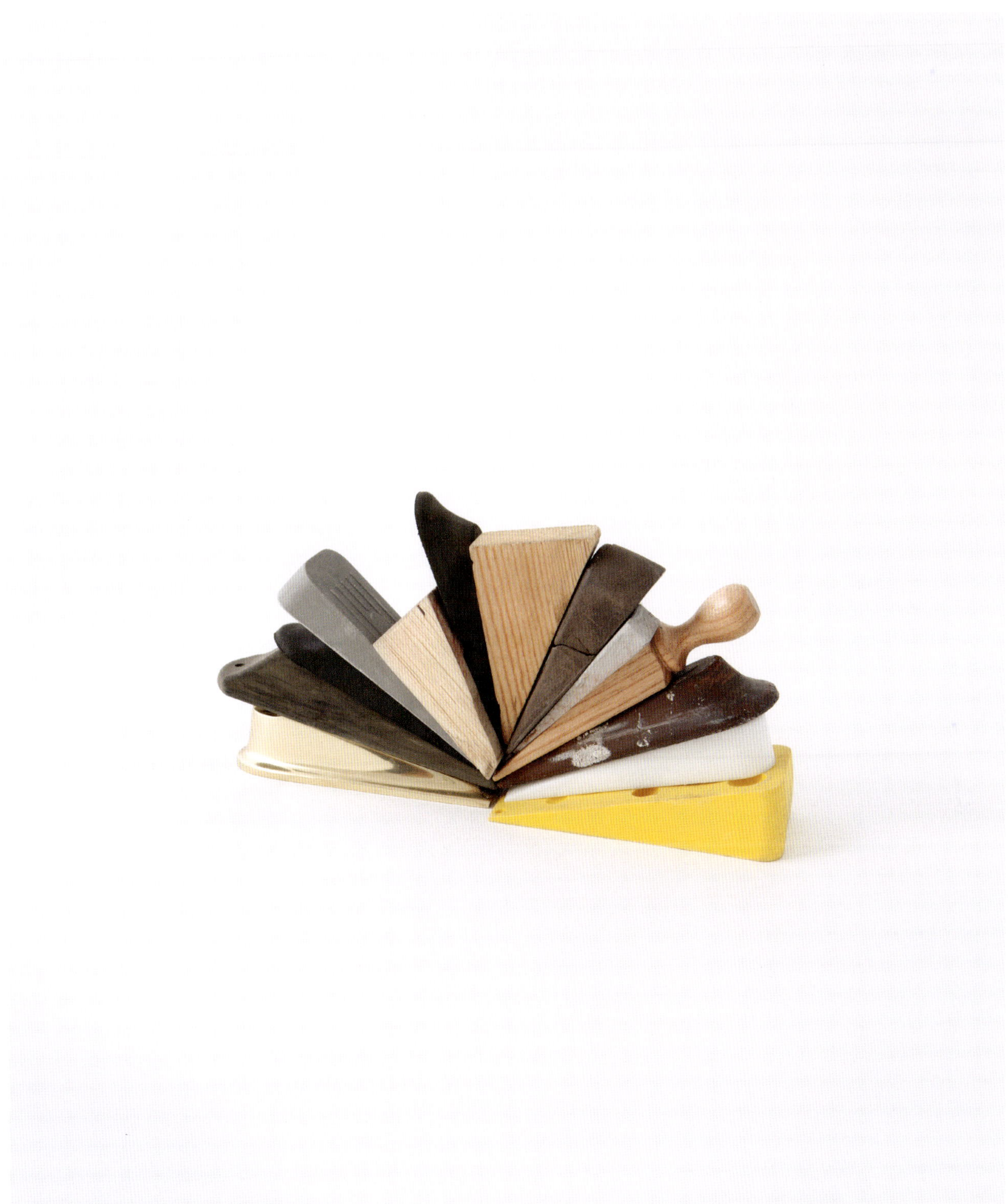

below

Cheese Wedge Used as a Doorstop 2000
Plaster and pigment,
11 × 15 × 11 cm

opposite

Wooden Cheese 2002
Wood,
7 × 12 × 7 cm

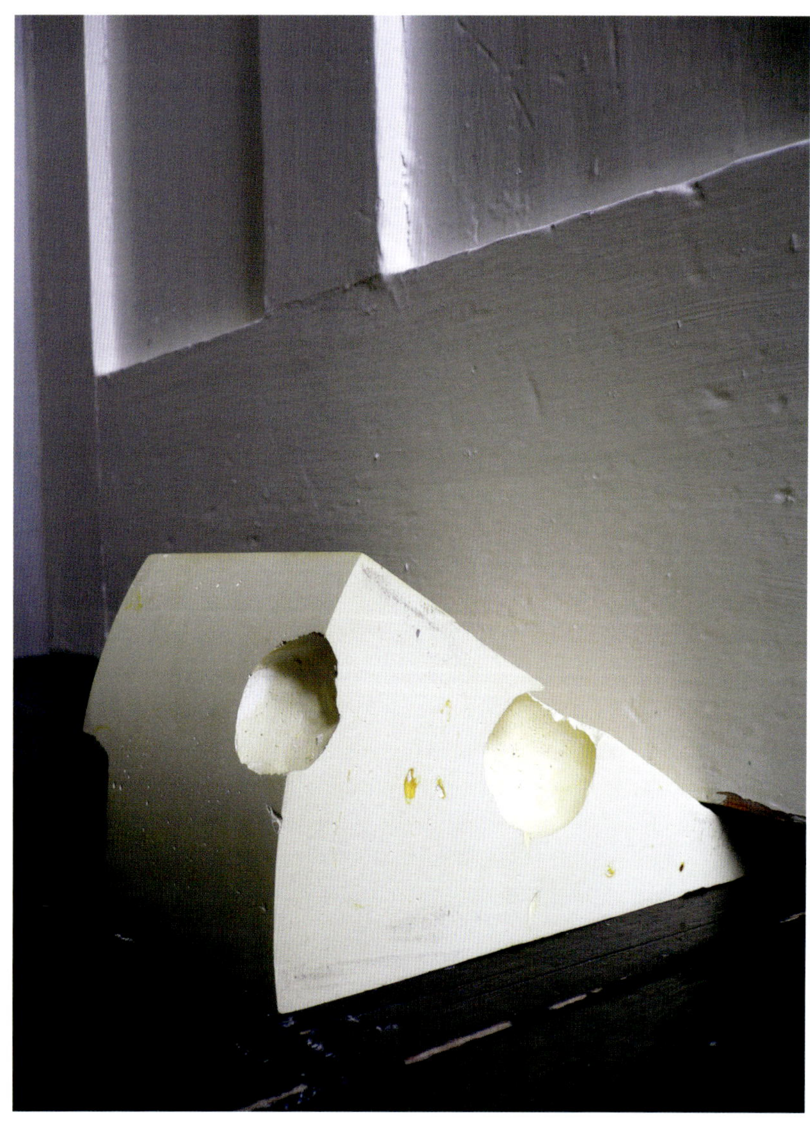

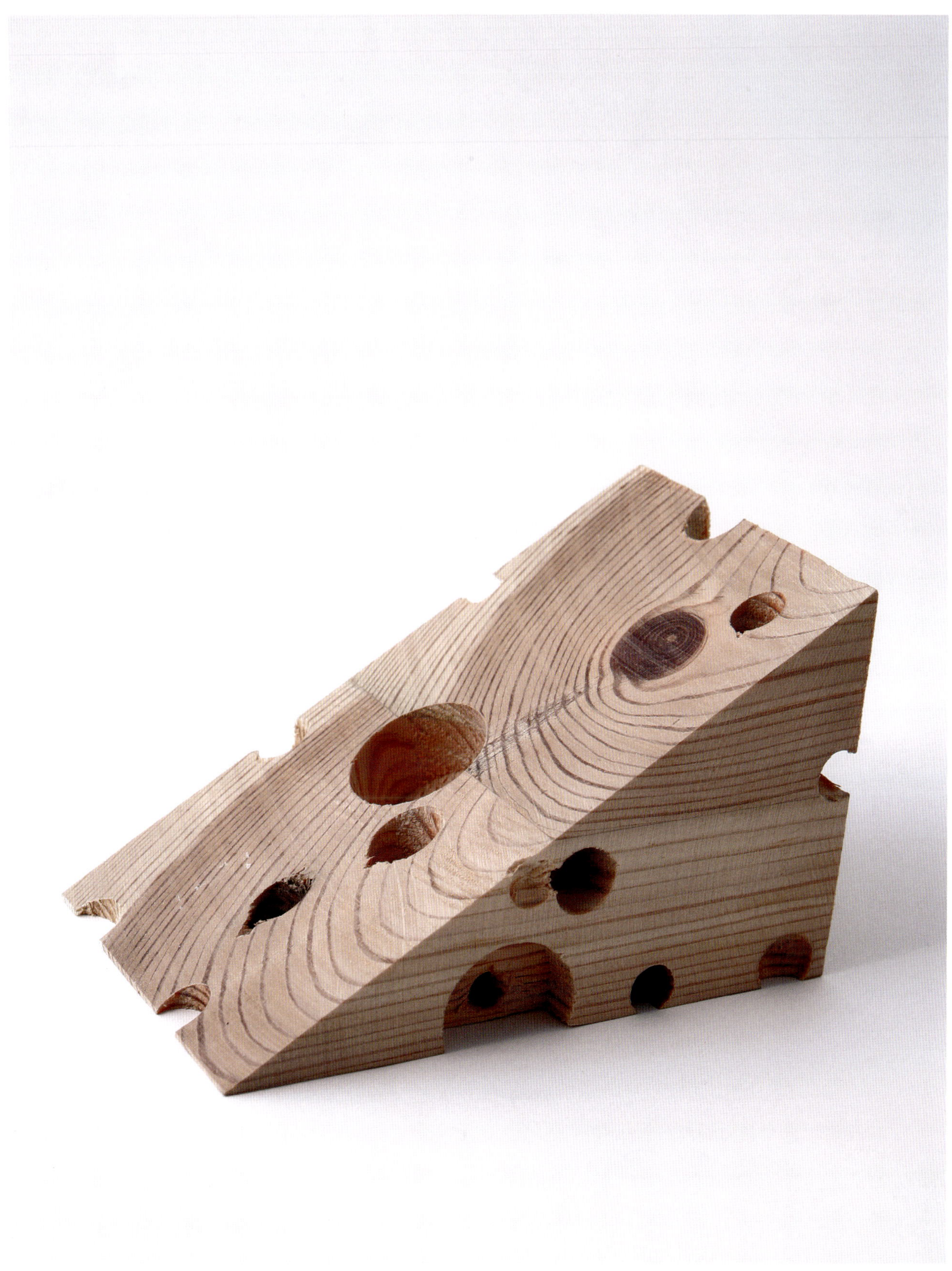

'I started making cubes by rolling small balls of clay and stacking them, beginning with a neat uniform edge at first and then enjoying the way that they would distort. Even though it seemed to be quite a rigorous system, and I'd try to make them as well as I could, because of the human error in the process, I always ended up with these wonky precarious rows that looked on the point of collapse. Because I'm colour blind, I'm always a bit reluctant to choose a colour, but the first few were about the size of marrowfat peas so that seemed like a good enough reason to use green.'

Pile of Peas 1997
Latex and pigment,
3 × 23 cm

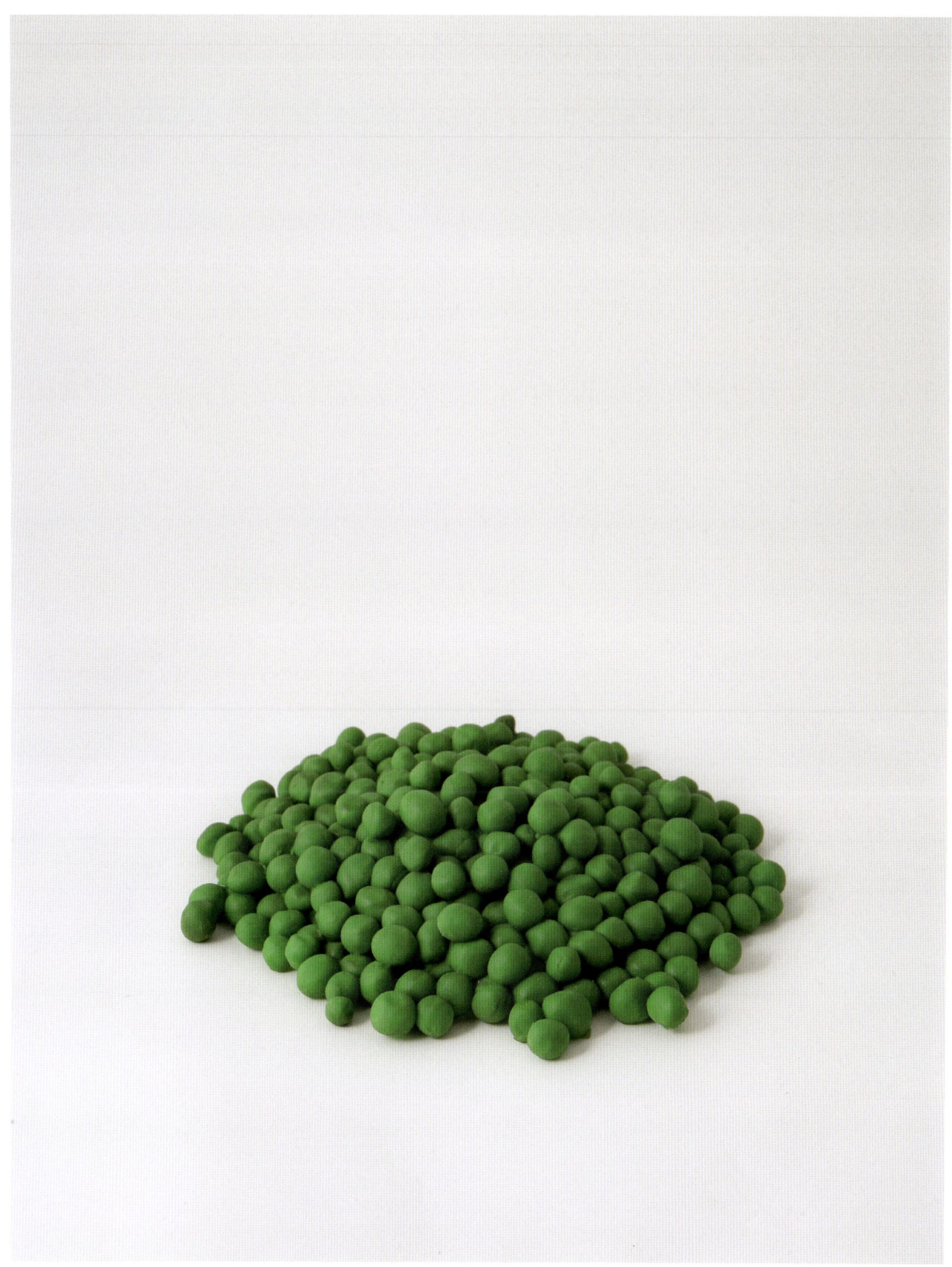

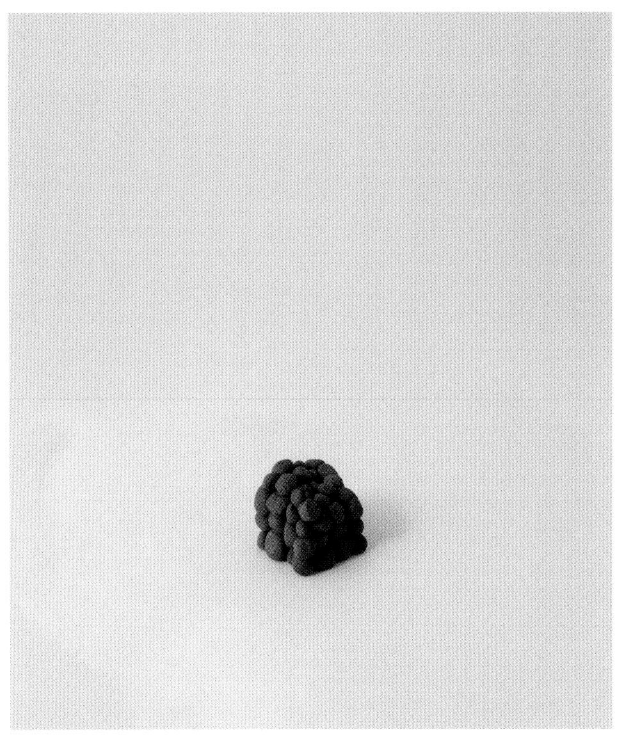

Pea Cube (Smallest) 1999–2001
Ceramic and stain, 3.5 × 3.5 × 3.5 cm

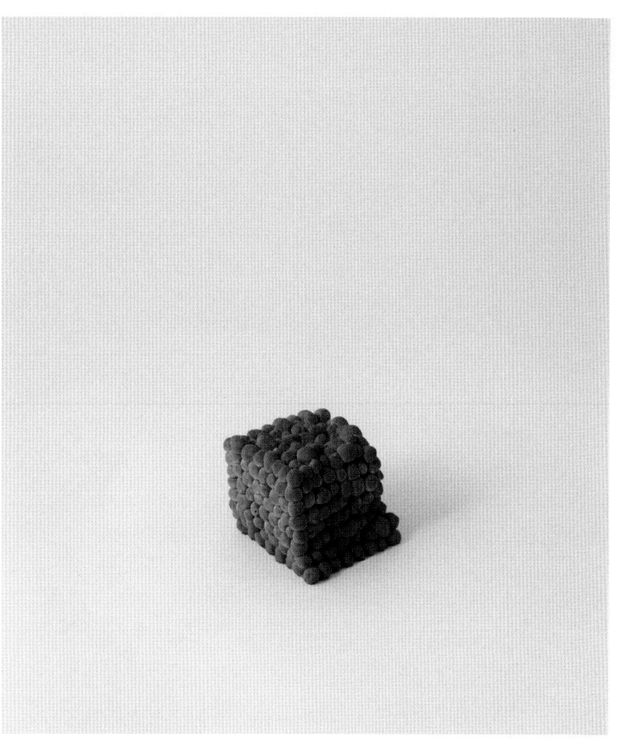

Pea Cube (Small Small) 1999–2001
Latex and pigment, 6 × 6 × 6 cm

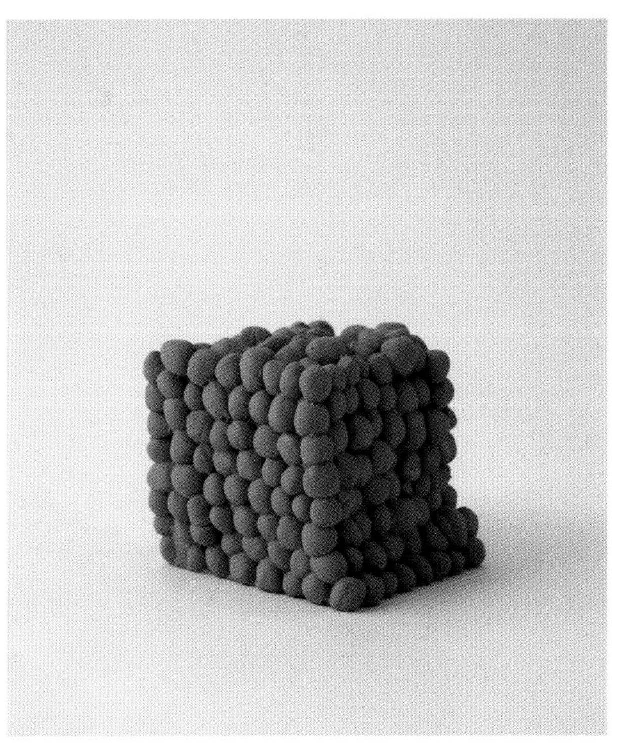

Pea Cube (Average) 1999–2001
Latex and pigment, 12 × 12 × 12 cm

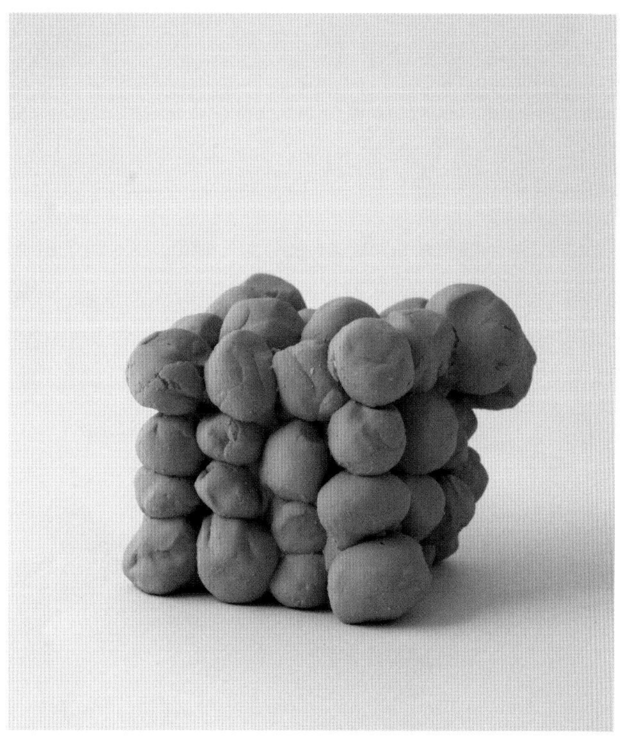

Pea Cube (Above Average) 1999–2001
Latex and pigment, 12.5 × 12.5 × 12.5 cm

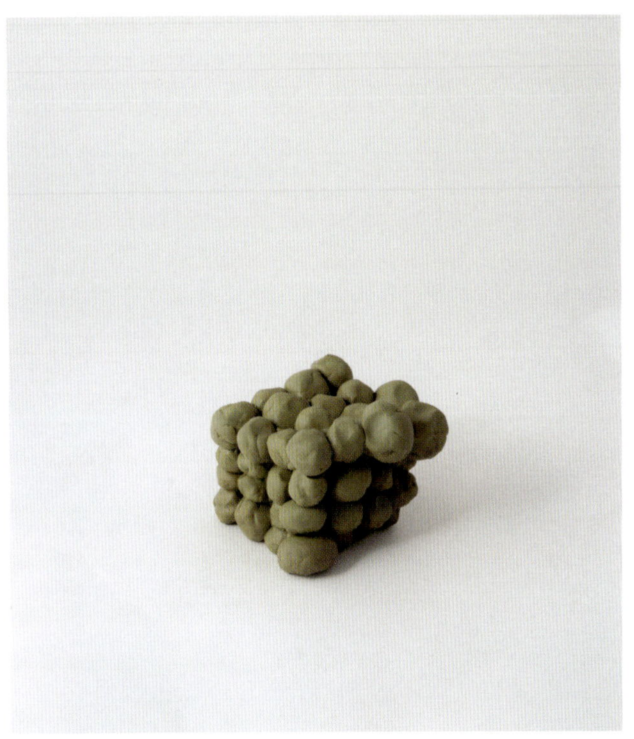

Pea Cube (Small Medium) 1999–2001
Latex and pigment, 9 × 9 × 9 cm

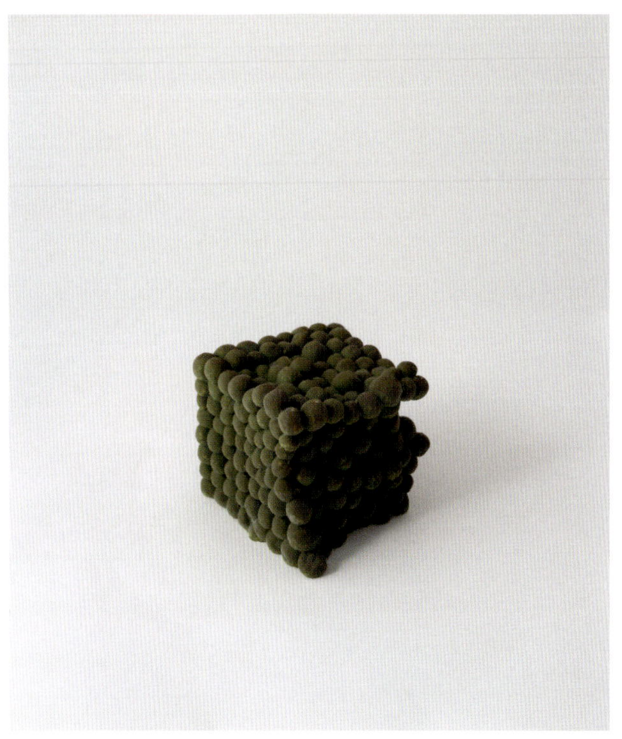

Pea Cube (Below Average) 1999–2001
Latex and pigment, 10 × 10 × 10 cm

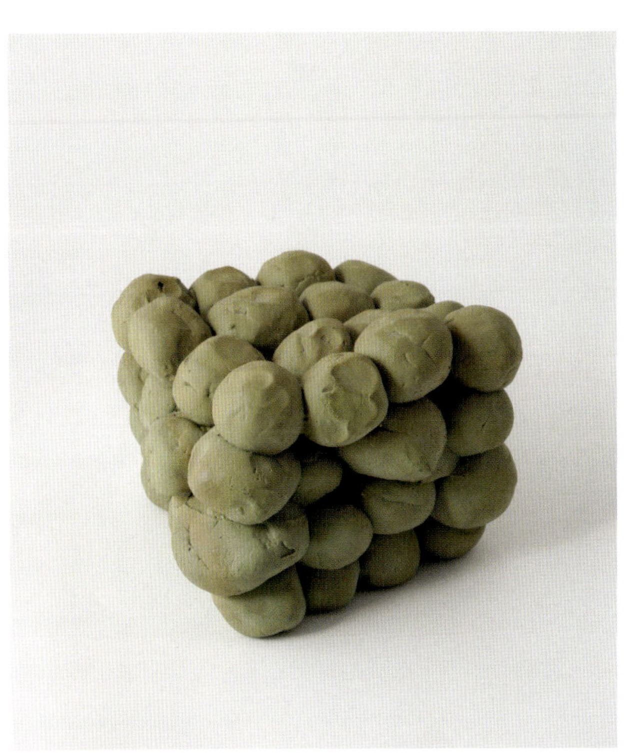

Pea Cube (Large Large) 1999–2001
Latex and pigment, 15 × 15 × 15 cm

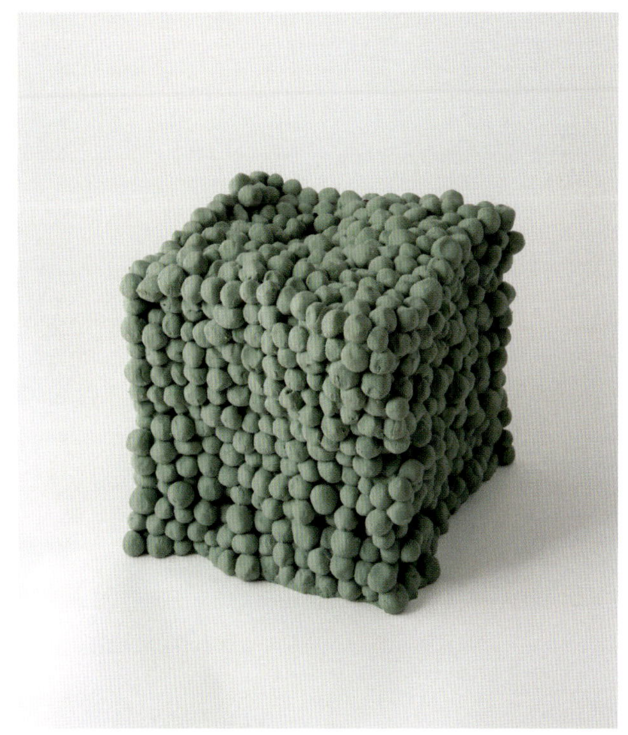

Pea Cube (Biggest Small) 1999–2001
Latex and pigment, 19 × 19 × 19 cm

'In 2003, I had a residency and an exhibition at The Showroom in Bethnal Green. I had the idea to produce a stained-glass window at the front of the space, a deep-set shop front. I thought for a while that it might be possible to make a wall of coloured glass by stacking bottles in the recess, similar to something I'd remembered from *Stig of the Dump*. I decided that as a tribute to the high jinks of the young art stars at the time I should drink all the wine myself. After a time of heavy drinking, I realized that I barely had enough to make a start. It looked like a pathetic effort. My dad started breaking into bottle banks for me, and developed a range of eccentric tools for the job, which ended up in the show. The bottles stacked perfectly and, without the need for glue, the last one tapped in to make a tight fit. The window was illuminated from the outside during the day, and from the inside at night.'

right
Model For Stained Glasses 2003
Resin, pigment and chipboard,
13 × 19 × 7 cm

below and below right
Stained Glasses 2003
Wine bottles,
approx. 300 × 300 cm. Installed
at The Showroom, London.

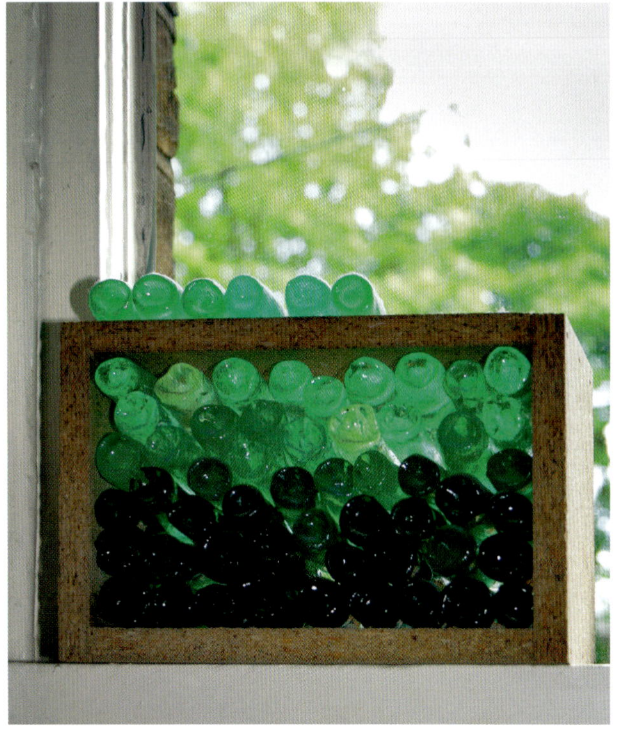

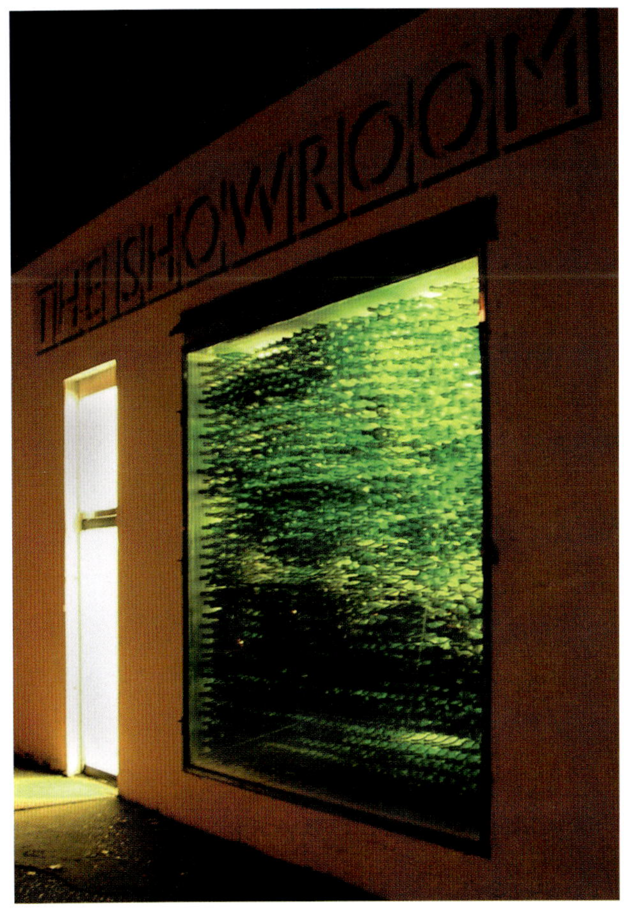

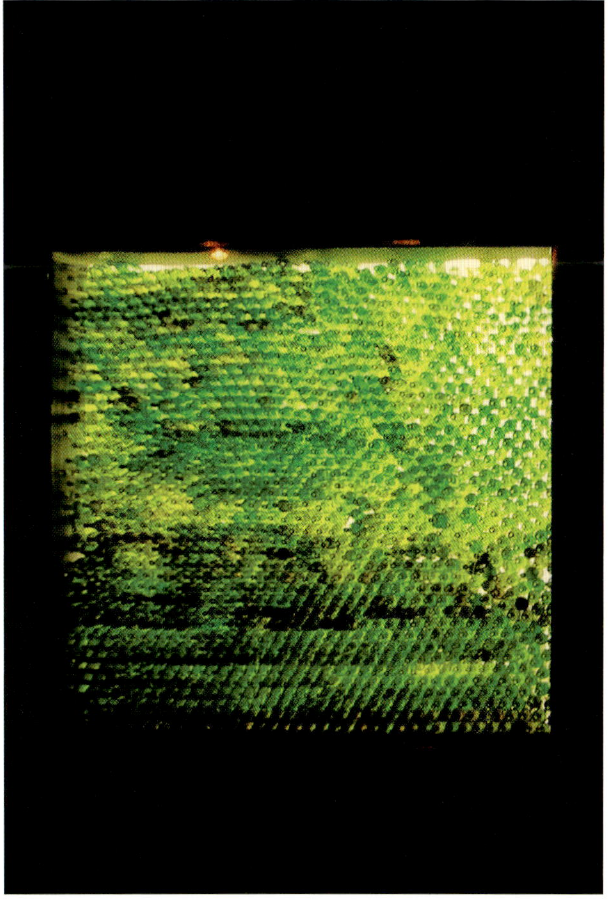

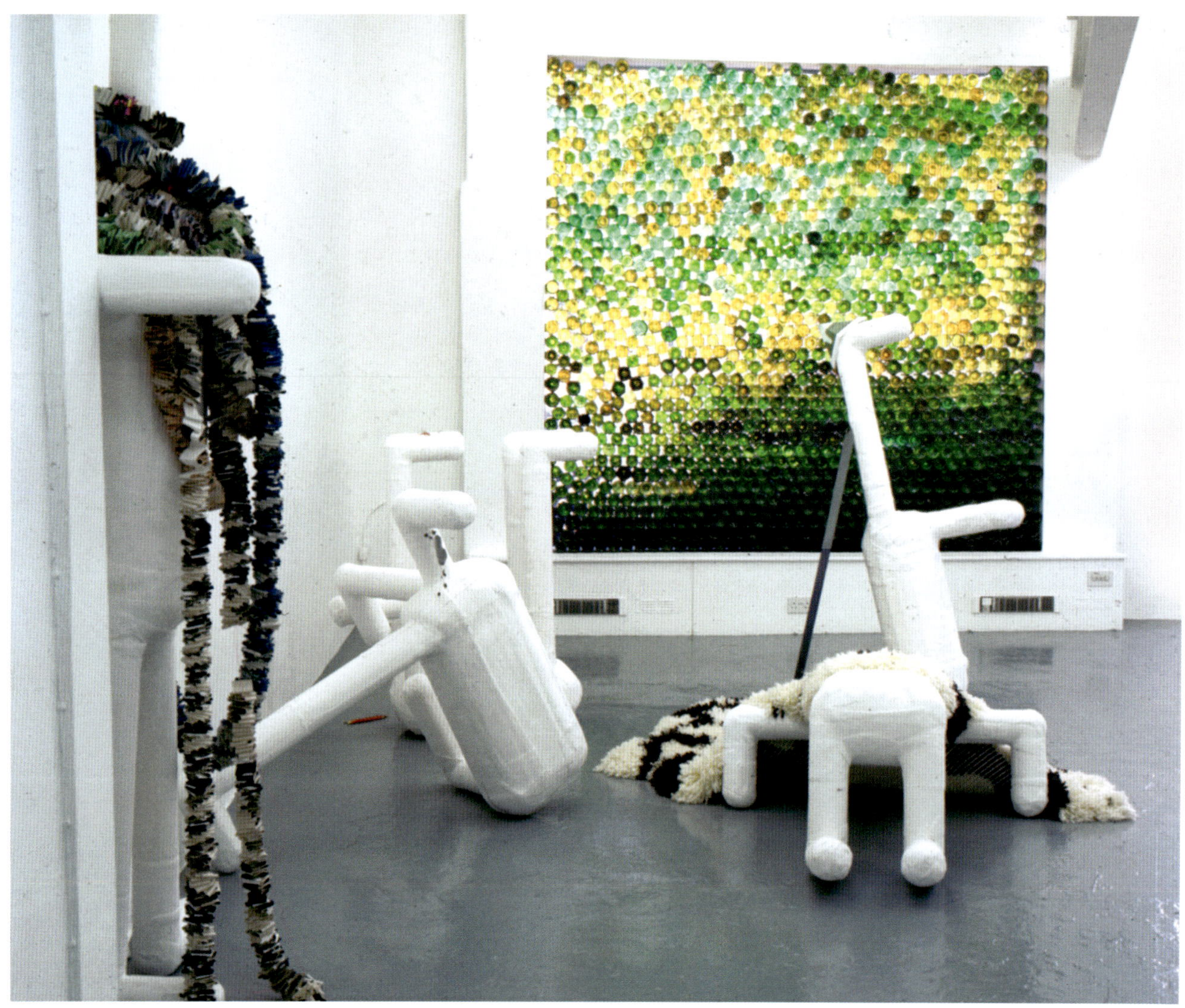

above and opposite
'**The Screaming Abdabs**' 2003
Mixed-media installation,
dimensions variable. Installed at
The Showroom, London.

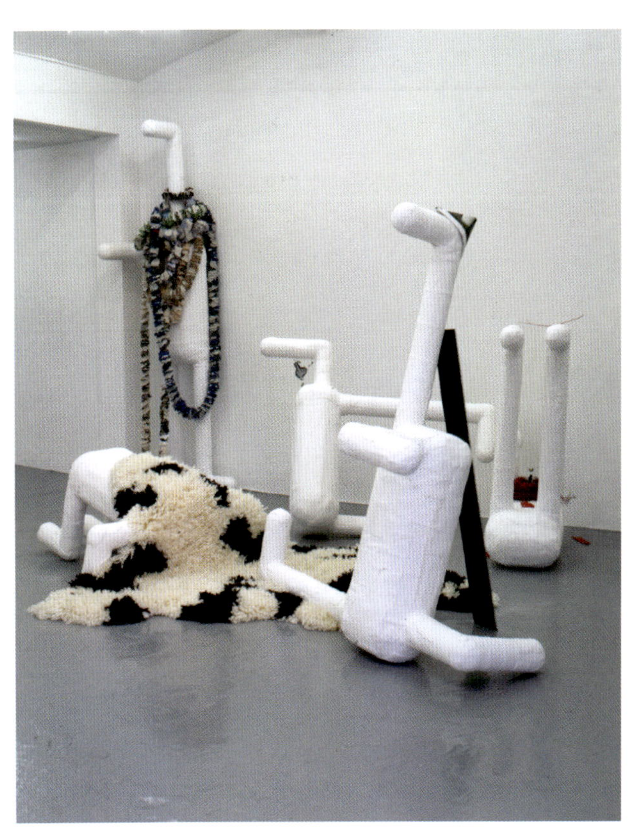

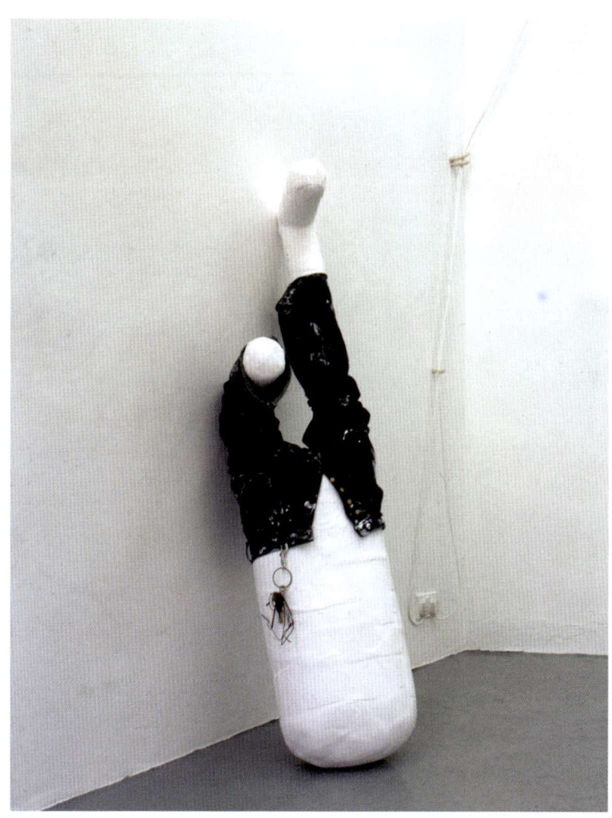

Ice Sculpture 2003
Clear resin and pigment cast
from ice-cube trays,
15 × 12 × 12 cm

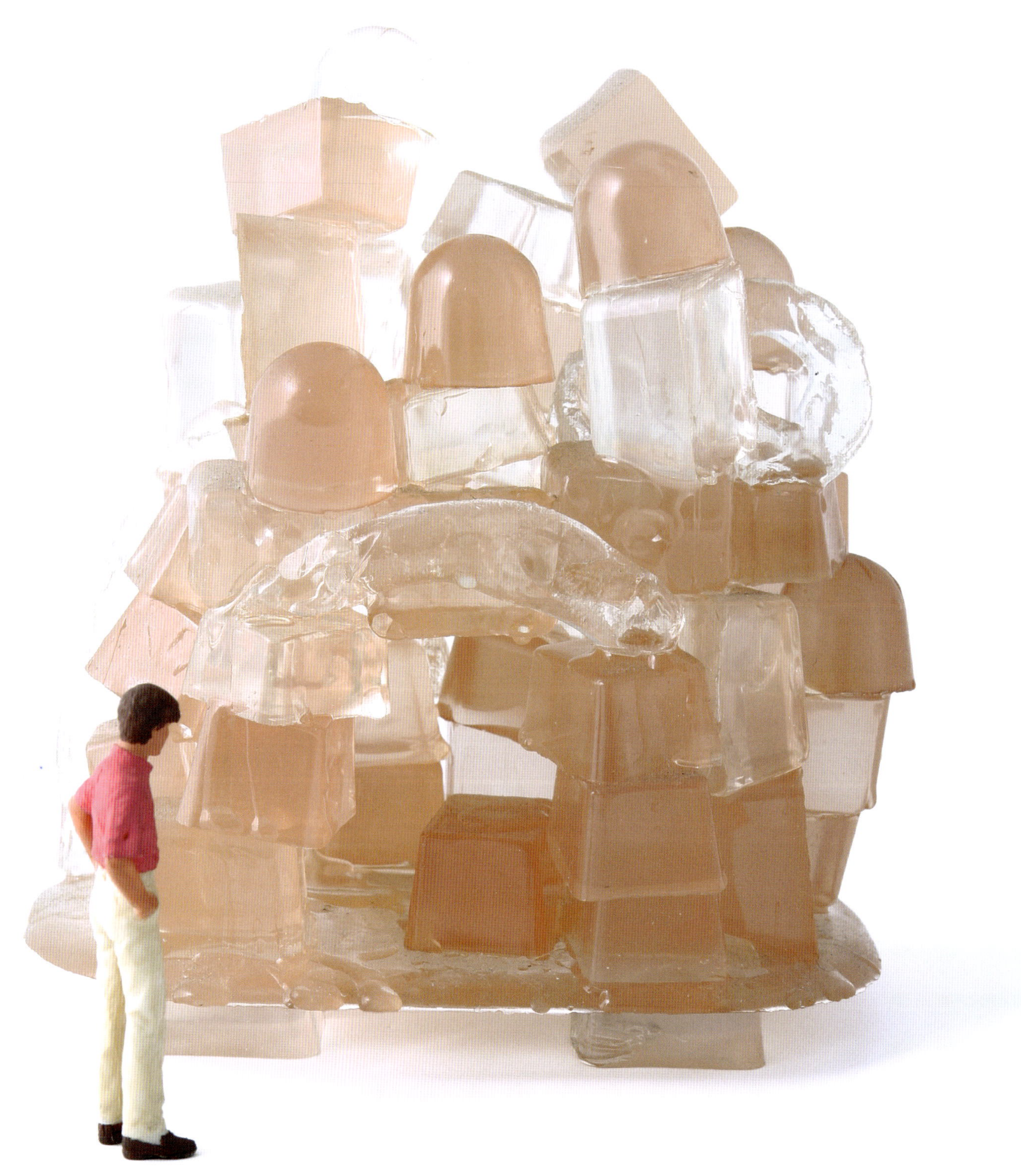

Dancing On The Dark 1994
Photographs and book,
18 × 11 × 5 cm

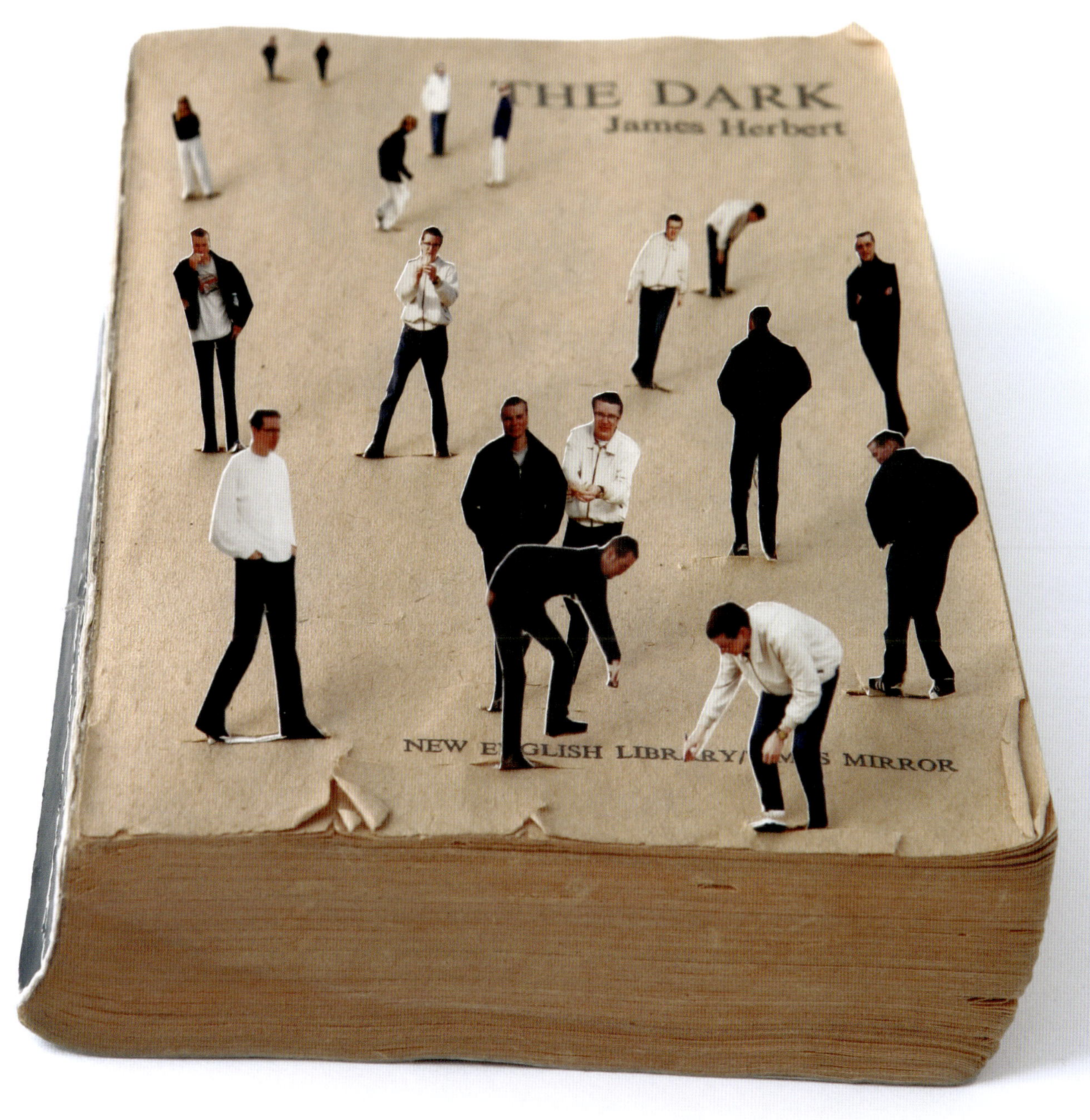

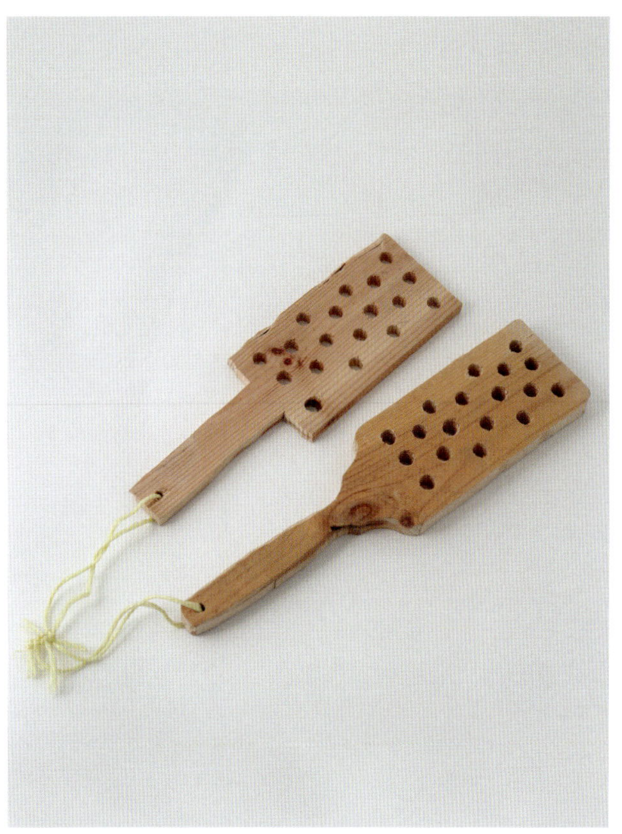

Tool for Loud Slapping 2004
Wood and string,
each 1.5 × 35 × 10 cm

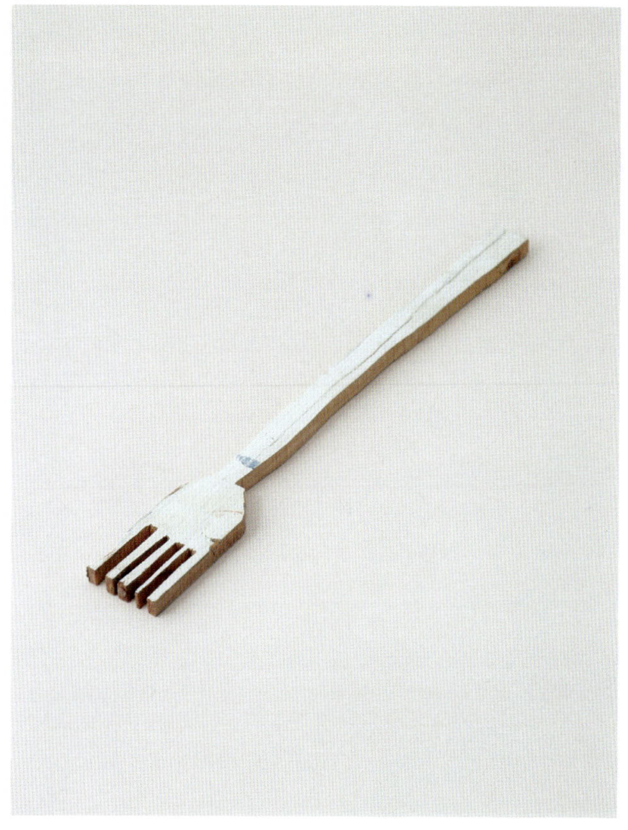

Tool for Forking 2004
Wood,
0.5 × 25 × 3 cm

Sculpture for Mice (in) 2006
Resin and marble powder,
10 × 9 × 5 cm

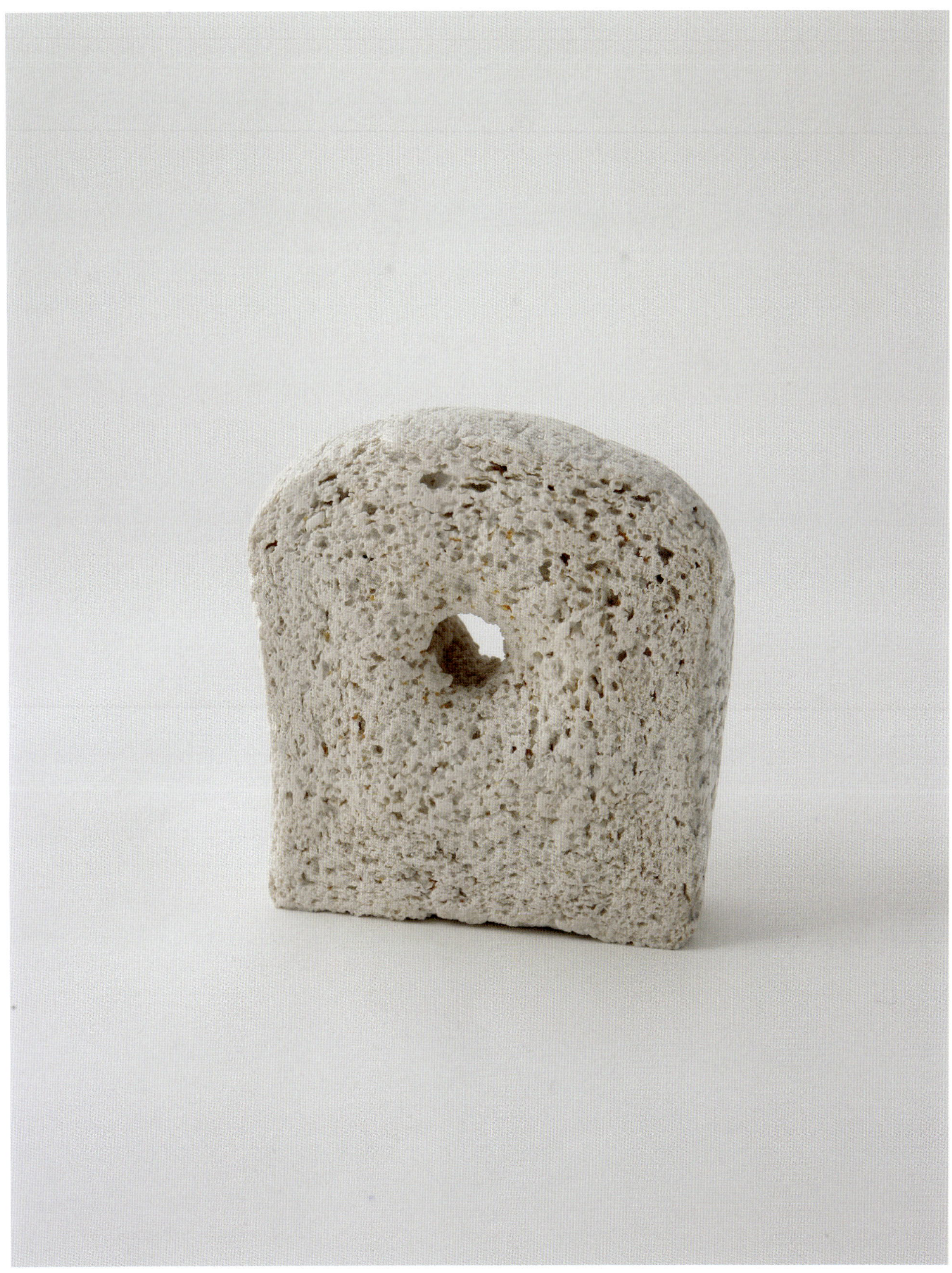

'These two headlines came together by chance, as so often happens, while I was filling up something by screwing up newspaper. The work is purely the connection between the headlines. Seemingly unconnected objects very often find themselves together as they move through the studio. It's a complete coincidence, like finding something in a skip, but it becomes important because there is a pattern or logic that someone else might not have noticed. I'm very glad when this happens and worry that it might stop. As a result, I now have a 'Dead Drawer' in the studio that is full of newspapers with dead celebrities on the cover. It is my responsibility not to miss any, as a collection insists that it must evolve if it is to remain interesting.'

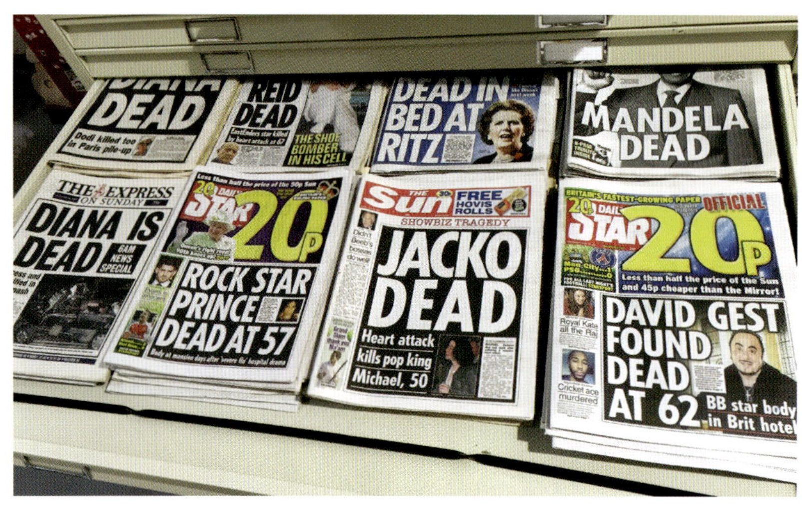

opposite
Living Dead 1998–2008
Framed newspaper page,
each 37 × 28 cm

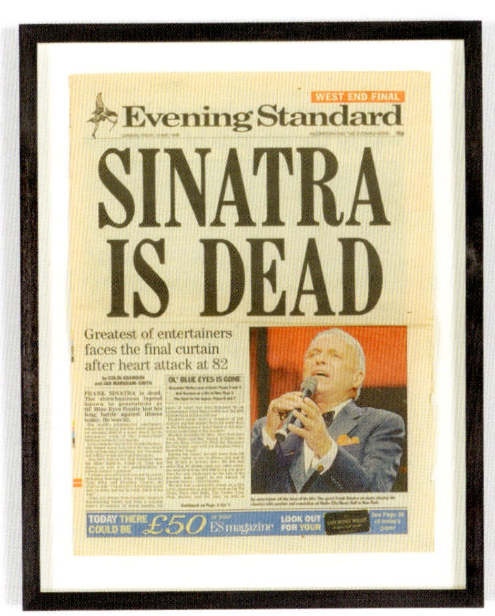

WEST END FINAL

Evening Standard

SINATRA IS DEAD

Greatest of entertainers faces the final curtain after heart attack at 82

OL' BLUE EYES IS GONE

TODAY THERE COULD BE £50 IN YOUR ES magazine

LOOK OUT FOR YOUR

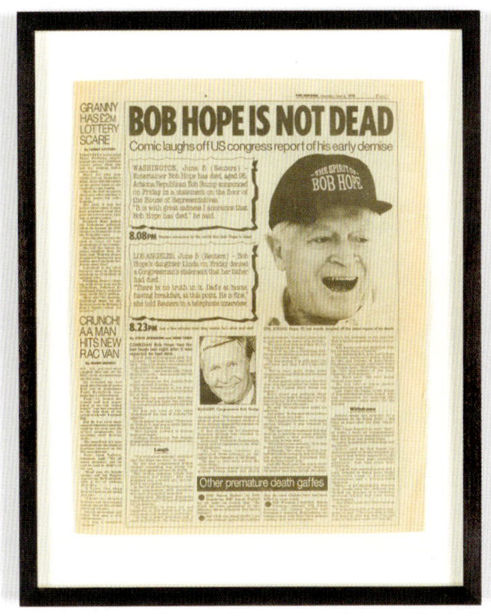

GRANNY HAS £2M LOTTERY SCARE

BOB HOPE IS NOT DEAD

Comic laughs off US congress report of his early demise

8.08PM

8.23PM

CRUNCH! AA MAN HITS NEW RAC VAN

Other premature death gaffes

Des Hughes is not dead

Born 1970 Birmingham

Education

2000–2
MA Fine Art Goldsmith's College, University of London

1990–4
BA (Hons) Fine Art (Sculpture) Bath College of Art

Selected solo exhibitions

2017
'Keeper of Heads', Martin Asbæk Gallery, Copenhagen

2016
'XXX', Bruce Haines Mayfair, London

2015
'Stretch Out and Wait', The Hepworth Wakefield
The Visitors, public art project for Wellington, New Zealand

2013
'Rust Never Sleeps', Buchmann Galerie, Berlin
Ancient & Modern, London

2012
'Everything's Inevitable', Manchester Art Gallery

2011
'Thems Please', 76 Chatsworth Road, London, curated by Measure

2010
'Endless Endless', Frame solo presentation, Frieze Art Fair
Small Collections Room, Nottingham Contemporary

2008
Des Hughes and Richard Hughes, Michael Benevento, Los Angeles

2007
Ancient & Modern, London

2005
'Boneless', Laing Art Gallery, Newcastle-upon-Tyne

2003
'The Screaming Abdabs', The Showroom, London

2002
'Unconvincing Sausages,' Kate MacGarry, London

1999
'Being Boring', Virgin Megastore, London

1998
'Wishing on a star', Tablet Gallery, London

1997
'I wouldn't normally do this kind of thing', Habitat, King's Road, London
'We hate it when our friends become successful', Southampton City Art Gallery

Selected group exhibitions

2018
'A Place on the Table', Plas Glyn-y-Weddw, Llanbedrog
'Malevolent Eldritch Shrieking', Paul Morrison Studio, Sheffield

2017
'Fifteen', Kate MacGarry, London

2016
'The Sleepers', Pallant House Gallery (two-person show with Clare Woods)
'Summer in the City', Martin Asbæk Gallery, Copenhagen
Royal Academy Summer Show, London
'Buffet d'Art', Berlin, London, Hestercombe House

2015
'Happy Valleys', Galerie Simpson, Swansea

2014
'Body and Void', Henry Moore Foundation, Perry Green

2012
'a thing is a thing is a thing', Minories Galleries, Colchester

2011
Sculpture Garden, Frieze Art Fair, London
'Dystopia', CAPC centre d'art contemporain de Bordeaux, France
'Sometimes I wish I could just disappear', David Risley Gallery, Copenhagen
'House of Beasts', Attingham Park, Shropshire (MeadowArts commission)
'Backbone: A Selection of Modern British Sculptors', New Art Centre, Roche Court, Salisbury
'Modern British Sculpture', Gimpel Fils, London

2010
'Never The Same River (Possible Futures, Probable Pasts)', Camden Arts Centre, London, curated by Simon Starling
'BigMinis, Fetishes of Crisis', CAPC centre d'art contemporarin de Bordeaux
'Newspeak, British Art Now Part II', Saatchi Gallery, London
Bart Wells Boutique, London, curated by Luke Gottelier and Francis Upritchard
'Undone: Making and Unmaking in Contemporary Sculpture', Henry Moore Institute, Leeds
'Rive Gauche, Rive Droite', various venues, Paris, curated by Marc Jancou
'The Nature of Things', Two Jonnys Projects, London

2009
'Art Now: Beating the Bounds', Tate Britain, London
'Fallen Out of Space', Jan Mol Collection, London
'Continuity', Gimpel Fils, London
'Friends & Family', Anton Kern Gallery, New York

2008
'Weißes Lächeln', Croy Neilson, Berlin

2007
'Strange Events Permit Themselves the Luxury of Occurring', Camden Arts Centre, London, curated by Steven Claydon
'Strange Weight', Martos Gallery, New York

2006
'Among the Ash Heaps and Millionaires', Ancient & Modern, London

2005
'Still Life With', Kate MacGarry, London
'Art Out of Place,' Castle Museum, Norwich
'The Wonderful Fund Collection', Musée de Marrekech

2004
'Wider Than The Sky', Commercial Street, London
'Mementoes & Other Curiosities', Farmiloes, London
'Death of Romance', Ganton Street, London
Bart Wells Institute, Hamish McKay, Wellington, New Zealand

2003
'The Unhomely', Kettle's Yard, Cambridge
'18%', Geoffrey Charles Gallery, London
'Twilight', Gimpel Fils, London

2002
'The Way To Happiness', VTO, London

Collections
Arts Council Collection, UK
David Roberts Foundation, UK
The Hepworth Wakefield, UK
Manchester Art Gallery, UK
Saatchi Collection, London, UK
Whitworth Art Gallery, Manchester, UK
and private collections in the United States, Canada, Denmark, Italy, France and Germany

Work is a four-letter word

Stephen Feeke is Director of the New Art Centre at Roche Court, Salisbury. He was previously a curator at the Henry Moore Institute in Leeds.

Bruce Haines is a gallerist, curator and researcher. He was formerly curator at Camden Arts Centre before co-founding Ancient & Modern in London and then opening Bruce Haines Mayfair.

Harry Thorne is a writer and editor based in Berlin. He is assistant editor of *frieze* magazine and a contributing editor of the *White Review*.

I live for your love

The artist would like to thank the following for their help in realizing this book: Andrew Brown; Stephen Feeke; Bruce Haines; Harry Thorne; Clare Woods; Sid Hughes; and Stripey Hughes. His sincere thanks go also to: Katharine Allard; Martin Asbæk; Michael Benevento; Madeleine Bessborough; Andre Buchmann; Anthon Maxus Christophersen; Helen Creese; Stuart Cumberland; Ruth Claxton; Eleanor Clayton; Alice Cowling; Rebecca Daniels; Simon Day; Mandy Fowler; Jackie Haliday; Erik Herkrath; Steve Lowe; Kate MacGarry; Simon Martin; Jane O'Connor; Kirsty Ogg; Michael Pennie; David and Indra Roberts; Andreas Rüthi; Michael Schultze; Helen Sear; Jane Simpson; Gavin Wade; Simon Wallis; Frederikke West; Stuart Whipps; Alice Workman; Ed Workman; Godfrey Worsdale; Nick Yeo; and Chris Weston at Castle Fine Arts Foundry; Chris Cox at Craven Dunnill Jackfield; Jaspal Singh and Helen Richardson at Fitting Frames.

Photography credits
Matthew Booth 151
Daniel Brooke 227–9
Gerard Hughes 19, 34–6, 63–7, 70–3, 88, 89, 174–7, 187, 189, 191, 198–200, 202, 203, 206, 207, 218–25, 230–3
Andy Keate 39, 42, 43, 87, 108, 110, 111, 184, 185, 194, 195, 197, 235
Roman März 6, 13, 124–7, 130, 131, 133–5
Andy Stagg 44 (top)
David Stjernholm 47, 51–6, 152
Joshua White 9, 10, 98–104, 107

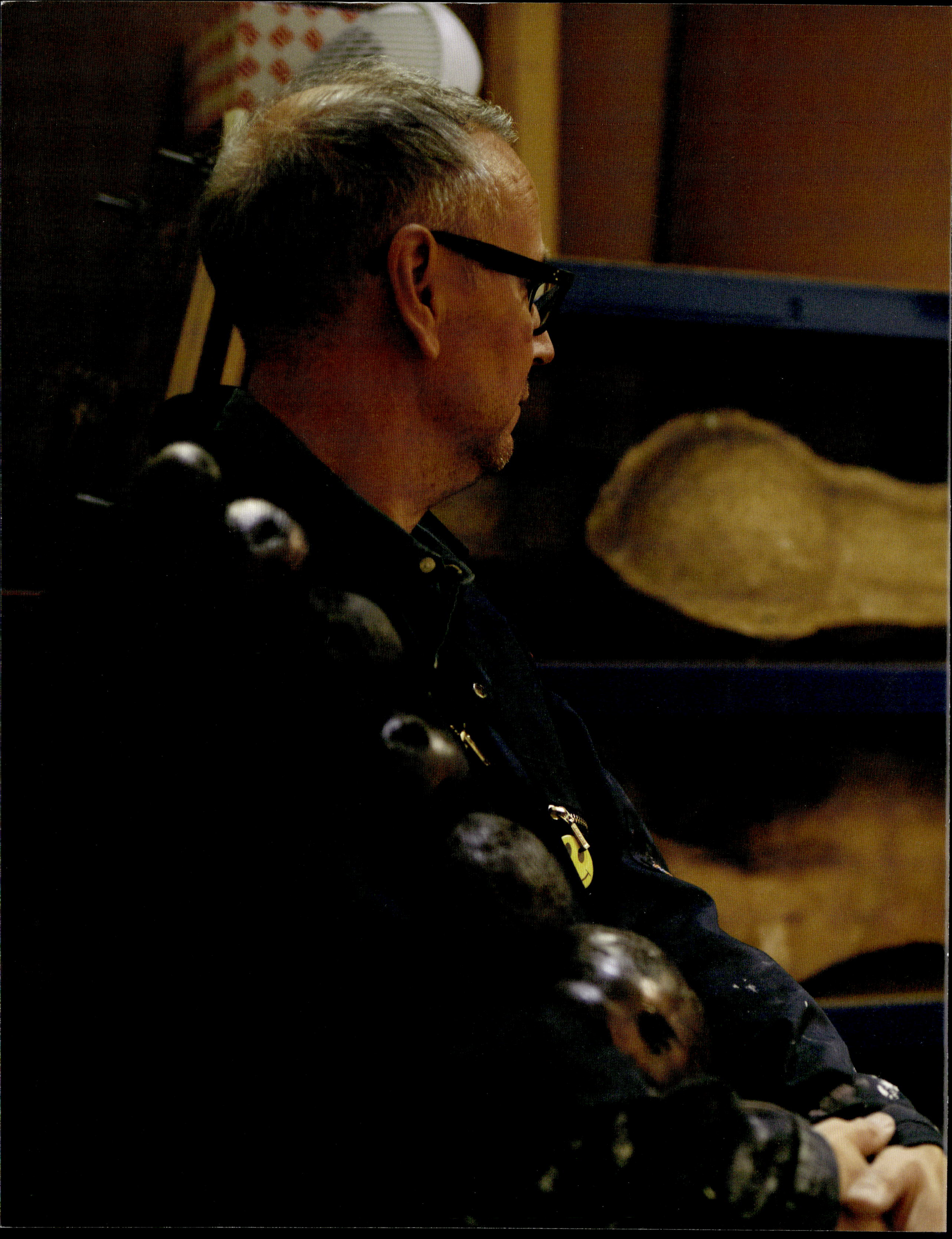

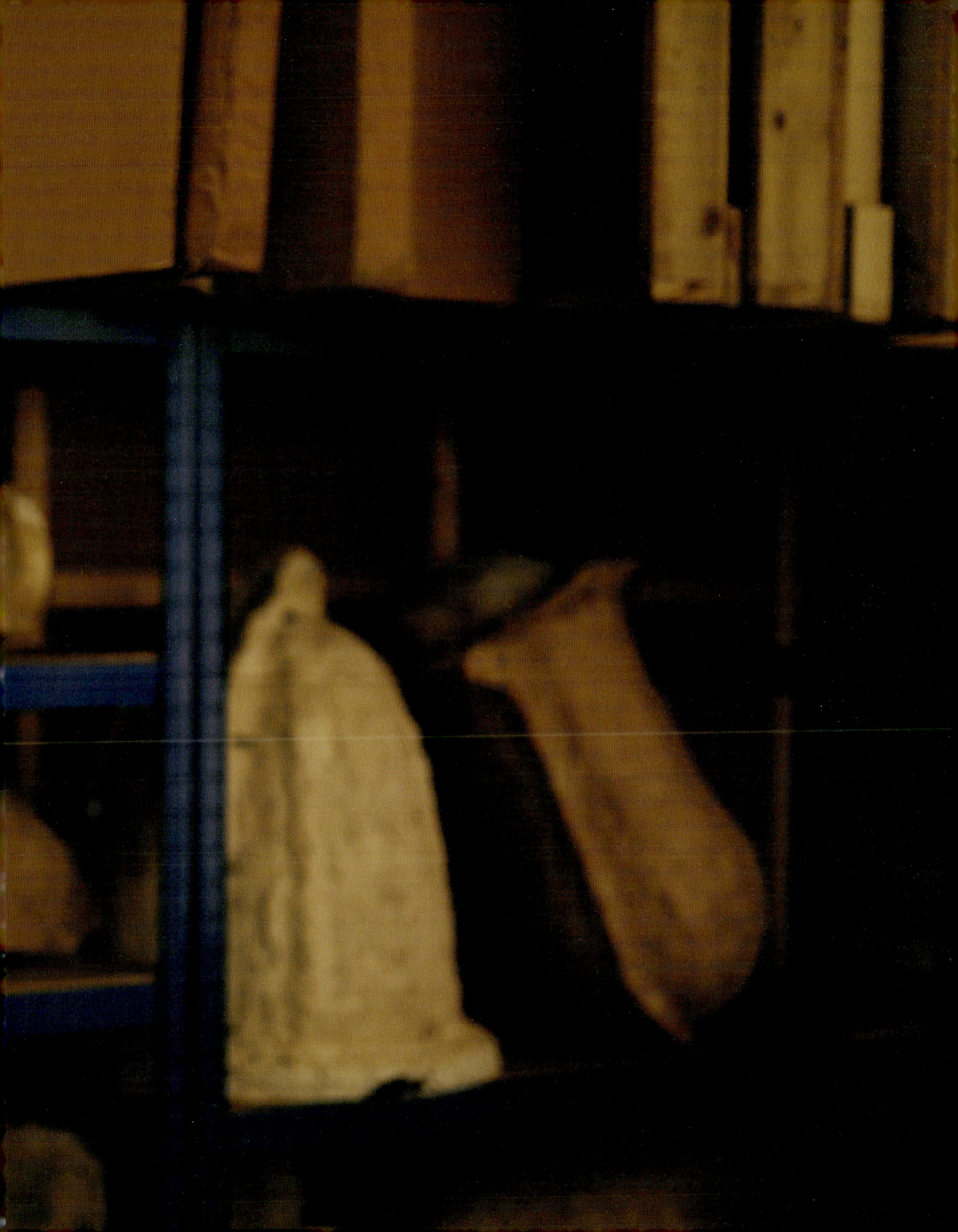

A Giving Glove 2015
Resin and iron powder,
24 × 12 × 1 cm

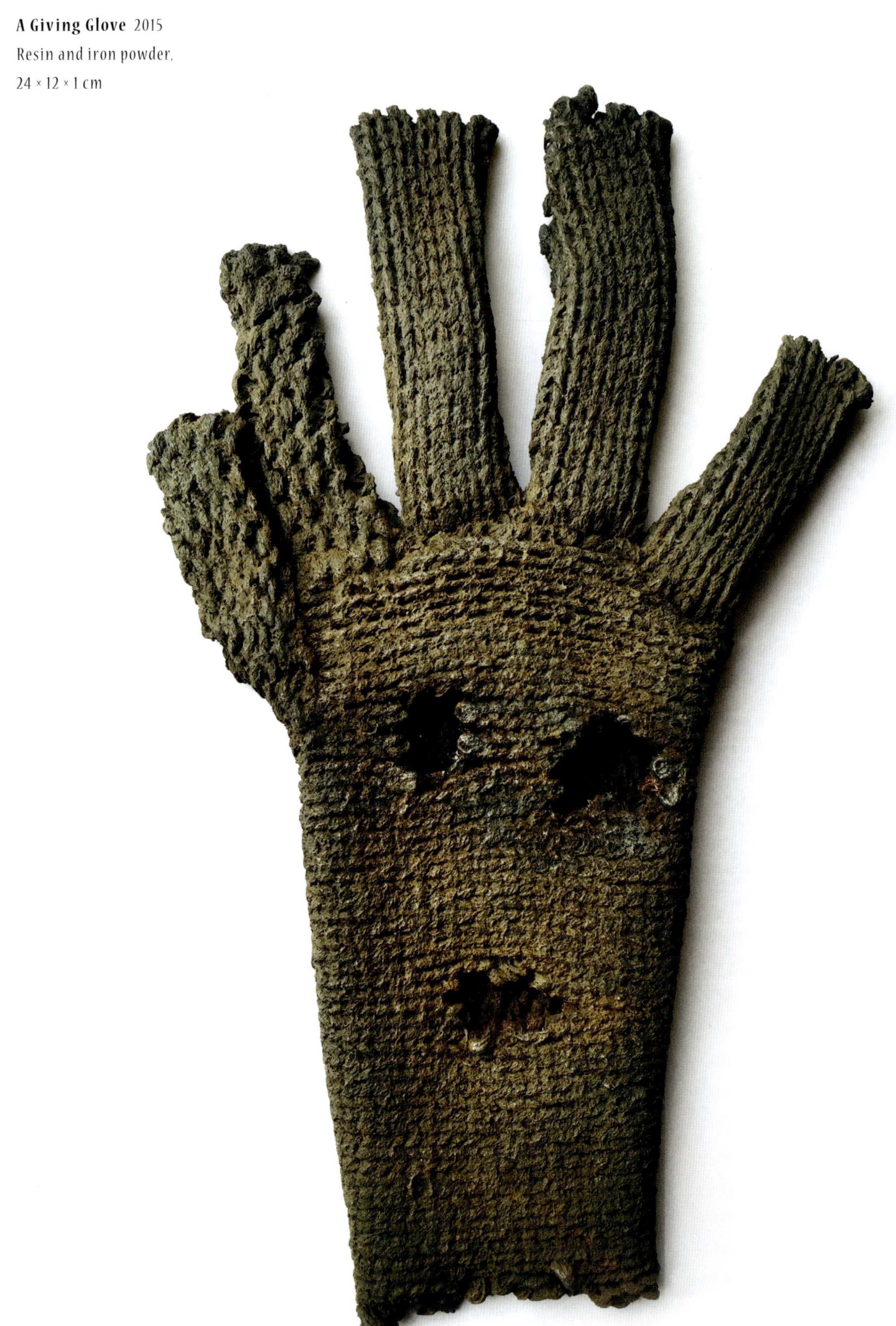